DATE DUE			

Do Taxes Matter?

Do Taxes Matter?

The Impact of the Tax
Reform Act of 1986

edited by
Joel Slemrod

The MIT Press
Cambridge, Massachusetts
London, England

This book was set in Palatino by Asco Trade Typesetting Ltd., Hong Kong, and printed and bounded in the United States of America.

Library of Congress Cataloging-in-Publication Data

Do taxes matter? : the impact of the Tax Reform Act of 1986 / edited
  by Joel Slemrod.
    p.   cm.
Papers from a conference held in Ann Arbor, Mich., Nov. 10–11,
1989.
Includes index.
ISBN 0-262-19302-7
1. Income tax—United States—Congresses. 2. United States—
Economic conditions—1981–   —Congresses. 3. Taxation—Law and
legislation—United States—Congresses. I. Slemrod, Joel.
HJ4652.D6   1991
336.2′00973—dc20   90-42398
                                                          CIP

Contents

List of Contributors   *vii*

Preface   *ix*

1   **The Economic Impact of the Tax Reform Act of 1986**   *1*

Joel Slemrod

2   **Investment, Tax Policy, and the Tax Reform Act of 1986**   *13*

Alan J. Auerbach and Kevin Hassett

COMMENTS Robert S. Chirinko   *41*

GENERAL DISCUSSION   *48*

3   **The Impact of the 1986 Tax Reform on Personal Saving**   *50*

Jonathan Skinner and Daniel Feenberg

COMMENTS Patric H. Hendershott   *80*

GENERAL DISCUSSION   *89*

4   **Effects of the Tax Reform Act of 1986 on Corporate Financial Policy and Organizational Form**   *91*

Roger H. Gordon and Jeffrey K. MacKie-Mason

COMMENTS R. Glenn Hubbard   *132*

GENERAL DISCUSSION   *139*

5   **Taxation and Housing Markets: Preliminary Evidence on the Effects of Recent Tax Reforms**   *141*

James M. Poterba

COMMENTS Michelle J. White   *161*

GENERAL DISCUSSION   *166*

290520

6 **The Impact of the Tax Reform Act of 1986 on Foreign Direct Investment to and from the United States**   *168*

Joel Slemrod
COMMENTS Kenneth A. Froot   *198*
GENERAL DISCUSSION   *201*

7 **The Impact of Tax Reform on Charitable Giving: A 1989 Perspective**   *203*

Charles T. Clotfelter
COMMENTS Don Fullerton   *236*
GENERAL DISCUSSION   *241*

8 **The Impact of the Tax Reform Act of 1986 on State and Local Fiscal Behavior**   *243*

Paul N. Courant and Edward M. Gramlich
COMMENTS Steven D. Gold   *276*
GENERAL DISCUSSION   *284*

9 **Foreign Responses to U.S. Tax Reform**   *286*

John Whalley
COMMENTS Richard A. Musgrave   *315*
GENERAL DISCUSSION   *319*

10 **Lessons for Tax Reform**   *321*

Henry J. Aaron
COMMENTS Charles E. McLure, Jr.   *332*
GENERAL DISCUSSION   *340*

Index   *343*

List of Contributors

Henry Aaron
The Brookings Institution

Alan Auerbach
University of Pennsylvania

Charles Ballard
Michigan State University

David Bradford
Princeton University

Gerard Brannon
Consultant

Robert S. Chirinko
University of Chicago

Charles Clotfelter
Duke University

Paul Courant
University of Michigan

Daniel Feenberg
National Bureau of
Econmic Research

Kenneth Froot
Massachusetts Institute of
Technology

Don Fullerton
University of Virginia

Steven Gold
National Conference of
State Legislatures

Roger Gordon
University of Michigan

Edward Gramlich
University of Michigan

Gilbert Harter
The Dow Chemical Company

Kevin Hassett
Columbia University

Robert Haveman
University of Wisconsin

Patric Hendershott
Ohio State University

Glenn Hubbard
Columbia University

Larry R. Langdon
Hewlett-Packard

Jeffrey MacKie-Mason
University of Michigan

Robert N. Mattson
International Business
Machines Corporation

Michael McIntyre
Wayne State University

Charles McLure
Hoover Institution

Paul Menchik
Michigan State University

Patrick Moran
Merck & Co., Inc.

Richard A. Musgrave
University of California-Santa Cruz

John Mutti
Grinnell College

James Poterba
Massachusetts Institute of
Technology

Fritz Scheuren
Internal Revenue Service

Matthew Shapiro
University of Michigan

Jonathan Skinner
University of Virginia

Joel Slemrod
University of Michigan

Burton Smoliar
Ford Motor Company

Randall Weiss
Deloitte & Touche

John Whalley
University of Western Ontario

James Wheeler
University of Michigan

Michelle White
University of Michigan

Ann Dryden Witte
Wellesley College

Martin Zimmerman
Ford Motor Company

Preface

The Tax Reform Act of 1986 was the most significant change in the income tax law since its conversion to a mass-based tax during World War II. Its likely effects on the economy were hotly debated in the two years before its passage. The economic record since its passage offers us a unique opportunity to address the question of whether taxes matter, or whether they matter in the ways we had thought prior to 1986. As of this writing, both the details and principles of TRA86 are undergoing serious legislative review. Before TRA86 is altered, it behooves us to examine closely the successes and failures of this momentous tax legislation.

To begin an assessment of these questions, the Office of Tax Policy Research commissioned nine studies of the impact of TRA86, which were presented at a conference held at the School of Business Administration of the University of Michigan, Ann Arbor. This volume begins with an overview chapter and then contains the nine commissioned papers plus for each paper the remarks delivered by a formal commentator and a synopsis of the general discussion that followed the conference presentations. The typical chapter examines one important sector of the economy that was directly affected by the 1986 tax reform. The expected impact of tax reform is addressed, and the evidence accumulated since its actual impact is carefully analyzed. The juxtaposition of theory and reality provides many surprises, and the authors draw out the lessons of this exercise for future tax reform. These studies represent the first systematic look at what the detailed impact of TRA86 has been.

We would like to thank the Sloan Foundation for its initial financial support, and to acknowledge contributions from Chrysler, Citicorp/Citibank, Dow Chemical Company, Ford Motor Company, Genentech, Inc., Hallmark Cards, Inc., Hewlett-Packard Company, International Business Machines Corporation, Merck & Co., Inc., Pepsico Inc., Union Pacific Corporation, and Xerox Corporation. Robert Mattson of IBM was instrumental in arranging the corporate financial support. The success of this project largely depended on the untiring efforts of Mary Molter and Elizabeth Meagher. Thanks are also due to Linda Burilovich, Laura Kalambokidis, and Doug Shackelford for helping to prepare the summaries of the conference discussion.

Do Taxes Matter?

1

The Economic Impact of the Tax Reform Act of 1986

Joel Slemrod

The Tax Reform Act of 1986 was signed into law by Ronald Reagan on October 22, 1986. Although there was widespread agreement at the time that it represented the most significant change in the U.S. income tax since its conversion to a broad-based tax during World War II, there was not widespread agreement on its likely economic impact. Critics linked it to the "deindustrialization of America"[1] or, less extremely and more specifically, to a reduction in the capital stock of 10% to 15%, a GNP of 5% less than otherwise, and a reduction in the rate of technical progress as well as the competitiveness of U.S. business.[2] For the most part, supporters stated its expected achievements in more abstract terms, for example, that it would "greatly improve the fairness of the tax system and remove major distortions from the economy."[3]

In hindsight at least one thing is clear—the sky has not fallen. There are no signs yet of the deindustrialization of America. On the contrary, since 1986 we have seen a continuation of the country's longest peacetime economic expansion in history. The ratio of real nonresidential fixed investment to real GNP is steady (and was up strongly in 1988), the saving rate in 1989 was at its highest level since 1984, and the unemployment rate has continued its downward trend begun in 1984 and now stands at its lowest rate since 1973.

Despite the encouraging economic performance since 1986, as of this writing the spirit of tax reform is under legislative attack. The Bush administration has proposed to restore a preferential tax rate for long-term capital gains. The Democratic congressional leadership has replied with a proposal to expand eligibility for IRA's and to pay for that by increasing the marginal tax rate for high-income taxpayers from 28% to 33%. Either change would move the tax system away from the principle of as broad a base as possible with as low rates as possible.

Before any such changes are enacted, it behooves us to carefully examine what the economic impact of tax reform has been. Three years of the postreform period, and less than three years of data about the postreform years, are hardly enough to tell a convincing story about its impact. We cannot say for sure how the economy would have evolved in the absence of tax reform, so isolating its effect is an imprecise exercise. But the policy process will not wait for our considered judgment on these issues. Moreover it is valuable to set out the methodological and conceptual issues that must be grappled with in order to assess the impact of tax reform, a task that should be revisited as more data becomes available.

To make an initial assessment of the economic impact of tax reform, the Office of Tax Policy Research of the University of Michigan commissioned nine studies. Each of the first eight studies reviewed the expected impact of tax reform on an important aspect of the U.S. economy, carefully considered what the actual impact has been, and, where the unexpected has happened, tried to reconcile theory and reality. The ninth study attempted to bring together the results and draw out the lessons for the future of tax reform.

A conference held in Ann Arbor, Michigan, on November 10 and 11, 1989, comprised the first systematic look at what the detailed impact of the Tax Reform Act of 1986 has been. This volume contains the papers presented at that conference, plus the comments of the discussants assigned to each paper and a summary of the general discussion that followed the presentation of each paper.

Before proceeding to a more detailed look at the results, it is worthwhile to recount the basic outlines of the tax reform. Its theme was to lower the statutory rates of tax and to recover the revenue thereby lost by broadening the tax base. By broadening the tax base in the direction of a more accurate measurement of income it was hoped that the differentials in taxation of different activities would be lessened—the playing field would be leveled—and the efficiency of the economy improved. The basic rate of corporate tax was reduced from 46% to 34%, accompanied by the elimination of the investment tax credit, a slight slowing of depreciation schedules, and the scrapping of several tax provisions that benefited certain specific sectors. On net, these provisions were projected to raise an additional $120 billion of corporate tax revenues in the five years after passage. On the individual side, both the standard deduction and personal exemption allowance increased significantly and tax rates were reduced, most dramatically at the top of the income distribution where the marginal rate fell from 50% to 28%. Some base broadening accompanied the decline in rates, including the full taxation of realized long-term capital gains, the elimination of the sales tax deduction, limits on passive losses, the abolition of the two-earner deduction, and limits on the deductibility of IRA contributions. All in all, the changes in the individual income tax were projected to reduce revenues by 7%. Taken together, the changes in the corporate and individual taxes were designed to be approximately revenue neutral.

During the debate about tax reform, its predicted impact on investment perhaps received the most attention. Most observers reasoned that the corporate rate cut did not offset the elimination of the investment tax credit and the longer depreciation lifetimes, leading to a higher effective tax rate on new investment. A declining rate of nonresidential investment was widely predicted. As chapter 2 by Alan Auerbach and Kevin Hassett documents, it has not turned out that way. Real investment in equipment, the category affected by the loss of the investment tax credit, has been strong since 1986. While office, computing, and accounting machinery dominated the growth in 1986 and 1987, equipment investment generally was strong in 1988. Investment in structures was weaker than expected in 1986–88, although total real nonresidential fixed investment as a fraction of real GNP was about the same as in the 1980–85 period. Auerbach and Hassett conclude from the post-TRA86 performance of investment that tax policy may have been given too much prominence in past discussions of investment behavior.

If for domestic investment a large predicted impact of tax reform has not materialized, the reverse is true in the case of foreign direct investment (FDI). Although tax reform did not set out to materially change the tax incentives for FDI, the post-TRA86 period has seen dramatic changes in FDI. Inward FDI to the United States reached an all-time high of $58.4 billion in 1988, continuing a secular increase that began in the late 1970s. Outward FDI also hit an all-time high of $44.2 billion in 1987, a sharp turnaround from the early 1980s, but fell back to $17.5 billion in 1988. However, in chapter 6 I argue that it is impossible to link conclusively the boom in FDI to changes in the tax system, both because the a priori net impact of the myriad changes is not clear and because one cannot, with less than three years of post-TRA86 data, sort out any tax effect from other influences on FDI. Nevertheless, several aspects of recent FDI performance are consistent with the expected effect of TRA86 on incentives, including the strength of outward FDI to low-tax countries, and the increase in net transfers of debt abroad. For inward FDI the predominance of Japanese and U.K. investment, the relative decline of debt transfer, and the increased reported rate of return on investment are consistent with the changed incentives of the new tax provisions.

TRA86 had significant implications not only for the real decisions of firms but also for their financial behavior and choice of legal status. Chapter 4 by Roger Gordon and Jeffrey MacKie-Mason argues that because TRA86 increased the tax cost of equity finance more than that of debt finance, debt-to-value ratios should have risen. This has in fact occurred, although to a lesser extent than they expected. Dividend payouts have increased as predicted, but surprisingly stock repurchases increased even more rapidly.

Because post-TRA86 the top individual tax rate lies below the corporate tax rate, there is a greater incentive for closely held firms to organize as subchapter S corporations and thereby to avoid corporate-level taxation. In fact there was a massive surge in S corporation elections immediately following TRA86—about 375,000 filings in the first half of 1987, compared to an average six-month rate of 150,000 during the four previous years. Furthermore preliminary data suggest that there may have been some movement of loss operations toward the more highly taxed corporate sector, while more gain operations are being taxed at the lower personal rates.

The story for personal saving sounds much like the story for investment. Many expected that tax reform would reduce saving, arguing that the reduction in individual tax rates would be outweighed by the increase in capital gains taxation and the tightening of restrictions on IRAs. In fact, although the personal saving rate fell from 4.1% in 1986 to 1.8% in the second quarter of 1987, it has since rebounded to 5.6% in the first quarter of 1989. This is the highest rate of personal saving since 1984, though it still lies well below the U.S. rates of the 1970s and the rate of saving in most other developed countries.

Chapter 3 by Jonathan Skinner and Daniel Feenberg concludes that the marginal tax rate on saving was definitely reduced by TRA86. Thus to the extent that saving is responsive to aftertax rates of return, it should have increased. The relatively high rate of saving since 1988 is consistent with this story. However, no clear empirical relationship between saving and aftertax rates of return has been apparent in recent decades, although the decade of the 1980s by itself supports such a relationship. The impact of TRA86 on the composition of saving is more clearly apparent, with taxpayers shifting a large fraction of their (no longer deductible) personal loans into (still deductible) home mortgage loans. There is little evidence, though, that the extraordinarily large volume of capital gains realizations in 1986 led to increased spending. Most gains were apparently reinvested, and largely shifted to interest-earning accounts, at least for the time being.

Not all sectors have fared well in the post-TRA86 economy. Multifamily housing starts fell sharply from 669,500 in 1985 to 406,800 in 1988, following the lengthening of tax depreciation lifetimes for real estate, the elimination of preferential capital gains tax rates, and the restrictions on tax shelter investments. But recall that one of the objectives of tax reform was to reduce the role of the tax system and restore the role of the market in the allocation of resources. Rental housing was clearly tax favored before TRA86, and any move toward a more level playing field was bound to adversely affect this sector. As chapter 5 by James Poterba points out, TRA86's reductions in marginal tax rates also increased the net cost of homeownership, holding nominal interest rates and inflation constant. But because this cost rose relatively less than the equilibrium cost of rental housing, the incentives toward homeownership probably increased. However, no pronounced shift toward homeownership is yet discernible, although in 1987 both single-family housing starts and real house prices started to decline, albeit in a much smaller way than for multifamily starts.

Of the many sectors that opposed the tax reform movement, the nonprofit sector was perhaps the most vocal. Many of the prominent reform proposals limited or even eliminated the deductibility of charitable contributions, and the move toward lower marginal rates reduced the tax incentive to make donations even if those donations remained deductible. Ultimately TRA86 did reduce marginal rates but retained the deductibility of contributions, although it abandoned the nonitemizer deduction which had been fully in place only for one year. Moreover the value of untaxed appreciation of donated gifts was added to the base of the alternative minimum tax.

As chapter 7 by Charles Clotfelter demonstrates, these changes dramatically increased the net-of-tax cost of making contributions, especially for high-income taxpayers, for whom it doubled. Economic models cited at the time forecast declines in giving on the order of 14% to 16%. In fact, aggregate giving has apparently increased each year since 1986, although contributions of appreciated assets to art museums and higher education, which traditionally rely on gifts from the wealthy, have declined since 1986. The distribution of contributions since 1986 has changed as expected, with a relative decline in gifts from those upper-income individuals who experienced the largest increases in the net-of-tax cost of making donations.

State and local govemments were faced with a much changed environment after TRA86. For those states that based their definition of taxable income on the federal concept, the base broadening provided a windfall of extra revenues. However, the net cost to residents of state and local spending rose because the deductibility of sales tax was eliminated and the federal tax rates against which other taxes could be deducted fell, and the number of itemizing taxpayers declined. The relative cost of revenue sources also changed, with the net cost of sales taxes rising relative to other revenue sources and the relative net cost of nondeductible revenue sources such as user fees decreasing.

In chapter 8 Paul Courant and Edward Gramlich's investigation of the post-TRA86 fiscal behavior of state and local governments uncovers little evidence of a change in the mix of tax revenues responding to changes in the net costs. Reliance on user fees has declined, and no clear shift away from sales taxes can be discerned in fiscal data. In fact, since 1987 twelve states have significantly increased their sales taxes, and a number had less significant increases. The authors conclude that the state and local response to price incentives has been smaller, and in some cases of an unexpected direction, than predicted. Many states did, though, increase the conformity between the state and federal income tax systems.

The movement toward broad-based low-rate systems became a worldwide phenomenon in the last half of the 1980s. Was TRA86 the catalyst for this rush to reform, or was it merely part of a trend inspired by a common intellectual spirit? After studying the tax reform movements of seven countries, John Whalley concludes in chapter 9 that the picture of TRA86 as catalyst is too simplistic. The United Kingdom initiated its corporate tax reform, and Canada was seriously considering reform, before the debate over TRA86 began. Moreover reform in some of the other countries had a quite different emphasis. For example, the Japanese reform emphasized a shift in the tax burden from income to sales tax, motivated in part by the perception that certain groups were unfairly evading their share of income tax. Nevertheless, the fear that lower tax rates in the United States would, if unimitated, lead to adverse economic consequences was clearly a motivating factor behind the Canadian and, to a lesser degree, the Japanese reduction in statutory corporation tax rates. However, in many other countries the direct economic impact of the U.S. tax system was apparently not a critical factor in the reforms. Whalley concludes that common intellectual influences were more important in the worldwide tax reform movement than the imperatives of an integrated world economy.

It is too early to discern the impact of tax reform in some important dimensions. Tax reform was designed to preserve the distribution of the tax burden across income groups (not considering the incidence of the increased corporation income tax). Whether this has been achieved, or whether unexpected behavioral responses of individuals have shifted the burden, must await the release of detailed tax data concerning the post-TRA86 years. One critical issue concerns capital gains. TRA86 could claim distributional neutrality at the top of the income distribution while sharply reducing the marginal tax rate from 50% to 28% only by at the same time eliminating the 60% exclusion of long-term capital gains, thus increasing their effective tax rate from 20% to 28%. Assuming a particular tax elasticity of capital gains realizations, these changes imply that the amount of revenue raised from the highest-income classes would be only slightly reduced. If, however, the elasticity assumption turns out to be incorrect, the observed distribution of tax burden may look quite different than was anticipated. In any event one has to be particularly careful about assessing the incidence of a tax that is levied on a voluntary financial transaction.

Another widely trumpeted goal of tax reform was simplification of the tax system. The most talked-about aspect of simplification—going from fourteen to three tax brackets—was probably the least significant. After all, once taxable income is calculated, it is a trivial exercise to use the tax tables to calculate tax liability, and one that doesn't much depend on the number of brackets. Other aspects of tax reform had a potentially larger impact on the complexity of the tax system. On the positive side, the increased standard deduction and limitations on itemized deductions implied that several million taxpayers no longer had to itemize deductions and millions more no longer had any tax liability, although many in this latter category continued to file returns in order to obtain the liberalized earned income credit. Lowered marginal tax rates reduced the incentive to seek out ways to reduce taxable income. The outright elimination of income averaging and the two-earner credit reduced the complexity of filing. Perhaps most important, taxing capital gains at the same rate as other income reduced the incentive to repackage income as capital gain and reduced the importance of the statutory dividing line between capital gain and ordinary income. More generally, less pronounced differences in the tax treatment of investments and flattened rate structure should reduce the need for, and incentive to, engage in complicated tax avoidance schemes. On the negative side, several aspects of the reform further complicated the tax system, including the employee benefit nondiscrimination rules, the limitations on passive losses, the expanded filing requirements for children, and modifications in both the alternative minimum tax and the foreign tax credit. The net effect of these many changes is unclear because quantifying the resource cost of collecting taxes at a given point of time is a tricky business, and accurately measuring any change in that cost is even more difficult.[4] Furthermore any time the tax law changes, the complexity of the system increases until the changes are digested.

What lessons can we draw from these studies of the impact of tax reform? In chapter 10 Henry Aaron offers several. First, TRA86 has had little apparent effect on the broad aggregates in which most economists are interested, and certainly less effect than had been previously expected. This does not necessarily imply that tax effects are unimportant because in some cases TRA86's many provisions had offsetting incentive effects. Also taxpayers could expect the changes to be short-lived or simply take a while to adjust their behavior to the changed environment. Nevertheless, there is a strong sense that behavioral elasticities are weaker than previously believed, and thus the efficiency cost of taxation is smaller than had been thought. As the relative importance of efficiency costs fades, Aaron believes that more attention should be given to the distributional effects of the tax system. Moreover current attempts to alter tax reform by restoring preferential treatment of capital gains or expanding eligibility for IRAs are likely to be largely ineffective in boosting saving and investment, and their strong distributional implications ought to be considered.

My own reading of the evidence about the economic response to tax reform suggests a hierarchy of responses. Standing at the top of the hierarchy, the most clearly responsive to tax incentives, is the timing of economic transactions.[5] In anticipation of the increase in the taxation of capital gains, realizations of long-term gains in excess of short-term losses jumped from $165 billion in 1985 to $325 billion in 1986, only to fall back to $135 billion in 1987. Foreign direct investment into the United States was $16.3 billion in the fourth quarter of 1986, more than double the rate of adjacent quarters, as investors raced to beat the expiration of tax rules favoring mergers and acquisitions. Donations of appreciated assets showed a large increase in 1986, followed by declines in 1987 and 1988 in response to the inclusion of otherwise untaxed appreciation in the alternative minimum tax base beginning in 1987. Firms accelerated the payment of dividends to shareholders and decelerated the payment of dividends from foreign subsidiaries. In these and other instances, the opportunity to realize temporarily available tax savings obviously dominated the cost of accelerating transactions.

In the second tier of the hierarchy are financial and accounting responses. There is substantial evidence of the reshuffling of individuals' portfolios and the repackaging of firms' financial claims. Individuals were quick to change the form of much of their debt away from personal loans once it lost its deductibility into still-deductible mortgage debt. Firms moved toward greater reliance on debt finance (although perhaps not as much as expected).

On the bottom of the hierarchy, where the least response is evident, are the real decisions of individuals and firms. Although its effective tax rate increased, nonresidential fixed investment has not declined relative to its trend and its strongest component in the post-TRA86 years, equipment, was the most penalized by the tax reform. Personal saving has exhibited no clear trend since 1986. One apparently clear real economic response is the decline in multifamily housing starts, although much of this drop may be related to the overbuilding of the early 1980s. This initial impression of little real response should be reevaluated as further evidence becomes available. But the short-term response has in most cases been less dramatic than many economists had expected.

Henry Aaron counsels us to look beyond the efficiency costs of taxation to its impact on the distribution of welfare. The hierarchy of responses to tax systems suggests that we pay closer attention to aspects of the tax code that provide rewards to taxpayers for changing the timing of transactions or to repackaging their financial claims. Such opportunities are likely to be quickly exploited by taxpayers, costing the Treasury revenues and encouraging socially unproductive behavior. In this category I put preferential rates on income in the form of capital gains (and even more so, temporarily low rates on capital gains) and IRAs.

Attention ought to be refocused on reducing the complexity of the tax system, an objective of tax reform that was honored more by its press than by its reality. The resource cost of collecting taxes is large[6] and may, if our estimates of the efficiency cost of taxation are to be revised downward, be the area where the most progress can be made.

What is the long-term viability of tax reform? Undoubtedly the passage of TRA86 in the first place surprised many historians of the tax law. Careful study of the history of tax reform, completed before the passage of TRA86, certainly leaves the reader with great pessimism about the likelihood of fundamental tax reform ever occurring.[7] Yet the fortuitous combination of a president committed to lowering tax rates, legislators committed to reform, and academics in the right place at the right time overcame the political system's historical resistance to fundamental change in the tax system.[8]

Of course when over $500 billion is at stake every year, forces for change of the income tax system will never be at rest. It may be, though, that a low-rate, minimal-preference tax system is somewhat self-perpetuating. With lower tax rates, there is a lower tax saving for any new preference that reduces taxable income by a dollar. Furthermore the intellectual defense against proposed special allowances is strengthened when it can reasonably be argued that the tax base has a coherent conceptual basis (in this case, income).[9]

As of this writing, two lines of attack against TRA86 have met with some success. The first line concerns the areas in which TRA86 complicated the law, and areas where it failed to simplify enough. There is wide agreement that the nondiscrimination rules for employee benefit plans, treatment of passive losses, the alternative minimum tax and the foreign tax credit, to name a few aspects of the new law, impose a severe compliance burden on taxpayers, with potentially adverse effects on compliance with the tax law. The benefit rules have already been substantially modified, and attention to the other areas is likely to come soon.

The second line of attack has been that TRA86 failed to provide enough encouragement to saving and investment. Proponents of this view have supported restoring preferential treatment of capital gains and expanded IRAs. But the evidence of the past three years should caution us that these measures may be more effective at inducing taxpayers to alter the timing of their asset sales and to reshuffle their portfolios than to significantly change their saving and investment patterns. One certain result is added complexity in the tax system.

To paraphrase from a poster I enjoy, tax reform is a not a station we arrive at, it is a way of traveling. My fond hope is that these early lessons learned about the impact of the 1986 version of tax reform can contribute to a better understanding of this reform and the tax reforms of years to come.

References

Brinner, Roger, and Jesse Abraham. 1986. The Packwood Tax Bill: What's Different? *Data Resources U.S. Review* (June): 11–15.

Hall, Robert E. 1988. Intertemporal Substitution in Consumption. *Journal of Political Economy* 96: 339–357.

Hulten, Charles R., and Robert A. Klayman. 1988. Investment Incentives in Theory and Practice. In Henry J. Aaron, Harvey Galper, and Joseph A. Pechman (eds.) *Uneasy Compromise: Problems of a Hybrid Income-Consumption Tax.* Washington, DC: Brookings Institution.

Pechman, Joseph A. 1987. Tax Reform: Theory and Practice. *Journal of Economic Perspectives,* 1, 1: 11–28.

Prakken, Joel L. 1986. The Macroeconomics of Tax Reform. Paper presented at a conference sponsored by The American Council for Capital Formation on "The Consumption Tax: A Better Alternative?" Washington, DC. September 3–5.

Roberts, Paul Craig. 1984. A Tax Scheme to Deindustrialize America. *The Wall Street Journal,* December 6.

Slemrod, Joel, and Nikki Sorum. 1984. The Compliance Cost of the U.S. Individual Income Tax System. *National Tax Journal* 37, 4: 461–474.

Summers, Lawrence H. 1987. A Fair Tax Act That's Bad for Business. *Harvard Business Review,* 65, 2: 53–59.

Swingen, Judyth A., and Susan B. Long. 1988. A Look Back at the 1988 Filing Season. *Tax Notes,* December 19, pp. 1343–1347.

Witte, John F. 1985. *The Politics and Development of the Federal Income Tax.* Madison, WI: University of Wisconsin Press.

Notes

1. Writing about the Treasury Department's tax proposal of November 1984, Paul Craig Roberts (1984) said that if it were implemented, "the U.S. would be deindustrialized within a decade." Although much changed about the tax reform between November 1984 and October 1986, the key aspects of the corporate tax reforms that Roberts criticized—the replacement of ACRS with slower depreciation schedules and the abolition of the investment tax credit—remained.

2. These forecasts are taken from Summers (1987). The large macroeconometric models generally concluded that the near-term impact of tax reform would be negative. For example, the Washington University macro model (Prakken 1986) forecast a sharp slowdown in economic activity, with business fixed investment off 10% by 1989, and in 1993 off by 17% and the unemployment rate three percentage points higher than otherwise. Data Resources forecast that the Senate Finance Committee version of tax reform, which was quite similar to the bill that eventually became law, would lower GNP by 0.7% in the short run and a few tenths of a percentage point in the long run. Fixed investment was predicted to fall by over 5% in 1990, before recovering. See Brinner and Abraham (1986).

3. This quote is from Pechman (1987), p. 17.

4. Swingen and Long (1988) report on survey evidence that indicates there was an 8% increase in return preparation costs between tax year 1986 and 1987. Because any change in the tax law is likely to increase compliance cost in the short run, one cannot be confident about the change in costs once the new law has been fully digested.

5. Here I purposely use the term economic *transactions* rather than economic *activity*. Recent econometric work (e.g., Hall 1988), as well as the evidence in the paper from this conference by Skinner and Feenberg, suggest that the timing of *consumption* is not very sensitive to its relative cost, the aftertax rate of interest. Consumer expenditures, which include spending on durable goods, is undoubtedly more sensitive than the flow of consumption.

6. Slemrod and Sorum (1984) estimated that the compliance cost of the individual income tax in 1983 amounted to between $17 and $27 billion, or from 5% to 7% of revenue raised.

7. See Witte (1985).

8. See Pechman (1987) for one view of how and why tax reform came to be.

9. For an elaboration of this view see Hulten and Klayman (1988).

2

Investment, Tax Policy, and the Tax Reform Act of 1986

Alan J. Auerbach and
Kevin Hassett

2.1 Introduction

The Tax Reform Act of 1986 shifted the U.S. tax burden from households to businesses while raising the overall tax burden facing new investment (Auerbach 1987). The tax burden on different types of investment also shifted. The repeal of the investment tax credit caused the effective tax rate on new equipment to rise, while the corresponding rate on business structures not qualifying for the investment tax credit fell, as the corporate rate reduction outweighed the impact of longer depreciation lifetimes.

These tax changes led many observers to predict that business fixed investment, especially investment in machinery and equipment, would suffer in the years that followed. However, a first glance at recent investment behavior suggests that such predictions failed to materialize. The continuing strength of the U.S. economy during the late 1980s was attributable in part to strong nonresidential investment, with equipment investment leading the way. This immediately suggests a problem for those who would attempt to explain investment behavior primarily in terms of responses to changes in fiscal policy.

Such difficulties have been recognized in the past. For example, Bosworth (1985) notes that the investment recovery following the recession of 1981–83, attributed by some to the Economic Recovery Tax Act of 1981, was led by investment in information processing equipment and automobiles, assets that did not benefit particularly from the 1981 changes.

Though it is a mistake to believe that fiscal policies largely determine the pattern of investment, one should not necessarily conclude that fiscal policy is entirely impotent in this area, either. Given the volatility of investment behavior, tax changes could significantly affect investment, without such effects being discernible from an examination of overall trends. Detection of such effects requires a model of investment behavior that controls for influences other than taxes so that one can estimate the marginal effects that tax policies have had. We use such a model in this chapter; the model is based on the theory of forward-looking investment behavior.

The model suggests that tax factors have influenced business fixed investment during the postwar period but that other factors, such as the profitability of investment and the real cost of funds, have played a significant role as well. It is also true, however, that much of the variation in investment cannot easily be explained statistically. Based on our analysis, we reach the following conclusions:

1. During the postwar years, tax factors have altered the pattern of U.S. fixed investment, particularly in machinery and equipment.

2. Before the Tax Reform Act of 1986, changes in taxation did not stabilize investment.

3. Aggregate equipment investment in 1986–87 was generally consistent with the model's predictions, as nontax factors outweighed the effects of the 1986 tax changes. However, equipment investment was stronger than predicted in 1988 and investment in nonresidential structures for the entire period 1986–88 weaker.

4. The growth in equipment investment during 1986 and 1987 can be fully explained by the 47% increase in expenditures on Office, Computing and Accounting Machinery. This suggests an important role for technological explanations of the recent performance of investment. The surge in 1988, however, was due in part to growth in other sectors as well.

We begin our analysis with a brief review of investment behavior during the past three decades. Section 2.3 sketches the model we use to estimate the effects of profitability, financial costs, and taxes on investment behavior and discusses the historical movements in each of these factors, showing how tax policy has influenced the overall incentive to invest over time. Using estimates of the impact of the sensitivity of investment to the cost of capital, we calculate in section 2.4 the impact that tax incentives have had over time on investment prior to the Tax Reform Act of 1986.

In section 2.5 we turn our analysis to the Tax Reform Act of 1986, discussing the relevant provisions of the act. Section 2.6 reviews the past few years' investment performance and considers how the incentive to invest and investment behavior itself might have looked had the Tax Reform Act of 1986 not been enacted. In our concluding comments, we discuss some of the limitations of the analysis and suggest other channels through which fiscal policy might affect investment beyond those considered here.

2.2   Postwar Investment Behavior

Table 2.1 presents statistics on U.S. nonresidential fixed investment during the past three decades, expressed in relation both to gross national product (GNP) and net capital stock estimates for equipment and structures.[1]

The patterns of behavior are different for the two investment aggregates. Expressed as a fraction of the capital stock, equipment investment has had two periods of weakness, from the late 1950s through the early 1960s and briefly during the early 1980s. Equipment investment was especially strong during the late 1960s, and again during the expansion of the late 1970s. Investment in structures, like that in equipment, strengthened in the mid-1960s. However, unlike equipment investment, its performance was relatively weak in the late 1970s and relatively strong in the early 1980s. Perhaps the most striking difference between the two investment series has been seen during the past few years. While equipment investment has, in each year, exceeded its average of the past three decades, investment in structures has experienced its three lowest annual levels (relative to the capital stock) during the entire period!

Relative to output, rather than capital, each investment series appears to have an upward trend, reflecting the increasing capital–output ratio over the period. However, there are few significant differences in the discernible patterns of investment.

2.3   Determinants of the Incentive to Invest

Given that tax policy shifted in favor of structures in 1986, it is immediately evident that one cannot explain the past few years' investment pattern with tax factors alone. Given the historical volatility of investment, however, a more relevant question is whether the act's influence was at all significant. To answer this question, we need a model that measures the impact of taxes, as well as other economic factors, on investment.

At least since the work of Jorgenson (1963), there has been a tension between the restrictions theory imposes on models of investment behavior and the difficulty of explaining investment behavior very well with such rigorous structural models. For example, a recent statistical evaluation of competing models of investment behavior by Bernanke, Bohn, and Reiss (1988) found that naive, atheoretical models performed as well as models suggested by economic reasoning. In particular, variables not predicted by theory to matter, such as output, have a statistically significant effect on investment. In addition the models' parameter estimates have been found to be quite sensitive to small changes in specification (Chirinko 1986).

Table 2.1
Investment behavior

Year	Relative to capital		Relative to GNP	
	Equipment	Structures	Equipment	Structures
1957	0.163	0.098	0.055	0.048
1958	0.134	0.088	0.048	0.046
1959	0.147	0.087	0.050	0.044
1960	0.147	0.090	0.050	0.046
1961	0.139	0.088	0.047	0.045
1962	0.151	0.090	0.049	0.045
1963	0.157	0.087	0.051	0.044
1964	0.172	0.091	0.054	0.045
1965	0.193	0.102	0.060	0.049
1966	0.205	0.103	0.065	0.049
1967	0.187	0.096	0.062	0.046
1968	0.185	0.095	0.062	0.046
1969	0.186	0.096	0.065	0.047
1970	0.171	0.090	0.063	0.046
1971	0.161	0.084	0.061	0.043
1972	0.172	0.084	0.064	0.042
1973	0.195	0.087	0.073	0.043
1974	0.185	0.083	0.074	0.042
1975	0.154	0.072	0.066	0.038
1976	0.156	0.071	0.066	0.037
1977	0.176	0.073	0.073	0.037
1978	0.189	0.079	0.078	0.038
1979	0.190	0.085	0.081	0.041
1980	0.168	0.086	0.076	0.043
1981	0.164	0.091	0.076	0.046
1982	0.143	0.085	0.071	0.045
1983	0.148	0.074	0.071	0.039
1984	0.176	0.082	0.080	0.041
1985	0.183	0.083	0.084	0.041
1986	0.175	0.070	0.082	0.035
1987	0.177	0.067	0.083	0.033
1988	0.190	0.067	0.090	0.032
Mean	0.170	0.085	0.067	0.043

Unfortunately, if one is to perform the sort of policy analysis done in this chapter, a structural model is necessary in which the coefficients of policy variables may be interpreted as the partial effects of such variables on investment. In view of this, and informed by the failures of previous structural modeling attempts, we adopt the approach developed in Auerbach and Hassett (1990), which provides a theoretical justification for inclusion of explanatory variables typically found to influence investment while at the same time incorporating these determinants in a structural framework that can be used to study the effects of policy. Moreover we consider alternative specifications to help ensure that our conclusions are not misleading.

The model we use is based on the assumption of forward-looking investment behavior by value-maximizing firms that are motivated by adjustment costs to smooth their capital expenditures over time. This behavior leads to a decision rule for investment that predicts that the ratio of current investment to the existing stock of capital should be determined by the present and expected future values of a composite term that is based on the various factors influencing both the cost of capital and the aftertax profitability of investment. Increases in this term, which we will call c, might be associated with increases in the costs of investment or declines in the cash flow such investment generates; either should decrease investment. One may view the term c as a comprehensive measure of the cost to the firm of a unit of capital services, controlling for fluctuations in productivity. The expression for c has five main determinants:

1. The price of investment goods relative to the price at which firms can sell their output g. The higher this ratio, the less attractive is investment.

2. The real cost of funds to the firm, which is expressed as a weighted average of the costs of equity and debt r. Increases make investment more expensive to finance.

3. The productivity of capital θ which can fluctuate due in part to business cycle factors. Decreases in productivity should discourage investment.

4. The tax treatment of investment. A higher marginal tax burden on the income from newly purchased capital should discourage investment.

5. The rate of capital depreciation δ. The higher this rate, the more expensive it is to use capital in production.

The formula for c is[2]

$$c = \frac{g(r + \delta)(1 - \Gamma)}{\theta(1 - \tau)},$$
(1)

where Γ is equal to the present value of aftertax depreciation allowances and investment credits received per dollar of capital purchased and τ is the corporate tax rate. The definitions of g, δ, and τ are straightforward. The terms r, θ and Γ require some further discussion.

The Real Cost of Funds (r)

Firms finance their investments using a mix of debt and equity. It is therefore logical to use some weighted average of the costs of debt and equity in computing the overall cost of funds for new investment. Using such a weighted average, rather than a simple interest rate or some constant assumed rate of return, is quite important given the gap between debt and equity returns and their potential to move independently because of such influence as individual taxes and risk.

Once one knows a firm's risk class, it is relatively straightforward to estimate the relevant interest rate associated with debt finance. We multiply this interest rate by the factor $(1 - \tau)$ to account for the deductibility of interest payments by business borrowers.

Computation of an equity cost of capital is considerably more difficult because we do not observe expected rates of return on equity the way we observe interest rates on bonds. There are a variety of possible proxies for the unobservable expected return to equity, and we have considered two in our research. One is the expected earnings–price ratio for the firm, after taxes and corrected for the capital consumption and inventory valuation adjustments. The other is the expected return to equity in the market, which is equal to the dividend yield plus rate of capital gain on shares. The latter is a more direct measure of the cost of equity funds but is more difficult to compute. In our empirical investigation we experimented with both definitions.[3] Because the results were generally similar, we report only those based on the earnings–price definition in order to conserve space.

A final issue in the computation of r concerns the inflation rate. Since we are interested in the real cost of funds, we must subtract an appropriate inflation rate from the weighted average of nominal required returns to debt and equity. In this context such an inflation rate equals the rate of increase in the effective price of investment goods. This price has two components. The first is a general price level, which we represent using the GNP deflator. The second is the out-of-pocket cost per dollar of capital expenditures Γ, which accounts for the effective price reduction provided by investment incentives. The full inflation rate is the sum of the rates of increase of these two components.

The Productivity of Capital (θ)

An important determinant of an investment's attractiveness is the additional cash flow such an investment would generate. Like the expected return to equity, this marginal return is not observable. As a proxy in our regressions for this marginal return to new capital, we use a corrected (to incorporate capital consumption and inventory valuation adjustments) measure of the average return to capital, earnings before interest and taxes, divided by the company's net capital stock. Auerbach and Hassett (1990) provide a theoretical justification for the use of this measure, although its relevance for investment is not difficult to understand: similar measures may be found in the previous investment literature (e.g., Feldstein 1982; Abel and Blanchard 1986).

The term θ will account for factors changing the profitability of capital, other than the capital intensity of production itself. Such factors will include supply disturbances, which will affect the productivity of capital directly, as well as demand disturbances, which, through the price of output, will affect the level of profitability, given the productivity of capital.

The Present Value of Investment Incentives (Γ)

The present value (per dollar of investment) of the tax benefits of investment tax credits and depreciation allowances equals:

$$\Gamma = k + \sum_{s=t}^{\infty} (1 + r)^{-(s-t)} \tau_s D(s - t), \tag{2}$$

where k is the rate of investment tax credit, and $D(a)$ is the depreciation allowance received by an asset of age a. It has been customary in past empirical analyses to assume that τ is constant. However, this formula is correct only if the tax rate τ does not change over time. It is true, of course, that future tax rate changes cannot be known with certainty, but our empirical analysis allows for this by using only predicted values of future costs of capital.

The Determinants of Investment over Time

Our model of investment predicts that current and future expected values of c, as defined in expression (1), should affect current investment. Their relative importance, in theory, should depend on the adjustment costs facing firms. With high costs of adjustment, future terms are very important because the firm must plan its investment far in advance. Based on evidence concerning adjustment costs as well as unconstrained regression estimates of the impact of future values of c on investment, we define a composite, smoothed measure of c, which we call ck, based on the current and three successive years' individual values, with each year's value given half the weight of the one before it.

The first column of table 2.2 presents our estimated costs of capital ck (with the equity cost of capital based on the earnings–price ratio) for the two components of nonresidential fixed investment, equipment and structures, over the period 1957–85.[4] To permit an evaluation of the importance of different factors, the table also provides measures of ck in which variations in productivity and tax parameters are held constant. The second column (no tax-1) is the estimated cost of capital absent all taxes. The third column (no tax-2) omits all tax effects except the deductibility of interest. Which of these numbers is more relevant depends on one's assumptions about the behavior of interest rates in response to rates of tax. The first no-tax variable corresponds to the assumption that before-tax interest rates are invariant with respect to corporate taxation, and the second corresponds to the assumption that aftertax interest rates are invariant with respect to taxation.[5] The last column of the table gives the cost of capital term with taxes but without the productivity term θ. This last term corresponds to the traditional user cost of capital. Figures 2.1 and 2.2 show these series for equipment and structures, respectively.

The means and standard deviations of each measure over the sample period are given at the bottom of each column. Dividing the standard deviation of a series by its mean yields its coefficient of variation, a measure of the series' volatility. Comparing the coefficients of variation for the total and no-tax costs of capital suggests that tax policy has not been used effectively as a tool for stabilizing investment. For both structures and equipment, each no-tax series is less volatile than the total series that incorporates the incentive effects of taxation. One major exception to this pattern occurs during the early 1980s, when low profitability and high real interest rates drove the cost of capital to historical highs. The generous provisions of Economic Recovery Tax Act offset this increase.[6]

Comparing figures 2.1 and 2.2, we also note a difference in the general trend of the cost of capital for equipment and structures. Since the late 1950s the cost of capital for structures has generally risen while there is a downward trend for equipment. The difference is due largely to the invest-

Table 2.2
Components of the cost of capital (using earnings—price measure)

Year	Total	No tax-1	No tax-2	No Θ
Equipment				
1957	0.234	0.124	0.125	0.250
1958	0.220	0.139	0.133	0.237
1959	0.231	0.140	0.140	0.244
1960	0.159	0.129	0.118	0.201
1961	0.207	0.144	0.139	0.228
1962	0.146	0.144	0.138	0.159
1963	0.128	0.131	0.120	0.152
1964	0.116	0.131	0.124	0.155
1965	0.130	0.122	0.113	0.160
1966	0.123	0.114	0.107	0.152
1967	0.146	0.109	0.101	0.178
1968	0.142	0.108	0.104	0.147
1969	0.131	0.109	0.099	0.132
1970	0.151	0.124	0.112	0.165
1971	0.176	0.136	0.124	0.179
1972	0.121	0.130	0.118	0.108
1973	0.114	0.132	0.119	0.107
1974	0.107	0.146	0.126	0.121
1975	0.196	0.151	0.131	0.171
1976	0.179	0.159	0.142	0.154
1977	0.136	0.163	0.145	0.136
1978	0.159	0.171	0.149	0.136
1979	0.153	0.183	0.154	0.124
1980	0.158	0.205	0.172	0.119
1981	0.129	0.222	0.190	0.088
1982	0.107	0.203	0.172	0.072
1983	0.130	0.228	0.198	0.104
1984	0.112	0.163	0.155	0.090
1985	0.112	0.122	0.111	0.083
Mean	0.150	0.148	0.134	0.150
Standard deviation	0.037	0.033	0.025	0.048

Table 2.2 (continued)

Year	Total	No tax-1	No tax-2	No Θ
Structures				
1957	0.074	0.041	0.042	0.089
1958	0.051	0.045	0.043	0.068
1959	0.054	0.024	0.029	0.071
1960	0.012	0.046	0.037	0.039
1961	0.095	0.041	0.039	0.104
1962	0.081	0.040	0.037	0.085
1963	0.081	0.051	0.043	0.088
1964	0.064	0.053	0.047	0.074
1965	0.074	0.061	0.051	0.081
1966	0.087	0.066	0.056	0.087
1967	0.087	0.070	0.060	0.087
1968	0.088	0.056	0.051	0.084
1969	0.066	0.062	0.051	0.070
1970	0.073	0.062	0.052	0.074
1971	0.075	0.054	0.046	0.073
1972	0.076	0.056	0.045	0.073
1973	0.088	0.060	0.050	0.083
1974	0.085	0.077	0.058	0.077
1975	0.134	0.068	0.048	0.114
1976	0.092	0.064	0.050	0.079
1977	0.075	0.075	0.061	0.069
1978	0.099	0.082	0.066	0.086
1979	0.125	0.111	0.085	0.099
1980	0.147	0.133	0.103	0.110
1981	0.155	0.144	0.116	0.101
1982	0.145	0.151	0.116	0.093
1983	0.056	0.154	0.127	0.057
1984	0.058	0.106	0.092	0.044
1985	0.077	0.086	0.072	0.073
Mean	0.085	0.074	0.061	0.080
Standard deviation	0.031	0.035	0.026	0.017

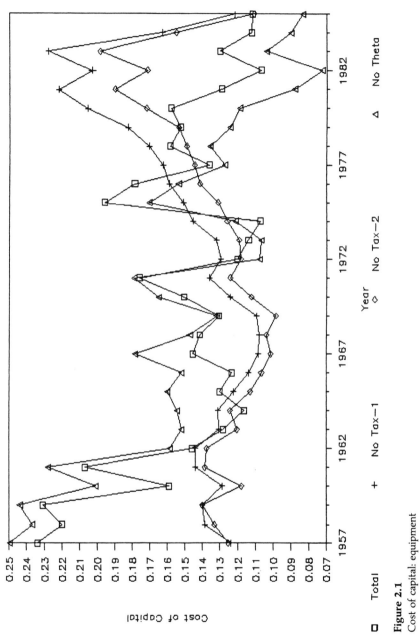

Figure 2.1
Cost of capital: equipment

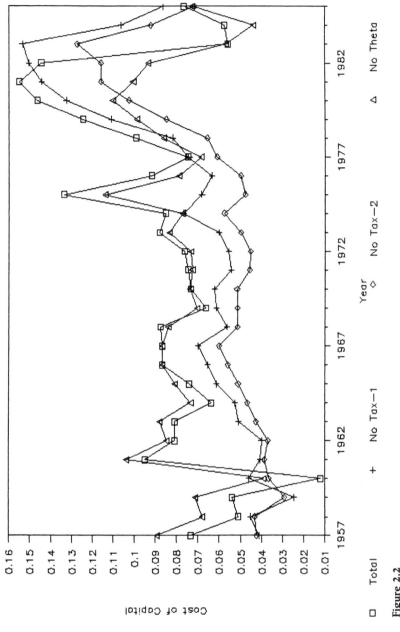

Figure 2.2
Cost of capital: structures

ment tax credit, which applied only to a small class of (public utility) structures but most equipment.

Although the analysis presented thus far is useful, it tells us only how the incentive to invest, and not investment itself, has been influenced by tax policy. Theory suggests that investment should be responsive to these incentives, but only empirical evidence relating to investment itself can enlighten us about the effects of tax policy on investment.

2.4 Explaining Actual Investment Behavior

The previous section described the determinants of investment behavior and how they have changed over time. This section provides estimates of how these determinants actually have influenced investment, showing in particular how investment in equipment and structures has been altered by tax policy. We focus on the general success of tax policy in stabilizing investment during the postwar period leading up to the Tax Reform Act of 1986.

In our empirical investigation, we considered several model specifications. Rather than present full details of the empirical results, we offer a summary of our general findings and then discuss the actual models we use to estimate the effects of tax policy on investment in structures and equipment.

General Findings

Empirical research has often found that cost of capital terms influence investment, but that other factors, such as output and business cash flow, do as well. Our specification including expected current and future profitability in the cost of capital expression provides a rationale for such findings in that (not surprisingly) these variables appear to exert less influence on investment once profitability is taken into account. However, one cannot rule out an independent effect for cash flow in all specifications.[7]

A second question that often has arisen in the past is whether taxes, when allowed to enter the estimated equation separately rather than being grouped together with other components of the cost of capital, help to explain investment. In a variety of models we found that the estimated importance of the cost of capital term was sensitive to whether a combined cost of capital expression alone was used or the influence of tax factors was estimated separately, but that tax factors typically were important in explaining investment behavior, particularly for investment in equipment.[8]

In general, our estimates were more satisfactory for equipment than structures, with coefficients in the structures equations typically more sensitive and less significant. It appears that investment in nonresidential structures does not conform as well to the predictions of our model. The better predictive power of the cost of capital for equipment expenditures is suggested by figures 2.3 and 2.4, which plot the cost of capital ck versus investment for equipment and structures, respectively. In figure 2.3 we observe many instances in which investment and the cost of capital move inversely, whereas the pattern of structures investment seen in figure 2.4 is much smoother and apparently less related to movements in the cost of capital.

A final empirical consideration is the relationship between equipment and structures investment. Since the two investment series have behaved quite differently over time, a disaggregate approach appears to be justified. However, one might still expect the structures and equipment investment decisions to be related, in that factors encouraging one type of investment might also cause a shift away from the other type.[9] To test this, we included the structures cost of capital term ck in the equipment investment equation and the equipment cost of capital term in the structures equation. In specifications that also included a cash flow term, such expressions had a significant, positive effect on investment.

Estimated Equations

The basic specifications we use for measuring the impact of the cost of capital on investment include as explanatory variables only the composite cost of capital ck and a constant.[10] Based on these equations, we simulate the historical effects of tax policy on investment under the assumption that our estimated no-tax cost of capital measures would have prevailed in the absence of taxation. In figures 2.5 (equipment) and 2.6 (structures), we plot series of the estimated impact of taxes on investment against investment itself. Due to the relatively small coefficients on the cost of capital, the estimated impact is not large relative to the variability of investment itself, particularly for structures.

What do these series tell us about the effectiveness of tax policy in stabilizing investment? Given the greater variability of the cost of capital due to taxes, it is not surprising that this increases the predicted variability of investment itself.

For equipment, the effects of taxes over the historical period is estimated to have lowered the average level of investment by 0.2% and increased the

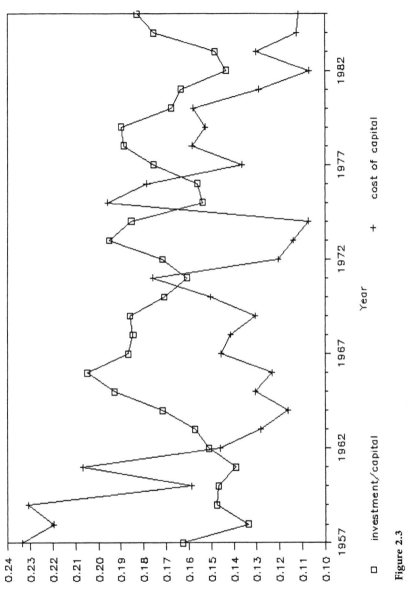

Figure 2.3
Investment and capital cost: equipment

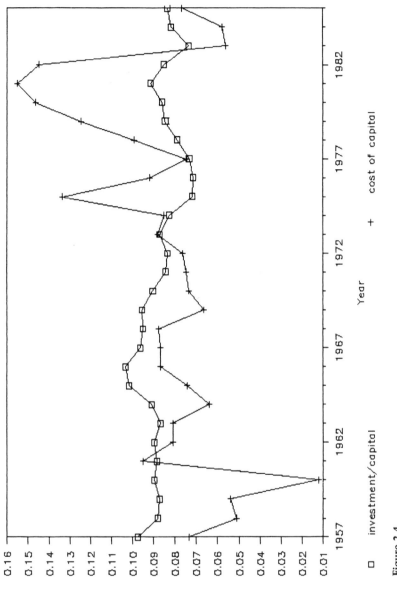

□   investment/capital   +   cost of capital

Figure 2.4
Investment and capital cost: structures

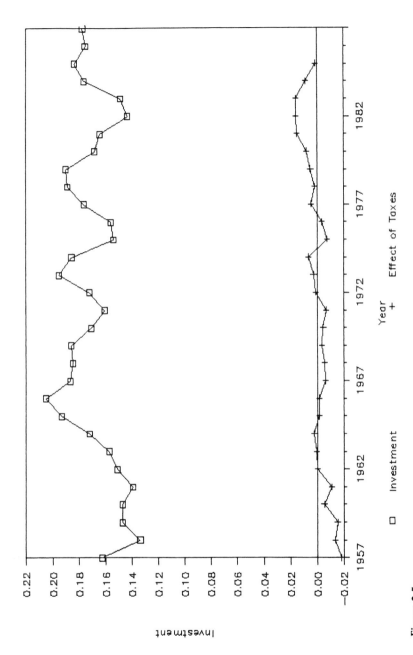

Figure 2.5
Effect of taxes: equipment

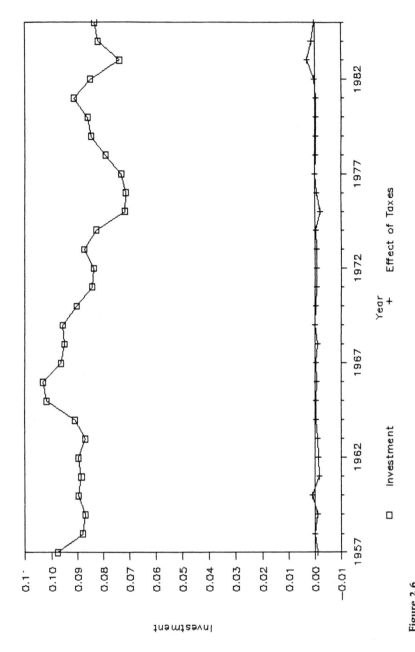

Figure 2.6
Effect of taxes: structures

standard deviation by 3.5%. Under the assumption that the real aftertax interest rate stays constant as taxes change (our no-tax-2 assumption discussed above), the estimated effects of taxes on both the mean and standard deviation of equipment investment are larger, with the mean of investment predicted to have been 1.6% lower and the standard deviation 10.5% higher. For structures, the impacts are considerably smaller.

Use of an alternative specification of investment, including cash flow and the other type of investment's cost of capital, led to a larger direct cost of capital coefficient.[11] However, it did not alter the general pattern of predicted investment for the post-1986 period. Therefore, although we recognize the uncertain pedigree of any particular model of investment, we are more confident that our characterization of the role of taxes after 1986 is accurate.

2.5   The Tax Reform Act of 1986

The Tax Reform Act of 1986 contained several provisions with potential effects on the incentive to invest. Among the most important of these were the reduction in the corporate tax rate, the lengthening of depreciation lifetimes, and the repeal of the investment tax credit.

The corporate tax rate, previously equal to 46%, was reduced to 40% for 1987 and 34% for 1988 and years thereafter. The investment tax credit, previously equal to 10% of qualifying investment expenditures, primarily those on new machinery and equipment, was repealed, with a retroactive effective date of January 1, 1986. Depreciation lifetimes for tax purposes, which had been 5 years for most equipment, 3 years for light equipment, and 19 years for business structures, typically increased, with most classes of equipment in the pre-1986, 5-year class being written off over 7 years and most nonresidential structures being written off over 31.5 years. For equity-financed investments, the drop in the corporate rate was outweighed by the reduced value of depreciation allowances and investment tax credits, with these provisions together leading to an increased tax burden on newly purchased equipment.

For nonresidential structures not previously qualifying for the investment tax credit, the cut in the corporate tax rate was more significant than the reduction in the value of depreciation allowances. However, some structures (generally public utility structures) had previously qualified for the credit. For this latter category, the effect of the act was like that for equipment, to increase the marginal tax burden.

There were many other ways in which the tax reform was expected to influence investment. The reduction of the corporate tax rate also lowered the benefits of the interest deduction associated with debt-financed investment, while the reduction in individual tax rates and repeal of the capital gains tax preference were expected to change the costs of equity and debt capital firms faced. Additional provisions, including the strengthening of corporate and individual minimum taxes, were generally expected to discourage investment. As we discuss below, it may be in this area that the effect of the tax policy was most evident.

Although careful calculations (e.g., Fullerton, Gillette, and Mackie 1987) showed relatively small increases in the total marginal tax burden on new investment, after taking account of all tax changes, there was a general consensus that the tax burden on business fixed investment had risen, particularly for machinery and equipment. Proponents of these provisions argued in terms of the potential gains from an improved allocation of capital, with few claiming that the change in law would encourage investment overall.

2.6 Recent Investment and the Tax Reform Act

Table 2.3 repeats, for convenience, the actual ratios of investment to the capital stock for equipment and nonresidential structures for the period 1986–88. As already mentioned, equipment investment has been strong during the period, apparently confounding the predictions that it would be stifled by the 1986 act. However, equipment investment during 1986 and 1987 was not out of line with our basic model's predictions, given in the second column of table 2.3.[12] In part, this is due to the relatively small

Table 2.3
Recent investment and the Tax Reform Act of 1986 (relative to the capital stock)

Year	Actual	Predicted	Due to reform
Equipment			
1986	0.175	0.176	0.0007
1987	0.177	0.174	−0.002
1988	0.190	0.174	−0.003
Structures			
1986	0.070	0.085	0.001
1987	0.067	0.084	−0.0002
1988	0.067	0.085	−0.0002

impact predicted by the model to have occurred because of the 1986 act, given in the last of column of the table.[13] In general, economic conditions for equipment investment were relatively good, even taking account of the Tax Reform Act. More difficult to explain are the strong growth of equipment spending in 1988 and the general weakness of structures spending throughout the past three years.[14]

At least part of the explanation for strong equipment investment may relate to changes in technology that are difficult to capture with our model. Table 2.4 provides a breakdown of equipment investment by category for the period 1985–88. As can be seen from the figures in this table, essentially all the real growth in equipment spending during 1986 and 1987 was attributable to investment in office, computing, and accounting machinery. While real (1982$) spending on this type of "high-tech" capital good rose from $65.0 billion in 1985 to $95.5 billion in 1987, the "low-tech" residual of nonresidential equipment spending was roughly constant, falling from $239.0 billion to $237.7 billion.

However, even this flat performance shines in comparison to the drop in real structures spending from $149.5 billion in 1985 to $122.3 billion in 1987. Moreover even "low-tech" equipment investment grew strongly in 1988, from $237.7 billion to $257.9 billion, a real growth rate of 8.5%. Nonresidential structures investment, on the other hand, declined slightly, from $122.3 billion to $122.2 billion.

Thus, even if one ignores the fast-growing information-processing equipment category altogether, equipment investment has grown more strongly than structures both during 1986–87 (when equipment spending was constant and structures spending fell considerably) and 1988 (when

Table 2.4
Nonresidential equipment investment, 1985–88 (billions of 1982$)

Category	1985	1986	1987	1988
Office, computing, and accounting machinery	65.0	73.1	95.5	113.7
Other information-processing and related equipment	54.3	55.6	57.4	60.5
Industrial equipment	64.6	62.3	61.9	68.4
Transportation and related equipment	61.5	59.9	58.9	65.7
Other equipment	58.6	57.4	59.5	63.3
Total	304.0	308.3	333.2	371.6

Source: *Survey of Current Business*, July 1989, table 5.7.

equipment investment rose considerably and structures spending was constant). This result is particularly important, given the uncertainty that some have expressed about the accuracy of the measure of the implicit price deflator. Although an understated quality-adjusted price for computers could lead to an overstatement of real computer purchases, it cannot explain the relative strength of other equipment investment.

A potential explanation for the weak performance of structures investment is that we may have left out of our model significant tax factors of the 1986 act affecting certain types of structures investment. For example, the act contained various provisions aimed at restricting the use by individual investors of tax losses generated by passive investments, including real estate.

In this regard, however, one must remember that in considering nonresidential structures investment, we have not even included the primary type of real estate investment against which such provisions were aimed—rental housing. This multifamily housing construction experienced a 34% drop in investment between 1986 and 1988 (from $29.1 billion to $19.3 billion in 1982$). Had we included this category in our measure of structures investment, the overall performance of the past few years would have been worse. Since construction of single-family housing units increased over the same period, this does provide evidence of an effect of the tax reform on residential investment but leaves us with our original puzzle unresolved.

A significant part of the answer can be found in a further disaggregation of nonresidential structures investment, given for the period 1985–88 in table 2.5. About two-thirds of the drop in real structures spending between 1985 and 1988 is attributable to one category of investment—mining,

Table 2.5
Nonresidential structures investment, 1985–88 (billions of 1982$)

Category	1985	1986	1987	1988
Industrial buildings	15.0	12.7	12.1	12.8
Commercial buildings	53.3	49.4	46.4	46.9
Public utilities	25.1	25.7	22.5	22.6
Mining exploration, shafts, and wells	35.2	20.7	18.2	17.2
Other structures	20.9	21.6	23.1	22.7
Total	149.5	130.1	122.3	122.2

Source: *Survey of Current Business*, July 1989, table 5.5.

exploration, shafts, and wells. The sharp decline in new oil exploration that occurred after the significant oil price decline in 1985, rather than any change in tax policy, seems to be the likely explanation here.

The remaining drop in investment since 1985 has been shared fairly uniformly by the other categories of structures investment, with purchases of industrial, commercial, and public utility structures declining by 15%, 12%, and 10%, respectively. However, if one considers the drop since 1986, when the tax reform act was passed, the decline is less evenly shared, as investment in public utility structures and commercial buildings declined, while industrial building construction has been roughly constant.

This pattern since 1986 is consistent with the relative tax treatment of these categories under the new law, as many utility structures had previously qualified for the now repealed investment tax credit and some of those commercial buildings not owned by corporations may have been subject to new rules limiting the deduction of real estate losses.

Perhaps the clearest tax incentive provided structures investment by the Tax Reform Act was in the industrial buildings category since few of these structures are owned by individuals potentially subject to the passive loss restrictions. However, as just indicated, investment in this category has been essentially constant in real terms, while investment in industrial equipment, which lost the investment tax credit, was growing by 10%.

Thus, certain obvious nontax factors, such as the boom in information processing and the decline in petroleum exploration, explain a significant part of the divergent performance of equipment and structures investment during the past few years. Within the structures category, there appears to be some change in composition consistent with the provisions of the new law. However, there remains an overall shift from structures to equipment investment that is not consistent with the incentives presented by the Tax Reform Act and for which there is no simple explanation.

Such a shift has been observed in the past. Looking once again at the last two columns of table 2.1, one can see a surge in the ratio of equipment to structures spending beginning around 1963 that, arguably, has carried through to the present. As we also noted, however, the cost of capital for equipment drifted lower through 1985, while the cost of capital for structures did not. Therefore a tax-related explanation for the shift was possible until 1986.

The evidence in this chapter, however, argues against such an explanation. First, our estimates of the impact of tax policy on investment are not strong enough to explain such a trend (see figures 2.5 and 2.6). Second, the trend has continued and, if anything, intensified during the past few years when tax factors pointed in the opposite direction.

2.7 Conclusions

Our primary findings in this chapter, as summarized in the introduction, are that tax factors have not stabilized nonresidential investment over the postwar period and that the Tax Reform Act of 1986 has played a relatively unimportant role in explaining the level and especially the pattern of investment in equipment and structures during the past few years.

It is important to exercise some caution when viewing these results. In analyzing the impact of tax policy, we have taken other macroeconomic factors, such as the level of profitability and the real interest rate, as given. To the extent that these factors would have been different under alternative tax regimes, our conclusions would require modification, although the size and direction of such corrections are not easily calculated. Nevertheless, our results suggest that tax policy may have been given too much prominence (relative to those other factors we consider here, such as interest rates and profitability, and those we don't, such as technological innovation) in past discussions of investment behavior.

Notes

We are grateful to Bob Chirinko, Joel Slemrod, and other participants in the conference for comments on an earlier draft, and to the OTPR and the Penn Institute for Law and Economics for financial support.

1. In this chapter we focus on *gross* rather than *net* investment. There has been a widening gap over the postwar period between these two figures as depreciation has become more significant. However, this is largely due to the shift toward investment in equipment. Because we focus separately on equipment and structures investment, the gross–net distinction is not as important.

2. This expression is basically the user cost of capital familiar from the investment literature and first derived by Jorgenson (1963), except that it includes the productivity term θ. This term replaces the frequent but ad hoc inclusion of cyclical measures such as output.

3. Because we do not observe expectations directly, we estimate them by regressing actual realized returns on observable variables such as past rates of return and output–capital ratios.

4. Estimated values are obtained by regressing ex post values of ck on information available at the current date, including a constant, a trend, lagged values of c, and the output–capital ratio.

In calculating the ex post values of c, we use the short-term commercial paper rate for the nominal cost of debt, the earnings–price ratio of the Standard and Poor's 500 companies for the cost of equity, and we calculate the tax parameters τ and Γ using the same methodology as Auerbach and Hines (1988).

5. When analyzing the effects of tax policy on investment, we use the no-tax-1 variable. Calculations based on the no-tax-2 variable did not differ significantly.

6. Through its impact on the federal budget deficit, the 1981 act may very well have contributed to the rise in real interest rates that occurred. However, in terms of revenue cost, the bulk of the 1981 tax cut came through reductions in individual tax rates (Auerbach 1982).

7. Other recent investment studies, notably the work of Fazzari, Hubbard and Peterson (1988), have found that cash flow does matter for a class of smaller firms when a more traditional measure of the cost of capital is included as an explanatory variable. The inclusion of cash flow can be justified as providing a proxy for capital market imperfections that makes internal funds less expensive to the firm than funds obtained at the market rates appearing in the cost of capital expression.

Whether cash flow matters for this reason or because of a general misspecification of the investment equation is an important question that deserves further attention.   .

8. We allowed for a separate tax effect in two different ways. One specification added either the no-tax-1 or no-tax-2 measure of ck to the basic equation including ck. In this case we typically found that both the no-tax and the total measure of ck had significant coefficients, suggesting that nontax factors may have a more important role than taxes relative to the theory. To control for the possibility that this weaker influence of taxes may have been due to our using poor measures of expected tax variables, we also tried including actual values of these future values. The results for this specification were similar to those of the first.

In each case the implied effects of taxes is typically not significantly different from the impact implied by the basic specification based on the combined cost of capital expression. It is this basic specification that we report in this chapter and use in our simulations.

9. One would expect this type of model to result from the specification of a general production function that includes the two types of capital, although we have not been able to obtain a simple closed form expression for investment in this case.

10. Our estimated equations are based on the measures of the cost of capital shown in figures 2.3 and 2.4. Since we are using annual data, the statistical theory of time aggregation (Working 1960) suggests that the aggregated equation will contain a first-order moving average, $ma(1)$, error term. Indeed, there is strong evidence of serial correlation, so we also correct for a first-order moving average process. It should be noted, however, that the point estimates of the moving average error terms are higher than is predicted by the theory, implying that the models may be omitting important explanatory variables.

The actual equations are (with standard errors given in parentheses)

for equipment,

$$\frac{I}{K} = 0.193 - 0.165 * CKE,$$
$$\quad\ (0.007) \quad (0.040)$$

$\bar{R}^2 = 0.520,$
$ma(1)$ Coefficient $= 0.879,$
Durbin-Watson statistic $= 1.79;$

for structures,

$$\frac{I}{K} = 0.089 - 0.029 * CKE,$$
$$\quad\ (0.002) \quad (0.024)$$

$\bar{R}^2 = 0.454,$
$ma(1)$ coefficient $= 0.971,$
Durbin-Watson statistic $= 1.92.$

11. The actual equations are (with standard errors given in parentheses)

for equipment,

$$\frac{I}{K} = 0.106 - 0.475 * CKEEQ + 0.428 * CKEST + 0.348 * CASH(-1),$$
$$\quad\ (0.031) \quad (0.127) \qquad\quad (0.155) \qquad\quad (0.083)$$

$\bar{R}^2 = 0.239,$
$ma(1)$ coefficient $= 0.301,$
Durbin-Watson statistic $= 1.85;$

for structures,

$$\frac{I}{K} = 0.019 - 0.070 * CKEST + 0.133 * CKEEQ + 0.258 * CASH(-1),$$
$$\quad\ (0.017) \quad (0.058) \qquad\quad (0.053) \qquad\quad (0.84)$$

$\bar{R}^2 = 0.249,$
$ma(1)$ coefficient $= 0.233,$
Durbin-Watson statistic $= 1.52,$

where CASH is retained earnings plus dividends plus depreciation divided by the capital stock, CKEEQ is the equipment cost of capital, and CKEST is the structures cost of capital.

The $ma(1)$ terms in this specification are more in line with those predicted from the theory of aggregation discussed in note 10.

12. These predictions are the fitted values for 1986–88 based on a reestimation of the model through 1988. Values of ck for the last three years depend on post-1988 values of c, which are not observable. For the estimation we use the actual 1988 value of c for these unobservable values.

13. The effects of the act are estimated by multiplying the coefficient from the basic investment equation, given in note 10, by the difference between the actual value of ck and the value that ck would have taken had the tax law been kept constant in 1986. The generally small effects are due in part to the small size of these coefficients.

The reason for the positive effect estimated for equipment in 1986 is that even though equipment had lost the investment tax credit, it still had and was about to lose accelerated depreciation allowances. This provided a powerful incentive to invest.

The negative effect for structures in 1987 and 1988 is attributable to the inclusion in this category of public utility structures that lost the investment tax credit in 1986.

14. The picture does not change appreciably if one uses the alternative investment equations that include both capital costs and cash flow. Again fixing each capital cost to its 1986 value with no tax change, and assuming that aftertax cash flow would have had the same ratio to before-tax cash flow in 1986 and 1987 as it did in 1985 (the last year before tax payments were affected by the change in law), the net effect of taxes on equipment investment in 1987 and 1988 is about 50% larger than before but still less than one-half percentage point (i.e., less than 3% of equipment investment) in each year. The effect on structures investment is also slightly larger in each year but still no more than about one-tenth of one percentage point (i.e., about 1.5% of structures investment) in each year.

When estimated over the full sample period 1957–88, these equations' predicted values of equipment and structures investment, like those of the basic model, fail to track the jump in 1988 equipment investment and the weakness of structures investment throughout the post-reform period.

References

Abel, Andrew B., and Olivier Blanchard. 1986. The Present Value of Profits and Cyclical Movements in Investment. *Econometrica* 54: 249–273.

Auerbach, Alan J. 1982. The New Economics of Accelerated Depreciation. *Boston College Law Review* 23: 1327–1355.

Auerbach, Alan J. 1987. The Tax Reform Act of 1986 and the Cost of Capital. *Journal of Economic Perspectives* 1: 73–86.

Auerbach, Alan J., and Kevin Hassett. 1990. Tax Policy and Fixed Business Investment in the United States. Mimeo.

Auerbach., Alan, J., and James Hines. 1988. Investment Tax Incentives and Frequent Tax Reforms. *American Economic Review* 78: 211–216.

Bernanke, Ben, Henning Bohn, and Peter Reiss. 1988. Alternative Non-nested Specification Tests of Time Series Investment Models. *Journal of Econometrics* 37: 293–326.

Bosworth, Barry. 1985. Taxes and the Investment Recovery. *Brookings Papers on Economic Activity* 16: 1–38.

Chirinko, Robert S. 1986. The Ineffectiveness of Effective Tax Rates: A Critique of Feldstein's Fisher-Schultz Lecture. *Journal of Public Economics* 32: 369–388.

Fazzari, Steven M., R. Glenn Hubbard, and Bruce C. Peterson. 1988. Financing Constraints and Corporate Investment. *Brookings Papers on Economic Activity* 19: 141–195.

Feldstein, Martin. 1982. Inflation, Tax Rules and Investment: Some Econometric Evidence. *Econometrica* 50: 825–862.

Fullerton, Don, Robert Gillette, and James B. Mackie. 1987. Investment Allocation and Growth under the Tax Reform Act of 1986. *Compendium of Tax Research 1986*. Washington, DC: U.S. Treasury.

Jorgenson, Dale W. 1963. Capital Theory and Investment Behavior. *American Economic Review* 53: 247–259.

Working, Holbrook. 1960. Note on the Correlation of First Differences of Averages in a Random Chain. *Econometrica* 28: 916–918.

COMMENTS

Robert S. Chirinko

For students of tax policy, a particularly embarrassing moment occurs when attempting to explain the empirical relation between tax incentives and business investment spending. Economic theory aside, movements in tax incentives are largely independent of, and occasionally run counter to, anticipated changes in investment. Such a moment confronts Auerbach and Hassett in their exploration of the effects of the 1986 Tax Reform Act on equipment and structures spending. In light of the provisions of this legislation and the implications of economic models, we would have expected that total business expenditures on fixed investment and the share devoted to equipment would both fall. The unfriendly facts are presented by Auerbach and Hassett in table 2.1. Stated as a percentage of GNP, equipment investment rose 7.1%, while structures investment fell 26.5% from 1985 to 1988.

Explanations for these facts can fall into two broad categories: the data are misleading or the models are inadequate. Auerbach and Hassett explore the latter possibility with an interesting extension of the user cost concept pioneered by Dale Jorgenson (1963). Before turning to their model, I would like to begin my remarks with a brief look at the data. I will then discuss their new analytic model and its application to understanding the effects of the 1986 Tax Reform Act.

In examining the growth of equipment spending, Auerbach and Hassett note that the growth in 1986 and 1987 can be explained by the behavior of one component—office, computing, and accounting machinery. Total equipment growth in 1988 was more balanced across assets. A similar decomposition for structures spending (relative to GNP) also proves informative, and is presented in table 2C.1. As shown in the fourth row, spending on mining exploration, shafts, and wells exhibited an enormous drop of 56.1%. During the same period the nominal price of crude energy fell by 27.2%. If investment in this category (as a percentage of GNP) had remained unchanged, then the ratio of total structures investment to GNP would have fallen by 13.3%, only one-half as much as the actual change. (The remaining decline might be explained by factors not usually considered in models of tax policy and investment spending, and these will be discussed in the final part of these remarks.) Thus, as with office machinery, examining the components can aid our understanding of the behavior of the aggregate and suggest what factors have been omitted from our theories.

Table 2C.1
Nonresidential structures investment as a percentage of GNP, 1985 and 1988

Category	1985	1988	% change
	(1)	(2)	(3)
Commercial	1.473	1.165	− 20.9
Industrial and not-for-profit	0.895	0.790	− 11.7
Public utilities	0.694	0.562	− 19.0
Mining exploration, shafts, and wells	0.973	0.427	− 56.1
Not elsewhere classified	0.097	0.092	− 5.2
Total	4.132	3.036	− 26.5

Source: Bureau of Economic Analysis, U.S. Department of Commerce. *Survey of Current Business* 69 (July 1989): GNP, table 1.2; Nonresidential Structures Investment, table 5.5.

Combined with the puzzling movements in the aggregates and the well-known success of the accelerator model, these disaggregate results suggest that we need to look beyond the effects of relative prices on investment, and this is the point of departure for the new model presented in this chapter. The Auerbach and Hassett model of a value-maximizing firm contains two dynamic elements—forward-looking behavior and convex adjustment costs penalizing the firm for rapid changes in the capital stock. In combination, these two assumptions force the firm to look into the future when formulating its investment plans and, with sufficient separability in the technology, lead to the following separate decision rules for equipment and structures investment as a percentage of their capital stocks (I_t/K_t):

$$\frac{I_t}{K_t} = \alpha + \beta ck_t + \varepsilon_t,$$

$$ck_t = 0.533 * c_t + 0.267 * c_{t+1} + 0.133 * c_{t+2} + 0.067 * c_{t+3},$$

where ε_t is a $ma(1)$ error term and the c_t's are defined by equation (1) in the Auerbach and Hassett paper.

Relative to the traditional Jorgensonian model of investment, there are four important differences. First, the c_t's defining ck_t are similar to the traditional user cost but for the productivity shock term θ. The inclusion of this latter term was motivated in part by the rapid increase in computing machinery and as a means for entering a cyclical measure (output, cash flow, etc.) into the model.[1] Recent research in macroeconomics has also used this concept, arguing that productivity shocks are a principal force in economic fluctuations.[2] In these models and in the empirical implementation of the current model, productivity shocks affect the technology uniformly and hence do not have differential effects on equipment and structures.[3] Although, in principle, there is no reason to preclude separate shocks for equipment and structures, such an approach might rob θ of any useful economic meaning.

Second, apart from θ, a cyclical variable does not enter the investment equation. I do not doubt that the maximization problem carries this implication, but it should be noted that, in contrast to the comments in section 2.3 and in note 2, the logic of the Jorgensonian model implies that output is an argument in the investment function. Indeed, the debate between Robert Eisner and Dale Jorgenson focused on, among other issues, whether output and user cost terms should enter separately or in combination.[4]

The remaining two differences stem from the greater pressure within the profession currently to derive econometric relations directly from the optimization problem. Third, in the Jorgensonian model, investment depends on current and past variables. In contrast, the two dynamic elements in the Auerbach and Hassett model result in today's investment depending on current, as well as future user costs, and lagged variables enter indirectly. In the estimation of the model and in the spirit of rational expectation econometrics, Auerbach and Hassett use only those variables that could be known by the firm before undertaking its current investment expenditures. These can be interpreted as instrumental variables, which include lags.

A final difference stems from the lack of consideration of delivery or gestation lags in the model presented by Auerbach and Hassett. In a formal optimization problem, these generally are rather 'messy' to deal with. Twenty-five years ago, equation specifications were not strictly tied to optimization problems, and lags could be imposed relatively easily, in what is now referred to—by the less than complimentary label—as ad hoc. Dynamics are imposed in the estimation by assuming that time aggregation induces a first-order moving-average error.

In general, I commend the authors' approach to specifying the econometric equations from first principles, and the model that arises has a clear interpretation based on neoclassical price theory. Since most investment models can be derived from the same optimization problem, it is interesting, though not surprising, to note that the specification of c_t in equation (1) bears a close resemblance to Tobin's Q. Measuring θ by pre-tax earnings relative to the capital stock, assuming that the marginal investment is equity financed, and setting the constant depreciation rate δ to zero, we can rewrite equation (1) as follows (omitting t subscripts):

$$c = \frac{K(1 - \Gamma)g'}{V} = Q^{-1},$$

where the numerator is the replacement value of the capital stock, adjusted for taxes $(1 - \Gamma)$ and the price of new capital goods (g'), and the denominator is the equity value of the firm.[5] Apart from the separate equations for equipment and structures, c is the inverse of Tobin's Q.

Given the parsimonious specification, the Auerbach and Hassett model does quite a good job of fitting the data and performs better for equipment than structures. One imagines that a good deal of this success can be traced to the large moving-average parameter (to be discussed further). Nonetheless, given the paths of the ck_t's in table 2.2, the model has difficulty explaining the upsurge in equipment and sharp drop in structures expenditure at the aggregate level. The effects of the 1986 Tax Reform Act, as reported in table 2.3, are extremely small, less than 2.7% of actual equipment investment and 0.6% of actual structures investment for 1987 and 1988. That is a conclusion with which I am most comfortable since it is consistent with my own investigations and with a good deal of the investment literature.[6]

However, I would like to take issue with the other major conclusions of the study: that tax policy has not stabilized investment spending. The stability issue cannot be assessed within the current framework for two reasons. First, as noted by the authors, the moving-average error term is much larger than can be ascribed to time aggregation as analyzed by Working (1960). Undoubtedly, this reflects the omission of some additional dynamics, such as delivery or gestation lags. The latter might be particularly important for structures, which has the poorer empirical performance and a larger ma parameter. When cash flow is entered as an additional regressor, the ma parameters drop substantially, but, as noted by the authors, the interpretation of this econometric equation with cash flow becomes uncertain (cf. notes 7 and 11). The strong suggestion from the econometric results of omitted dynamics casts suspicion on any analysis involving the timing of investment with this estimated model.

Second, Lucas' work on econometric methods and policy analysis has an important bearing on the stability analysis. In that paper Lucas (1976) highlighted the problems with using investment equations in assessing temporary changes in tax policy. Since the equations in the Auerbach and Hassett model are based on an explicit technology, the estimated parameters will be immune from the Lucas Critique. However, ck_t is defined above as a weighted-average of current and future c_t's, where the weights have been prespecified. These prespecified parameters (and possibly the moving-average parameter) are determined by the expectations process, and that is the process that Lucas argued would likely be volatile in the face of policy changes. Whether this phenomenon is empirically important for the experiments that the authors are undertaking remains an open question.[7]

Returning to the assessment of tax policy and the modeling of investment expenditures, there still remain, despite the spirited efforts of Auerbach and Hassett, the puzzles concerning rising equipment and falling structures investment in the late 1980s. I would like to conclude with some observations as to what factors may have been operative in this period and how they might affect future models of firm behavior and tax analysis.

Apart from the enormous decrease in mining exploration, table 2C.1 highlights that investment in commercial structures also fell sharply. In attempting to understand this decline, I pursued the underutilized—though occasionally highly informative—research strategy of contacting a practitioner, who in this case is a Chicago developer of both residential and nonresidential properties. Her view of the decline was that despite the drop in corporate and personal tax rates, the dominant effect of the 1986 Tax Reform Act was that it precluded the possibility of taking passive losses through partnerships. A second factor, unrelated to the 1986 legislation, was the "overhang" of existing buildings.

Neither factor is captured by the econometric models routinely employed in assessing investment and taxes. The former effect could be reflected in a higher discount rate, as firms find it increasingly difficult to raise funds, and suggests more attention to the issues of finance and clienteles (e.g., Auerbach, 1983). The latter effect is not easily incorporated into existing dynamic models. In a stock-adjustment framework, "overhang" can be represented by the lagged capital stock. Although these models are quite successful in fitting the data, they cannot be derived in a consistent manner from a model where the firm is forward-looking. This thus limits their usefulness in generating a deeper understanding of firm behavior and, most important for present purposes, in assessing how firms will react to changes in their tax environment. The "overhang" issue highlights the inattention to the supply side of the market for capital goods and to the distinction between the demand for the stock of capital and the demand for the flow of investment.[8]

In regard to equipment spending, the distinction between old and new capital is made frequently but has not had sufficient impact on empirical models. As suggested by Auerbach and Hassett equipment may have enjoyed favorable technology shocks. In turn, these would lead to the obsolescence of old capital and hence an increased demand for new capital observed in the data.[9] Thus there may exist complicated interactions between θ, an endogenous rate of depreciation, and tax parameters not captured adequately by standard models.

The lesson for investment and tax analysis from the 1986 Tax Reform Act is that we are in need of an expanded view of the firm and the markets in which it operates. That expanded view would recognize

1. the effects of financing clienteles,

2. sharp distinctions between supply and demand and stocks and flows in the market for capital goods,

3. the possibility of endogenous depreciation,

4. the role of technology shocks and their effects on old and new capital, as modeled in the Auerbach and Hassett paper.

Reference

Auerbach, Alan J. 1983. Stockholder Tax Rates and Firm Attributes. *Journal of Public Economics* 21: 107–127.

Baily, Martin N. 1981. Productivity and the Services of Capital and Labor. *Brookings Papers on Economic Activity* 1: 1–50.

Chirinko, Robert S. 1986. Business Investment and Tax Policy: A Perspective on Existing Models and Empirical Results. *National Tax Journal* 39: 137–155.

Chirinko, Robert S. 1987. The Ineffectiveness of Effective Tax Rates on Business Investment: A Critique of Feldstein's Fisher-Schultz Lecture. *Journal of Public Economics* 32: 369–387.

Chirinko, Robert S. 1988. Business Tax Policy, The Lucas Critique, and Lessons from the 1980s. *American Economic Review* 78: 206–210.

Chirinko, Robert S., and Robert Eisner. 1983. Tax Policy and Investment in Major U.S. Macroeconometric Models. *Journal of Public Economics* 20: 139–166.

Jorgenson, Dale W. 1963. Capital Theory and Investment Behavior. *American Economic Review* 53: 247–259.

Lucas, Robert E. 1976. Econometric Policy Evaluation: A Critique. In Karl Brunner and Allan H. Meltzer (eds.), *The Phillips Curve and Labor Markets*. Amsterdam: North-Holland, pp. 19–46. Reprinted in *Studies in Business Cycle Theory*. Cambridge: MIT, 1981, pp. 104–130.

Mankiw, N. Gregory. 1989. Real Business Cycles: A New Keynesian Perspective. *Journal of Economic Perspectives* 3: 79–90.

Plosser, Charles I. 1989. Understanding Real Business Cycles. *Journal of Economic Perspectives* 3: 51–78.

Poterba, James M. 1984. Tax Subsidies to Owner-Occupied Housing: An Asset Market Approach. *Quarterly Journal of Economics* 99: 729–752.

Shapiro, Matthew D. 1986. Investment, Output, and the Cost of Capital. *Brookings Papers on Economic Activity* 1: 111–152.

Topel, Robert, and Sherwin Rosen. 1988. A Time-Series Model of Housing Investment in the U.S. *Journal of Political Economy* 96: 718–740.

Working, Holbrook. 1960. Note on the Correlation of First Differences of Averages in a Random Chain. *Econometrica* 28: 916–918.

Notes

In preparing these remarks, the author has benefited from helpful conversations with Matthew Shapiro and Linda Vincent.

1. It is not necessarily the case that productivity shocks will lead to a cyclical variable in an investment equation. See Shapiro (1986), pp. 115–121.

2. See the recent surveys of real business cycle models by Mankiw (1989) and Plosser (1989).

3. This is one reason why the errors terms are likely to be correlated, a relation that could be exploited in estimation.

4. Auerbach and Hassett (section 2.4 and note 8) find that entering tax terms separately or in combination with other components of c was important empirically.

5. With these assumptions, we obtain the following relation,

$$c = \frac{[(1 - \Gamma)(g'/p)(E/S)]/(V/S)}{(E/p)/K} = \frac{K(1 - \Gamma)g'}{V} = Q^{-1},$$

where p = a price deflator, $g = g'/p$, E = earnings, S = number of shares, and V = the equity value of the firm.

6. See Chirinko and Eisner (1983) and Chirinko (1987) for empirical evidence and Chirinko (1986) for a survey of the literature.

7. See Chirinko (1988) for some evidence that the Lucas Critique, as an empirical proposition, is not of first-order importance.

8. Some important advances along this line can be found in the models of the housing market by Poterba (1984) and Topel and Rosen (1988).

9. See Baily (1981) for further discussion.

GENERAL DISCUSSION

Michael McIntyre asked whether the investment figures used by the authors were for *expenditures* or for *commitments*. Because there are significant lags in producing structures, commitment data would be misleading. Alan Auerbach responded that expenditure figures had been used.

Matthew Shapiro noted that the impact of the tax legislation of the early 1980s may continue to appear in more recent figures. Auerbach agreed that overhang can be a problem but claimed that its effect is picked up by the profit variable used in the study.

Shapiro continued the discussion with a comment about the authors' use of an average, rather than a marginal, measure of the incentive to invest. Finally, he noted that θ, the variable representing the productivity of capital, would be correlated with tax changes in an important way.

Don Fullerton recommended that the authors reevaluate the level of asset aggregation. He saw an overemphasis on equipment and structures, which together represent only one-half of the corporate capital stock. Future studies should also include analyses of land, inventories, and intangibles. The tax changes affecting these assets are especially noteworthy because such investments did not lose the investment tax credit to offset the reduction in tax rates.

Expressing doubt that tax change tests have sufficient power to measure the impact of nontax events, James Poterba wondered how the effect of recent economic changes are fed through the model. He also cautioned that we have only a poor ability to predict and measure investment.

Glenn Hubbard encouraged researchers to explore the effect of uncertainty over tax parameters on investment behavior. Uncertainty about the reenactment of the investment tax credit, for instance, could be an important factor in investment decisions. Other studies have used models that attempt to capture these effects by randomizing tax variables. Hubbard also noted the distinction between productivity shocks and technology shocks, and asked how productivity shocks are introduced into the model.

Randall Weiss observed that pinning down the effective dates for tax changes for which there are elaborate transition rules, such as the treatment of depreciation and the investment tax credit, poses difficulties for this kind of study. For example, in the presence of binding contracts, there would be some delay before the new rules would become generally effective, with the outcome that some of the investment observed during the test period may actually have been installed under the old rules. Weiss added that this may be of particular importance for public utilities.

Referring to the experience of Dow Chemical, Gilbert Harter claimed that TRA did not significantly change the return standards for the chemical industry. Between 1981 and 1987 the industry had been operating under capacity, resulting in few capital acquisitions during this period. In 1988 industry demand increased quickly, stimulating Dow's current heavy capital investment program. Thus the change in investment came not in response to tax changes but in response to demand. With this in mind, Harter encouraged the inclusion of demand factors in investment studies, as well as an exploration of how taxes affect product demand.

Charles McLure made several points. First, he proposed the fall in the price of oil as an explanation for the authors' observed drop-off in investment in structures used for mining exploration, shafts, and wells. Second, he recommended carrying the time series on investment in structures back to 1981 to see what happened to commercial building since that time as a result of the encouragement of tax shelters by the 1981 tax act. Finally, he emphasized the importance of considering risk in an investment model.

Henry Aaron asked how the authors handled the "office equipment controversy." This issue of falling prices for computer equipment, responded Auerbach, is part of the larger question of whether the study uses the correct price deflator. Jack Mutti added that for its current account projections the Fed deals with this problem by breaking computers out of the aggregate data.

Responding to the several comments about treatment of risk, Auerbach explained that risk is treated by linearizing the model. He also pointed out that in this study the cost of capital values were calculated in any given year based on what tax rules actually followed. The model uses past interest and profit rates as instrumental variables in the estimating equation for the cost of capital.

3

The Impact of the 1986 Tax Reform on Personal Saving

Jonathan Skinner and
Daniel Feenberg

3.1 Introduction

The 1986 Tax Reform Act was viewed by some critics as discouraging saving.[1] While marginal rates were reduced, the preferential treatment of capital gains was erased and IRAs largely shut down. At first, the pessimistic view of tax reform seemed to be borne out by the statistics; personal saving rates plunged from an already low 4% in 1986 to 1.8% in the second quarter of 1987. But since that time the saving rate has rebounded; by the second quarter of 1989, the personal saving rate stood at 5.4%.

One of the most difficult tasks in economics is to establish a causal relationship, and in the case of a structural change as recent as the 1986 tax reform, the task is particularly difficult. The first question that must be addressed is, Were there large changes in the incentives to saving under the 1986 tax reform? We find that the changes in marginal household saving incentives were substantial.[2] For example, 27% of taxpayers, weighted by dividend income received, experienced a decline in marginal tax rates on dividend income of more than 20 percentage points. We also find that the decline in marginal rates and the increase in the tax on capital gains largely offset one another, leaving the effective household tax rate on investments largely unchanged or even lowered. Furthermore investments held for a long period of time were most favored under the 1986 tax reform, even when accrued capital gains comprised a substantial fraction of the total return.

The second question is, How do these marginal incentives to save—as summarized by the aftertax rate of return—affect saving rates? The evidence that interest rates affect saving is weak, although for the most part the evidence excludes the latter part of the 1980s.[3] We reevaluate the evidence, first with simple saving regressions that imply a *negative* interest elasticity of saving during the postwar period and, second, with the Euler equation approach to consumption which implies essentially no effect of the real aftertax return on saving (Hall 1988). But when the sample is restricted to the 1980s, both the saving and consumption regressions show a positive and significant effect of the aftertax return on saving. These results either suggest a fundamental shift in saving behavior during the 1980s or a simple statistical artifact.

If the aftertax rate of return has had little historical impact on aggregate personal saving, then why should the 1986 Tax Reform Act (TRA86) be expected to affect saving? There are three reasons. First, TRA86 sharply restricted IRA eligibility to higher income taxpayers, and IRA contributions fell by 62% between 1986 and 1987. Generally, microeconomic studies have been supportive of the view that IRAs represent new saving, so TRA86 could have reduced household saving by restricting IRAs.[4] But the evidence from aggregate personal saving suggests that IRAs, if anything, reduced saving. Between 1982 when IRAs became generally available and 1986 when they were curtailed, personal saving declined from 6.8% to 4%; since 1986 the saving rate has rebounded by two percentage points.

One explanation for the sharply different results between the microeconomic studies suggesting that IRAs increase saving, and the aggregate data suggesting that they do not, is the measurement of saving. Saving can be measured in two ways: either as the difference between the flow of income and the flow of consumption—which is how personal saving is usually measured—or as the change in net wealth. Theoretically the two measures are identical. But in practice they are quite different.[5] And saving rates calculated as the difference in net wealth tell a different story of asset accumulation during the period when IRAs were available; this measure of saving remained high during 1982–86 and dropped off slightly after 1987. Obviously many factors accounted for this increase in net wealth, such as the stock market boom, but the point remains that household asset accumulation was strong during the mid-1980s. Hence it is difficult to make any conclusions about the effect of IRAs on saving based only on an examination of aggregate saving rates since alternative measures of saving tell such different stories.

The second way that TRA86 affected saving behavior was by phasing out the deduction for personal interest payments and thereby increasing the net cost of borrowing. As a result of TRA86 both total consumer credit (excluding house mortgages) and revolving credit fell sharply between the latter half of 1986 and the first quarter of 1987. Holding other factors constant, this would imply that TRA86 stimulated saving, since a dollar not borrowed is a dollar saved. But taxpayers did not hold their home mortgages constant. Using a panel of taxpayers for the years 1985 to 1987, we found that taxpayers shuffled their reduced personal credit into home equity lines of credit or increased home mortgages. Our estimates suggest that of every dollar reduction in personal interest payments, between 67 and 86 cents went back into increased home mortgage payments. Perhaps this is one reason why the ratio of home mortgages to housing value reached 48% in 1988, a sharp rise from the 40.4% ratio in 1984 (Federal Reserve Board 1989). At least for the wealthy taxpayers in our sample, the reduction in personal credit deductibility had little effect on overall saving.

The third effect of TRA86 on the level and composition of household saving was the controversial decision to ease the distinction between long term capital gains and ordinary income. The top marginal rate on capital gains rose from 20% to 33%, while the statutory rates on ordinary income declined. Once it became clear that the new law would raise capital gains taxes in 1987, taxpayers rushed to realize long-term gains in 1986. A lively debate still continues on whether increased capital gains taxes raise revenue (Lindsey 1987; Cook and O'Hara 1987; Auerbach 1988), but a different, and neglected, question is how announced changes in the capital gains tax affected household saving. The primary impact of TRA86 on saving could have been to encourage taxpayers to unlock their long-term gains and spend them (Summers 1989). Results from the panel survey of taxpayers provide little support for the view that the capital gains realization in 1986 reduced saving, although we do find evidence that taxpayers shifted their capital gains into interest-bearing assets. In summary, the Tax Reform Act of 1986 had a stronger impact on the composition of saving and credit than on the actual level of aggregate household saving.

3.2 The Effect of TRA86 on the Marginal Return to Saving

The objective of TRA86 was to broaden the tax base and lower marginal rates. These lower rates were phased in during 1987, and by 1988 taxpayers faced top marginal rates of 33%, with the wealthiest individuals paying a marginal tax of 28%. For many taxpayers the changes in marginal rates were quite small. For example, in a 1987 study Hausman and Poterba evaluated the overall impact of TRA86 on marginal rates:

Our calculations suggest that in 1988, over 40 percent of the taxpaying population will face marginal tax rates equal to or higher than the rates they would face under current law. Only 11 percent of taxpayers receive marginal tax rate reductions of ten percentage points or more. In part, these findings account for our conclusion that the tax reform will have relatively small aggregate effects. (pp. 101–102)

Our calculations focus less on the absolute number of taxpayers and more on those taxpayers who are actually receiving a large fraction of interest, dividend, or capital gains income. Our measure of marginal tax rate changes weights each taxpayer by the amount of relevant income that they received in 1986. Since a large fraction of saving is done by those whose tax rates are affected most by TRA86, we find substantial shifts in the marginal tax rates on a "representative" or average dollar of capital income.

The distribution of these changes may be seen in figures 3.1 and 3.2 (and in table 3.1) as calculated by NBER's TAXSIM program. The 1986 tax model is a stratified random sample of 75,400 U.S. individual income tax returns weighted to replicate the 1986 universe of tax returns.[6] Figure 3.1 shows the distribution of changes in the marginal tax rate on dividends and capital gains between 1986 and 1988, weighted by dividend and capital gains income, respectively. For example, taxpayers who in total account for 27 cents of every dollar received in dividend income experienced a decline

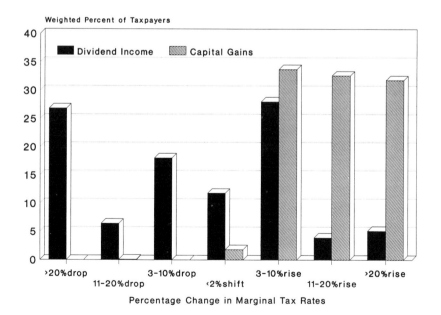

Figure 3.1
Change in tax rates for dividend and capital gains income. Source: NBER TAXSIM.

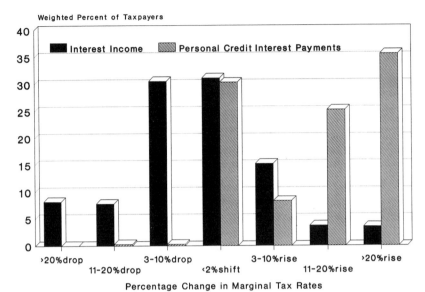

Figure 3.2
Change in tax rates for interest income and personal credit interest payments. Source:
NBER TAXSIM.

Table 3.1
Distribution of changes in marginal tax rates on interest, dividend, capital gains income,
and personal credit interest

Percentage point change in marginal tax rates	Interest income	Dividend income	Capital gains	Personal credit
Decline greater than 20	8.2	26.8	0.0	0.0
Decline between 11 and 20	7.8	6.4	0.1	0.3
Decline between 3 and 10	30.5	18.0	0.0	0.3
Change between −2 and 2	31.1	11.8	1.8	30.3
Increase between 3 and 10	15.2	28.0	33.7	8.3
Increase between 11 and 20	3.7	3.9	32.6	25.2
Increase greater than 20	5.1	3.5	31.8	35.6

Note: Calculated using NBER TAXSIM. Interest, dividend, and capital gains changes weighted
by their respective sources of income, with negative AGI taxpayers excluded. Personal
interest tax rate changes weighted by AGI.

in their marginal tax rate of more than 20 percentage points. This number largely reflects those taxpayers formerly in the 50% bracket now subject to the 28% bracket. But almost all taxpayers experienced a sharp rise in their capital gains tax; the rate jumped by at least 10 percentage points for taxpayers receiving 74 cents of every dollar in capital gains.

The corresponding figures are shown for the marginal tax rates on interest income and personal credit in figure 3.2. In the first case the percentage of taxpayers experiencing a shift in their marginal tax rates is weighted by interest income received; in the second case we weight by AGI (since total personal credit is unavailable). There is an overall decline in the marginal tax on interest, but it is less in magnitude than that for dividend income because a smaller fraction of interest income is held by the wealthiest taxpayers. Only 6.2% of interest income was taxed at the 50% marginal rate in 1986, compared with 25% of dividend income in the same year. Finally, the reduction in deductions allowed on personal credit—from 100% to 40% in 1988, coupled with the lower marginal tax rates in 1988—sharply increased the aftertax cost of personal borrowing. Taxpayers who together accounted for 61% of AGI experienced at least a 11 percentage point decline in the marginal subsidy for personal interest.

While marginal dividend tax rates went down and capital gains taxes went up, what was the overall impact of TRA86 on investments that pay a combination of dividends and realized capital gains? The popular view was that assets which appreciated in value, especially over the long-term, would suffer under TRA86 because of the higher capital gains tax rate. A simple calculation suggests otherwise. Consider an investment which retains ψ and pays in dividends $(1 - \psi)$ of every dollar in net business profits. In the calculations that follow, we assume that the fixed after-corporate-tax nominal return is r, that the holding period is n years, and that dividends paid in each year are reinvested in the same investment.

Consider a two-year investment purchased for $1. In the first year the accumulated value of the investment (after the first-year dividend has been reinvested) is $1 + \psi r + z$, where $z = (1 - \psi)r(1 - \tau_y)$ is the aftertax dividend rate and τ_y is the income tax assessed on the dividend. At the end of the second year, the investment is sold, the capital gains tax is paid, and net of the principal of $1, the investor is left with

$$(1 + \psi r + z)^2 - [(1 + \psi r)(1 + \psi r + z) - (1 + z)]\tau_c,$$

where the second term in brackets represents the portion of the investment subject to the capital gains tax rate τ_c. In general, the realized return n years in the future (net of the principal) on an investment of $1 is

$$R(\tau_c, \tau_y) = (1 + \psi r + z)^n - [(1 + \psi r)(1 + \psi r + z)^{n-1} - B]\tau_c - 1,$$

where the accumulated tax basis of the principal plus reinvested dividends is given by

$$B = 1 + \frac{z}{\psi r + z}[(1 + \psi r + z)^{n-1} - 1].$$

To measure the effect on incentives of TRA86, we first calculate the aftertax return R for a representative taxpayer under prior law. For example, the aftertax rate of return R on a $1 investment held for five years, paying 12%, and with a retained earning percentage of 50% is $0.47 at a marginal income tax rate τ_y of 50% and a capital gains tax τ_c of 20%. The next step is to consider the effect on the rate of return R of a tax reform that taxes capital gains and dividends at the single rate τ^* along the lines of TRA86. In particular, we calculate the value of τ^* such that the return $R(\tau^*, \tau^*) = R(0.4\tau_y, \tau_y)$ so that the investor is *indifferent* between paying τ^* under the new regime without preferential treatment of capital gains and τ_y under the old regime with preferential treatment of capital gains. Returning to our example above, a tax rate of $\tau^* = 0.36$ on both dividends and capital gains would yield the same aftertax return of $0.47.

Taxpayers always prefer to pay lower taxes: If the taxpayer's true marginal rate under TRA86 is *below* τ^*, they are better off; if it is *above*, they are worse off. In the above example every taxpayer with a marginal rate below 36% is better off under TRA86. Note that we do not need to specify the inflation rate or the internal rate of return on the investment to make this comparison.

The calculations are presented in table 3.2 for a variety of parameters. In the first row and first column of results, the reported value of τ^*, 0.35, is the marginal tax rate that would leave the investor indifferent to the original 50% tax bracket with 60% exclusion of capital gain; nearly every investor under TRA86 will be subject to marginal rates below 35%, and therefore will be better off. For longer holding periods the marginal rate τ^* *rises* as the holding period increases. That is, even when half of all profits are retained, and hence subject to capital gains tax, nearly every taxpayer previously in the 50% tax bracket will benefit under TRA86 for long-term investments.[7]

The intuition is that as the holding period increases, reinvested dividends account for a larger fraction of the overall return. Under TRA86

Table 3.2
The hypothetical tax rate τ^* under TRA86 that provides aftertax returns equal to those under the prior law

Interest rate, r	Prior law tax rate, τ_y	Holding period			
		1	5	10	25
Retained earnings $\psi = 0.50$					
0.12	0.5	0.35	0.36	0.37	0.40
0.12	0.4	0.28	0.29	0.30	0.33
0.08	0.5	0.35	0.36	0.37	0.39
0.08	0.4	0.28	0.29	0.29	0.31
0.04	0.5	0.35	0.35	0.36	0.37
0.04	0.4	0.28	0.28	0.29	0.30
Retained earnings $\psi = 0.70$					
0.12	0.5	0.29	0.30	0.31	0.35
0.12	0.4	0.23	0.24	0.25	0.28
0.08	0.5	0.29	0.30	0.31	0.33
0.08	0.4	0.23	0.24	0.25	0.27
0.04	0.5	0.29	0.29	0.30	0.31
0.04	0.4	0.23	0.24	0.24	0.25

Note: Column 1 is the gross return on the investment; column 2 is the initial income tax rate τ_y under pre-TRA86 tax law; and columns 3 through 6 are the marginal tax rates τ^* that under TRA86 (with full taxation of capital gains) leave the taxpayer with an equal aftertax return.

those aftertax dividends are larger, and hence augment the overall rate of return.[8] For a wide range of interest rates and holding periods, TRA86 benefits household investors previously in marginal tax brackets of 40% or 50%. We have also calculated τ^* for a 30% dividend payout rate ($\psi = 0.7$). In this case the calculated τ^*'s are lower, but even the wealthy taxpayer formerly in the 50% bracket and now in the 28% bracket will be almost uniformly better off under TRA86.

Although these calculations suggest that conventional saving vehicles were relatively unharmed at the household level by TRA86, there were a number of investment categories that experienced sharp increases in tax liability, such as investments generating passive losses and real estate.

It is not surprising that partnership and S corporation net losses fell by 40% and rental property by 23% between 1986 and 1987 (Hostetter and Bates 1989). Thus there was some evidence that TRA86 was successful in discouraging household saving in these formerly tax-favored investments.

Nevertheless, for orthodox financial investments, and particularly those with low levels of retained earnings, TRA86 generally reduced marginal tax rates on household saving. Whether these lower tax rates translated into higher saving rates is the topic of the next section.

3.3   The Aftertax Rate of Return, Saving, and Consumption

The impact of a change in the interest rate on saving is ambiguous. The substitution effect induces investors to save more in response to a higher return, but a higher return provides the investor with more future income for a given level of saving; this income effect may lead to a reduction in overall saving. On theoretical grounds, however, the lower marginal rates under TRA86 might be expected to increase saving. First, the tax reform was designed to be revenue neutral, so the overall income effect will be nearly zero. Second, as Summers (1981) has demonstrated in a life cycle model, the endowment effect—that an increased interest rate will reduce the present value of future earnings and thus depress current consumption —tends to imply a positive saving elasticity.[9] Yet the empirical evidence for any positive correlation between the aftertax rate of return and the saving rate is very weak. Some studies have found positive effects of the interest rate on saving (Boskin 1978; Summers 1982), but they are not robust to alternative empirical specifications (Howrey and Hymans 1978; Hall 1988; also see Friend and Hasbrouck 1983). As a first step it is useful to reexamine the evidence in light of new data from the 1980s.

We adopt as our measure of personal saving the Commerce Department (NIPA) saving measure plus contributions to government pension plans,[10] divided by disposable personal income plus the government pension contributions. We include government pensions for consistency with the convention of including private pensions in saving (Hendershott and Peek 1989). There are alternative measures of saving (discussed below), but we adopt this measure of saving because it addresses a well-defined question: Are U.S. households generating sufficient saving to finance domestic investment? If personal (along with corporate business plus government) NIPA saving are low, then foreign inflows are necessary to finance domestic investment. Although the economic effect of large foreign capital inflows is not necessarily harmful (just that foreign investors own a larger share of the U.S. capital stock), politicians do appear to be concerned with the foreign ownership of large, visible U.S. corporations.

Figure 3.3 shows personal saving rates, both quarterly and a three-quarter moving average, for the NIPA measure of saving with the adjust-

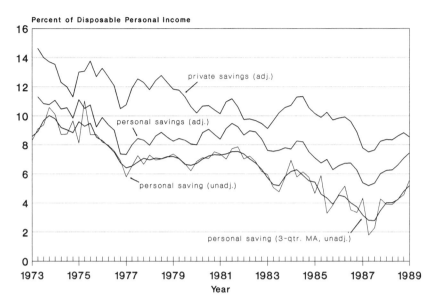

Figure 3.3

Private saving, personal saving, and adjusted personal saving rates, 1973–89. Adjusted saving rates are three-quarter moving averages. Sources: *Survey of Current Business*, Federal Reserve, Z.7 (various issues); and CITIBASE.

ment for government pension contributions. The adjustment increases the overall saving rate by one or two points but has no strong effect on the general trend, which at least until 1987 was downward. Since 1987 saving rates have increased, but they still remain below rates during the 1970s.

Although our primary interest is in personal saving rates, we include the three-quarter moving average of private saving (which also includes the government pension contributions) because, in both theory and practice, it is often difficult to distinguish between business and private saving. First, on theoretical grounds, business saving could substitute for personal saving since the ultrarational consumer would care little whether the corporation in which she owned stock was saving directly or issuing dividends so that she could save at the household level. Second, and more practically, the personal saving rate is a hybrid of business and household saving because it includes profits from unincorporated businesses (Hendershott and Peek 1989). But private saving follows the broad pattern of personal saving: Both rates decline, and both rebound at roughly the same time.

Figure 3.3 may suggest that TRA86 encouraged personal and private saving since saving rates rebounded during 1987, the first year of its implementation. But there were many factors that affected saving in recent years. To list only three, (1) farm support payments were large (and not seasonally adjusted) in 1988 and could account for roughly half of the increase (Koretz 1989); (2) strong automobile sales fell in 1988, leading to a decline in consumer durable sales and hence a "rebound" in saving (Koretz 1989); and (3) tax collections were high during 1987 (perhaps as a result of TRA86 or payments on capital gains made during 1986) which temporarily depressed disposable personal income. In short, one cannot make inferences about the success or failure of TRA86 by looking at short-term quarterly changes in personal saving rates. Nevertheless, the evidence is clear that although personal saving may have stemmed its downward slide, it still remains below its level of the 1970s.

Another approach to measure the impact of TRA86 on saving is to statistically estimate the impact of the aftertax rate of return on saving during the postwar period and then to use these structural estimates to evaluate tax reform. As a first step, we define the aftertax return to be the return on a three-month treasury bill less the average marginal tax rate on interest income, less expected inflation.[11] The expected inflation measure is taken from Hamilton (1985), who used a Kalman filtering technique to estimate the implied expectations by financial markets of next-period inflation. There are two advantages of this method for measuring expected inflation over the commonly used Livingston inflation survey. The first is that the Hamilton measure of expected inflation is generated every three months, unlike the Livingston survey which applies over a six-month period. The second is that Livingstone surveys do not use all the financial information available in making inflation forecasts.[12] We extend the Hamilton measure through the 1980s, using data on treasury bills and the GNP implicit price deflator.[13]

Three-quarter moving averages of the personal saving rate and the real aftertax rate of return are shown in figure 3.4. The most striking relationship between the two is the long-term negative correlation between the saving rate and the interest rate: Interest rates were low in the 1970s and high in the 1980s, whereas saving rates were high in the 1970s and low in the 1980s. But *within* the 1980s saving rates appear to be positively correlated with the aftertax real return.

Table 3.3 provides a few simple statistical tests of the correlation between saving and the aftertax return. We also include two other factors to explain saving: the fear of nuclear war as proxied by "minutes to midnight," a measure that Slemrod (1986) found to be significant in explaining the postwar saving rate,[14] and the quarterly change in log disposable

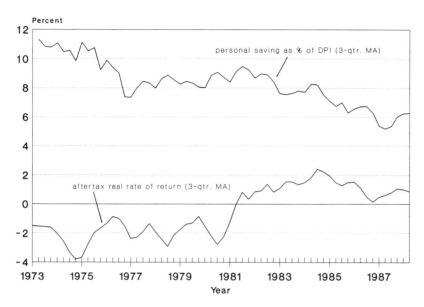

Figure 3.4
Adjusted personal savings rate and the aftertax real return. Sources: *Survey of Current Business*; Federal Reserve, *Bulletin* (various issues); CITIBASE; and Hamilton (1985).

income to reflect transitory income shifts absorbed by variation in saving. Regression 1 shows that a reduction in the risk of nuclear war has a strong positive effect on saving rates, but as is suggested by the graph, there is a negative (and significant) correlation between interest rates and saving rates.

The same regression using data after 1982, shown in row 3, yields different results. The regression implies that every one percentage point increase in the aftertax return will increase saving by 0.66 percentage points; this result is somewhat stronger when the other explanatory variables are excluded. A transitory income shift is predicted to have a strong positive impact on the saving rate, whereas lower fear of nuclear war leads to less, rather than more, saving. It is not clear whether these estimates imply a fundamental shift in saving behavior during the 1980s. For example, the growth of money market funds and interest-bearing accounts during the late 1970s could have forged a stronger link between saving and interest rates, but the possibility remains that it is simply a statistical anomaly. But even for this saving elasticity, large by empirical standards, the implied impact of TRA86 on saving is very small. The shift in marginal tax rates on interest income between 1986 and 1988 was 7.8 percentage

Table 3.3
Consumption and saving regressions

Dependent variable	Coefficients Interest rate	Minutes to midnight	Change in log income	C	$\bar{R}^2$	Sample period
1. Saving rate	−0.437 (5.88)	0.127 (4.28)	0.183 (1.71)	5.602 (25.10)	0.33	1951:2−1988:3
2. Saving rate	0.663 (2.71)	−0.385 (2.22)	0.658 (3.47)	4.262 (5.87)	0.60	1983:1−1988:3
3. ΔCons	0.040 (0.76)	0.007 (0.34)		0.587 (4.20)	−0.01	1951:2−1988:3
4. ΔCons (adjusted)	0.040 (0.66)	0.007 (0.31)		0.704 (4.00)	−0.01	1951:2−1988:3
5. ΔCons* (adjusted)	0.038 (0.52)	0.006 (0.22)		0.730 (3.99)	−0.01	1951:2−1988:3
6. ΔCons (adjusted)	0.255 (4.02)			0.389 (3.87)	0.29	1979:1−1988:3
7. ΔCons (adjusted)	0.163 (1.92)	−0.120 (1.60)		0.997 (2.54)	0.31	1979:1−1988:3

Note: Equation (5) which is starred was estimated using 2SLS. The saving rate is defined as personal saving divided by disposable personal income (uncorrected for government pension contributions), and t-statistics are in parentheses. Consumption (ΔCons) is the log change in real quarterly nondurable nonservice consumption. Adjusted consumption is

$$\Delta Cons_t - 0.27\ \Delta Cons_{t+1} + 0.07\ \Delta Cons_{t+2}$$

(from Hall 1988).

points; at the average interest rate during this period of 6.2, the regression equation predicts an increase in saving of only 0.3 percentage points.

Most macroeconomists have eschewed saving regressions in favor of the Euler equation approach to estimating the interest sensitivity of consumption. The Euler equation approach, as pioneered by Hall (1978), relies upon the notion that consumption at time t will reflect all information known to individuals at time t, so any deviation from planned consumption at $t + 1$ must be the result of a random surprise—in income, for example—between year t and year $t + 1$. The interest rate affects the time path of planned consumption because a higher rate, for example, increases the incentive to defer consumption until the next period. One might therefore expect that if consumption and saving are sensitive to the interest rate, there would be a positive correlation between the growth rate in consumption and the expected interest rate during the period.

Using Euler equation regressions, Hall (1988) found that the interest rate has little or no impact on the time path of consumption, or equivalently, that the intertemporal interest elasticity of consumption is essentially zero. Row 3 in table 3.3 confirms his results. Consumption is defined to be the log change in real nondurable (nonservice) consumption, and the estimated intertemporal elasticity is only 0.04, with a t-statistic of 0.76. Fear of nuclear war also has little effect on consumption, and the adjusted R^2 is negative. One problem with using quarterly data is time aggregation bias; even if monthly consumption follows a random walk, quarterly consumption will not. Hall suggests a simple correction from Hayashi and Sims (1983); the regression using this correction is shown in row 4 in which the coefficients are roughly similar. Finally, in row 5 we instrument the ex post aftertax return with lagged values of the interest rate and two-quarter lagged consumption changes with unchanged results.

Surprisingly, Euler consumption regressions in the subperiod 1979–88 show a strong positive effect of the real aftertax interest rate on consumption. Row 6 presents the regression result without the nuclear war variable; the estimated elasticity of substitution is 0.26 with a t-statistic of 4.0. While in row 7 the elasticity estimate drops to 0.16 after including the nuclear war variable, the coefficient remains significant at conventional levels. The result was not sensitive to replacing the ex post for the ex ante aftertax return, but the use of the full instrumental variable procedure in this subperiod led to an insignificant (and negative) coefficient on the aftertax real return.

The general consensus in the literature is that positive interest elasticity estimates, either of consumption or saving, are fragile and fleeting. The evidence from the later 1970s, when interest rates were strongly negative yet saving rates relatively high, lends support to this view. Nevertheless, regressions restricted to the 1980s show a significant correlation between consumption and saving and the aftertax rate of return.

3.4 IRAs and the Measurement of Saving

The 1986 Tax Reform Act should be judged on more than how it affected the aftertax rate of return. In this and the sections that follow, we will examine how TRA86 affected other policies toward saving.

The tax reform placed restrictions on Individual Retirement Accounts (IRAs) for single taxpayers with income over $25,000 and married taxpayers with income over $40,000. Some critics viewed these cutbacks on IRA eligibility as a major blow to saving. For example, a recent report by the Joint Committee on Taxation suggested that the drop in the saving rate between 1986 and 1987 was caused by the restrictions on IRAs (*New York Times* 1989).

There is no question that TRA86 cut back sharply on IRA enrollment, even for those who remained eligible to contribute (Summers 1989; Gravelle 1989). There was at least a 25% decline in contributions between 1986 and 1987 for taxpayers at all but the very lowest income levels.[15] Summers (1989) attributes this decline to the fall in aggressive marketing of IRAs after TRA86.[16]

There is no question that IRAs contributions fell, but there is still some question whether the lost IRAs reduced personal saving. That is, if taxpayers simply shuffle assets from taxable accounts into IRAs, then restricting the use of IRAs will have no impact on saving—if anything, the restrictions will increase national saving by easing the budget deficit. But much of the evidence from microeconomic studies of IRAs and saving is consistent with the view that IRAs increase saving. Estimates from Venti and Wise (1986, 1987, 1989) and Hubbard (1984) imply that a large fraction of IRA saving comes from consumption rather than other (taxable) forms of saving. Feenberg and Skinner (1989) compare the taxable interest and dividend income of taxpayers before and after the introduction of IRAs and find no evidence of simple shuffling. Some recent studies have criticized the econometric specification used by Venti and Wise (Gravelle 1989), while preliminary results from Gale and Scholz (1990) suggest that some shuffling may have occurred. In general, however, the microeconomic evidence does not contradict the view that IRAs are new saving.

The macroeconomic evidence seems to contradict the view that IRAs are new saving. As is shown in figure 3.3, the personal saving rate slid downward during 1982–86, precisely the period during which IRA contributions averaged roughly $30 billion per year. Once IRAs were restricted in 1987, the saving rate recovered to its current rate of 5.4%.[17] Can the microeconomic data be reconciled with the aggregate data?

One potential reconciliation is to account for broader measures of aggregate wealth accumulation. The Federal Reserve Board compiles yearly measures of household wealth. The Haig Simons definition of saving is the change in household wealth (adjusted by the implicit GNP price deflator) over the year. In practice, this measure of saving is much different from NIPA saving, primarily because capital gains are included in the household balance sheet (see Bradford 1989; Hendershott and Peek 1989). Which saving series one uses depends on what question is being asked. As we noted above, our primary concern is whether TRA86 has stimulated the supply of funds for domestic investment, and for this type of question, the NIPA saving measure (with the government pension adjustment) is adequate. But in looking at household purchases of IRAs, we are asking how purchases of IRAs affected other forms of household assets, so a measure of saving that emphasizes total household wealth may be more appropriate. Figure 3.5 shows annual household saving rates as calculated for households and nonprofit institutions (Federal Reserve Board 1989). Because there is a great deal of fluctuation in year-to-year saving rates (caused by shifts both in the value of the stock market and in the implicit price deflator), we have constructed three-year averages of saving rates, excluding durables and divided by disposable personal income plus capital gains as calculated from the Federal Reserve balance sheets.[18] The saving rates calculated in this way differ sharply from the traditional measures; household wealth declined during the late 1970s and early 1980s (in large part because of the laggard stock market), before recovering in the 1980s. But by 1988 saving rates had stagnated.[19] Although it is difficult to pick turning points in saving patterns from three-year averages, these results are not inconsistent with the view that IRAs were positively associated with household saving. Note that we do not regard these aggregate results as

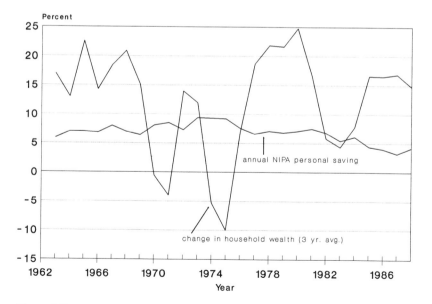

Figure 3.5
Personal saving: NIPA and household wealth measures. Sources: *Survey of Current Business* (various issues) and Federal Reserve, *C.9* (April 1989).

proving in any sense that IRAs stimulated saving during 1982–86. Instead, we question whether aggregate saving statistics can be used to test whether IRAs are a success or failure in encouraging saving since the answer depends so crucially on how one decides to measure saving.

3.5 Personal Credit Interest and Home Mortgage Interest

Phasing out deductions for personal interest payments to reduce borrowing is one way to stimulate net saving. The transition from the pre-1986 tax law allowing full deductibility was gradual, with 65% deductible in 1987, dropping gradually to 10% deductible in 1990, and completely phased out thereafter. The combination of the partially phased out personal interest deduction and the much lower marginal tax rates led in 1987 to a substantial decline in the tax advantage of borrowing. For example, a taxpayer in the 50% bracket in 1986 would pay only half the gross borrowing rate after taxes; the same taxpayer in 1987 in a 28% bracket would pay 82% of the gross rate after taxes. In this section we present evidence from both aggregate and panel data that taxpayers sharply reduced their outstanding personal credit. Hence TRA86 was successful at reducing taxpayers' reliance on personal borrowing. But TRA86 was unsuccessful at reducing overall borrowing. We show that for wealthier taxpayers, much of the reduction in personal credit was simply shuffled into home mortgage loans, leaving total credit nearly unaffected.[20]

First, consider the aggregate impact of TRA86 on total consumer credit (excluding home mortgages), revolving credit, and mortgages on one-to four-family dwellings (Federal Reserve Board *Bulletin*). Figure 3.6 shows the four-quarter change in outstanding credit for each of these measures during 1982–88, with a vertical line in the first quarter of 1987 to show the transition to the new tax regime. There is considerable fluctuation from year to year depending on interest rates and other factors, but the sharp decline in personal credit between the latter half of 1986 and the first quarter of 1987 is substantial. By contrast, home mortgage credit expanded during the period immediately following TRA86 and thereafter returned to its previous growth rate.[21]

It is difficult to make strong inferences based on the aggregate time-series data since there are so many factors that affect consumer credit. A clearer picture of how TRA86 affected the composition of consumer debt comes from a panel survey of taxpayers during the years 1984–87. Although there is no public use sample of 1987 tax returns as of this writing, John Scholz has kindly made available to us a nonrandom sample of

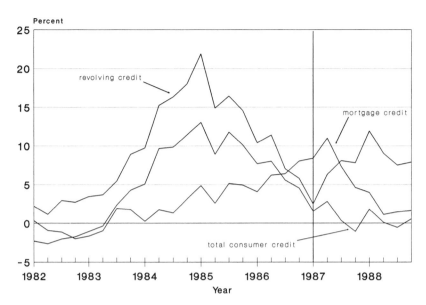

Figure 3.6
Four-quarter change in total consumer credit, revolving credit, and mortgage credit.
Sources: Federal Reserve, *Bulletin* (tbls. 1.54 and 1.55, May 1989, and various issues), and
CITIBASE.

approximately 20,000 largely well-off taxpayers collected for a different
study. The sample is nonrandom because the choice of the sample was
based on their residence. The information available for each taxpayer is
essentially the same as for the ordinary public use tapes. Our sample of
7,165 excludes nonitemizers, individuals with AGI less than $10,000, and
AGI in excess of $1 million. The average income of the sample was
$63,760 in 1985.

One advantage of a panel data set is that we observe individual taxpayers before and after the tax reform, so we can correct for individual
differences across taxpayers. Column 1 of table 3.4 shows a least squares
regression of the change in personal credit interest as a function of the tax
price (i.e., one minus the effective marginal rate), the real change in AGI,
and marital status. The tax price exerts a positive and significant impact on
personal credit; a 5 percentage point increase in the tax price is predicted
to reduce personal interest payments by $570. For example, a taxpayer
previously facing a marginal rate of 50% who after TRA86 faces a 28% rate
would be predicted to reduce personal credit interest payments by $2,507
in 1987. All regressions report heteroscedastic-consistent standard errors as

Table 3.4
Personal credit and mortgage interest regressions, 1985–87

Dependent variable	Δpersonal interest (OLS)	Δmortgage interest (OLS)	Δmortgage interest (2SLS)
ΔPrice of mortage interest		−6,581.0 (1.4)	−7,105.0 (1.4)
ΔPrice of personal interest	−11,394.0 (3.4)		
ΔIncome	−0.010 (1.4)	0.015 (1.2)	0.014 (1.0)
ΔPersonal interest		−0.673 (2.7)	−0.864 (2.54)
Marital status	−860.0 (5.0)	335.0 (1.3)	129.0 (0.4)
C	1,702	16	144
$\bar{R}^2$	0.02	0.18	0.17

Note: $N = 7,165$; t-statistics are reported in parentheses. All OLS regressions report heteroscedastic-consistent t-statistics.

adjusted by the White (1980) technique; in some cases this adjustment reduced t-statistics by a factor of 10.[22]

The next question is whether the reduction in personal debt was shifted into home mortgage debt. Table 3.4 also includes OLS regression results for the change in home mortgage interest payments. Column 2 tests whether the change in personal credit interest had an impact on changes in home mortgage interest payments. The coefficient implies that a reduction in personal interest payments of $1 is associated with 67 cent increase in mortgage payments.[23] That is, only 33 cents of every dollar reduction in interest payments reflects a cutback in spending.

There is a potential simultaneity bias when the change in personal credit is used as an exogenous explanatory variable for the change in mortgage interest payments since both variables will be affected by individual-specific unobservable factors. To correct for this, we estimate a two-stage least squares regression in which the change in personal interest payments is identified by the shift in its own tax price. Results are shown in column 3 of table 3.4; they imply an even larger (and significant) shuffling effect of 86 cents for each dollar reduction in personal credit payments.

These results may not be stable with respect to the model specification. If the variance of the error term is proportional to income, then a correction for heteroscedasticity is to weight each observation by the inverse of the square root of AGI. Regressions using this correction resulted in similar results for the least squares regression but resulted in insignificant results for the 2SLS regressions.

In sum, the evidence suggests that itemizing taxpayers who owned a house circumvented the restrictions on personal interest payments by shuffling their consumer debt into home mortgages. This may be one reason why the ratio of home mortgages to home market value has risen in 1988 to 48%, 10 percentage points higher than the average ratio during the 1970s (Federal Reserve Board 1989).

3.6   Capital Gains and Saving

There is a some evidence on how capital gains tax rates affect revenue, although there may be little agreement over how to interpret it.[24] But there is little evidence on how capital gains taxation affects saving. One view is that lower capital gains taxation encourages saving, and in particular saving in high-risk enterprises such as venture capital (see Poterba 1989). Another view is that temporarily low capital gains tax rates will reduce saving rates as investors who realize long-term capital gains are tempted to spend the cash on big-ticket consumption items rather than reinvest it (Summers 1989). In this view the 1986 tax reform had its primary impact on saving rates *before* it became effective as investors realized gains just prior to the 1987 capital gains tax increase.[26]

We use the Scholz panel of taxpayers to gain some indirect evidence on what individuals did with their capital gains realized in 1986: Did they spend or reinvest them? To do this, we compare interest and dividend income before and after TRA86 to see whether large capital gains are associated with a decline in asset income. This finding would suggest that the money was spent rather than reinvested. The test is not perfect since we are using information only from a subset of the taxpayer's total assets. For example, a taxpayer taking capital gains on owner-occupied housing would experience no decline in asset income even if the entire proceeds were spent on a new car. An additional question is whether investors who realized capital gains in 1986 reinvested them in interest-bearing assets which, relative to capital gains, are relatively favored under the new tax law.

Table 3.5 presents regression results which casts some doubt on the hypothesis that those taking capital gains spent them. The first regression (row 1) uses as the dependent variable a measure of imputed wealth,

Table 3.5
Capital gains and wealth regressions

Dependent variable	Capital gains in 1986	Capital gains in 1985	Dependent variable in 1985	Δearnings	C	$\bar{R}^2$
1. Wealth* in 1987	0.385 (8.50)	1.056 (1.62)	1.245 (23.92)	1.559 (5.25)	4,270	0.63
2. Wealth in 1987	0.378 (8.62)	1.182 (10.29)	1.225 (21.02)	1.667 (5.72)	11,295	0.59
3. Interest + dividends in 1987	0.037 (12.18)	0.046 (5.75)	0.752 (14.00)	0.102 (5.02)	2,615	0.51
4. Interest in 1987	0.038 (12.54)	0.014 (1.83)	0.640 (10.97)	0.075 (3.74)	2,412	0.40
5. Dividend in 1987	0.0002 (0.23)	0.033 (12.25)	0.995 (24.71)	0.026 (3.73)	76	0.55
6. Interest in 1986	0.014 (14.15)		0.840 (49.78)	0.001 (0.40)	772	0.26

Note: The sample size is 9,368. The sample excludes long-term capital loss returns, and t-statistics are reported in parentheses. The sample is weighted by 1/(square root of 1985 AGI) unless noted by an asterisk.

defined to be interest income divided by the average interest rate in that year plus dividend income divided by the average dividend yield. The null hypothesis that all capital gains are reinvested is that the 1986 capital gains coefficient should be zero; capital gains should have no impact on future asset income. Should the capital gains tax be paid out of the realizations in the same year, then the coefficient should be negative. Alternatively, if the capital gains are taken on assets that pay neither interest or dividend income, but the proceeds are shifted into taxable accounts, then the coefficient on capital gains would be positive. For example, if private investors dissolved a real estate partnership and invested the proceeds in bonds, imputed taxable wealth would rise.

The regression coefficients in table 3.5 are consistent with this latter story. The effect of an increase in capital gains of $1 during 1986 is to increase 1987 imputed wealth by 38 cents. Thus the evidence provides little support for the view that investors who took capital gains in 1986 spent them. Instead, it appears that investors shifted their assets which previously yielded little taxable income into interest-bearing accounts or stocks.

One possible explanation for this result is that investors park their capital gains in relatively liquid (and taxable) instruments for a year or so before choosing a new investment; hence the coefficient of 0.38 on 1986 capital gains is simply a short-run adjustment effect. In this view the coefficient on 1985 capital gains should be less than the coefficient on 1986; in fact it is substantially more. Although the 1985 capital gains coefficient is not significant in the regression in row 1, it is in row 2 when the regression is weighted by the inverse of the square root of AGI to correct for potential heteroscedasticity of the error term. Row 3 which uses as the dependent variable the sum of interest and dividend income yields similar results.

Rows 4 and 5 in table 3.5 enter interest and dividend income separately as dependent variables. These regressions suggest that TRA86 had a stronger impact on the composition of saving than on the overall level of saving. The interest regression shows that for every dollar of 1986 capital gains, interest income rose by 3.8 cents. With average returns on interest-bearing assets roughly double this value, the coefficient implies that almost half of the realized capital gains were shifted into interest-bearing accounts. By contrast, capital gains taken in 1985 had little or no effect on interest income in 1987.

The regressions explaining dividend income in 1987 (row 5) suggest a much different pattern. Capital gains in 1986 had no effect on dividends, although past capital gains from 1985 affected 1987 dividends. Taxpayers appear to have taken capital gains on assets and shifted them into alternative investments with a heavier reliance on interest income.

An alternative explanation for this pattern is that capital gains are parked in interest-bearing accounts, so the correlation between 1986 capital gains and 1987 interest income simply reflects short-run adjustment. To test for this, we regress 1986 interest income on 1985 capital gains to get a measure, untinged by tax code changes, of the normal propensity to place capital gains in temporary interest-bearing accounts (row 6). The coefficient is 0.014, implying that nearly two-thirds of the capital gains shift into investments paying interest income $(1 - [1.4/3.8])$ represented a permanent shift associated with TRA86.

In conclusion, we find more evidence supporting the view that taxpayers shifted capital gains into assets favored under TRA86. Although our test for the hypothesis that investors spent some fraction of their 1986 capital gains on consumption is not a strong one, there is little evidence that supports the hypothesis. Further the tests are likely contaminated by other factors occurring during this volatile period in financial markets, but at least one—the stock market rise during most of 1987—would have discouraged investments in interest-bearing assets.

3.7 Conclusion

Stimulating the saving rate was never the primary objective of the 1986 Tax Reform Act. Instead, TRA86 was designed to close down abusive tax shelters, equalize the tax treatment of different assets, and lower marginal rates. Did the tax changes in TRA86 designed to meet these objectives encourage or discourage saving? We have argued in this chapter that TRA86 was successful at the household level in reducing the marginal tax rates on household saving, even for long-term investments with much of its return paid as capital gains.

Whether one can detect the effect of these improved incentives on measured aggregate saving rates is another matter. Saving is usually defined as income less consumption. Small percentage changes in either income or consumption can lead to large fluctuations in saving rates, so that attributing the two percentage point rise in aggregate personal saving since 1987 to TRA86 is speculative at best. Furthermore the historical record seems quite clear in indicating little effect on saving of the aftertax real interest rate, although in the 1980s we did find a correlation between the real aftertax interest rate and both saving and consumption. Nevertheless, it is difficult to conclude from aggregate time-series data that TRA86 had any impact—negative or positive—on aggregate personal saving.

If the link between the aftertax rate of return and personal saving is weak, then has TRA86 affected saving behavior in other ways? TRA86 favored some forms of saving over others, and the evidence is clear that TRA86 did affect the composition of saving. For example, the eligibility rules were tightened for IRAs, which lead to a 62% decline in tax deductible contributions between 1986 and 1987. If IRAs represented new saving, rather than shuffled saving, then TRA86 would be viewed as discouraging retirement saving. Yet standard measures of personal saving show low levels of saving during 1982–86 when IRAs were widely available and an increase in saving since 1987. Once again, we suggest that one cannot infer a great deal from aggregate saving rates since an alternative measure of saving from household wealth data tells an entirely different story in which saving rates were quite strong during the golden age of IRAs.

The 1986 tax reform also gradually phased out the deductibility of interest on personal credit. Personal credit declined sharply after 1986, which might by itself be expected to increase net national saving. But we found strong evidence that wealthier taxpayers successfully shifted a large fraction of their personal loan reductions into home mortgage loans. This type of shuffling from consumer credit into housing credit had little impact on saving.

The Tax Reform Act of 1986 also increased the tax on capital gains in 1987 and, by doing so, set off a stampede to cash in gains under the prior law (Auerbach 1988). There is little evidence that our sample of taxpayers spent their realized capital gains; instead, they appear to have largely reinvested them. But they did shift a larger fraction of the 1986 capital gains into interest-bearing accounts to take advantage of their relatively more favorable tax treatment.

We have ignored one very important factor, the change in tax rules for business investment, in evaluating the effect of TRA86 on saving. Some observers during the mid-1980s predicted declines of up to 200 basis points in after-corporate-tax rate of return owing to the lengthening of asset lives for depreciation and the repeal of the investment tax credit (Hausman and Poterba 1987), and this lower rate of pre-tax return could affect household saving. Yet the aftertax real return should reflect changes in corporate as well as personal income taxes, and there is little evidence that the rate of return available to households has fallen dramatically since TRA86.

Recent developments in Congress suggest that the tacit agreement to resist tinkering with the 1986 tax reform may have now been broken. If there is a lesson, then, from just a few years experience with the 1986 tax reform, it is that the tax code has a stronger and more immediate impact on the financial composition rather than the absolute level of personal saving.

Notes

We are grateful to Don Fullerton, Kevin Hassett, Pat Hendershott, Andrew Lyon, Joel Slemrod, conference participants, and the Public Finance seminar at Columbia University for very helpful suggestions. Richard McGrath provided excellent research assistance, and we especially thank John Scholz for allowing us to use his taxpayer survey.

1. For example, in late 1986 Murray Weidenbaum stated that under tax reform, "Investment incentives are clobbered.... [The tax bill] depresses saving and investment, and that reduces economic growth." (quoted in the *National Journal*, October 11, 1986, p. 2457).

2. This chapter focuses only on household saving incentives, although the 1986 Tax Reform Act had a major effect on corporate tax incentives. For reviews, see Auerbach (1987) and Bovenberg (1989).

3. See Hall (1988), Boskin (1978), Howrey and Hymans (1978), Summers (1982), and Friend and Hasbrouck (1983).

4. See, for example, Venti and Wise (1986, 1987, 1989), Feenberg and Skinner (1989), and Hubbard (1984); for criticisms of these studies see Gravelle (1989) and preliminary work by Gale and Scholz (1990).

5. For recent discussions of this issue, see Auerbach (1985), Boskin (1988), Bradford (1989), and Hendershott and Peek (1989).

6. The TAXSIM data include all information (except taxpayer identification) from the 1040 form and a few items from important supporting schedules. The very rich are oversampled to provide more accurate estimates of tax liabilities, with sampling rates of up to one in three for the highest income levels. To the extent feasible, complexities of the tax code, including income averaging and the minimum tax, are accounted for in the calculation of tax liabilities and marginal tax rates. The tax return data is as rich in income information as it is poor in demographic information. Race, sex, and exact age are pointedly not available.

7. The calculations presented in the text refer only to new investments made after 1987. Old investments that pay ordinary income tax on capital gains will obviously be disadvantaged by TRA86.

8. The timing of the tax collection differs as well. Under TRA86 a larger portion of the tax is collected at realization in year n.

9. Defined benefit pension plans are a perfect example of "target" saving since a higher interest rate will reduce the contributions necessary to meet future benefit payments. Hence the importance of pension funds in personal saving would tend to reduce the interest elasticity of saving (Bernheim and Shoven 1985; Makin and Couch 1989).

10. Line 6 in the sector statements of saving and investment from the Flow of Funds Accounts of the Federal Reserve (various issues).

11. We are grateful to Joe Peek for providing the tax rate series. He used the *Statistics of Income* in various years to calculate an average marginal tax rate weighted by interest income received for married taxpayers filing jointly. The rates for 1987 and 1988 were projected using 1986 weights.

12. Brown and Maital (1981) suggest that adding additional information, such as money supply changes, would result in inflation forecasts more accurate than the Livingstone predictions. For a discussion of the Livingstone stock market forecasts, see Dokko and Edelstein (1989).

13. Most of the updated financial variables and aggregate data come from Citibase through the third quarter of 1988. More recent figures come from the *Survey of Current Business* (August 1989) and *Federal Reserve Bulletin* (May 1989). Interest rates were measured in February, May, July, and October. There was some difference between Hamilton's (1985) interest rate figures from Salomon Brothers and the overlapping Citibase rates during the volatile early 1980s, due to differences in how the monthly rate was calculated from daily rates.

14. We used the unadjusted personal saving rate for the regression analysis. The "minutes to midnight" measure is an 11-quarter moving average of the actual count to reflect the relative infrequency of its shifts. Note that high values of the index are associated with lower fear of nuclear war. We are grateful to Joel Slemrod for providing the measure.

15. Some part of this reduction may have been caused by the reduction in marginal rates. The tax subsidy is lower when marginal rates are lower, and one advantage of an IRA—deducting the contribution at a high marginal rate while working, and paying the tax at a low marginal rate while retired—was sharply diminished by TRA86.

16. The tax reform also restricted the maximum contributions to 401(k) plans, although few enrollees were affected by the restrictions. Salisbury (1989) suggested that after TRA86, 401(k)s were used to substitute for IRAs.

17. Kevin Hassett suggested an alternative test of whether IRAs affected saving and consumption: Include an IRA dummy in the Euler equation consumption model to test whether individuals' adjusted consumption plans during 1982–86 take advantage of the IRA:

$$c = 0.0622 + 0.184 \times \text{IRA} - 0.0001 \times R + 0.012 \times \text{nuke},$$
$$\quad (3.24) \qquad (1.07) \qquad\qquad (0.01) \qquad\qquad (0.49)$$

where the t-statistics are in parentheses and the adjusted R^2 is -0.01. The coefficient on the IRA variable is positive but not significant.

18. Household capital gains were calculated as the difference between the change in real household net worth minus net investment by households.

19. It is difficult to use the Federal Reserve saving data in regressions since the savings rate fluctuates so wildly. But it is interesting to note the following pattern in the three-year saving rate and the three-year average real aftertax rate of return:

	Saving rate	Real aftertax return
1974–76	0.068	−2.23
1977–79	0.216	−1.92
1980–82	0.058	−0.43
1983–85	0.166	1.42
1986–88[a]	0.147	0.83

a. Third quarter data.

A pattern similar to that found with the Commerce Department saving rate can be seen: a negative correlation between saving and the aftertax real return in the 1970s and a slight positive correlation in the 1980s.

20. Manchester and Poterba (1989) suggest that home equity loans were used to finance consumption expenditures as well as to reduce other types of nontax-deductible credit.

21. The ratio of consumer credit to mortgage credit (for one- to four-family homes) fell from 39% in 1985 to 33% in the third quarter of 1989.

22. The sensitivity of the standard error to the White correction suggests mispecification of the equation. We examine this further later when we weight by the inverse of the square root of AGI.

23. If home equity interest rates were lower than personal credit interest rates, the shuffling effect would be even larger.

24. See Cook and O'Hare (1987), and in particular Auerbach (1988) for reviews of recent literature.

25. Note that this story of taxpayers spending their capital gains because the cash is at hand is not entirely consistent with a model of rational investor behavior. A rational investor separates investment transactions to maximize wealth from consumption decisions to maximize utility. Strictly speaking, the decision to realize expected capital gains should have little effect on consumption choices.

References

Auerbach, Alan J. 1985. Saving in the U.S.: Some Conceptual Issues. in Patric Hendershott (ed.), *The Level and Composition of Household Saving*. Cambridge, MA: Ballinger, pp. 15–38.

Auerbach, Alan J. 1987. The Tax Reform Act and the Cost of Capital. *Journal of Economic Perspectives* 1: 73–86.

Auerbach, Alan J. 1988. Capital Gains Taxation in the United States—Realizations, Revenue, and Rhetoric. *Brookings Papers on Economic Activity* 2: 595–631.

Auerbach, Alan J., and Kevin Hassett. 1989. Corporate Savings and Shareholder Consumption. NBER Working Paper No. 2994 (June).

Bernheim, Douglas, and John Shoven. 1985. Pension Funding and Saving. NBER Working Paper No. 1622.

Boskin, Michael. 1978. Taxation, Saving, and the Rate of Interest. *Journal of Political Economy* 86: S3–S27.

Boskin, Michael. 1988. Issues in the Measurement and Interpretation of Saving and Wealth. NBER Working Paper No. 2633 (June).

Bovenberg, A. Lans. 1989. Tax Policy and National Saving in the United States: A Survey. *National Tax Journal* 42: 123–138.

Bradford, David F. 1989. Market Value vs. Financial Accounting Measures of National Saving. NBER Working Paper No. 2906 (March).

Brown, Bryan W., and Shlomo Maital. 1981. What Do Economists Know: An Empirical Test of Experts' Expectations. *Econometrica* 49: 491–504.

Carroll, Chris, and Lawrence H. Summers. 1987. Why Have Private Saving Rates in the U.S. and Canada Diverged? *Journal of Monetary Economics* 20: 249–280.

Cook, Eric W., and John F. O'Hare. Issues Relating to the Taxation of Capital Gains. *National Tax Journal* 40: 473–488.

Dokko, Yoon, and Robert H. Edelstein. 1989. How Well Do Economists Forecast Stock Prices? A Study of the Livingstone Surveys. *American Economic Review* 79: 865–871.

Feenberg, Daniel, and Jonathan Skinner. 1989. Sources of IRA Saving. In Lawrence Summers (ed.), *Tax Policy and the Economy 3*. Cambridge: MIT Press and NBER.

Federal Reserve Board. 1989. Balance Sheets for the U.S. Economy 1949–88. Publication C-9 (April).

Follain, James R., Hendershott, Patric H., and David C. Ling. 1987. Understanding the Real Estate Provisions of Tax Reform: Motivation and Impact. *National Tax Journal* 40: 363–372.

Friend, Irwin, and Joel Hasbrouck. 1983. Saving and After-tax Rates of Return. *Review of Economics and Statistics* 65: 537–543.

Fullerton, Don, Shoven, John B., and John Whalley. 1983. Replacing the U.S. Income Tax with a Progressive Consumption Tax. *Journal of Public Economics* 20: 3–23.

Gale, William G., and John Karl Scholz. 1990. Effects of IRAs on Household Saving. Mimeo (May).

Gravelle, Jane G. 1989. Capital Gains, IRAs, and Savings. Congressional Research Service Report 89–543.

Hall, Robert E. 1978. Stochastic Implications of the Life Cycle–Permanent Income Hypothesis: Theory and Evidence. *Journal of Political Economy* 86: 971–987.

Hall, Robert E. 1988. Intertemporal Substitution in Consumption. *Journal of Political Economy* 96: 339–357.

Hamilton, James D. 1985. Uncovering Financial Market Expectations of Inflation. *Journal of Political Economy* 93: 1224–1241.

Hausman, Jerry A., and James M. Poterba. 1987. Household Behavior and the Tax Reform Act of 1986. *Journal of Economic Perspectives* 1: 101–119.

Hayashi, Fumio, and Christopher Sims. 1983. Nearly Efficient Estimation of Time Series Models with Predetermined, But Not Exogenous, Instruments. *Econometrica* 51: 783–798.

Hendershott, Patric H., and Joe Peek. 1989. Aggregate U.S. Private Saving: Conceptual Measures and Empirical Tests. In Robert E. Lipsey and Helen Stone Tice (eds.), *The Measurement of Saving, Investment, and Wealth.* Chicago: The University of Chicago Press and NBER, pp. 185–286.

Hostetter, Susan, and Jeffrey Bates. 1989. Individual Income Tax Returns, Preliminary Data, 1987. *SOI Bulletin* (Spring): 5–18.

Howrey, E. Philip, and Saul H. Hymans. 1978. The Measurement and Determination of Loanable Funds Saving. *Brookings Papers on Economic Activity* 2: 655–685.

Hubbard, R. Glenn. 1984. Do IRAs and KEOGHs Increase Saving? *National Tax Journal* 37: 43–54.

Koretz, Gene. 1989. Are Fatter Piggy Banks Merely an Illusion? *Business Week* May 15, p. 24.

Lindsey, Lawrence B. 1987. Capital Gains Taxes under the Tax Reform Act of 1986: Revenue Estimates under Various Assumptions. *National Tax Journal* 40: 489–504.

Makin, John H., and Kenneth A. Couch. 1989. Saving, Pension Contributions, and the Real Interest Rate. *Review of Economics and Statistics* 71: 401–407.

Manchester, Joyce, and James Poterba. 1989. Second Mortgages and Household Saving. *Regional Science and Urban Economics* 19: 325–346.

New York Times. 1989. IRAs Effect on Savings. September 18, p. D2.

Poterba, James. 1989. Venture capital and capital gains taxation. In Lawrence Summers (ed.), *Tax Policy and the Economy 3*. Cambridge: MIT Press and NBER.

Salisbury, Dallas L. 1989. Testimony before Senate Finance Committee. September 29.

Slemrod, Joel. 1986. Saving and the Fear of Nuclear War. *Journal of Conflict Resolution* 30: 403–419.

Summers, Lawrence H. 1981. Capital Taxation and Accumulation in a Life-cycle Growth Model. *American Economic Review* 71: 533–544.

Summers, Lawrence H. 1982. Tax Policy, the Rate of Return, and Savings. NBER Working Paper No. 995 (September).

Summers, Lawrence H. 1989. How Best to Give Tax Incentives for Saving and Investment? Testimony before Senate Finance Committee. September 29.

Venti, Steven F., and David Wise. 1986. Tax-deferred Accounts, Constrained Choice, and Estimation of Individual Saving. *Review of Economic Studies* 53: 579–601.

Venti, Steven F., and David Wise. 1987. Have IRAs Increased U.S. Saving? Evidence from Consumer Expenditure Surveys. NBER Working Paper No. 2217 (April).

Venti, Steven F., and David Wise. 1989. The Saving Effect of Tax-Deferred Retirement Accounts: Evidence from SIPP. Mimeo.

White, Halbert. 1980. A Heteroskedasticity-Consistent Covariance Matrix and a Direct Test for Heteroskedasticity. *Econometrica* 48: 721–746.

COMMENTS

Patric H. Hendershott

Though I admire the courage of the authors, I question their sanity in agreeing to undertake this task. Estimating the impact of the 1986 tax act on personal saving seems to me to be near impossible for two reasons. Little agreement exists in the profession on either how personal saving should be measured or how strongly personal saving responds to changes in aftertax rates of return. It's hardly reasonable to expect an analysis of the 1986 tax act to resolve the questions that the profession has been struggling with, not very successfully, for the past decade.

Further the 1986 tax act contains numerous provisions with offsetting impacts on the returns to saving. Marginal income tax rates were cut sharply, but the deductibility of retirement contributions (IRAs and supplemental retirement accounts) and consumer credit interest payments were sharply restricted, passive loss rules for real estate investments were introduced, the individual minimum income tax was strengthened, and the capital gains exclusion was eliminated. Even if we knew how saving responds to changes in aftertax returns, the combined effect of all these changes on "the marginal aftertax return to saving" is a real mystery. Not surprisingly, Skinner and Feenberg don't make strong statements about the net impact of the tax act on personal saving but rather play around the edges, discussing what effect individual provisions of the act might have had.

I will address the measurement issue here and provide my view of the saving record of the United States in the 1980s. Then I will turn to the possible impact of the 1986 tax act on household saving.

Net Saving and Investment in the 1980s

National saving and investment have declined sharply in the 1980s. Because official personal saving data have also exhibited a significant fall, it is easy to attribute the decline in U.S. national saving (and investment) to reduced household saving. However, this view is incorrect because the saving data are incomplete. Households have not reduced their saving in the 1980s; they have simply shifted its composition from the accumulation of assets officially counted as saving (financial assets, real estate, and private pensions) to the accumulation of those not counted (consumer durables and government pensions, including social security). Let me dwell for a moment on the misclassification of contributions to government retirement plans and durable outlays.

The national income and product accounts treat household investment in retirement accounts and real assets in an inconsistent manner (Hendershott and Peek 1989). When a household contributes dollars to a private retirement plan set up either by itself (e.g., IRAs) or its private sector employer, these dollars are counted as household, not business, saving. However, when the dollars are contributed to a government retirement plan, including social security, the dollars are counted as government saving. Consistency requires treating these contributions similarly, and logic requires counting all of them as household saving.[1]

When a household purchases a house, rather than renting one, the purchase is classified as saving (and investment). When an automobile is purchased, however, the acquisition is treated entirely as consumption (if a business purchases automobiles to rent to households the acquisition is labeled investment). Similarly, if appliances, bookcases, carpeting, etc., are part of the house purchased, they are saving, but if these goods are bought separately, they are consumption. Consistency requires treating these purchases similarly, and logic dictates that purchases net of depreciation be counted as saving.

Data on sectoral net saving and investment (as a percent of net national product) are listed in table 3C.1 for the decade 1979–88.[2] The data in the top of the table indicate that household net durables purchases and net contributions to government retirement plans increased by 3 percentage points in 1985–88 period relative to 1980–81, totally offsetting the 1980s plunge in personal saving. In contrast, moving net contributions to government retirement plans from government saving to household saving lowers the government saving rate by 1.5 percentage points in 1988 versus 1980–81. As a result total household saving is flat between 1979 (the last year in which the U.S. economy was operating at full employment) and 1988, while total government saving is down a full 5 percentage points.

The problem of a low U.S. national saving rate is shown in the lower part of the table—the 3 percentage point decline since 1979 in net investment, all of which has taken the form of reduced business, not household, capital formation. The direct cause of the problem is the huge negative government dissaving (and to a lesser extent the biases in the tax code against business investment and in favor of household investment).

Table 3C.1
Net saving and investment as a percent of net national product

	1979	1980	1981	1982	1983	1984	1985	1986	1987	1988
Household saving										
Personal	5.8	6.1	6.4	6.0	4.7	5.3	3.8	3.6	2.7	3.6
Durables	2.7	1.4	1.5	1.4	2.3	3.2	3.5	3.6	3.1	3.2
Government retirement	1.2	1.4	1.6	1.7	1.9	2.2	2.5	2.4	2.6	3.1
Total household[a]	9.7	8.9	9.5	9.2	8.9	10.7	9.8	9.6	8.4	9.9
Business saving[b]	3.0	1.7	1.7	0.8	2.3	3.0	3.1	2.4	2.0	2.0
Government[c]	−0.6	−3.0	−2.8	−6.0	−6.5	−5.6	−6.5	−6.5	−5.5	−5.5
Foreign	−0.1	−0.5	−0.4	0.0	1.2	2.9	3.4	3.9	4.0	2.9
Total saving	12.0	7.1	8.0	3.9	5.9	11.0	9.8	9.4	8.9	9.3
Net business investment[d]	5.4	3.3	4.6	1.2	1.2	5.1	3.4	2.6	2.3	2.4
Net household investment										
Owner housing	3.9	2.7	2.1	1.3	2.6	2.9	2.8	3.1	3.4	3.5
Durables	2.7	1.4	1.5	1.4	2.3	3.2	3.5	3.6	3.1	3.2
Total investment[e]	12.0	7.4	8.2	3.9	6.1	11.2	9.7	9.3	8.8	9.1

Note: Net national product equals gross product less capital consumption, including that on consumer durables.
a. Net contributions to government insurance programs, including social security.
b. Retained earnings plus CCA and IVA.
c. Federal and state and local "surpluses" less net household contributions to government retirement and insurance programs.
d. Net private domestic investment excluding owner housing (and consumer durables).
e. Total investment and saving differ by the statistical discrepancy.

The 1986 Tax Reform Act and Personal Saving

Skinner and Feenberg (S&F) consider many, but not all, aspects of the 1986 tax law as it relates to household saving. They present some evidence that restrictions on the deductibility of consumer credit are being largely offset by substitution of mortgage debt for consumer credit. On the other hand, they argue that IRA contributions under old law were not largely funded by households shifting existing assets into IRAs and thus contend that the restrictions on IRA contributions in the 1986 act are significantly reducing saving.[3] Note the asymmetry: Households largely rearrange their liability structures in response to tax changes but only rearrange their asset portfolios slightly. S&F also compute the importance of the cut in marginal income tax rates relative to the increase in the capital gains tax rate. They do not consider the impacts of the reduction from $30,000 to $7,000 in the maximum deductible annual contributions to 401(k)s, the new passive loss rules that restrict the deduction of real estate losses from other income, the strengthened minimum tax, or the increased taxation of corporations.

At one point S&F do venture tentatively toward a statement regarding the overall impact of TRA86. They plot some data (figure 3.4) and report some regression equations (table 3.3) that suggest a positive response since 1983 of personal saving to the real aftertax three-month Treasury bill rate. They describe this result as either a fundamental shift in saving behavior (the relationship does not hold before 1983) or a statistical artifact. Because marginal tax rates on interest income were significantly decreased by the 1986 tax act, S&F's empirical result would suggest a positive impact of the tax act on personal saving.

I am uncomfortable with the Skinner-Feenberg result and this suggestion for two reasons. First, their measured return to saving reflects the single tax change in the 1986 act that favors saving—the cut in marginal tax rates on interest and dividends—but ignores all the negative changes—the increase in the capital gains tax rate, the lost deductibility of retirement accounts and consumer credit interest, and the attacks on tax shelters. When all the tax changes are accounted for, I have no doubt that the marginal aftertax return to saving fell, not rose. Second, the saving series is inappropriate. As I emphasized above, I do not believe that household saving has declined in the 1980s. Thus I don't think either of the two positively correlated series is relevant to the issue of the impact of TRA86 on personal saving.

Relative Importance of the Income and Gains Tax Rate Changes

As S&F emphasize, the impact of the 1986 tax act on returns to savers is
unclear for mixed income-gains investments because regular income tax
rates were cut but capital gains tax rates were raised. Assuming no change
in pretax returns, taxes on pure capital gains assets would rise, while taxes
on pure income assets would fall. But how would mixed income-gains
assets held for different holding periods fare? Skinner and Feenberg report
some calculations for mixed assets, but the calculations are not the traditional effective tax rates, so I have computed the latter.

Skinner and Feenberg consider an asset that earns a return before personal taxes of r, pays $1 - \psi$ of the return in "dividends" to the investor who
reinvests them in the asset after personal taxes are paid at the rate τ_y, and
reinvests the remaining ψr for the investor. At the settlement date (end of
the holding period), the capital gain derived from the reinvestment of
retained earnings, the ψr, is taxed at the capital gains rate τ_c. The question
is, What is the effective tax rate on the asset under the old and new tax
laws? The answer is obtained by computing what single tax rate τ^* applied
to a dollar invested at the return r would yield the same final value (at the
settlement date n) as a dollar invested in the mixed income-gains asset
described above. That is, what τ^* solves

$$A^n - \tau_c \sum_{j=0}^{n-1} \psi r A^j = [1 + r(1 - \tau^*)]^n,$$

where $A = 1 + r[1 - \tau_y(1 - \psi)]$? A^n represents the initial dollar investment plus the accumulation of aftertax returns that allows for the avoidance of taxes by the retention of income, including the capital gain
through period n. The summation on the left is the capital gains tax due on
the retentions at the time of sale.

Table 3C.2 contains the effective total tax rates on mixed assets (retention rate varying from 0.3 to 0.7) for holding periods of 1 to 25 years under
the 1985 and 1986 tax laws for investors whose marginal regular income
tax rates were cut from 0.5 to 0.28 and from 0.4 to 0.33. The ratios of the
τ^*'s under the 1986 and 1985 tax laws are also shown. As long as the
retention rate is less than 30%, both investors pay lower tax rates under
1986 tax law. The highest income household pays a lower tax rate unless
the retention rate is over 70%; the current 33% tax rate investor pays a
higher tax rate if the retention rate is over 50%. Of course we would expect
retention rates to decline due to the 1986 tax act (Gordon and MacKie-

Table 3C.2
Effective tax rates for 1985 and 1986 tax law under different retention ratios and holding periods ($r = 0.12$)

	Regular tax rate	Holding period (years)			
		1	5	10	25
30% of earnings retained					
1985 tax law	0.5	0.410	0.403	0.395	0.379
	0.4	0.328	0.321	0.315	0.302
1986 tax law	0.28	0.280	0.268	0.255	0.232
	0.33	0.330	0.316	0.302	0.275
Ratio of 1986 to	0.28/0.5	0.68	0.67	0.65	0.61
1985 τ^* values	0.33/0.4	1.01	0.98	0.96	0.91
50% of earnings retained					
1985 tax law	0.5	0.350	0.336	0.323	0.295
	0.4	0.280	0.268	0.256	0.234
1986 tax law	0.28	0.280	0.259	0.238	0.199
	0.33	0.330	0.307	0.283	0.237
Ratio of 1986 to	0.28/0.5	0.80	0.77	0.74	0.67
1985 τ^* values	0.33/0.4	1.18	1.15	1.11	1.01
70% of earnings retained					
1985 tax law	0.5	0.290	0.269	0.249	0.210
	0.4	0.232	0.214	0.197	0.166
1986 tax law	0.28	0.280	0.251	0.221	0.165
	0.33	0.330	0.297	0.264	0.198
Ratio of 1986 to	0.28/0.5	0.97	0.93	0.89	0.79
1985 τ^* values	0.33/0.4	1.42	1.39	1.34	1.19

Mason 1989) and pretax returns on capital gains assets to rise relative to returns on regular income assets.

The tax rates decline with the holding period due to the deferral of the capital gains tax and, under 1985 tax law, the gains exclusion. Interestingly, the effective tax rates decline even faster under 1986 law than under 1985 law, as is witnessed by the monotonic decline in the ratios of the 1986 τ^*'s to the 1985 τ^*'s.

The Impact of Decreases in Business Saving on Household Saving

As is well known, the 1986 tax act financed a roughly $140 billion five-year household tax cut with a comparable increase in business taxes. As a result business saving would be expected to decline, and looking back at table 3C.1, a decline has in fact occurred. Between 1984–85 and 1987–88 the business saving rate fell by one-third (recall that the investment tax credit was unavailable throughout 1986). The question here is how household saving might have been expected to change in response to the reduction in business saving.

There are two keys to how household saving is affected. The first is how the market value of corporations responds to the tax increase, and this largely depends on how existing, rather than new, investments are affected by the tax change. If existing capital is taxed more heavily, stock prices will decline, presumably by the present value of the future expected tax payments (Downs and Hendershott 1987), and thus households could increase their saving sufficiently to offset a substantial part of the reduction in business saving. In contrast, if new investments are taxed more heavily, firms will require higher pretax returns on new investments, and thus investment will slow. This slowdown will raise returns on old investments as well as new ones, tending to raise the market value of existing capital and thus lead to a decline in household saving.

The second key is how businesses change their payout rate. If the payout rate is increased, as Gordon and MacKie-Mason (1989) indicate it has been, then stock values will decline relatively, and households should increase their saving. The household increase will roughly equal the business decrease if the payout increase is viewed as permanent but will be only a fraction of the business decrease if the decline is temporary (Hendershott and Peek 1989).

The form of the increased business taxation in the 1986 tax act should have been extremely negative for household saving. The corporate tax rate cut reduced the taxation of existing capital, while elimination of the investment tax credit and lengthening of tax depreciation schedules raised the investment hurdle rate and thus pretax incomes on new investments. The pretax income on existing capital would of course rise sympathetically. The value of existing capital, and thus of the stock market, rose owing to both higher pretax incomes and lower taxes. Thus households should have been expected to reinforce, not offset, the decline in business saving. On the other hand, households might be expected to offset the increase in the corporate payout rate.

Conclusion

The 1986 tax act directly lowered private saving by taxing corporations more and households less, the former having a higher propensity to save than the latter. The act also taxed new corporate investments more, and existing corporate capital less, heavily, a combination almost certain to raise stock market values and lower household saving through a wealth effect. Finally, the economic incentive for households to save is likely reduced. While tax rates on interest and dividend income are lower, capital gains are taxed more heavily, deductible contribution limits for retirement accounts are sharply lower, and tax shelters are restricted (new passive loss rules and a more inclusive minimum income tax base). Observing reduced household saving might be difficult because of enormous errors in the measurement of saving.

Notes

1. The correct measurement of net contributions to social security is impossible to obtain with the data available (Hendershott and Peek 1989). In table 3C.1 I have simply shifted the well-known buildup in social security funds from the government sector to households.

2. A number of economists have advocated adding real capital gains to, and subtracting real losses from, household saving. But only real capital gains that reflect a more productive capital stock and thus greater future consumption possibilities should be added to saving, and only real losses that reflect reduced future consumption possibilities should be subtracted (Hendershott and Peek 1985). It is not obvious that routinely adding all real gains (or subtracting losses) to traditional saving numbers would improve our measure of saving (see Hendershott 1989 on this point). Until explicit measures of real capital gains or losses that are associated with productivity changes are obtained, we should continue to work with flow saving data.

3. The decline in the IRA uptake rate in 1986 and 1987 by families with incomes under $40,000 (whose IRA contributions were not affected by the 1986 tax act) has been attributed to reduced IRA advertising rates. The decline could instead reflect the completed transfer of existing liquid saving.

References

Downs, Thomas, and Patric H. Hendershott. 1987. Tax Policy and Stock Prices. *National Tax Journal* (June): 183–190.

Hendershott, Patric H. 1990. U.S. National Saving and Real Capital Gains. In C. E. Walker, M. A. Bloomfield, and M. Thorning (eds.), *The U.S. Savings Challenge*. Boulder, CO: Westview Press.

Hendershott, Patric H., and Joe Peek. 1985. Real Household Capital Gains and Wealth Accumulation. In Patric H. Hendershott (ed.), *The Level and Composition of Household Saving*. Cambridge, MA: Ballinger.

Hendershott, Patric H., and Joe Peek. 1989. Aggregate U.S. Private Saving: Conceptual Measures and Empirical Tests. In Robert E. Lipsey and Helen Stone Tice (eds.), *The Measurement of Saving, Investment and Wealth*. Chicago: University of Chicago Press.

GENERAL DISCUSSION

Charles Ballard expressed skepticism that the introduction of IRAs did much toward stimulating savings. He noted that some recent research has concluded that IRAs had little effect on the rate of savings.

Alan Auerbach recommended that research focus on explaining the behavior of consumption rather than savings. Studies of savings must struggle with difficult definitional issues. However, the result that consumption as a percent of net national product rose over the relevant period is robust to different measures of consumption. He also asked how the authors treated purchases of consumer durables in composing their savings measures.

Commenting on the relationship between capital gains realization decisions and savings behavior, Auerbach observed that when taxpayers sell assets, they sell a range of taxable and tax-free assets, and then decide where to reinvest the return. He agreed that the study's results were consistent with this realization and reinvestment activity, but that they may not be indicative of a long-run change in savings behavior.

James Poterba argued that focusing on the simple savings rate may still have some value, but that the flow of funds invested in the financial sector should also be analyzed. His own work has shown that there appears to be a correlation between realizations resulting from corporate takeovers and household outlays.

Skeptical about using the change in net wealth as a measure of saving for a study such as this, Charles McLure noted that wealth may increase without capital formation having occurred. Consider the recent case of Japanese investors purchasing Rockefeller Center in New York. As a direct result of this transaction the value of property in the surrounding area skyrocketed, increasing the wealth of the property owners, without any capital formation having occurred.

McLure also noted that because the ability to substitute still-deductible mortgage debt for nondeductible personal debt is confined to homeowners, these taxpayers have access to a tax-reducing scheme that is unavailable to the remaining one-third of the public.

David Bradford supported Auerbach's argument that consumption, rather than saving, should be the object of study. He also responded to McLure's discussion of wealth changes without capital formation—as businesses certainly regard land to be as productive at the margin as other kinds of assets, perhaps we *should* consider an increase in land value as being capital formation.

Bradford also recommended that researchers look at the ratio of consumption to wealth, rather than consumption to income. The ratio of consumption to wealth, defining wealth to include government debt, has been fairly constant over the last eight or nine years, and has increased if wealth is defined to exclude government debt. This ratio *should* have fallen, as we would expect it to fall when the economy experiences "good times," such as we have seen in recent years. In Japan and the United Kingdom, this ratio *has* fallen. It would be interesting to explore what these data are revealing.

Adding to the discussion of deductible mortgage interest, Martin Zimmerman proposed that a lot of the debt associated with recent home equity loans is being used for the same purposes as the traditional second mortgage. If we include home equity loans in the analysis, the ratio of mortgage debt to the value of housing stays about the same over the test period.

Henry Aaron brought up a broad issue by asking how the observed responses to TRA are affecting economists' expectations of the effectiveness of tax policy.

Michael McIntyre recommended certain other variables to be controlled for in the time-series analysis of saving behavior, such as demographic changes that may have favored an increase in savings and the continued overfunding of pension programs.

4

Effects of the Tax Reform Act of 1986 on Corporate Financial Policy and Organizational Form

Roger H. Gordon and Jeffrey K. MacKie-Mason

The Tax Reform Act of 1986 (hereafter TRA86) included the most extensive changes in the U.S. tax law since the dramatic increase in corporate and personal tax rates during World War II. For many years tax economists have found that it is difficult to estimate the effect of taxes on corporate behavior because there has been so little variation in corporate tax policy. The major changes introduced by the TRA86 offer an opportunity to assess how well previous analyses succeeded in predicting the effects of tax changes and to obtain new understanding about taxes and corporate behavior.

The objective of this chapter is to examine the effects of the tax reform on the financial decisions made by firms. Taking as given its real decisions, a firm has substantial flexibility in deciding on the source of finance for its operations, and even on the legal form of ownership. To begin with, corporations can finance themselves through both debt and equity. Additional equity finance can be obtained either through retained earnings or through new share issues. When payments get made to equity holders, they can take the form of dividends or share repurchases. Shares of other firms as well as of one's own firm can be repurchased. More fundamentally, a firm need not necessarily set itself up as a corporation for both legal and tax purposes. By becoming a subchapter S corporation, its income is taxed solely under the personal income tax, even though it retains many of the others benefits of the corporate form of organization. In addition it can become a partnership or proprietorship for tax or legal reasons.[1]

Past work has presumed that taxes play an important role in these decisions. If so, then the extensive changes in the tax law that were enacted in 1986 should have led to noticeable changes in these decisions. What was forecasted, and what happened?

In section 4.1 we focus on a corporation's decision to use debt rather than equity finance. We present various theoretical models that have been developed to describe a firm's decisions and then use the models to forecast what should have happened as a result of the 1986 tax reform. We find that the actual change in debt-to-value ratios has been substantially smaller than the models predict. We discuss some reasons for the surprise. In addition we raise some new issues, including the implications for the effective tax on retained earnings that follow from optimal trading strategies and the incentives provided by the new interest allocation rules for multinational corporations to shift their borrowing abroad.

In section 4.2 we examine the decision to pay dividends rather than use the same funds to reduce new share issues or to repurchase existing shares of one's own firm or of other firms. Finally, in section 4.3 we examine the choice of organizational form. We summarize the results briefly in section 4.4.

4.1 Debt versus Equity Finance

Forecasts from the traditional theory

During the last decade there have been a variety of approaches in the theoretical literature to the determinants of a corporation's debt–equity ratio. To begin with, Miller-Modigliani (1961) emphasized that interest payments but not dividends are deductible under the corporate income tax, implying that a shift of a dollar from equity to debt finance lowers corporate tax payments each year by τi, where τ is the corporate tax rate and i is the nominal interest rate. This tax savings from additional use of corporate debt would be traded off with the increased risk of costly bankruptcy that results. As the literature developed, real bankruptcy costs included not only administrative costs[2] but also a variety of extra monitoring and agency costs arising from the conflicts of interest between different classes of creditors in bankruptcy, and even in anticipation of the possibility of bankruptcy.[3] Suppose the additional costs that arise from the marginal dollar of debt can be expressed as a general function of the existing debt–value ratio $C(D/V)$, where $C(\cdot)$ is assumed to be increasing in D/V. If the firm adds debt until the extra tax savings are just offset at the margin by extra bankruptcy costs, then in equilibrium $\tau i = C(D/V)$.

Miller (1977) pointed out that this model entirely ignores personal taxes. Yet under the personal income tax all nominal income from debt (interest payments) is taxed at ordinary rates, while nominal income from equity consists not only of dividends, which are also taxed at ordinary rates,[4] but also of capital gains, which are not. Capital gains are taxed only when the asset is sold, allowing a gain from deferral of tax payments. Further, prior to the TRA86 capital gains were taxed at only 40% of the ordinary rate if the asset had been owned for over six months and were entirely tax exempt if the asset was held until death.[5] The less favorable tax treatment of debt income under the personal income tax offset to some degree the more favorable tax treatment of debt under the corporate income tax.

To understand the implications of taking personal taxes into account, let t represent the ordinary tax rate of the marginal investor in corporate debt, and let e represent the net taxes on a dollar of income to equity, received in some combination of dividends and capital gains.[6] If a firm owns an asset earning i before tax and finances this asset by debt, then no corporate taxes are due on the resulting net income, but personal tax liabilities equal ti. In contrast, if the asset were financed with equity, corporate tax liabilities would be τi, leaving net of corporate tax income of $(1 - \tau)i$ received by equity holders. They pay a tax at rate e on this income, implying total tax payments $[\tau + (1 - \tau)e]i$ of under equity finance.[7] If additional debt is used to finance the firm until the tax savings that result are just offset at the margin by additional bankruptcy costs, then in equilibrium[8]

$$[\tau + (1 - \tau)e - t]i = C\left(\frac{D}{V}\right). \tag{1}$$

In order to summarize the incentives to use debt finance under the tax law immediately prior to the 1986 reform, each of these tax parameters must be measured. Consider first the marginal effective tax rate on income at the corporate level. During this period corporations with substantial income faced a statutory tax rate equal to 0.46. Corporations with losses were allowed to use these losses to offset any profits earned during the previous 3 years, or profits they may earn during the following 15 years. In addition corporations with taxable income below $100,000 in a year faced lower statutory corporate tax rates. Furthermore the effective marginal tax rate was reduced by the limitation on use of the investment tax credit to 85% of tax payments.[9] Using time-series data available internally at the Treasury, Altshuler and Auerbach (1990) calculated that on average the corporate tax rate that applied to interest deductions was only 0.318 during the early 1980s.

Measuring the ordinary tax rate faced by the "marginal investor" in corporate debt is even more difficult since investors in many different tax brackets invest in bonds. Gordon and Bradford (1980) show that the tax rate on interest income embedded in the market's evaluation of bonds is a weighted average of the marginal tax rates of all investors active in the bond market. One possible approach to measure this weighted average of marginal tax rates is to compare the interest rates on taxable and tax-exempt bonds that otherwise have similar characteristics. Poterba (1989) compares the yield on long-term Treasury bonds to state and local municipal bonds and finds that the average t over 1981–85 is 0.202.[10]

We now estimate the marginal tax rate on equity income. If the fraction d of the nominal income accruing to equity holders takes the form of dividends, and capital gains are always realized long term, then $e = dt + (1 - d)g\alpha t$. Here g measures the fraction of long-term gains that are taxable implying that $g = 0.4$ prior to 1986, and α is intended to capture the benefits from deferring the payment of accruing tax liabilities on capital gains until the asset is sold as well as the benefits of being exempted from tax on gains on assets still held at death. The conventional assumption in the literature has been to assume that the effective tax rate on capital gains is halved due to deferral, and halved again due to the exemption at death, implying that $\alpha \approx 0.25$.[11]

We estimate d by taking the average ratio of aggregate corporate dividend payments to aftertax corporate profits during 1984 through 1986, as reported in the National Income and Product Accounts, which equals 0.560.[12] Given these parameter values, $\tau + (1 - \tau)e - t = 0.199$.[13] Therefore $.199 more is paid in taxes on a dollar of pretax corporate income if this income belongs entirely to equity-holders than if it belongs entirely to debt-holders.

What would have happened to the tax incentive to use debt under the TRA86, as calculated using this traditional approach? Many incentives changed under the TRA86. To begin with, the maximum statutory corporate tax rate was cut from 46% in 1986 to 40% in 1987 and 34% in 1988 and thereafter. This rate now applies to income over $75,000 rather than $100,000, so fewer firms are likely to face the lower bracket rate. In addition the likelihood that a corporation will have tax losses has fallen due to the reduction in initial depreciation allowances on purchases of new physical capital.[14] The repeal of the investment tax credit also eliminates the effect of the limitation on allowed tax credits, which had lowered the effective marginal tax rate.

All of these changes raise the fraction of corporate income taxable at the maximum rate. However, the TRA86 also increased the importance of the alternative minimum tax. Companies paying the alternative minimum tax face a marginal tax rate of 20%. Some of the companies paying the alternative minimum tax may otherwise have faced a lower marginal rate due to tax losses and progressivity in the rate schedule, while some would have faced a 34% marginal tax rate. Without access to confidential tax returns, we cannot redo the calculations reported in Altshuler and Auerbach (1990) for post-1986 data. Thus we simply assume that the average corporate tax rate that applied to interest deductions during 1987–88 was 85% of the maximum statutory rate rather than 69.2%, as found during the early 1980s by Altshuler and Auerbach.

The cut in personal tax rates in 1986 should also have reduced t. Using municipal bond return data, Poterba (1989) implicitly estimates that the personal tax rate on the marginal investor in taxable bonds was 19% in 1987, and 15.5% in 1988. In addition individuals could no longer exclude the first $100 in dividend income, though for the most part this should not affect marginal incentives.

The remaining parameters to be estimated are d, α, and g. Using the estimated equation for dividends in Poterba (1987), we forecast that the TRA86 should increase the dividend payout rate by 12.3% in 1987 and by another 4.7% in 1988, raising d from 0.588 to 0.711 and 0.758 in 1987 and 1988, respectively.[15] In addition long-term gains became fully taxable, so $g = 1.0$. While the timing of realizations is likely to change under the new law, we initially maintain the conventional assumption that $\alpha = 0.25$.

We have collected our calculations in table 4.1. According to the above discussion, the tax rate (corporate and personal) on equity is $\tau + (1 - \tau)e$,

Table 4.1
Tax advantage to debt finance

Tax rate on equity: $\tau + (1 - \tau)e$
Tax rate on debt: t

Parameter	1986	1987	1988
τ: effective marginal corporate tax rate on interest deductions	0.318	0.340	0.289
e: effective marginal personal tax rate on equity income $= dt + (1 - d)g\alpha t$	0.122	0.149	0.127
t: tax rate of marginal investor in debt	0.202	0.190	0.155
d: dividend payout ratio	0.560	0.711	0.758
g: fraction of taxable long-term capital gains	0.400	1.000	1.000
α: present-value factor for capital gains deferral	0.250	0.250	0.250
Equity tax	0.401	0.438	0.379
Debt tax	0.202	0.190	0.155
Difference	0.199	0.248	0.224

Sources: τ from Altshuler and Auerbach (1987) for 1986; 0.85* statutory rate for 1987–88. t from Poterba (1989). d from NIPA for 1986 (average 1984–86); forecasts based on Poterba (1989) for 1987–88. α from Feldstein, Dicks-Mireaux, and Poterba (1983). Other parameters calculated as described in text.

while the tax rate (personal only) on debt is t. Comparing 1988 to 1986 shows that the tax rate on income to debt is estimated to fall from 0.202 to 0.155, while the tax rate on income to equity falls only from 0.401 to 0.379, implying a net increase in the tax advantage of debt from 0.199 to 0.224. Therefore, the TRA86 provided some incentive to increase debt financing.

Why does debt look more attractive? The estimated magnitude of the fall in the tax cost of debt is not surprising, given the general drop in both personal and corporate statutory tax rates.[16] Why did the tax cost of equity fall by less? There are two factors at play here. First, the estimated personal tax rate on equity income is estimated to increase slightly from 0.122 to 0.127. Although personal tax rates were cut, Poterba forecasts that more equity income will be in the form of dividends, which remain more highly taxed than capital gains (because capital gains taxes are still deferred until realization or forgiven at death). The shift from capital gains to dividends more than compensates for the decrease in the tax rate on the marginal investor's income.

The second factor in the tax cost of equity is the effective corporate tax rate. We believe that the fall in this rate was also relatively small (from 0.318 to 0.289) despite the deeper cut in statutory rates (from 0.46 to 0.34) because of the simultaneous changes in depreciation and investment tax credits. With a broader tax base and no credits firms will be less likely to face a zero tax rate (tax exhaustion). The statutory rate fell, but the likelihood of actually paying that tax rate increased, with the net effect that the expected corporate tax rate did not fall by much.

Thus offsetting changes in the corporate tax rules and in the composition of equity income should limit the change in the tax cost of equity, while the debt cost appears to have fallen more substantially. The combined effect is for firms to have a higher incentive to borrow.

What effect should this change in incentives have on the average corporate debt–value ratio? To our knowledge, no one has attempted to estimate directly the relationship between the debt incentive of equation (1) and firm debt ratios. There are two reasons why such studies have not been feasible. First, there has been very little time-series variation in many of the tax parameters during the period since World War II. Second, it is difficult to measure accurately many of the tax parameters, as evidenced by the work of Altshuler and Auerbach (1990). As a result many authors have attempted to estimate the effect of various partial proxies for the effective marginal tax advantage of debt on debt ratios. Typical proxies with sufficient time-series variation include depreciation deductions, loss carryforwards, and investment tax credits.[17] However, most of these studies have not carefully specified the relationship between the proxies and the marginal tax advantage of debt, and in fact many of them have obtained estimated coefficients that have the wrong sign according to the theory.[18] Thus it would be very difficult to use these estimates to forecast the effects of the 1986 tax changes.

Another approach was taken by Gordon (1982), who tested the sensitivity of debt–value ratios to changes in market interest rates, through running a regression of the form $D/V = b_0 + b_1 i + \ldots$ using time-series data. As seen in equation (1), the incentive to use debt should instead be a function of the product of the market interest rate and a tax term. However, if the tax term were unchanging during the sample period, then the debt–value ratio is simply a function of the market interest rate, and we can interpret b_1 as equalling $b_1^*[\tau + e(1 - \tau) - t]$. The specification then implies that b_1^* should remain constant over time, even if tax rates do change. We therefore assume that the tax incentive term had been constant during the sample period 1956–80 at our estimated 1986 value of 0.199. We then infer from the estimated parameters that the debt–value ratio should have increased by 0.234 from 1986 to 1987, but only by 0.155 from 1986 to 1988, due to both the changes in the tax law and the observed increase in market interest rates.

MacKie-Mason (1989, 1990) takes a different approach to studying the determinants of financing decisions. Rather than estimate models of firm debt–value ratios, he studies incremental choices: the first study considers the choice between stock and bonds when a firm publicly issues securities, and the second considers the choice between private and public sources of funds. The econometric results indicate that the public debt–equity choice depends significantly on implicit variation in a firm's effective marginal tax rate. Specifically, if a firm has high nondebt tax shields (loss carryforwards and investment tax credits) when it is near tax exhaustion, then those shields have a substantial probability of crowding out interest deductions on new debt. The first study finds that those firms are less likely to issue bonds. In essence the analysis uses publicly available information to identify those firms likely to have a low expected marginal corporate tax rate, and then estimates the difference in debt–equity choices for those firms.

We have used the estimates in MacKie-Mason (1990) to forecast the ratio of new debt issues to equity issues after the tax reform. We first calculated the predicted fraction of debt issues in 1987 and 1988 using the observed values for firm characteristics. We then attempt to forecast what the fraction of debt issues would have been if there had been no tax reform.

Table 4.2
Predicted fraction of debt issues in public offerings

	1986	1987	1988
With TRA86[a]	0.46	0.54	0.43
Without TRA86[b]	0.41	0.52	0.37
Difference	0.05	0.02	0.06

Source: Based on model estimates in MacKie-Mason (1990).
Note: The estimates in MacKie-Mason (1990) were based on a sample of individual firms with a much higher debt fraction in 1986 (72%) than the population mean (46%). The discrete choice estimation method used sets the intercept to correctly predict the mean fraction of debt issues. To correct for the different mean in the full population, we subtracted an intercept dummy equal to −0.2 from the regression function.
a. Predictions use observed values for all explanatory variables.
b. Predictions replace actual ITC–ZPROB (investment tax credits interacted with a tax exhaustion predictor) with an estimate of its value without the tax reform.

To do this, we used the following method to estimate what loss carry-forwards and ITC would have been. We assumed that ITC would have been the same fraction of new capital expenditures as in 1985[19] and that tax loss carryforwards would remain unchanged in 1987 and 1988 from its previous value.[20] The results are shown in table 4.2. The forecast is that the effect of the TRA86 on the fraction of new issues that are debt rather than equity should be an increase in the debt share of 0.02 in 1987 and 0.06 in 1988. With the TRA86, debt issues in 1987 are forecast to increase over 1986 by 8% but then fall by 11% from 1987 to 1988 due to variation in other factors.

We shall return later in this section to the forecasts and compare them with actual financing practices in 1987 and 1988. We now continue our survey of theory and forecasts, considering some elaborations on the theory presented above, some new issues raised by the TRA86, and some alternative theories.

Further Elaborations on the Traditional Model

In the preceding discussion we assumed that the costs of extra debt, as measured by the function $C(D/V)$, do not change as a result of the Tax Reform Act. These costs are presumed to arise primarily from conflicts of interest between debt- and equity-holders, giving the firm the incentive to make value-reducing decisions that aid equity-holders at the expense of debt-holders and leading debt-holders in response to spend resources monitoring the firm. To the degree to which debt-holders and equity-holders are the same people, however, this conflict of interests is reduced since redistribution among securities no longer implies redistribution among investors. Under the tax law prior to 1986, portfolio holdings were highly segmented, with interest-bearing assets held by individuals and institutions in low or zero tax brackets and equity held by those in high tax brackets—those in high tax brackets benefited much more from the favorable treatment of capital gains on equity.[21] As a result of the TRA86, however, the tax benefit of capital gains was substantially reduced, reducing tax distortions to portfolio choice. If portfolios become more balanced, conflicts of interest between debt-holders and equity-holders should become less important. As a result the costs of extra debt are less (the function $C(D/V)$ shifts downward) and use of debt should increase by more than forecast using the above model.[22]

Another weakness of the traditional theory is its naive treatment of capital gains. Recent research on optimal trading strategies suggests that the effects of the tax treatment of capital gains can be far more complicated than presumed in the above discussion.[23] The effective tax rate on additional retentions depends heavily on the trading strategies followed by investors. For example, under both the old and the new laws, investors would have the incentive to sell immediately securities that have dropped in price in order to claim the tax loss without delay. In addition calculations reported by Constantinides (1984) suggest that under the old law investors also had the incentive to sell gains as soon as they become long term rather than hold gains to defer the capital gains tax. By selling as soon as gains become long term and then reinvesting, the investor acquired the right to realize any drop in price during the following year as a short-term loss, a right that was valuable enough that it paid to realize the long-term gain. If investors did follow this strategy of selling losses short term and gains just after they became long term so that all securities were turned over each year, then the *ex ante* expected increase in capital gains taxes when a firm retains an extra dollar would be $t\beta + 0.4t(1 - \beta)$, where β is the probability that the value of the firm falls during the year.[24] Under this trading rule the value of α should be $1 + 1.5\beta$ rather than 0.25 as assumed above.[25] For a variety of reasons actual trading strategies are likely to involve much less trade, implying a lower value of α but not necessarily one close to 0.25.

Under the Tax Reform Act of 1986 long-term capital gains are no longer taxed at a lower rate, eliminating the attractiveness of selling gains. The optimal trading strategy now becomes selling losses and holding gains.[26]

The change in trading strategy implies a drop in α after 1986. How large a drop is difficult to judge, but any drop makes equity more attractive. Suppose, for instance, that the correct value for α pre-TRA86 was 0.50 but that the value then dropped to 0.25 after the reform. Then the forecasted change in D/V between 1986 and 1988 decreases from 0.155, the value calculated above, to 0.127.

New Issues Raised by the Tax Reform Act of 1986

The Tax Reform Act of 1986 included several new provisions not present in previous legislation, which could also affect corporate debt–equity ratios. Understandably, previous theories did not examine the effects of such provisions. The first provision restricts interest deductions on schedule A under the personal income tax to mortgage interest on a first or second house and investment interest up to the amount of investment income. The deductibility of consumer interest payments (except those related to a business) is being phased out during 1987–90. What should the effects of these provisions be?

To begin with, individuals have the incentive to convert nonmortgage debt into mortgage debt, thereby making the interest payments deductible, or alternatively to use any holdings of taxable bonds to repay nonmortgage debt. As long as an individual's total net debt has been less than the allowed amount of mortgage debt under the statute, this conversion is feasible and should be the only effect of the new provision.[27] To the extent that there are transactions costs from this conversion, the net tax effect can be no larger than these transactions costs.

What happens if the individual's total net debt had been greater than the allowed amount of mortgage debt?[28] This is most likely to occur for the wealthiest individuals who for tax reasons have had the incentive to borrow heavily and invest the funds in more lightly taxed assets such as corporate equity. These individuals would prefer borrowing by the corporations in which they own shares to personal borrowing. At the margin they face a tax rate on interest income of $t = 0$, so equation (1) implies a very strong incentive for corporations to make increased use of debt finance.[29] As in the proof of the Modigliani and Miller (1958) theorem, corporate borrowing replaces individual borrowing. In particular, corporations can borrow to repurchase the shares of these individuals, who then use the proceeds to repay their excess debt.

In table 4.3 we present some evidence on personal borrowing patterns. There was a dramatic increase in mortgage borrowing in 1986 and 1987,

Table 4.3
Flow of borrowing and interest deductions by individuals

Year	Flow of total borrowing (billions of nominal dollars)		Interest reported on Schedule A (millions of nominal dollars)	
	Nonfarm mortgages	Consumer credit	Mortgages	Consumer credit
1980	96.4	2.6		
1981	73.8	16.9		
1982	52.9	16.4		
1983	120.4	49.0		
1984	136.7	81.6		
1985	157.0	82.5		
1986	216.7	58.0	122.2	71.7
1987	233.9	32.9	134.5	65.3
1988	219.6	51.1	138.5	62.3
1989:1	187.0	34.9		

Sources: Borrowing flows: Board of Governors of the Federal Reserve System, *Flow of Funds Accounts, First Quarter 1989*, June 2, 1989. Interest tabulation provided by Brain Erard, IRS, from IRS tax reform panel study sample.
Note: 1989 data are at an annual rate for first quarter only. Nonmortage interest reported is the interest deducted on Schedule A grossed up by the allowable fraction of total interest (100%, 65%, and 40% in 1986–88, respectively).

as expected. Mortgage borrowing has fallen off in 1988 and the first quarter of 1989, but the level is still substantially higher than it was pre-TRA86. Consumer credit reached its peak during 1984–85 and fell off considerably from 1986 on. Thus it appears that there was significant substitution from consumer credit to mortgage borrowing. In addition total borrowing had been increasing almost linearly from 1980 to 1986 but fell well below the trend line after the TRA86.

The aggregate flows in table 4.3 are for all individuals in the United States, but the interest deduction provisions of the TRA86 affect only those individuals who itemize. Most individuals with mortgages are itemizers, but many who use consumer credit are not, and nonitemizers faced no change in the tax cost of borrowing. The other part of table 4.3 reports preliminary data on interest deductions claimed by itemizers during 1986–88. Mortgage interest paid by itemizers has steadily increased, while consumer interest paid by itemizers (*i.e.*, deductions grossed up by the fraction that is deductible under the new law) has fallen significantly. The ratio of nonmortgage to mortgage interest for itemizers has fallen from 59% in 1986 to 45% in 1988.[30]

A related provision of the new law limited the tax deductibility of losses arising from "passive" investments such as shares in a limited partnership or income from rental housing.[31] These losses arise in part because of the deduction of interest payments on debt incurred as part of the business activity. Again, these individuals could attempt to substitute mortgage debt for the passive business debt. If this is not feasible, however, then they would face a reduced marginal tax rate on income from these passive activities. For passive investments undertaken after October 1986 that incur net tax losses, the marginal tax rate is zero. For earlier passive investments that have losses, phase-in rules allow some fraction of these losses to be deducted from taxable income. Simple calculations suggest that the marginal tax rate on this income is approximately $0.825t$ in 1987 and $0.5t$ in 1988.[32] If these individuals are also corporate shareholders, they would again have an increased incentive to substitute corporate borrowing for personal borrowing due to the drop in the personal tax rate applying to interest deductions. This new provision therefore should also increase corporate incentives to issue debt.

A third provision in the new law requires that affiliated corporations eligible to file a consolidated return allocate worldwide interest deductions across the various companies in proportion to their assets to determine domestic and foreign source income. Previously, an affiliated group could calculate income separately for each company, allowing it to allocate interest deductions to particular firms in order to minimize total tax payments by the group. As long as most other countries continue to follow the previous accounting practice, there will be complicated interactions between the provisions in different countries. In fact the rules may have a "beggar-thy-neighbor" effect, by increasing tax payments to the United States at the expense of tax payments to foreign governments.

Consider the following example: In the simplest terms a U.S. firm with foreign branch operations pays a total tax bill consisting of foreign taxes plus precredit U.S. taxes minus foreign tax credits:

$$\tau_f y_f^f + \tau_u(y_u^u + y_f^u) - \min[\tau_f y_f^f, \tau_u y_f^u],$$

where τ_i is the tax rate in country i with f the foreign country and u the United States, and y_i^j is source income in country i as defined by country j's tax law. Suppose that a U.S. multinational has domestic capital K_u and foreign branch capital K_f, and increases borrowing enough to make additional interest payments of i. U.S. precredit tax payments fall by $\tau_u i$ regardless of where the borrowing takes place since tax is levied on worldwide income. If the firm has excess foreign tax credits ($\tau_u y_f^u < \tau_f y_f^f$), then the foreign tax credit falls by $\tau_u i(K_f/(K_u + K_f))$ under the new interest allocation rules, again regardless of the location of the borrowing. However, foreign tax payments may depend on the borrowing location: With a source-based deduction, foreign taxes fall by $\tau_f i$ only when the borrowing is done abroad. Thus a multinational with excess foreign tax credits and foreign branch operations will reduce its total tax liability by doing all borrowing abroad. In contrast, if the firm does not have excess foreign tax credits, then the location of the interest deductions does not affect total tax payments.[33]

Other Theories of Corporate Financial Policy

In response to the poor performance of empirical tests of the traditional model of corporate financial policy used above, Myers and Majluf (1984) developed an alternative model, focusing on the conflicts of interest between existing equity-holders and new creditors (both equity and debt). They argued that a firm's manager has better information about the true value of the existing firm than the market does and wants to use this information to the advantage of existing equity-holders. As a result the manager may issue new shares either because the market overestimates the true value per share or because the firm in fact needs further funds to finance valuable new investment projects. Investors therefore must react cautiously when the firm issues new securities since the fact that the firm chooses to make the new issue suggests that the firm's share price may be too high. This caution makes it more expensive for the firm to go to the market for new funds, and more so for new equity than for new debt since the return on equity is much more sensitive to the true value of the firm. Myers and Majluf then conclude that the firm would always prefer to issue debt rather than equity and would find internal finance preferable (if available) to outside finance.[34] Firms may also concentrate their issues of new securities during periods in which the market is relatively well informed about the situation of the firm, thereby lessening the need for caution on the part of purchasers of these new issues.

The theory did not directly focus on tax effects. It would appear that taxes reinforce the firm's preference for new debt issues over new equity issues but create an incentive to issue new debt even when internal finance is available for needed projects.

What would the Tax Reform Act of 1986 do to corporate financial policy according to this theory? Under the reform, corporate tax payments should go up, at least during the first few years. As a result the internal funds available for new investment projects would drop. Firms therefore would be forced to seek outside finance more frequently, where outside finance normally takes the form of debt. Therefore debt–equity ratios should grow, at least for those firms in which internal funds are not sufficient to finance desired investment projects.

Evidence on Debt–Equity Ratios after the Reforms

What in fact happened to debt–value ratios in response to the TRA86? Table 4.4 reports figures calculated from the balance sheet data of 996 firms on the Compustat tape.[35] The first row reports debt–value ratios from 1985–88, using data on book debt and the market value of equity. Here we find that debt–value ratios did increase as forecast, but that the increase

Table 4.4
Average debt–value changes since 1985 (996 Compustat firms; book debt and market equity)

	1985	1986	1987	1988
Debt–value[a]	0.398	0.403	0.441	0.439
Changes since 1985				
All firms		0.005	0.043	0.041
1985 ITC: low[b]		0.000	0.036	0.030
1985 ITC: high		0.010	0.050	0.052
1985 ZPINV: low[c]		0.011	0.068	0.069
1985 ZPINV: high		−0.001	0.018	0.014
Foreign operations: yes[d]		0.014	0.038	0.040
Foreign operations: no		0.006	0.052	0.060

Source: 1988 Compustat Primary, Secondary and Tertiary tape. Sample size is 996 firms, except for foreign operations for which only 778 firms had nonmissing data.
a. The debt–value ratio is calculated as (book debt)/(book debt + market value of equity), with the market value of equity measured on 12/31, and with book debt equal to the sum of short-term and long-term debt.
b. Firms split approximately at median value of ITC/(aftertax income), which was 0.0445; 491 firms are in "low."
c. ZPINV is 1/ZPROB, where ZPROB is Altman's (1966) predictor of firm bankruptcy. Firms split approximately at median value of ZPINV, which was 0.504; 495 firms are in "low".
d. We determine whether a firm has foreign operations based on whether it reports any foreign income tax payments on its Form 10K; 404 firms are classified as having foreign operations.

was only 0.041 from 1985 to 1988, in contrast to the forecasted increase of 0.155.[36] Why might the theory have forecast a much larger change than in fact was observed? One possible explanation is that the adjustment of corporate capital structure is a costly process that is likely to occur gradually. Auerbach (1985) makes a simple attempt to model dynamics and finds that only 27.4% of the adjustment takes place each year, implying that 52.7% of the adjustment should have taken place after two years. This would imply a long-run increase in D/V of only 0.078, which still seems very small.

A second possible explanation is that some of our tax parameters are estimated poorly, leading us to overestimate the size of the tax change. For example, our estimate of the effective corporate tax rate in 1986 was based heavily on calculations by Altshuler and Auerbach for the early 1980s, when the state of the economy was much different,[37] while our estimate for the corporate tax after 1986 was simply a guess. Had the ratio between the effective and the statutory corporate tax rates not changed as a result of the TRA86, then debt–value ratios would have been forecast to decrease.[38] To explore the possible importance of this explanation, we compared what happened to firms that were more or less likely to face a lower effective corporate tax rate. In particular, we compared firms whose ITC credits in 1986, as a fraction of aftertax profits, were below with those whose credits were above the median value for firms in the sample. Firms with large ITC's were more likely to face a binding restriction on credits in 1986, reducing their effective corporate tax rate then but not (to the same degree) in 1988. As a result they should have increased their debt–value ratios more in response to the tax change, and this is indeed what we find. But even for those firms with larger ITCs in 1986 that should have faced a time pattern of tax rates similar to those used in our calculations, the observed increase in use of debt was small relative to the forecasts.

Similarly, little is known about the effective capital gains tax rate, given its heavy dependence on trading strategies which themselves are affected by the tax law. We showed above that the forecasted change in D/V was sensitive to the assumptions made about the values of α before and after the reform. Before the reform, more trade should have occurred due to the favored treatment of capital gains. This raises the effective tax rate on retained earnings, making debt finance more attractive. Perhaps we underestimated the magnitude of the change in trading strategies brought about by the tax reform, causing us to overestimate the increased tax incentive to issue debt. To test the plausibility of this explanation, we would need data before and after the reform on the fraction of shares sold each year, both long term and short term, but such data are not currently available.

In addition the above calculations assumed a closed economy. Yet corporate securities are increasingly being purchased by foreign investors. Equity is no longer as favored under the U.S. personal income tax, due to the increased tax rate on capital gains and the general reduction in the importance of taxes due to the drop in tax rates,[39] but barring similar changes in foreign tax laws, foreign holding of U.S. equities should remain as favored as before.[40] We would therefore forecast an international shift in portfolios, with foreigners increasingly owning the equity in U.S. firms, implying on net a smaller drop in the personal tax advantage of equity after 1986. As a result debt–value ratios should not have increased by as much as was previously forecast, assuming a closed economy. How important this effect should be is hard to judge. Was there any observable shift toward foreign ownership of the equity in U.S. firms? Scholes and Wolfson (1988) report a large and sustained increase in foreign acquisitions of U.S. firms starting in the fourth quarter of 1986. International portfolio shifts may therefore be part of the explanation for the small change in debt–value ratios.

A third possible explanation follows from some of the other complications discussed earlier in this section. Some of those factors would have led us to forecast an even larger increase in D/V, so they do not help directly in explaining the smaller than expected increase. One complication that does lead to a reduced forecast of D/V is the interest allocation rule for multinationals. To test the importance of this complication, we calculated the change in debt–value ratios for the subsample of firms that reported no foreign income tax payments, which presumably were firms unaffected by this complication.[41] For these purely domestic firms, D/V increased by 0.060 from 1986 to 1988, which is still small relative to the above forecasts.[42]

Perhaps the poor forecasts simply result from the limits of past empirical work on firms' responsiveness to tax incentives rather than weaknesses in the procedures used for calculating tax incentives. If so, we have learned that corporate debt policy is quite insensitive to tax incentives.

One possible direction in which to seek an explanation for the small increase in the D/V ratio is through nontax changes in the bankruptcy and agency cost function, $C(D/V)$. If $C(D/V)$ shifted up, debt would be relatively less desirable. A number of factors may have changed bankruptcy and agency costs. For instance, the October 1987 stock market crash may have increased the perceived level of risk, leading to higher required risk premia on debt. Other factors to consider include recent institutional developments such as the emergence of a market for below-investment-grade debt ("junk" bonds) and the growth of leveraged buyouts of firms, though the timing of these events would themselves need to be explained.

We also examined the degree to which firms that faced higher bankruptcy risk in 1985 behaved differently in response to the TRA86. These firms presumably had a higher debt–value ratio than desired in 1985, so they would be trying to reduce it during the following few years, leading to a smaller increase in D/V.[43] For a bankruptcy indicator we used $1/\text{ZPROB}$, where ZPROB is a discriminant function predictor of bankruptcy estimated by Altman (1966); a high value of $1/\text{ZPROB}$ indicates a relatively high probability of declaring bankruptcy. We find that firms facing a higher risk of bankruptcy (high ZPINV in table 4.4) did not change their debt–value ratios much in response to the TRA86, whereas firms facing little risk responded much more.[44]

We also tested the accuracy of the forecasted effects of the tax reform on the fraction of new public issues that are debt, based on the estimates in MacKie-Mason (1990). In table 4.5, we report the number of new stock and bond issues from 1980 to 1988. As predicted, we observe an increase in the

Table 4.5
Stock and bond issues

	Number of issues			Amount in $ billion		
	Stocks[a]	Bonds[b]	Debt fraction	Stocks	Bonds	Debt fraction
1980	826	515	0.38	12.7	40.0	0.76
1981	1135	423	0.27	14.2	34.7	0.71
1982	746	595	0.44	13.4	42.3	0.76
1983	1765	589	0.25	29.8	43.6	0.59
1984	1038	587	0.36	8.8	56.1	0.86
1985	1175	1020	0.47	18.4	81.7	0.82
1986	1846	1551	0.46	34.2	168.6	0.83
1987	1676	1851	0.53	37.6	181.7	0.73
1988[c]	983	1885	0.66	22.2	170.4	0.89

Source: U.S. Securities and Exchange Commission, *SEC Monthly Statistical Review*, vol. 48, tables M-371 and M-375, various issues.
a. Stocks are primary, public offerings of conventional common stock.
b. Bonds are primary, public offerings of nonconvertible bonds.
c. December 1988 data used in calculating 1988 totals are preliminary.

fraction of debt issues from 46% in 1986 to 52% and 66% in 1987 and 1988, respectively, implying an increase of 6% by 1987 and 20% by 1988. The forecasts were for 54% and 43% debt issues in 1987 and 1988. The 1987 forecast was very accurate, but 1988 was extremely underforecast. Since we don't know if the poor forecast in 1988 is due to bad estimates of the tax or other effects, it is difficult to infer whether the estimated impact of TRA86 on debt issues (an additional 2% in 1987 and 6% in 1988) is reasonable.

How do we reconcile a large shift toward debt issues with a rather small change in debt–value ratios? First, as seen in the right-hand side of table 4.5, the amount of capital raised by debt as opposed to equity did not change much during the time period, due presumably to changing relative sizes of issues. In addition the change in the market value of equity depends not only on new issues but also on stock repurchases, dividend payments, as well as revaluations of existing capital by the market; book debt changes include private borrowing as well as public issues. The value of most equities rose dramatically during the first three quarters of 1987 and then crashed, leaving average equity values at about the same level at the end of 1988 as at the time of the tax reform. Therefore the revaluation effect may not be important during this period, but changes in share repurchases and dividend payout rates were important, as seen below.

One important uncontrolled factor in all of the analysis is the effect of the 1987 stock market crash on short-run financing choices.[45] Even if psychological and institutional effects do not persist in the long run, they may have affected financing behavior substantially during 1987 and 1988, which are the only years we have data for. Casual reading of the *Wall Street Journal* suggests that the crash led to a dramatic drop in the rate of equity financing during 1988. If so, debt–value ratios would have been even lower without the crash. This only reinforces the puzzling lack of change in debt–value ratios.

4.2 Corporate Distributions through Dividends, Share Repurchases, or Mergers

Traditional Story

Under the tax law prior to the TRA86, most corporations faced a tax incentive to make payments to shareholders in the form of share repurchases rather than dividend payments.[46] When payouts are made via share repurchases, the distribution is taxed as a capital gain under the personal income tax but would be taxed at ordinary rates if the payout had taken the form of a dividend payment.[47] Since at least long-term capital gains were taxed at a lower rate prior to the TRA86, dividend payments were discouraged by the tax law. Even when the tax rate is the same on dividends and capital gains, there would still be a tax advantage to share repurchases. Whichever form of payout occurs, shareholders are not taxed on the return of their initial investment. With share repurchases, this exemption takes the form of a deduction of the initial purchase price (basis) when each share is sold. With dividend payments, if payouts have been so large that all accumulated earnings within the firm have been paid out, then any further dividend payments are classified as "return of capital" and are untaxed. With either form of payout, the total nominal tax exemption is the same, but the exemption occurs much earlier in time when share repurchases are used.

As a result of this tax advantage to share repurchases, economists have long been puzzled why corporations pay dividends at all.[48] Attempts to explain the payment of dividends have normally assumed some nontax benefit from dividend payments that can offset the tax disadvantage of dividends. One story that has been explored in several papers is the use of dividends to signal the current profitability of the firm.[49] Although these papers do not attempt to distinguish dividends from share repurchases, Gordon and Malkiel (1981) argue that dividends rather than share repurchases might be preferable as a signal because the tax disadvantage of dividends implies that in equilibrium less payout will occur, implying lower cash-flow pressure on the firm than if repurchases are used as a signal.[50] Another approach, explored in Poterba and Summers (1985), is to assume that shareholders want dividends for liquidity reasons and that liquidity is valuable enough that shareholders desire dividends despite the tax disadvantage. Share repurchases are less attractive than dividends since investors must spend the time and brokerage costs to sell some fraction of their shares.

Under either story the lower is the tax rate on dividend income, the larger is the amount that should be paid as dividends. Poterba (1987) estimates the sensitivity of the dividend payout rate to the tax treatment of dividends, using a simple time-series model with a dynamic structure. From his estimates we forecast that the TRA86 should have resulted in an 8.5% increase in corporate dividends in 1987 and an additional 10.8% increase in 1988.[51]

Alternative Story of Dividends

An alternative approach to explaining dividend payments, known as the "new view," appears in Auerbach (1979), Bradford (1981), and King (1977). These papers assume that a corporation cannot in fact repurchase shares. Either it pays dividends or it reinvests the funds in new physical capital, resulting in capital gains to shareholders.[52] If it pays dividends, it does so until it is indifferent between that and reinvesting another dollar, implying that the capital gains q that result from reinvesting an extra dollar satisfy $(1 - g\alpha t)q = (1 - t)$. Here the right-hand side represents the net-of-tax income shareholders receive if an extra dollar is paid as dividends, while the left-hand side measures the net-of-capital-gains-tax income that results from retaining and reinvesting an extra dollar. If q is greater than $(1 - t)/(1 - g\alpha t)$ even when all profits are reinvested, no dividends would be paid.

Under this theory, what effects should the TRA86 have on the dividend payout rate? Since dividends equal corporate net-of-tax cash flow minus expenditures on new investment, dividends change due to a change in the investment rate, in tax payments, or in pretax cash flow. But changes in investment incentives were relatively minor in the TRA86.[53] The TRA86 increased tax payments of firms, at least in the first few years following the tax reform. Any effects of the TRA86 on pretax cash flow would be indirect, arising from general equilibrium effects. If in fact pretax cash flow and investment are little affected by the TRA86, then this theory forecasts that corporate dividends should fall by the same amount that corporate tax payments went up.[54]

Dividends versus Purchase of Shares in Other Firms

Rather than repurchasing its own shares, a firm could instead purchase the shares of other firms. Such portfolio investments, funded by forgone dividends, would have slightly different tax consequences than repurchase of the firm's own shares. Both would save taxes that would have been paid on the forgone dividends,[55] and both would lead to personal capital gains taxes on the sale of shares to the firm. However, the firm will owe some taxes on any dividend income it receives on the shares it purchases,[56] as well as capital gains taxes if it sells any of these shares. In addition the firm can be subject to an accumulated earnings tax if it receives earnings from financial assets beyond the reasonable needs of the business.

These various corporate taxes can be avoided, however, if the firm acquires at least 80% of the stock of any given company. Doing so, though, can lead to yet different tax implications than simply repurchasing one's own shares, as summarized in Auerbach and Reishus (1988). To begin with, if either firm had unused tax losses, then these losses can be used to offset the taxable profits of the other firm. This potential gain from a merger should become less important as a result of the TRA86 since tax losses will become less common, and also since the act itself restricted the ability of the merged firm to make use of tax losses built up by one of the separate firms.

Furthermore the acquiring firm can step up the basis of any assets it purchases, though in exchange the shareholders of the selling firm would owe capital gains taxes on the increase in basis. Letting ΔB represent the step-up in basis, z represent the present value of depreciation deductions per dollar of initial cost of an asset,[57] and c represent the effective capital gains tax rate on the sale, then the overall tax savings equals $\Delta B(\tau z - c)$, which is positive as long as $\tau z > c$.[58] The TRA86 included several changes which together should have eliminated any tax saving from such a step-up in basis. First, tax lifetimes for depreciation purposes were generally lengthened, the discount rate used in calculating z was increased as a result of the drop in tax rates, and τ was cut, all reducing τz. Prior to the TRA86, capital gains taxes were generally paid just under the individual income tax, based on the General Utilities doctrine, and at a maximum tax rate of 20%. If an installment sale were used, the capital gains tax payments could be postponed, reducing the effective tax rate yet further. Under the TRA86, personal capital gains tax rates on long-term gains generally increased, though they were cut on short-term gains. In addition the General Utilities doctrine was repealed, so capital gains are now taxed at both the corporate and personal levels if a firm liquidates some or all of its assets as part of the takeover. Also installment sales are usually disallowed under the act. In combination these increases in capital gains tax rates should be sufficient to guarantee that $\tau z < c$, implying a tax loss from a step-up in basis.[59]

These tax changes should all make mergers less attractive. How large an effect would be expected? Auerbach and Reishus (1988) found that tax incentives were not capable of explaining the pattern of mergers that occurred prior to 1986, and they forecast that little change in merger behavior should be expected.

Evidence on Dividend Payout and Merger Rates

We now examine how the pattern of payouts from corporations to equity investors has changed since the TRA86. Corporate aftertax profits and

Table 4.6
Corporate Payouts of Equity (billions of dollars)

	1984	1985	1986	1987	1988	1989:1[a]	1984–86 average
Aftertax profit	147.9	154.2	152.8	137.2	142.4	123.4	151.6
Dividends	81.0	84.0	89.9	95.5	103.3	109.6	85.0
Forecast dividends[b]				97.5	108.0		
Payout ratio[c]	0.548	0.545	0.588	0.696	0.725	0.888	0.560
Forecast ratio				0.711	0.758		
Net repurchases[d]	74.5	81.5	80.8	76.5	130.5	180.0	78.9
Total payouts	155.5	165.5	170.7	172.0	233.8	289.6	163.9
Dividends/payouts	0.521	0.508	0.527	0.555	0.442	0.378	0.518

Source: Board of Governors of the Federal Reserve, *Flow of Funds Accounts, First Quarter 1989*, June 2, 1989.
a. 1989 data are at an annual rate for first quarter only.
b. Dividend forecast is based on Poterba (1987), table 5. The forecast used actual values for all explanatory variables, converted to 1982 dollars. The results were then reinflated to nominal dollars.
c. Payout ratio is defined as (net dividends)/(aftertax profit + CCA + IVA). This is the dividend payout of book income, not payout of cash flow (which includes depreciation).
d. Repurchases are net of new equity issues.

dividend payments for 1984—89 (first quarter) are given in table 4.6. The table also presents our forecasts of the effect of the TRA86 on dividend payments based on Poterba's (1987) econometric estimates.[60]

The first thing to note is that dividends have dramatically increased as a fraction of aftertax profits.[61] This is consistent with the traditional view that there is some nontax benefit to paying dividends so that dividends will increase when the tax cost falls. The increase contradicts the "new view" discussed earlier in this section.[62] In fact the forecasts based on Poterba's estimates are quite reasonable. The payout ratio was forecast to increase 12% in 1987 and another 3% in 1988 (from 0.59 to 0.71 and 0.76, respectively); the actual ratio increased 11% in 1987 and 3% in 1988.

The theory forecasts, however, that dividends will increase relative to share repurchases. At the bottom of table 4.6, we report the net amount spent on share repurchases during the same time period,[63] the total payouts to equity holders (dividends plus share repurchases), and the fraction of total payouts to equity holders that took the form of dividends. Total payouts to equity holders increased dramatically in 1988 and again in the first quarter of 1989. Although dividends increased slightly as a fraction of total payouts in 1987, they fell sharply relative to total payouts in 1988 and even more so in 1989—despite the increase in nominal dividend payments, share repurchases increased much more quickly.

How is this sharp increase in share repurchases to be explained? The traditional theory unambiguously forecasts that dividends should have increased relative to repurchases of both a firm's own shares and purchases of shares in other firms. The forecasts based on the Auerbach-Bradford-King model are also sharply inconsistent with the evidence since their models would forecast a drop in payouts, in contrast to the observed increase; they also assume that repurchases are not possible. Perhaps firms have only recently learned about the advantages of repurchases (see, e.g., Shoven 1987), or only recently realized that the IRS will not reclassify these capital gains as dividends. If firms have been so unsophisticated about the tax law, this would undermine much of the research on corporate taxation. Dividend behavior continues to be a puzzle to tax economists.

We did not expect the TRA86 to have major effects on merger activity since tax effects appeared to be small in the past. However, in a recent paper Scholes and Wolfson (1988) claim to find significant changes in merger activity following the act. In table 4.7 we reproduce some of the data that they present on acquisitions of U.S. firms by U.S. firms (we have extended their series from 1987:4 to 1989:1). The numbers are striking,

Table 4.7
Domestic merger and acquisition activity (billions of 1987:4 constant dollars)

Quarter	U.S. acquisition of U.S. firms
1985:4	48.60
1986:1	31.65
1986:2	46.22
1986:3	35.33
Average	40.45
1986:4	67.44
1987:1	22.02
1987:2	31.65
1987:3	32.98
1987:4	33.96
1988:1	27.71
1988:2	42.18
1988:3	28.86
1988:4	57.74
1989:1	28.62
Average	33.97

Sources: Nominal merger values from *Mergers and Acquisitions*, various issues. CPI-Urban from U.S. Department of Commerce, Bureau of Economic Analysis, *Survey of Current Business*, various issues. This table reproduces and extends part of table 1 in Scholes and Wolfson (1988).

and they challenge the forecasts. The constant dollar volume of acquisitions jumped dramatically in the fourth quarter of 1986, after the TRA86 passed but before its relevant provisions took effect. The one-quarter jump is not that surprising: Firms that were already planning mergers may simply have rushed to beat the General Utilities deadline, and thus to save substantial amounts on capital gains taxes. However, there seems to have been a persistent reduction in the level of U.S. acquisitions following 1986. The mean rate of acquisitions is $34 billion per quarter, versus $40 billion per quarter during the prior year. It is hard to believe that the lowered rate of activity as late as 1989:1 is still due to the rush to beat General Utilities two years earlier. On the other hand, the rate began increasing again toward the end of this period, and the difference in means is not statistically significant.[64]

4.3 Effects on the Choice of Organizational Form

Theoretical Considerations

Following the assumptions made by Harberger (1962), much of the literature on the incentive effects of the corporate income tax has assumed that production is done by corporations in certain industries and by unincorporated firms in others. In fact firms can choose among several different organizational forms for tax and legal purposes. Gravelle and Kotlikoff (1988, 1989) emphasize that many industries contain a sizable number of both corporate and noncorporate firms and that these proportions shift over time. Interest in a firm's choice of organizational form is starting to receive more attention.[65]

What affects a firm's choice of organizational form? Taxes clearly are one consideration. If a firm is an ordinary (C) corporation, its income is taxed first at corporate rates with the remainder taxed again at personal rates when received as dividends or when capital gains are realized. Losses can be carried backward or forward across time to offset taxable profits in other years, but they cannot directly result in tax refunds. In contrast, the income of a partnership, sole proprietorship, or subchapter S corporation is taxed each year at the personal income tax rate of each owner. Losses can be used to offset taxes on other personal income.[66]

Whether a firm would pay less in taxes as a corporation or as a partnership/proprietorship depends on its circumstances. If the corporate income tax rate were below the personal income tax rate of the owners, if the personal taxes paid on corporate aftertax income were low enough (e.g., if little is paid in dividends and shares are not sold), and if the firm has taxable profits, then the firm would pay less in taxes by incorporating.[67] Similarly, if the firm has losses that can be deducted against corporate profits of other affiliated firms and the corporate tax rate is higher than personal tax rates, then the corporate form of ownership incurs lower tax liability. In other cases the firm would pay less in taxes by remaining unincorporated (or operating as an S corporation).

Another tax consideration potentially enters when some of the income of the firm is taxable as capital gains, such as sales of property by a real estate firm. The relative tax rate on capital gains has been different under the corporate income tax than under the personal income tax. In general, capital gains have been more favorably treated under the personal income tax, making the corporate form less attractive if the firm receives a nonnegligible fraction of its income in the form of capital gains. However, suppose a corporation separately incorporated an asset about to be sold and then made a liquidating payment of the sales proceeds to the shareholders. Prior to the TRA86 the General Utilities doctrine allowed the resulting capital gains to be taxed only at the personal level, implying no difference in the effective tax treatment of capital gains from such sales under corporate versus partnership forms of organization.

Taxes are obviously not the only consideration affecting a firm's choice of organizational form. We focus on the choice between C corporations and S corporations. To begin with, there are some eligibility requirements for S corporations: no more than 35 shareholders, not part of an affiliated group, only individual (not corporate) shareholders,[68] only one class of stock, and not a domestic international sales corporation (DISC). In addition, some states tax S corporations under their state corporate tax, rather than under the personal tax, requiring these companies to maintain two sets of tax accounts, one for state and one for federal taxes. Except for these considerations, however, C and S corporations are treated the same—for example, both have limited liability. There are presumed to be many important nontax distinctions between corporations and partnerships, however. For example, corporations have limited liability, they can trade ownership shares more easily, and they can base compensation of managers on the price of a publicly traded ownership share.[69] There has been little careful economic analysis, however, of the nontax factors that are likely to be important.

The TRA86 had conflicting effects on a firm's choice between C and S status. We discuss first the new advantages of an S election. To begin with, in most cases the personal tax rate was cut by more than the corporate tax rate, increasing the attraction of receiving income as an S rather than as a C corporation.[70] Perhaps more important, the General Utilities doctrine was repealed for corporations. Thus the capital gains on a sale of assets in corporate form will now be taxed first at the full corporate rate and then again at the full personal rate. Since no corporate tax applies to an S corporation, capital gains are taxed only at the personal rate of the shareholders. Any firm that earns substantial income from capital gains, or that is liquidated or purchased in a taxable takeover, will reap large tax savings from choosing S status.[71]

In addition S corporations are not subject to the new alternative minimum tax (AMT) faced by C corporations. This factor will be especially important for firms with substantial tax deferrals and accounting practices that lead to large book income relative to taxable income because the AMT includes 50% of that difference in the alternative tax base. Second, income from a C corporation cannot be used to offset "passive" losses, whereas income (to nonmanagers) from an S corporation can be.[72]

These gains were emphasized by Scholes and Wolfson (1988) and Plesko (1988), who predicted as a result that S corporations would become a much more important form after the TRA86. The TRA86 also introduced some offsetting costs to the choice of S corporation status, however. For instance, most fringe benefits that are deductible from C corporation income will be deductible for S corporations only to the extent that these deductions are allowed under the personal income tax. The higher floors set on many personal deductions mean that some expenses will generate lower tax savings in S corporation form. In particular, health and accident benefit insurance can be fully deducted by a C corporation, but only medical expenses in excess of 7.5% of adjusted gross income are deductible from the personal tax base. In addition the new passive loss restrictions can work against some S corporations: If the firm earns losses, then passive shareholders cannot use those losses to offset ordinary personal income. Although the same loss carryback and carryforward provisions are available for C and passive S corporations, this is an unfavorable change for passive S shareholders from the pre-TRA86 rules.

One significant provision may make a switch from C to S status less appealing than the choice of S status for a new firm. With the repeal of the General Utilities doctrine, Congress expected that many C corporations would retain their status but then strategically switch to S status just before a major asset sale or liquidation in order to avoid the corporate capital gains tax. Section 1374 was enacted to remove this incentive. Under Section 1374, firms that convert to S status must pay tax at the top corporate rate on any "built-in gains" realized during the ten years following conversion. Built-in gains are defined to include any difference between the fair market value of the firm at conversion and the C corporation tax basis at that time. Thus a firm that switches to S status and liquidates the next day will pay the full corporate tax on the entire capital gain. In principle, this provision should not make the incentives for choosing S status different for existing and new firms since in both cases the favorable capital gains treatment for an S corporation applies equally to all gains incurred after the date of S election. However, the added transactions costs of bookkeeping and negotiating with the IRS about the amount of the built-in gains from a conversion may be sufficient to reduce the desirability of converting from C to S status.

Empirical Evidence

How large an effect would these changes in tax incentives likely have on firms' choices of organizational form? Unfortunately, the quantitative importance of tax incentives relative to the various nontax considerations has not yet been explored.[73] However, on the assumption that the TRA86 provided the only change in the incentives for choosing a particular form since 1985, we can attempt to forecast the direction of the effects and to compare the forecasts to the data.

We showed above that the TRA86 changed both the benefits and costs of electing noncorporate tax status. Although there are no careful measurements of the relative value of the different provisions to firms, it seems plausible to think that for a typical firm the choice of S status looks more favorable than it did before 1986. The main benefits are the lower tax rates available at the personal level and the single taxation of new capital gains; the main costs appear to be the reduced deductibility of some noncash forms of compensation and increased transaction costs arising from the taxation of built-in gains when a company shifts from C to S status. If this judgment is correct, then there should be a shift of economic activity toward the noncorporate sector. Of course any given firm would be more likely to shift to S status if it can satisfy the eligibility requirements described above without substantial changes.

In figure 4.1 we present data from the NIPA accounts on profits plus interest in various corporate and noncorporate sectors of the economy

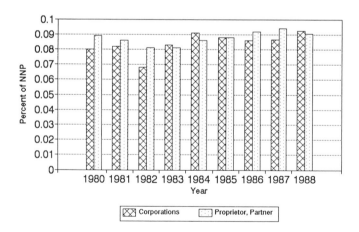

Figure 4.1
Profits and interest from corporate and noncorporate sectors

since 1980. Except for the bad year for corporations in 1982, the level of capital income is almost the same in the corporate and noncorporate sectors. These magnitudes suggest that more attention to noncorporate business taxation and organizational choice incentives may well be warranted. However, the TRA86 had no apparent impact on the relative levels of activity. Capital income has been relatively stable since 1986, with no trend in either series.[74]

Unfortunately, the tax incentives that are our primary interest make it unlikely that measures of net income can be very informative. Given differences in corporate and personal tax rates, and the varying treatment of capital gains, the choice of organizational form will depend in part on whether the firm is earning profits or losses. In fact, the aggregate taxable income of partnerships has been negative since 1981. The same firm may be organized in different forms at different times precisely because of its time path of gains and losses. For example, S corporations were often recommended as an initial status for new firms that expected losses (while depreciation on initial investment was high and revenues low) because the losses could immediately offset personal income, but a change to C status would follow as the need for broader ownership increased. Thus annual net income may be a poor measure of the amount of economic activity undertaken in various organizational forms.

Information about the assets of firms choosing each form of organization would be much more informative. For example, in 1985 partnerships had 1/10 as much in assets as corporations, but corporations had taxable income of $266 billion while partnerships reported income of −$17 billion. Unfortunately, this information is not yet available for the period after the TRA86.

Another piece of evidence about post-TRA86 activity is available. Firms electing to be taxed as an S corporation must file Form 2553 with the IRS. We present semiannual data on these filings for recent years in figure 4.2. Two points are striking. First, there was a massive surge in S elections immediately following the TRA86: about 375,000 filings during the first six months of 1987, compared to an average six-month rate of about 150,000 during 1983−86. Second, no trend was apparent before 1987, but the filing rate has been higher during every period after the reform than during any prior period. Thus we see evidence both that a large number of existing firms elected to convert from C to S status (the initial surge) and that many more firms are continuing to choose S status (presumably both further conversions and a higher rate of new S incorporation).

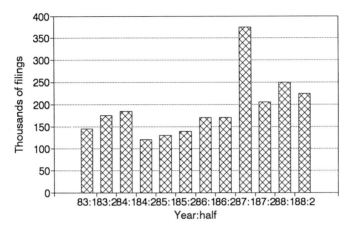

Figure 4.2
S corporation elections (form 2553), 1983–88

However, just looking at the number of firms does not indicate the amount of economic activity. For example, many of the new S corporations may be very small, with most assets remaining under C status despite the increased number of S corporations.

One bit of evidence from tax returns is available at this time. The net income from partnerships and S corporations reported on individual tax returns is presented in table 4.8. From 1981 to 1986 this reported income averaged − $2.2 billion. In a remarkable turnaround, $32 billion in positive (net) income was reported in 1987. Although we cannot tell the extent to which assets and activities moved among different forms, it appears that the nature of activity changed dramatically. Much of the difference could be due to passive losses borne by individuals who did not have offsetting passive gains. However, the total profits for the subset of partnerships with positive income were only $32 billion in 1985. Thus, to explain the 1987 reported profits in table 4.8, either almost all passive losses were not deductible, or more likely a substantial amount of loss activity was shifted into corporate form, where it could be deducted at a higher tax rate, while gains were left to be taxed at the lower personal rates.

4.4   Conclusions

How successful were the traditional models of corporate financial policy in forecasting the response of corporations to the Tax Reform Act of 1986? Results are mixed at best.

Table 4.8
Income from partnerships and S corporations reported on individual income tax returns
(billions of nominal dollars)

Year	Net reported income
1980	10.1
1981	−0.9
1982	−1.7
1983	−0.5
1984	−2.2
1985	−2.2
1986	−5.9
1987	32.1

Source: U.S. Internal Revenue Service, *Statistics of Income Bulletin*, various issues.

To begin with, traditional models implied that the tax incentive to use debt instead of equity increased substantially as a result of the tax reform. From the available empirical evidence on the responsiveness of debt–value ratios to tax incentives, and using the traditional approach, we forecast that debt–value ratios would increase by 0.155; the observed increase was only 0.041. Although the actual change was in the forecasted direction, its magnitude was far smaller than forecast.

We discussed some possible explanations for the lower-than-expected changes in debt–value ratios, but available data and models are inadequate to test their plausibility. Of particular interest is the possibility that the effective tax on retained earnings has been underestimated in the past because of naive assumptions about optimal trading strategies. Recent developments in trading theory suggest that a lower capital gains tax rate encourages higher share turnover and thus a higher tax on retentions, giving firms an incentive to rely more heavily on debt. If so, then TRA86 may have reduced the penalty on retained earnings by equalizing the taxation of capital gains and ordinary income.

In addition some aspects of the Tax Reform Act raised interesting new issues for future research. One possibly important effect is the change in the relative desirability of overseas borrowing for multinational corporations. The "one-taxpayer" interest allocation rules will allow many firms to reduce their foreign tax liability (without affecting U.S. tax liability) by borrowing through their foreign branch operations rather than domestically.

We also examined the implications of the tax reform for the form of corporate payouts. Dividend payments were discouraged by the tax law far more before the reform than after, leading most traditional theories to forecast an increase in the fraction of payouts taking the form of dividends. Although dividends did increase, and by an amount quite consistent with the forecasts in Poterba (1987), repurchases of shares increased at a much faster rate, implying a sharp drop in the fraction of payouts taking the form of dividends. We have no convincing explanation. The Auerbach-Bradford-King model of dividend policy would have forecast a fall in dividend payments, which was also inconsistent with the evidence.

What about a firm's choice of organizational form? Our assessment was that the existing theory was not capable of forecasting how the changes in the tax law would affect the attractiveness of the corporate relative to various noncorporate forms of organization. The data show that a large number of firms elected S corporation status, but we do not yet know how much economic activity these firms represent. The first piece of available tax evidence suggests that loss operations have shifted toward the more highly taxed corporate sector, while gain operations are being taxed at the lower personal rates. Further analysis awaits the release of post-TRA86 tax data by the IRS.

One of the main problems in developing and testing models of the effects of taxes on corporate financial policy prior to the Tax Reform Act had been the lack of variation in tax policy since World War II. Given the sharp changes in incentives created by this act, economists will now be in a much better position to refine their understanding of the determinants of corporate financial policies. Our results show that they need to.

Notes

We are grateful for helpful comments from Glenn Hubbard and Joel Slemrod. Brian Erard of the IRS provided us with some unpublished summary statistics based on individual returns. MacKie-Mason gratefully acknowledges financial support from a Rackham Faculty Research Grant.

1. Firms can make choices about organizational form when they are first formed; later they can choose to shift from one form to another, though with some costs.

2. Warner (1977) presented data indicating that these were small.

3. See, for example, Myers (1977), Jensen and Meckling (1976), Bulow and Shoven (1978), and White (1980, 1989).

4. Prior to the TRA86 the first $100 in dividends received by an individual were tax free. Since virtually all dividends are received by shareholders with more than $100 in dividend income, this provision should have no effect on marginal tax rates.

5. Prior to July 1984 the holding period for long-term gains was one year, and prior to October 1979 the long-term rate was 50% of the ordinary income tax rate.

6. For capital gains we use the accrual equivalent tax rate rather than taxes currently paid.

7. If the asset earned more than i, with the additional income accruing to the original equity holders, then the same amount of taxes would be paid on the additional income, regardless of the choice of debt or equity finance at the margin.

8. See Gordon (1982) for a formal derivation.

9. Given this limitation, tax payments equal $\tau Y - \min(0.85\tau Y, C)$, where Y equals taxable income and C equals the amount of investment tax credits. The marginal tax rate in a given year drops to 0.15τ when the limitation on investment tax credits is binding. Carryover of credits complicates this calculation, however.

10. Gordon and Malkiel (1981) compare the yields on taxable and tax-exempt bonds issued simultaneously by the same corporation by looking at firms that issued tax-exempt industrial revenue bonds (IRBs) along with ordinary bonds with the same nontax provisions. This alternative approach ensures that the comparison holds everything other than tax status constant. They estimated t to be 0.225 in 1978. The TRA86 restricted the use of IRBs for private investment, so we cannot use this superior method to estimate the implicit tax rate post-TRA86. We thus rely on Poterba's approach, which he uses to estimate t for 1987–88.

11. See, for example, Feldstein, Dicks-Mireaux, and Poterba (1983).

12. Aftertax corporate profits include the inventory valuation adjustment and the capital consumption adjustment. We exclude financial sector firms throughout this study.

13. Miller (1977) argued that in equilibrium t would adjust until this expression equals zero, whereas DeAngelo-Masulis (1980) argued that τ should adjust until in equilibrium this expression equals zero. Rather than relying on their theoretical results, which depend on the assumption that marginal bankruptcy costs are zero, we used the best empirical estimates we could find for each parameter.

14. For a sample of approximately 1,400 firms with complete data in Compustat, average loss carryforwards have fallen since 1986 from about 30% of net sales to 8% in 1988, even though aftertax corporate profits have fallen during this same period from $191 billion to $186 billion according to the *Survey of Current Business* (table 1.16), July 1989.

15. We report increases in the dividend payout rate relative to 1986 values. However, to calculate the pre-TRA86 tax incentive for debt, we used the average value for 1984–86.

16. Financial intermediaries are important investors in bonds, implying that changes in corporate tax rates can also affect the tax rate on debt.

17. Examples include Titman and Wessels (1988), Ang and Peterson (1986), Auerbach (1985), Bradley, Jarrell and Kim (1984), and Long and Malitz (1985).

18. MacKie-Mason (1990) discusses these problems in more detail.

19. We use 1985 as the base year because the repeal of ITC was retroactive to January 1, 1986.

20. Alternative assumptions about TLCF made no difference to the forecasts.

21. For evidence on portfolio holdings, see, for example, King and Leape (1984). Note, however, that if equity is owned directly by investors in high-tax brackets, but corporate bonds are owned by corporate defined-benefit pension funds, where the corporation is the residual claimant on the assets, then the income from both the equity and the debt accrue to those in high-tax brackets.

22. For further discussion, see Gordon (1989).

23. See, for example, Constantinides (1984) and Stiglitz (1983).

24. One omitted complication is that the tax law forces individuals to use long-term capital gains to offset short-term capital losses, with only the *net* loss deductible. Another is that only $3,000 in net losses can be deducted from other income. Some ways to relax these constraints are discussed in Stiglitz (1983).

25. The value of α is the factor that converts the capital gains tax rate on long-term gains gt into an accrual-equivalent tax rate. The factor is greater than one with frequent trading because incremental retained earnings in gain years are taxed at gt, but retentions in loss years are taxed at the full personal rate t.

26. In addition the probability of experiencing a capital loss on a particular asset would change due to changes in debt—equity ratios, changes in dividend payout rates, and the change in trading strategy. Trading strategy matters because of the longer holding period for gains. The conditional probability of an asset experiencing a capital loss—a drop in price below the original basis—falls the longer the asset is held as long as the asset has a positive expected nominal rate of return.

27. Of course the individual must also hold enough home equity to secure the necessary mortgage debt. Manchester and Poterba (1989) estimate that there was a potential stock of $2.5 trillion in unused mortgage borrowing in 1985 and that, if the $100,000 limit on tax-deductible second mortgage debt had been in place, only 10.5% of homeowners would have been constrained.

28. "Net" debt does not include debt used to finance portfolio investments, since interest on this debt is still deductible.

29. Feldstein (1989) also makes this argument about the effects of the limitation of interest deductions on corporate borrowing.

30. See chapter 3 by Skinner and Feenberg in this volume for further evidence on shifts from consumer credit to mortgage borrowing.

31. Note that aggregate partnership income reported on individual returns has been negative since 1981.

32. Under the phase-in rules, 65% of the losses in 1987 could be deducted, 40% of the losses in 1988, 20% of those in 1989, and 10% of those in 1990. The figures in the text use these rules but take into account the benefit of carryover of losses disallowed in an earlier year assuming a 10% discount rate.

33. If foreign governments adopt the same tax provision for the allocation of interest deductions, then the location of the interest deduction becomes irrelevant, but the effective corporate tax rate applied to interest deductions becomes $(K_f \tau_f + K_u \tau_u)/(K_f + K_u)$, which is simply a weighted average of the foreign and domestic tax rates, rather than τ_u as assumed above.

34. If the firm cannot issue new debt, due perhaps to credit rationing as described by Stiglitz and Weiss (1981), then it may choose to issue new equity.

35. We only selected firms from the Primary, Secondary, and Tertiary tape, so our sample is biased toward large firms. Our selection criteria were that the firms be nonfinancial and that they have complete data for all of the variables in each comparison. Book debt is the sum of short and long term, and the market value of equity is measured using the price on the last trading day of the year.

36. The debt–value ratios for our sample are very similar to the values for the entire nonfinancial corporate sector as reported by the Federal Reserve—0.24 in 1985 and 0.29 in 1988 (*Balance Sheets for the U.S. Economy*, April 1989)—so our reliance on a sample does not appear to introduce important bias.

37. For instance, the importance of tax loss carryforwards was likely much higher during the middle of a deep recession in the early 1980s than in 1986, after several years of relative prosperity.

38. For example, if the ratio of the effective to the statutory tax rate remained equal to the Altshuler and Auerbach estimate for the early 1980s, then the tax incentive favoring debt would drop from 0.199 in 1986 to 0.177 in 1988.

39. According to our figures in table 4.1, the difference in the personal tax rates on income from debt versus equity had been $(0.202 - 0.122) = 0.08$ in 1986 but only $(0.155 - 0.127) = 0.028$ in 1988.

40. As Whalley shows in chapter 9 of this volume, many other countries have also recently revised their tax systems, usually in a manner similar to the U.S. tax reform. Thus U.S. equity may now also be less favored in other countries.

41. If multinationals shift borrowing abroad in response to the new interest allocation rules then domestic debt/value ratios might decline. However, in many cases the data are reported on a consolidated basis, in which case there may be no effect on the observed D/V. Because of the data complications we focus here only on firms with no foreign operations.

42. However, if we also take into account Auerbach's (1985) estimated adjustment rate, the predicted long-term change is 0.114, which is not too far from the 0.155 predicted by the theory.

43. On the other hand, they should have faced a lower effective corporate tax rate in 1985, reducing their optimal debt–value ratio then, causing the forecasted change to be larger.

44. Further results on the pattern of response across firms are available in Givoly, Hayn, Ofer, and Sarig (1989). They regress changes in debt–value ratios between 1986 and 1987 on a variety of variables. Their results agree with our inferences: Different firms were affected by the reform in accordance with the standard theories of bankruptcy cost and nondebt tax shield effects. However, several of the explanatory variables in their analysis include book debt or the market value of equity, which are also in the dependent variable, so the results of their OLS regressions are likely to be biased and inconsistent. We avoid endogeneity by using 1985 values to classify the firms.

45. The crash may be one reason that we underpredicted the fraction of debt issues (overpredicted equity issues) for 1988.

46. Since new share issues are simply negative share repurchases, the theory forecasts a tax savings from simultaneously reducing new share issues and dividend payments.

47. To prevent a wholesale shift from dividend payments to share repurchases, the IRS holds that if a corporation repurchases shares at regular time intervals or proportionately from all shareholders, then the capital gains that result would be taxed at ordinary rates. Corporations can easily avoid having their repurchases taxed as ordinary income, however, simply by repurchasing shares on the open market and not at regular intervals.

48. Perhaps corporations had not yet fully realized the tax benefits from shifting to share repurchase. Shoven (1987) and MacKie-Mason (1989) report that corporations were in fact increasing their reliance on share repurchases during the early 1980s.

49. See, for example, Bhattacharya (1979) and Miller and Rock (1985).

50. Bernheim (1988) presents a formal model of this effect. Barclay and Smith (1987) point out that repurchases may be costly because of an adverse selection problem: Repurchases may exploit superior information available to managers who hold shares at the expense of other shareholders.

51. Poterba forecasts an immediate 8.1% increase in dividends after the TRA86, but his forecast holds everything else constant. We calculated a one-period static forecast using actual values for corporate earnings and lagged values of earnings and dividends since these weren't constant.

52. Use of debt finance is assumed to be constrained by exogenous factors.

53. For a discussion of the implications of the TRA86 for investment incentives, see Auerbach (1989). Investment in fact increased, implying a larger forecasted fall in dividends under this view.

54. Note the parallel between this argument and that resulting from the Myers and Majluf (1984) model of debt policy. Myers and Majluf took dividend payments as exogenous and tied debt finance to corporate cash flow, whereas this model of dividend policy takes debt finance as exogenous and ties dividend payments to corporate cash flow. There has not yet been an explicit marriage of these two theories.

55. If these share purchases had instead been funded by debt issues, then both would lead to the same increase in interest deductions.

56. Under the previous law 15% of dividend receipts were included in taxable income. This fraction was increased to 20% by the TRA86.

57. We assume implicitly here that assets are depreciated using some form of declining balance formula, but without a switch to straight-line depreciation.

58. If $\tau z < c$, then the firms can engage in a nontaxable merger to avoid the resulting tax increase.

59. See the appendix in Scholes and Wolfson (1988) for a more complete discussion of the effects of the TRA86 on merger incentives.

60. We report data for the nonfinancial corporate sector on a national income basis. Poterba (1987) estimated his dividend regressions on a gross domestic product basis.

61. Dividends are generally much more stable than aftertax profits, implying that the payout rate rises when aftertax profits fall as they did after 1986. We did not attempt to estimate to what degree the increased payout rate was larger than would be expected given this fall in aftertax profits.

62. Poterba (1987) also rejects the "new view" for the pre-TRA86 period.

63. These data from the Flow of Funds Accounts do not distinguish between purchases of a firm's own shares and purchases of shares of other firms.

64. Scholes and Wolfson (1988) also show changes in the types of domestic acquirers. Notably they argue that management unit buyouts and going-private transactions increased because these transactions are likely to rely more on nontax factors and thus do not suffer as much from the TRA86. They also show striking effects for acquisitions of U.S. firms by foreign companies, with a large and sustained increase beginning in fourth quarter 1986.

65. For other references, see Scholes and Wolfson (1987) and Gravelle (1988).

66. The TRA86 introduced restrictions on the use of some losses to offset other sources of income; we discuss these restrictions later.

67. See, for example, Feldstein and Slemrod (1980) for further discussion.

68. Some estates and trusts can be shareholders.

69. If a firm is organized as a limited partnership, all investors except the general partner can have limited liability. Further the general partner can be a corporation, giving it limited liability. Also ownership shares in some partnerships have been publicly traded; however, the 1987 tax law requires that most new publicly traded partnerships be taxed as corporations.

70. The first $50,000 of corporate income is still taxed at less than the 28% and 33% marginal personal rates. However, that income will be subject to double taxation, so the desirability of C status still depends on the degree of tax deferral through retaining earnings in the corporation.

71. Changing to a partnership may not be as favorable because disincorporation is a taxable event subject to the capital gains tax. However, the partnership form may be more desirable after the repeal of General Utilities for new firms just starting up.

72. In some cases, an identical result can be achieved by having the C corporation purchase the activity generating the passive loss. These losses then offset the income of the C corporation, and the same amount of corporate tax is avoided. However, transactions costs may be lower if individuals own some partnership and some S corporation shares, tailoring their portfolio to individual needs rather than arranging ownership of C corporations so that the shareholders collectively benefit from the merger of corporate gains and passive losses.

73. See Plesko (1988) for an exception. We are currently attempting such empirical work.

74. NIPA measures of capital income since 1986 are still preliminary because they do not yet reflect actual corporate tax collections. The July 1990 revisions will be the first to incorporate actual 1986 corporate tax data. Thus we cannot be confident about the apparent lack of change in the series after 1986.

References

Altman, E. I. 1968. Financial Ratios, Discriminant Analysis, and the Prediction of Corporate Bankruptcy. *Journal of Finance*, 23: 589–609.

Altshuler, R., and A. J. Auerbach. 1990. The Significance of Tax Law Asymmetries: An Empirical Investigation. *Quarterly Journal of Economics*, forthcoming.

Ang, J. S., and D. R. Peterson. 1986. Optimal Debt Versus Debt Capacity: A Disequilibrium Model of Corporate Debt Behavior. In A. W. Chen (ed.), *Research in Finance*, vol. 6. Greenwich, CT: JAI Press.

Auerbach, A. J. 1979. Wealth Maximization and the Cost of Capital. *Quarterly Journal of Economics* 93: 433–446.

Auerbach, A. J. 1985. Real Determinants of Corporate Leverage. In B. M. Friedman (ed.), *Corporate Capital Structures in the United States*. Chicago: University of Chicago Press.

Auerbach, A. J., and D. Reishus. 1988. The Effects of Taxation on the Merger Decision. In A. J. Auerbach (ed.), *Corporate Takeovers*. Chicago: University of Chicago Press.

Barclay, M., and C. W. Smith, Jr. 1987. Corporate Payout Policy: Cash Dividends versus Share Repurchases. Working Paper. William E. Simon Graduate School of Business, University of Rochester.

Bernheim, B. D. 1988. Dividends versus Share Repurchases as Signals of Profitability. Working Paper. Stanford University.

Bhattacharya, S. 1979. Imperfect Information, Dividend Policy, and the "Bird in the Hand" Fallacy. *Bell Journal of Economics* 10: 225–235.

Bradford, D. F. 1981. The Incidence and Allocation Effects of a Tax on Corporate Distributions. *Journal of Public Economics* 15: 1–22.

Bradley, M., G. A. Jarrell, and E. H. Kim. 1984. On the Existence of an Optimal Capital Structure: Theory and Evidence. *Journal of Finance* 39: 857–878.

Bulow, J., and J. Shoven. 1978. The Bankruptcy Decision. *Bell Journal of Economics* 9: 437–456.

Constantinides, G. M. 1984. Optimal Stock Trading with Personal Taxes. *Journal of Financial Economics* 13: 65–89.

DeAngelo, H., and R. W. Masulis. 1980. Optimal Capital Structure under Corporate and Personal Taxation. *Journal of Financial Economics* 8: 3–29.

Feldstein, M. S. 1989. Excess Debt and Unbalanced Investment: The Case for a Cash Flow Business Tax. Testimony before the Committee on Ways and Means. U.S. Congress. January 31.

Feldstein, M. S., and J. Slemrod. 1980. Personal Taxation, Portfolio Choice, and the Effect of the Corporation Income Tax. *Journal of Political Economy* 88: 854–866.

Feldstein, M. S., L. Dicks-Mireaux, and J. Poterba. 1983. The Effective Tax Rate and the Pretax Rate of Return. *Journal of Public Economics* 21: 129–158.

Givoly, D., C. Hayn, A. R. Ofer, and O. Sarig. 1989. Taxes and Capital Structure: Evidence from Firms' Response to the Tax Reform Act of 1986. Northwestern University Graduate School of Business Working Paper.

Gordon, R. H. 1982. Interest Rates, Inflation, and Corporate Financial Policy. *Brooking Papers on Economic Activity* 2: 461–488.

Gordon, R. H. 1989. Do Publicly Traded Corporations Act in the Public Interest? Working Paper. University of Michigan.

Gordon, R. H., and D. F. Bradford. 1980. Taxation and the Stock Market Valuation of Capital Gains and Dividends. *Journal of Public Economics* 14: 109–136.

Gordon, R. H., and B. G. Malkiel. 1981. Corporation Finance. In H. J. Aaron and J. A. Pechman (ed.), *How Taxes Affect Economic Behavior*. Washington, DC: Brookings Institution.

Gravelle, J. G. 1988. Corporate Taxation and the Efficiency Gains of the 1986 Tax Reform Act—A New Look. Working Paper, Congressional Research Service.

Gravelle, J. G., and L. J. Kotlikoff. 1988. Does the Harberger Model Greatly Understate the Excess Burden of the Corporate Income Tax? NBER Working Paper No. 2742.

Gravelle, J. G., and L. J. Kotlikoff. 1989. The Incidence and Efficiency Costs of Corporate Taxation When Corporate and Noncorporate Firms Produce the Same Goods. *Journal of Political Economy* 97: 749–781.

Harberger, A. C. 1962. The Incidence of the Corporation Income Tax. *Journal of Political Economy* 70: 215–240.

Jensen, M. C., and W. H. Meckling. 1976. Theory of the Firm: Managerial Behavior, Agency Costs and Ownership Structure. *Journal of Financial Economics* 3: 305–360.

King, M. A. 1977. *Public Policy and the Corporation*. London: Chapman and Hall.

King, M. A., and J. I. Leape. 1984. Wealth and Portfolio Composition: Theory and Evidence. NBER Working Paper No. 1468.

Long, M. S., and I. B. Malitz. 1985. Investment Patterns and Financial Leverage. In B. M. Friedman (ed.), *Corporate Capital Structures in the United States*. Chicago: University of Chicago Press.

MacKie-Mason, J. K. 1990. Do Taxes Affect Corporate Financing Decisions? *Journal of Finance*, forthcoming.

MacKie-Mason, J. K. 1989. Do Firms Care Who Provides Their Financing? In R. G. Hubbard (ed.), *Asymmetric Information, Corporate Finance and Investment*. Chicago: University of Chicago Press.

Manchester, J., and J. Poterba. 1989. Second Mortgages and Household Saving. *Regional Science and Urban Economics* 19: 325–346.

Miller, M., and K. Rock. 1985. Dividend Policy under Asymmetric Information. *Journal of Finance* 40: 1031–1051.

Miller, M. H. 1977. Debt and Taxes. *Journal of Finance* 32: 261–275.

Miller, M. H., and F. Modigliani. 1961. Dividend Policy, Growth and the Valuation of Shares. *Journal of Business* 34: 411–433.

Modigliani, F., and M. H. Miller. 1958. The Cost of Capital, Corporation Finance, and the Theory of Investment. *American Economic Review* 48: 261–297.

Myers, S. C. 1977. Determinants of Corporate Borrowing. *Journal of Financial Economics* 5: 147–175.

Myers, S. C., and N. S. Majluf. 1984. Corporate Financing and Investment Decisions When Firms Have Information That Investors Do Not Have. *Journal of Financial Economics* 13: 187–221.

Plesko, G. A. 1988. Choice of Corporate Entity: The Use of S Corporations before and after the Tax Reform Act of 1986. Working Paper, Office of Tax Analysis, U.S. Department of Treasury.

Poterba, J. 1987. Tax Policy and Corporate Savings. *Brooking Papers on Economic Activity* 2: 455–503.

Poterba, J., and L. Summers. 1985. The Economic Effects of Dividend Taxation. In E. I. Altman and M. G. Subrahmanyam (ed.), *Recent Advances in Corporate Finance*. Homewood, IL: R. D. Irwin.

Poterba, J. M. 1989. Tax Reform and the Market for Tax-Exempt Debt. NBER Working Paper No. 2900.

Scholes, M. S., and M. A. Wolfson. 1987. Taxes and Organization Theory. Working Paper, Stanford Graduate School of Business.

Scholes, M. S., and M. A. Wolfson. 1988. The Effects of Changes in Tax Laws on Corporate Reorganization Activity. Working Paper, Stanford Graduate School of Business.

Shoven, John B. 1987. The Tax Consequences of Share Repurchases and Other Non-dividend Cash Payments to Equity Owners. In L. H. Summers (ed.), *Tax Policy and the Economy*. Cambridge: MIT Press.

Stiglitz, J. E. 1983. Some Aspects of the Taxation of Capital Gains. *Journal of Public Economics* 21: 257–294.

Stiglitz, J. E., and A. Weiss. 1981. Credit Rationing in Markets with Imperfect Information. *American Economic Review* 71: 393–410.

Warner, J. B. 1977. Bankruptcy Costs: Some Evidence. *Journal of Finance* 32: 337–347.

White, M. J. 1980. Public Policy toward Bankruptcy: Me-First and Other Priority Rules. *Bell Journal of Economics* 11: 550–564.

White, M. J. 1989. The Corporate Bankruptcy Decision. *Journal of Economic Perspectives* 3: 129–151.

COMMENTS

R. Glenn Hubbard

Questions of the effects of taxation on decisions by firms regarding organizational form and capital structure have traditionally been a bread-and-butter research topic for public finance economists. Empirical evidence has not always been illuminating, however. In part, this is because there have been few identifiable tax regime shifts to provide variation for econometric analysis. Loosely speaking, the requirement for such an experiment is that the nontax part of a model of economic behavior stays constant while there is a significant change in the tax price of certain activities. Examples from the past include the Undistributed Profits Tax of 1936–37 and the introduction of the investment tax credit in 1962.

The implicit claim here is that the Tax Reform Act of 1986 is such an experiment. Like the undistributed profits tax or investment tax credit experiments, there is of course debate about what the appropriate underlying model is (and the influence of the choice of underlying model on the estimated or predicted tax effects). Roger Gordon and Jeff MacKie-Mason have taken a sensible approach here—to analyze the effects of tax reform on corporate financial decisions within the framework of consensus models. I want first to review their approach and then to suggest an alternative underlying model for analyzing corporate financial choices.

Let me begin by saying that this is a very well exposited paper, and the careful reader will benefit not only from the analysis of bread-and-butter issues but also from the discussion of thoughtful tangents, many of which are topics for future study.

Taxation and Firms' Leverage Decisions

The Authors' Approach

Gordon and MacKie-Mason begin by going back to the traditional theory in which the (corporate) tax benefits of leverage are traded off against bankruptcy costs. At this juncture the standard complaints are three:

1. The underlying model cannot be right. There was, after all, "debt" before "taxes."

2. Pure bankruptcy costs are not usually estimated to be large (though, of course, agency costs of financial distress may well be).

3. Personal taxes—which carry with them a different set of incentives for *holding* debt or equity—are ignored.

The authors address the third reservation most directly. In the first part of their chapter, they incorporate personal taxes and calculate the total tax advantage to debt (to finance a hypothetical new investment project) prior to and following the Tax Reform Act of 1986 (TRA86). They are very careful in calibrating the tax parameters, building on recent work that tries to estimate effective corporate and personal tax rates.

The chapter's conclusion is that debt finance became more attractive after TRA86. (If anything, this estimate is probably an understatement because the effective tax rate for bondholders is likely to be less than the average rate they use.) The strategy here is to calculate the predicted fraction of debt issues in 1987 and 1988 using the observed values for firm characteristics. Then the authors forecast what the fraction of debt issues would have been if there had been no tax reform.

I like the approach taken here (and in earlier work by MacKie-Mason 1989), which considers incremental financing choices. In that approach finance contracts can be considered along alternative dimensions—such as debt versus equity or public versus private. In previous work MacKie-Mason found that the *public* debt-equity choice (the choice we usually consider) is sensitive to variation in firms' effective marginal tax rates.

At this point Gordon and MacKie-Mason review the predictions of one alternative to the traditional model—the "financing hierarchy" approach suggested by the work of Myers and Majluf (1984) and others. In that approach, because of particular problems of asymmetric information, managers (in financing an investment project) *prefer* internal funds to debt issues and debt issues to new equity issues. The prediction for the effects of TRA86 on leverage would be that—holding constant investment opportunities—since internal funds decreased (i.e., since the average corporate tax burden increased), leverage should increase.

The authors find that the ratio of debt to the market value of equity did increase after 1986 but by substantially less than their approach would have predicted. They review a number of potential explanations, including (1) slow adjustment to changes in desired leverage, (2) poor estimates of tax parameters, and (3) changes in bankruptcy risk. I will focus my remarks on the following points: the likely effects of shifts in the bankruptcy cost function, the measurement of the effective tax rate on capital gains, and the complications introduced by new rules on borrowing for multinational corporations.

With respect to the first, the authors calibrate bankruptcy costs relative to firms' debt-to-value ratios—in a function $C(D/V)$. Shifts in this function could explain movements in leverage. For example, development of more efficient debt markets could lower these costs, increasing allowable leverage. One must be careful here. Private debt has a lower $C(D/V)$ than public debt (because it is monitored), yet most of the increase in borrowing has been public. In fact private debt has declined sharply after 1986 as a source of funds for the nonfinancial corporate sector.

With respect to the second issue, there are certainly problems in measuring the effective fraction of gains that are long-term (the α parameter in their model). The trading-strategy points here are noteworthy and would help explain a smaller increase in leverage than the authors predicted. It is difficult to know whether the transactions costs faced by most taxable investors would have permitted full tax arbitrage.

Third, the discussion of potential changes in foreign versus domestic borrowing by U.S. multinationals is interesting. After TRA86 affiliated corporations eligible to file a consolidated return allocate worldwide interest deductions across the various companies in proportion to their assets to determine domestic and foreign source income. For a firm with *excess* foreign tax credits, borrowing overseas can decrease total tax payments. This is potentially important. A number of firms had excess foreign tax credits prior to TRA86, and more were likely to afterward because of the reduction in the U.S. statutory corporate tax rate (see Hines and Hubbard 1990). To the extent that overseas borrowing by multinationals is imperfectly documented in domestic data, observed leverage data could be misleading.

I have three general quibbles with the approach taken by Gordon and MacKie-Mason, the last of which I elaborate below:

1. In gauging firms' responses to tax prices, uncertainty about future tax policy is ignored. To the extent that tax regimes alternate between high and low tax prices for particular activities, observed responses would be lower than a simple model might predict.

2. The leverage experiment is the correct one for the decision to finance a new investment project. The tax wedge (in favor of debt finance) on pure corporate restructurings is smaller.

3. There are important questions about the underlying model of leverage, which depends critically on taxation. There was leverage prior to taxation. In fact debt–equity ratios were higher in 1913 than until after World War II (Taggart 1985). Understanding leverage decisions will in general contribute importantly to an analysis of the effects of tax incentives.

A "Modified View" of Corporate Financial Decisions

By the late 1980s it is difficult to talk about leverage in the sense of pure debt and equity. Many interesting real-world finance contracts involve features of both, suggesting that the notion of a debt–equity measure may be hard to evaluate.

Much of the concern about traditional descriptions of leverage has been cast in economic models in which there is asymmetric information among firm claimants. The authors talk about one such approach, the "lemons" model of Myers and Majluf (1984). Additional discussions in the financial and academic communities have centered on agency problems between firms' insiders and outsiders. One feature has been to evaluate the use of financial contracts to mitigate incentive problems in corporate governance. When some inside activities and components of firm expenditures are not observable to outsiders, financial contracting patterns may be determinate, even apart from tax considerations.

In particular, if all risk were firm-specific, payments from outsiders to insiders should be fixed relative to common (industry or economywide) movements in earnings. That is, debt is the efficient contract. In the more general case in which there is a mixture of firm-specific risk and common risk, payments from the firm will be both fixed (debt) and common state contingent (equity). Discussions of recent financing patterns in this respect can be found in Jensen (1989) and Gertler and Hubbard (1990).

The effect of taxation on leverage is more subtle in this framework than in the traditional model. For example, the threat of reorganization is less a cost than an important device for corporate control. Asymmetric tax treatment of debt and equity leads to a choice of contract that fits the tax-favored definition. The distortion is as follows: If debt were costlessly renegotiable ex ante or ex post (the former ruled out by the tax code and the latter by real-world complications), there would be no distortion, even though "leverage" would be higher. If this renegotiation is complicated, a debt overhang can be motivated endogenously. It may be in a firm's interest to cut production, investment, or employment during a downturn because of excessive leverage.

Such a view can be called upon to rationalize the greater reliance on interest to get funds out of the corporate sector, the realignment of debt and equity in corporate capital structures, and the recent concern that many new corporate debt contracts (e.g., junk bonds) may not be easily renego-tiable during a business recession. This view also stresses the need to distinguish among secured debt, public (arm's-length) debt, and private (more closely monitored) debt in making debt-to-value calculations.

Problems in testing the predictions of the generalized agency-cost view complement those put forward in the empirical evidence in the Gordon–MacKie-Mason chapter. It is likely that tax and nontax factors have changed in recent years—the latter corresponding to fundamental changes in debt markets, including, but not restricted to, the development of secondary markets for risky debt. Measurement issues are nonetheless important. The appropriate measure of leverage may be model specific; just looking at debt-to-value ratios per se may be too narrow. Much more empirical work is needed here.

The Tax Reform Act and Corporate Distributions

To justify the payment of dividends in the presence of more tax-favored means of getting corporate funds back to shareholders, one must appeal to some intrinsic valuation of dividends (for liquidity reasons, to minimize agency cost, etc.). In such a framework (the so-called traditional model), the perceived benefits of dividend distributions are traded off against the tax cost. Hence the lower dividend tax rate after 1986 should stimulate dividend payout. The alternative tax capitalization view of dividends make such distributions a residual, equaling aftertax cash flow less new investment. Since average corporate tax burdens increased after TRA86, dividend payout should decrease.

Gordon and MacKie-Mason find that both the level of dividends and dividend payout rates increased after 1986, casting doubt on the tax capitalization view. Share repurchases went up by even more.

The agency-cost approach I sketched previously has implications for distributions as well. First, large-scale share repurchases facilitate realignment of the optimal payout pattern (loosely speaking, between debt and equity contracts). Second, depending on the mixture of firm-specific risk and common risk, firms have some target level of dividends (i.e., a pattern desired by suppliers of funds). In that sense the required return hinges on the payout decision as in the traditional model. Lowering the tax price of dividends would lead to greater payout, as Gordon and MacKie-Mason find.

The Tax Reform Act and Organizational Form

A number of organizational-form questions are of interest here. Largely for reasons of data availability, Gordon and MacKie-Mason focus on the effects of changing tax incentives for ordinary corporations versus subchapter S corporations. In favor of the S corporation are the considerations that (1) personal tax rates were reduced by more than corporate tax rates, (2) repeal of the General Utilities doctrine means double taxation of gains on the sale of assets in corporate form, and (3) S corporations would not be subject to the alternative minimum tax. Working in the other direction, ordinary corporations will incur personal tax obligations, for most fringe benefits that are deductible from income. On net, Gordon and MacKie-Mason find a large increase in S corporation filings after 1986, as well as a significant increase in income reported by S corporations.

What might be the implications of the agency-cost–incentives approach? One should expect the greatest responsiveness to tax price changes here; indeed, the margin of organizational form may well become increasingly sensitive to changes in taxation. The past decade has witnessed a trend toward more active investors and concentrated ownership of firms (in part for reasons of monitoring and aligning incentives). Hence it may become easier for partnerships or S corporations to be an alternative to larger-scale ordinary corporate activity.

Summary

I liked the Gordon–MacKie-Mason chapter very much for both its scope and details, and I concur with the authors' concluding remarks that much more work needs to be done here. Incorporating considerations of tax policy uncertainty and refining underlying (nontax) concepts of corporate financial policy will be important future steps.

Notes

1. A cautionary note is in order here. Estimates based on the work in MacKie-Mason (1989) were from a sample of firms with greater leverage than the population of firms. Hence in table 4.2, it may not be appropriate to adjust means (intercepts) if sample firm characteristics are materially different from the rest of the population.

References

Gertler, Mark, and R. Glenn Hubbard. 1990. Taxation, Corporate Capital Structure, and Financial Distress. In Lawrence H. Summers (ed.), *Tax Policy and the Economy*, vol. 4. Cambridge: MIT Press.

Hines, James R., and R. Glenn Hubbard. 1990. Coming Home to America: Dividend Repatriations by U.S. Multinationals. In Assaf Razin and Joel B. Slemrod (eds.), *Taxation in the Global Economy*. Chicago: University of Chicago Press.

Jensen, Michael C. 1989. Active Investors, LBOs, and the Privatization of Bankruptcy. *Journal of Applied Corporate Finance* 2: 35--44.

MacKie-Mason, Jeffrey K. 1990. Do Firms Care Who Provides Their Financing? In R. G. Hubbard (ed.), *Asymmetric Information, Corporate Finance, and Investment.* Chicago: University of Chicago Press.

Myers, Stewart C., and Nicholas S. Majluf. 1984. Corporate Financing and Investment Decisions When Firms Have Information That Investors Do Not Have. *Journal of Financial Economics* 13: 187−221.

Taggart, Robert A. 1985. Secular Patterns in the Financing of U.S. Corporations. In Benjamin M. Friedman (ed.), *Corporate Capital Structures in the United States.* Chicago: University of Chicago Press, 13−75.

GENERAL DISCUSSION

Alan Auerbach questioned the proposed decline in conflict of interest between shareholders and debt–holders when investors balance their portfolios by holding both equity and debt. He argued that the conflict would continue within each firm because an investor's portfolio would not necessarily include equity and debt *in the same firm.*

Auerbach also noted that firms that shift out of the corporate sector post-1986 will incur costs associated with the repeal of the General Utilities doctrine. Therefore we should not expect to see substantial reorganizations from the corporate to the noncorporate sector of firms with accumulated capital gains.

David Bradford observed that the rapidly rising stock market over the study period would have in itself caused large decreases in debt–value ratios.

Bradford also questioned whether the "new view" of corporate dividend policy would predict that greater cash flow for a corporation will result in greater dividend payout. Larry Langdon remarked that because a one-time increase in dividends influences market expectations about future dividends, a firm with excess cash would be more likely to repurchase shares than to pay out dividends.

In a related comment, James Poterba suggested that a higher capital gains tax rate might lead to a prodividend policy. He also argued that share repurchases are more often related to changes in corporate control than to tax issues. Researchers therefore should analyze separately that part of share repurchases that is related to corporate control.

Burton Smoliar made two points about the authors' claim that multinationals now have the incentive to borrow through their foreign affiliates. First, the interest allocation rules refer only to a corporation's domestic consolidation group, and second, most firms borrow overseas as a hedge against currency fluctuations.

Matthew Shapiro wondered about the relationship between observed increases in debt and technological change in the investment banking industry. The shape of the marginal cost-of-debt financing function may be important. For example, small technological innovations on Wall Street may have big effects on optimal debt ratios.

Roger Gordon agreed with the suggestions of several people that we should worry more about the nontax theories of corporate debt. He also observed that financial policy is the fastest changing tool firms can use to respond to changing tax policy.

Jeffrey MacKie-Mason agreed with Auerbach's assessment of the costs associated with disincorporation after the repeal of the General Utilities doctrine. He concluded by emphasizing that despite observed increases in leveraged buyouts and general corporate borrowing, we really are not seeing *as much* corporate debt as the theory would suggest.

5 Taxation and Housing Markets: Preliminary Evidence on the Effects of Recent Tax Reforms

James M. Poterba

Housing accounts for one-sixth of consumption expenditure in the United States, second only to food among major budget categories. It is also the expenditure category most directly affected by federal tax policy. The federal income tax subsidizes homeownership because imputed rent is not included in the tax base, whereas mortgage interest payments are tax-deductible. Renters also receive tax subsidies since landlords have historically received generous depreciation allowances that subsidize investment in rental properties relative to other real assets.

The tax reforms of the last decade have significantly affected incentives for housing consumption. Reductions in marginal tax rates have reduced the value of tax-exempt imputed income for homeowners, with particularly large changes for high-income individuals whose tax rates were 70% at the beginning of the 1980s but are 28% today. The changes in the tax incentives for rental investment have been even more dramatic. The 1981 Economic Recovery Tax Act liberalized depreciation provisions for rental property, but the Deficit Reduction Act of 1984 and the Tax Reform Act of 1986 reversed these changes. The 1986 act included provisions designed to reduce investment in tax shelters, including real estate shelters. The net effect of these reforms has been a reduction in the net tax incentives to rental construction.

The effects of these changes are just becoming manifest in U.S. housing markets. In the long run, reduced incentives for housing consumption will raise rents, lower the housing stock, and potentially affect the division of the population between homeowners and renters. In the short run, however, the effects of tax reform are most likely to appear in house prices and new construction of rental and owner-occupied properties.

This chapter describes the tax reforms of the last decade and presents preliminary evidence on their housing market effects. The chapter is divided into five sections. Section 5.1 documents the importance of analyzing how tax changes affect housing markets, demonstrating that these changes have an important influence on more general incidence calculations. Section 5.2 presents a framework for analyzing how the tax system affects housing markets, developing the concept of the user cost for both owner-occupied and rental housing. Section 5.3 describes the various tax reforms of the last decade, focusing on how these reforms altered the incentives for home-ownership and investment in rental properties. Section 5.4 examines the reaction of housing starts, real rents, house prices, and homeownership rates to recent tax changes. Trends in U.S. housing markets, as well as comparisons between the United States and Canada, provide some evidence on the sensitivity of housing markets to tax policy. Section 5.5 provides a brief conclusion.

5.1 Why Study Tax Policy toward Housing?

Three factors make changes in the tax treatment of housing a critical component of applied tax incidence analysis. First, there are important differences in housing tenure across groups with different economic status. Table 5.1 illustrates this using tabulations from the 1986 Consumer Expenditure Survey. Households are divided into deciles based on their total expenditures, with higher outlays indicating better economic circumstances.[1] More than 60% of the households in the lowest expenditure decile are renters, compared with only 15% of those in the highest outlay category. The bottom third of the expenditure distribution contains half of all renter households, and the probability of owning a home increases throughout the expenditure distribution. Changes in the relative tax treatment of owner-occupied versus rental housing therefore have important distributional effects. Higher subsidies to rental accomodation benefit poorer households, whereas subsidies to homeownership yield benefits that are more concentrated among better-off households.

Second, for low-income households the changes in real rents that result from tax reforms can easily outweigh the direct changes in tax liability. Table 5.1 shows that in the bottom expenditure decile, average federal tax payments are $133 per year and average rent payments by households who rent are $978. A 5% change in real rents can therefore offset a 30% change in taxes. Results presented below suggest that the 1986 Tax Reform Act will ultimately increase real rents by nearly 10%, more than the actual reductions in tax payments for low-income households.

Table 5.1
Housing consumption by expenditure deciles, 1986

Consumption decile (average)	Average pretax income	Average federal taxes	Average rent (if renters)	Percent renters
1 ($4,008)	$5,785	$133	$978	63.3%
2 (7,260)	9,212	285	2,170	60.0
3 (9,641)	13,989	723	2,802	51.5
4 (11,941)	16,691	1,062	3,380	49.7
5 (14,260)	20,974	1,316	3,952	45.3
6 (17,009)	25,847	1,772	4,114	34.9
7 (20,410)	29,650	2,374	4,643	30.8
8 (24,739)	36,752	2,801	4,438	27.3
9 (31,624)	40,519	3,298	5,528	17.5
10 (58,477)	51,499	4,841	5,506	15.2

Source: Tabulations from the Consumer Expenditure Survey, 1986 (first quarter expenditure data). Parenthetic values in the first column are average consumption within each decile. Average rent is per year.

Finally, tax reform can induce significant changes in house prices. Since houses are the primary asset of most elderly households and many younger middle-income households, these effects must be included in any complete analysis of tax redistribution. For a household with an annual income of $50,000, a home worth $200,000, and a $125,000 mortgage, lowering the personal income tax rate from 35% to 30% would reduce annual tax payments by less than $500. The capitalized reduction in the value of mortgage interest deductions, however, could reduce home values by at least 5%, or $10,000 in this example. Because asset prices are forward-looking and reflect the present value of changes in renter or homeowner costs, the revaluation effects fall on households who own homes when the tax reform takes effect. They are frequently an order of magnitude larger than the effects on current income and expenditure which are typically modeled in applied incidence studies.

5.2   Taxation and Housing Markets: Analytical Framework

The net effect of the tax code on incentives for tenure choice and for housing consumption can be formalized by computing the aftertax user costs of owner-occupied and rental housing under various tax regimes. The user cost of homeownership measures the marginal cost of an incremental amount of owner-occupied housing, including the forgone return on the owner's equity. The user cost for rental property reflects the landlord's cost of investing in the property; in equilibrium the landlord must earn rents equal to his user cost.

The user cost of homeownership is defined as

$$c_o = [(1 - \theta)(i + \tau_p) + \delta + \alpha + m - \pi_e]P_o, \tag{1}$$

where i is the the nominal interest rate, τ_p is the property tax rate per dollar of property value,[2] θ is the household's marginal federal income tax rate, δ is the physical decay rate for the property, α is the risk premium for housing investments, m is the cost of home maintenance as a fraction of house value, π_e is the expected rate of house price appreciation, and P_o is the real price of owner-occupied housing.[3] This expression applies only to households who itemize for federal income tax purposes. For the nearly half of all homeowners who do not, the marginal user cost sets $\theta = 0$ in equation (1).

The user cost of homeownership varies across households and, for itemizers, is inversely related to a household's marginal tax rate. Although it reflects the *marginal* cost of additional housing purchases, it may not reflect the *average* cost. The latter is the key determinant of whether owner-occupied or rental housing is the most cost-effective way for a given household to obtain housing services. The distinction between average and marginal costs arises because some households may itemize if they are homeowners, but not if they are renters. Many such households have itemized deductions excluding housing costs equal to less than the standard deduction; they forgo the tax saving associated with the standard deduction when they become homeowners.

The user cost for rental property is

$$c_r = \left\{ [(1 - \tau)i + \delta + \alpha - \pi_e] \left(\frac{1 - \tau^* z}{1 - \tau} \right) + \tau_p + m \right\} P_r, \tag{2}$$

where the parameters not defined above are τ, the marginal income tax rate of the rental landlord, P_r, the real price of rental property, and z, the present value of tax depreciation allowances.[4] In equilibrium the rent charged must equal c_r so that the landlord is willing to hold the rental property.

Two parameters in the rental user cost are controversial. The first is τ, the marginal tax rate of the rental landlord. Some studies, such as Titman (1982) and Scholes, Terry, and Wolfson (1989), assume that the landlord is a top-bracket individual investor. Such an investor receives maximum advantage from the depreciation allowances on rental property since these allowances generate deductions that reduce taxable income. If the marginal supplier of funds to the rental industry is in a lower-tax bracket, however, this will reduce the value of these deductions and therefore raise equilibrium rents.[5] Particularly when the dispersion of marginal tax rates is large, as it was prior to the 1981 tax reform, assumptions about the identity of the marginal investor could have important effects on estimated user costs.

Second, the measurement of z, the present discounted value of depreciation allowances, is complicated because buildings may be depreciated more than once. Particularly during inflationary periods when there are substantial gains to selling a building and redepreciating its increased nominal basis, investors may "churn" their properties. This can substantially increase the present value of depreciation allowances for investors in rental property,[6] lowering the user cost and the equilibrium rent demanded by landlords.

5.3 Tax Reform Provisions Affecting Housing Markets, 1980–88

The Economic Recovery Tax Act of 1981 and the Tax Reform Act of 1986 changed residential investment incentives. This section sketches the five most important provisions of these bills and describes their effects on both owner-occupied and rental housing.

Marginal Tax Rates

Both tax reforms lowered personal income tax rates. Holding constant the pretax interest rate at which households borrow and lend,[7] this *raises* the aftertax cost of homeownership. In 1980 the weighted-average marginal federal tax rate on mortgage interest deductions was 32%. By 1984, when the rate reductions of 1981 had taken full effect, this average tax rate was 28%.[8] Lower tax rates reduce the value of homeowners' deductions for mortgage interest payments and property taxes. The 1981 reform should therefore have lowered the quantity of housing demanded by some homeowners and (holding other factors constant) reduced home prices. This downward price pressure should have been greatest for high-priced homes whose owners received the largest marginal rate reductions.[9]

Standard Deductions

The 1986 reform reduced the fraction of the population who would itemize if they were not homeowners. For a joint filer the standard deduction rose from $3,670 to $5,000. As noted above, the average tax benefit to home-ownership, and the tax incentive for owning rather than renting, depends on the difference between a household's total itemized deductions and the standard deduction. This difference falls when the standard deduction increases. This effect is particularly important for lower- and middle-income households with relatively few nonhousing itemized deductions. Higher standard deductions reduce the incentive for a household to own, but conditional on deciding to own, they do not affect the marginal cost of additional housing services.

Depreciation Provisions

The 1981, 1984, and 1986 reforms affected tax depreciation benefits for rental property and thereby changed the incentives for households to own rather than rent their accomodation. Table 5.2 shows the recent history of depreciation policy for rental property. ERTA shortened the tax lifetime for residential rental property from 32 to 15 years.[10] The 1986 act reversed this policy, extending the lifetime to 27.5 years and requiring straightline depreciation rather than more accelerated 175% declining balance. The reduction in marginal tax rates in 1981 partly counteracted the expanded depreciation benefits in ERTA, but in 1986 less generous depreciation rules combined with lower marginal tax rates to significantly reduce the value of depreciation benefits. Since the present value of depreciation tax benefits is a key consideration in rental investment decisions, these changes should affect rental markets. Real rents should increase because of the 1986 Tax Reform Act.

Table 5.2
Depreciation provisions for residential structures, 1969–88

	Lifetime	Depreciation schedule
1969–81	32 years	150% declining balance
1981–84	15 years	175% declining balance
1984–85	18 years	175% declining balance
1985–86	19 years	175% declining balance
1986–	27.5 years	Straight line

Source: Author's compilation based on U.S. Internal Revenue Code.

Capital Gains Tax Rates

Both major tax reforms affected capital gains tax rates, although in opposite directions. The 1981 tax reform reduced the marginal tax rate on long-term capital gains for top-bracket investors from 28% to 20%, whereas the 1986 act eliminated the distinction between capital gains and other types of income and raised the top tax rate to 28%. Although the capital gains tax may have little effect on homeowners, except for those in top-income brackets for whom the $125,000 lifetime exclusion on taxation of housing gains is inframarginal, it is potentially important in the rental market. There is no tax exemption for capital gains on rental property, and a substantial fraction of the returns to property investment often accrue as capital gains. In addition the capital gains tax has an important effect on the incentive to "churn" real property. When capital gains taxes are low, the tax burden on the initial asset owner is reduced and the incentives for churning are greater. This implies that the capital gains reduction in 1981 further enhanced the depreciation benefits in ERTA, whereas the higher rates in 1986 magnified the reduction in these benefits.

Antishelter Provisions

The Tax Reform Act of 1986 included several provisions designed to restrict tax shelter investments, including investments in real estate. The most important restrictions were passive loss limitations. Prior to 1986 investors in rental properties that generated tax losses could use these losses to shelter taxes on other income. The 1986 act restricted this practice, allowing only other passive income to be offset by passive losses.[11] This provision raises the aftertax risk of rental projects since it provides limited loss-offset in unprofitable projects. It also discourages high-leverage rental projects because the interest deductions in these projects are no longer as valuable to investors.

    Table 5.3 provides evidence on the efficacy of the antishelter provisions in the 1986 act. The table presents data on sales of publicly traded real estate partnerships in each year since 1981. Although not all tax shelters are publicly traded and not all real estate partnerships invest in rental property, these data provide some guide to the level of tax shelter activity. The table shows a 37% real decline in real estate partnership sales between 1985 and 1988. While other types of partnerships (e.g., oil and gas leasing) have also been discouraged by recent tax changes, real estate has declined more than the others. Real estate related partnerships accounted for over 55% of new sales before the 1986 Tax Reform Act but only 44% in 1988.

Table 5.3
Investment in publicly registered real estate limited partnerships

Year	Amount	Percent of public limited partnerships
1981	1,799.4	28.6
1982	2,612.6	39.1
1983	4,202.2	43.1
1984	5,346.7	57.8
1985	6,737.8	53.3
1986	6,132.2	55.6
1987	4,789.1	43.4
1988	4,249.0	44.0

Source: *The Stanger Report*, various issues. Data in column 1 reflect sales of publicly registered limited partnerships, excluding a small number of master limited partnerships (with traded shares) that have appeared in the late 1980s. Real estate partnerships holding mortgages are also excluded. Dollar values are in 1989 prices.

The foregoing list of tax provisions affecting housing markets is far from exhaustive. Many other legal changes—such as removal of amortization of interest on "builder bonds," limits on tax-exempt financing for housing projects, and changes in the minimum tax—also affected incentives for housing consumption. In addition this discussion ignores the particular provisions affecting low-income housing.[12] The 1986 change in depreciation benefits for such housing was even more dramatic than that for other rental housing, with a switch from double-declining balance depreciation on a 15-year lifetime to straight-line depreciation on a 27.5-year life. My analysis, however, will focus on the change in rents for units that do not qualify for low-income provisions.

To illustrate how recent tax reforms have affected the housing market, table 5.4 reports the user cost of homeownership for three households at various times during the last decade. The first panel considers the user cost for a fixed pattern of interest and expected inflation rates, thereby identifying the effect of tax changes. The second panel evaluates the tax code of each year since 1980, using interest and expected inflation rates that prevailed at that time and thus indicating the net change in incentives for homeownership.[13] Other auxiliary parameters, such as the property tax rate and the cost of maintaining the home, are assumed constant throughout the calculations.

The results illustrate that recent reforms had their most pronounced effect on the cost of homeownership for high-income households. For a family with adjusted gross income (AGI) of $250K in 1988, the Tax Reform

Table 5.4
User costs of owner-occupied and rental property, 1980–88

	1980	1982	1984	1986	1988
Case 1: Fixed parameters i = 0.07, π_e = 0.03					
User cost of homeownership					
1988 AGI = $25,000	0.120	0.122	0.125	0.125	0.126
1988 AGI = $45,000	0.110	0.113	0.117	0.117	0.114
1988 AGI = $250,000	0.081	0.094	0.094	0.094	0.114
Rental user cost	0.129[a]	0.118	0.118	0.120	0.132
Case 2: Prevailing interest and inflation rate					
User cost of homeownership					
1988 AGI = $25,000	0.110	0.125	0.128	0.145	0.139
1988 AGI = $45,000	0.094	0.107	0.119	0.134	0.125
1988 AGI = $250,000	0.047	0.072	0.079	0.104	0.125
Rental user cost	0.096	0.096	0.104	0.137	0.149
Parameter values					
Nominal rate	0.127	0.151	0.124	0.103	0.091
Expected inflation	0.085	0.093	0.072	0.037	0.034

Note: Calculations for both cases assume that τ_p = 0.02, δ = 0.014, α = 0.04, and m = 0.025. Rental user costs assume no churning, with marginal tax rates for the rental landlord of 0.50 in 1980–86 and 0.28 in 1988. Owner calculations assume that taxpayers itemize and claim average itemized deductions for their income class.
a. The 1980 rental user cost does *not* assume the highest possible marginal tax rate for the rental landlord; it assumes a 50% rather than a 70% marginal rate.

Act of 1986 lowered the marginal tax rate from 0.50 to 0.28 and raised the user cost of homeownership from 0.094 to 0.114, assuming the base case with an interest rate of 7% and a 3% expected inflation rate.[14] The actual change in the user cost of homeownership since 1986, recognizing variations in interest rates and inflationary expectations, is from 0.104 to 0.125 for this household. Assuming a price elasticity of demand of −1.0 for owner-occupied housing,[15] this tax change could have large effects on both demand and house prices. Although precise results depend on the tax experiment, simulation evidence[16] suggests that the percentage change in house prices is approximately half as large, and of opposite sign, as the change in user costs. This analysis would therefore predict roughly a 10% decline in real house prices for the homes typically demanded by very high-income households.

The post-1986 change in user costs for high-income households, however, is small relative to the change from the beginning of the 1980s when the estimated user cost was 0.047. Despite this substantial change there is no evidence that house prices for the homes typically owned by these taxpayers have collapsed. This may be because households did not expect the low user cost of 1980 to prevail forever. This would make them reluctant to pay as much for a home as this user cost would suggest since higher future user costs would lead to capital losses. If households expected inflation to decline, for example, then the user cost for 1980 understates the cost for a typical housing purchase. Households may view tax changes as more permanent than other sources of variation in user costs, although, given the experience of the 1980s, this perception may be changing.[17]

The effect of rate reductions on homeownership incentives for those in lower-income brackets is much smaller since the decline in tax rates in the 1986 reform was less pronounced. For the household with AGI of $25,000 in 1988, the tax reform lowered the marginal tax rate from 16% to 15% and raised the user cost (in the benchmark case) from 0.125 to 0.126. Some middle-income households such as the $45,000 example presented here even experience increases in their marginal tax rates, and for them housing costs decline.[18]

The results in table 5.4 show that the combination of high expected inflation rates and high marginal tax rates at the beginning of the 1980s made user costs relatively low, particularly for high-income households. For the household with AGI of $45,000 in 1988, the user cost of home-ownership increased nearly 30%—from 0.094 to 0.125—during the eight years following 1980. This reflects rising real interest rates as well as the decline in tax incentives.

User costs of rental housing are also reported in table 5.4.[19] Assuming that the marginal supplier of rental units was an individual in the top marginal tax bracket, the rental user cost rose from 0.137 to 0.149, or 9%, between 1986 and 1988. The increase would have been larger if the real interest rate had not declined during this period. The change in user costs in the early 1980s is smaller. If the nominal interest rate and expected inflation rate had been at their 1980 levels in 1982, rental user costs would have declined from 0.096 (assuming a landlord tax rate of 50% in 1980) to 0.089, or by 7.3%. The increase in real interest rates between 1980 and 1982, however, counteracted this effect, so the reported user costs in the lower panel of table 5.4 show no change.[20]

The results for rental user costs during the late 1980s are sensitive to different assumptions about the "marginal investors" in rental prop-erties. If corporations are the marginal suppliers of rental housing, for example, then the adverse effects of the 1986 Tax Reform Act on real rents would be much smaller. Corporate investors face smaller reductions in marginal tax rates, and are less affected by passive loss limits, than are individual investors.

It is essential to recognize the partial equilibrium nature of the foregoing calculations, and the limitations this places on the analysis. The 1981 and 1986 tax reforms changed the tax treatment of housing as well as many other assets. In particular, the 1986 reform raised the tax burden on corporate assets while bringing tax burdens on equipment, structures, and other assets into closer alignment. If tax rates on housing and all other assets rise and capital is incompletely mobile internationally, so changes in the U.S. system affect aftertax returns to U.S. investors, then a tax change of this type should reduce real aftertax interest rates. The amount of such a decline is crucial for calibrating the actual changes in housing user costs. General equilibrium simulations of the type performed by Hendershott (1987) or Berkovec and Fullerton (1989) are needed to aggregate the different tax changes for different assets into the single summary measure, the change in the interest rate, through which other aspects of tax reform affect the housing market. For some of the tax-induced changes in user costs isolated in table 5.4, notably those for high-income individuals and those for landlords, however, implausibly large changes in interest rates would be needed to offset the reported effects.

5.4 Housing Market Response to Tax Reforms

The housing market adjusts slowly to external shocks from the tax system and other sources. The tax changes of 1981 were only in force for five years, and many of the changes in the Tax Reform Act of 1986 have only been fully effective for two years. It is unreasonable to expect large changes in the housing stock or in the fraction of households who rent as a result of these tax reforms. This section nevertheless examines the available evidence on changes in prices and quantities after the major tax reforms.

Table 5.5 displays single-unit and multiunit housing starts for the United States during the period since 1970. The data support the view that taxes affect the rental housing market. The table shows a sharp decline in multifamily starts since 1986: Starts in 1988 were only 62.5% as large as in the 1983–86 period.[21] The data also show an increase in rental construction in the 1983–84 period. This may reflect incentives for new construction that are not captured in the user cost measure of the last section, particularly the opportunities for "churning" rental properties during this period.

Table 5.5
Housing starts in the United States and Canada, 1970–88 (in thousands)

	United States		Canada	
	Single family	Multifamily	Single family	Multifamily
1970–74	1,058.6	786.5	107.6	125.4
1975–79	1,226.6	463.5	117.9	117.9
1980	852.2	440.0	87.9	70.9
1981	705.4	378.8	89.1	88.9
1982	662.6	399.6	54.5	71.4
1983	1,067.6	635.5	102.4	60.3
1984	1,084.2	665.4	83.7	51.2
1985	1,072.4	669.4	98.6	67.2
1986	1,179.4	626.0	120.0	79.8
1987	1,146.4	474.0	140.1	105.8
1988	1,081.3	406.8	128.5	94.1
1989	1,019.1	385.5	—	—

Source: Data are from the U.S. Commerce Department and Statistics Canada.
Note: Columns 1 and 3 report single-unit residential starts, and columns 2 and 4 the sum of all starts for residential structures with more than two units.

Predictions of how the recent tax reforms should affect owner-occupied housing starts are less clear than those with respect to rental housing. The 1986 tax reform raises homeownership costs for more than half of the taxpaying population, but the real rent increase which should also result blunts this effect. On balance the reform encourages homeownership. The data neither support nor contradict this prediction. Single-family housing starts were low in the early 1980s when real interest rates were at record heights; they were lower in 1988 than in either 1986 or 1987, but the decline is much smaller than that for multifamily starts.

Simply comparing the number of housing starts before and after tax reform is a weak test because it fails to control for other changes that may alter the incentives for housing construction. One way of accounting for such changes is through international comparison, particularly between the United States and Canada. Canada provides a natural "control" since it has a similar demographic mix and is subject to economic shocks similar to those in the United States, but it has quite different and relatively stable tax policy with respect to housing. Canadian homeowners are not permitted to deduct mortgage interest from their taxable income, although they are permitted to use tax-deferred saving accounts to facilitate downpayment accumulation.

Canadian housing starts are also shown in table 5.5. The comparison of the two nations strengthens the evidence for a tax-related slowdown in U.S. rental construction after 1986. Since 1986 the Canadian data display an upturn in multifamily building; in 1988 the number of multifamily starts was 45.6% *larger* than the number in 1983–86. The pattern of single-family housing starts in the two nations is similar, however.

Tax changes that affect housing demand should affect the prices of existing rental and owner-occupied structures. A reform such as that in 1986 which reduces incentives for housing consumption should reduce the prices of these assets, thereby discouraging new investment and eventually leading to a smaller housing stock. Table 5.6 presents data on house prices and real rents during the last two decades in both the United States and Canada.[22]

Movements in the real price of single-family homes in the United States are only partially consistent with the tax-based analysis described above. Price patterns in the 1970s and late 1980s accord with the earlier discussion. Although table 5.4 did not present information before 1980, the rapid rise in inflationary expectations in the late 1970s reduced user costs relative to their levels in prior years. At the same time table 5.6 shows that real house prices increased 18% between 1976 and 1980. Similarly, in the two years after the 1986 Tax Reform Act when user costs increased for most households, prices declined by more than 5%.

Real house price movements in the early 1980s are difficult to reconcile with the aftertax user cost analysis, however. Although real interest rates increased and tax rates declined, raising user costs for households throughout the income distribution, real house prices declined only 3% between 1980 and 1983. The explanation of this price pattern must involve shifts in demand which are not related to aftertax real interest rates. The entry of the "baby boom" generation into their homebuying years, a demographic shift that increased the demand for owner-occupied housing, is one potential explanation.[23]

The view that slowly changing demographic factors explain robust house prices in the early 1980s, however, is difficult to reconcile with the Canadian data in the third column of table 5.6. These data show a 25% decline in real house prices between 1981 and 1984, the period when real interest rates increased. Although both aftertax real housing costs and demography probably affect real house prices, still other factors may be needed to account for the U.S. and Canadian price trajectories in the 1980s.

Table 5.6 also shows the time series for real rents in the United States and Canada. Since 1986 real rents in the United States have increased by less than 2%. This increase is smaller than that in the four years leading up

Table 5.6
Real house prices and real rents, 1970–88

	United States		Canada	
	Real house prices	Real rents	Real house prices	Real rents
1970	77.9	123.9	84.0	155.1
1971	79.0	124.3	86.0	153.1
1972	81.2	124.3	90.0	148.0
1973	83.4	122.2	101.6	139.3
1974	82.6	115.3	116.7	129.0
1975	84.0	111.4	116.5	122.7
1976	85.7	111.2	119.6	122.1
1977	89.4	110.7	114.9	120.2
1978	94.7	109.9	108.0	116.2
1979	99.7	105.8	102.7	111.2
1980	99.5	101.6	100.6	105.7
1981	100.0	100.0	100.0	100.0
1982	97.7	101.4	88.1	98.4
1983	96.7	103.8	80.7	100.0
1984	96.8	104.5	77.8	100.7
1985	96.3	106.7	75.7	100.9
1986	96.7	110.6	79.2	100.8
1987	95.2	111.7	86.2	100.2
1988	91.7	112.6	91.6	100.1
1989	90.6	111.9	—	—

Source: House prices provided by the Census Department and Statistics Canada.
Note: Real house prices are the ratio of constant-quality house price indexes to the personal consumption deflator. Real rents are the ratio of the rental component for the consumer price index in each country to the total CPI.

to the 1986 reform, when real rents rose 8% in a tax environment that was favorable to rental housing.[24] The user costs in table 5.4 suggest that rising real interest rates in the early 1980s largely offset the tax incentives for rental housing investment during this period, potentially explaining this pattern. Real rents in Canada decline throughout the 1970s, in part because of rent control which began in the early 1970s. They are relatively stable in the 1980s.

The relatively slow increase in U.S. real rents since 1986, however, despite the sharp decline in new rental construction, is puzzling. One explanation for this pattern is that rental markets in many regions were overbuilt during the early 1980s, and this reduced real rents in the latter part of the decade. Rental vacancy rates provide some support for this view. These rates averaged 7.7% in 1988, a substantial increase from 5.7% in 1983 . For large properties, those with five or more units, the increase in vacancies was even more pronounced: 11.4% in 1988, compared with 7.1% five years earlier.[25] The lags in construction, coupled with the sharp rise in multifamily *starts* earlier in the 1980s, could explain these changes. This view implies that recent tax changes may not be reflected in real rents for several years.

The tax changes of the last decade should affect homeownership rates. The 1986 reform should lead to a larger fraction of the population owning their homes rather than renting, although these changes may materialize even more slowly than the effects on housing investment and house prices. The homeownership rate changes very little from year to year, and it has remained stable at 63.8% since 1986.[26] It is probably too soon to detect the effects of the recent reform on tenure choice. The homeownership rate declined in the years prior to the 1986 Tax Reform Act, falling from 65.6% in 1980 to 64.5% in 1984 to 63.8% in 1986 . This shift was during a period when the user cost of homeownership increased faster than that for rental housing. The decline in homeownership was concentrated among younger households. For example, the homeownership rate for households headed by individuals between ages 25 and 29 declined from 43.8% to 36.2% between 1980 and 1988; for households aged 30 to 34, the decline from 61.1% to 52.6% was even more pronounced. These changes may have resulted more from the difficulties first-time buyers faced in meeting high nominal mortgage payments during this period than from tax incentives for owning rather than renting.

The tax changes of the last decade are only one of the factors that may have altered the affordability of homes for young buyers. The decline in nominal interest rates in the late 1980s has lowered the minimum income needed to qualify for a mortgage on a given-sized home. The rise of adjustable rate mortgages, which in many periods reduced still further the carrying costs for new homebuyers, has reinforced this pattern. It is difficult to separate these effects from the changes due to the tax law.

5.5   Conclusion

The tax changes of the 1980s altered the incentives for housing consumption. Marginal tax rate reductions in both 1981 and 1986 reduced the attraction of homeownership, particularly at high-income levels. Reduced depreciation allowances, lower marginal rates, and anti-tax-shelter provisions in the 1986 Tax Reform Act lowered the net tax benefit for rental landlords. This should ultimately increase real rents, and the data on housing starts already suggest that rental construction has been adversely affected by the tax reform.[27]

These changes have important implications for analyzing the incidence of the recent tax reforms. The increased cost of housing for high-income households should translate into reduced demand for high-priced homes. The capital losses for the current owners of these homes could be substantial, offsetting part of the benefit these households received from rate reductions in the 1986 tax act. For low-income households the higher rents that result from reduced investment in rental housing could have more important welfare effects than the direct changes in tax payments from these reforms. The effects of housing market considerations are least important for middle-income households, where the 1986 reform had little effect on marginal tax rates.

This chapter has not examined the efficiency gains in capital allocation that may result from the recent reforms. The tax incentives for housing consumption in the pre-1986 tax code led to more housing investment than a neutral tax code. Such distortions in the size and allocation of the capital stock have efficiency costs, and some estimates suggest these costs are significant.[28] Resolving the questions this chapter raises about how taxes affect house prices and real rents, however, seems logically prior to estimating deadweight burdens that result from tax incentives.

Notes

I am grateful to Gary Engelhardt for excellent research assistance, to Hilary Sigman for assistance with the Consumer Expenditure Survey data, and to Joel Slemrod, Michelle White, and the participants at the Office of Tax Policy Research Symposium on the Tax Reform Act of 1986 for helpful comments. This research was supported by the National Science Foundation and is part of the NBER Research Program in Taxation.

1. Poterba (1989) argues that consumption provides a more satisfactory basis than annual income for classifying households. The results in table 5.1 are insensitive, however, to the choice of income or expenditure to define the deciles.

2. Only the part of the property taxes that is *not* a "benefit tax" (a fee for local public service provision) should actually be included in the user cost.

3. This equation assumes that all capital gains on owner-occupied dwellings are untaxed. Since each household is eligible for $125,000 in untaxed lifetime gains, this assumption may not be unrealistic. If it were not satisfied, π_e would be replaced with $(1 - \tau_g)\pi_e$, where τ_g is the effective capital gains tax rate. A more heroic implicit assumption is that the household faces identical borrowing and lending rates. Further discussion of these assumptions and information on plausible parameter values for the components of equation (1) may be found in Poterba (1984).

4. Equation (2) treats the government as sharing the risk associated with rental investments, an assumption that may be incorrect. If the government is not a partner to such risk, the α term would no longer be multiplied by $(1 - \tau z)/(1 - \tau)$.

5. Gravelle (1985) argues that corporations, not individuals, are the marginal suppliers of capital to the rental housing industry. Poterba (1986) reports that corporations held only 4.5% of residential rental property in 1985, compared with 38.6% for partnerships and sole proprietorships that are taxed at individual rates. The relative unimportance of corporate investors casts doubt on the view that they are price-setters in this market.

6. The significance of churning for rental user costs is explored by Hendershott and Ling (1985), Gordon, Hines, and Summers (1987), and Scholes, Terry, and Wolfson (1989).

7. Major tax reforms can affect pretax returns. Slemrod (1982), Goulder and Summers (1989), and Berkovec and Fullerton (1989) report general equilibrium simulation results that recognize these effects.

8. These estimates are based on data reported in the IRS *Statistics of Income: Individual Tax Returns* for 1980 and 1984.

9. While the 1981 tax reform raised the price of owner-occupied housing for high-income households, it also raised the aftertax income of these households. This positive income effect should have partly offset the demand reduction.

10. Hendershott (1987) discusses in detail the changes in depreciation provisions and their likely effects.

11. Special provisions apply to passive losses of small landlords, those with adjusted gross incomes below $100,000. These landlords may deduct $25,000 in passive losses against other income.

12. Since 1986 low-income housing has been defined as rental construction in which 20% of the tenants are below 50% of a community's median income, or 40% are below 60%. The qualification rules prior to 1986 were more complex.

13. The first set of user cost changes reflects the effects of tax reform but in a counterfactual setting, whereas the second convolutes the effects of tax changes with the effects of other shocks—for example, changes in monetary policy—that are unrelated to the tax system. A more complete analysis would involve general equilibrium analysis of tax policy, in particular, with an endogenous real interest rate.

14. The reform would have to lower real interest rates by nearly three hundred basis points to offset the lost value of tax deductions.

15. Rosen (1986) and Olsen (1987) survey the voluminous housing demand literature.

16. More detailed treatment of the asset price changes that follow from housing tax reforms may be found in Poterba (1984).

17. It is also possible that the user cost expression misstates the true costs for some high-income households. The assumption that the opportunity cost of funds is $(1 - \theta)i$, for example, may be incorrect if high-tax-bracket households invest in tax-exempt debt, with a yield above $(1 - \theta)i$, at the margin.

18. Hausman and Poterba (1987) find that only 59% of all taxpayers received marginal tax rate reductions as a result of the 1986 Tax Reform Act.

19. These user costs do not reflect capital gains taxes on rental property appreciation, and they assume that structures are depreciated only once.

20. If the marginal investor in rental property in 1980 was in the 70% tax bracket, then the net change from 1980 to 1982 is an *increase* in rental user costs since the reduction in the landlord's tax rate outweighs the increasingly generous depreciation provisions.

21. Multifamily starts include both apartment buildings and condominiums. Both declined between 1986 and 1988, with condominium starts falling from 143 (thousand) to 99 and rental starts from 483 to 307. Weakness in the condominium market may in part reflect the changing incentives for homeownership by young households.

22. Data on the real price of rental structures are not compiled by the Commerce Department.

23. Mankiw and Weil (1989) present evidence that demographic factors have an important influence on house prices, even when they are forecastable long in advance. Their results, along with those of Case and Shiller (1989), call into question the premise that houses sell for the present discounted value of their rationally forecast imputed rents.

24. The accuracy of the Bureau of Labor Statistics Rental CPI component as a measure of rental costs for a constant-quality unit is somewhat controversial. Apgar (1988) argues that failure to control for quality change leads to systematic understatement of rental inflation rates in the CPI, whereas Randolph (1988) argues for the BLS assumption of a stable quality distribution on the grounds that it is difficult to identify depreciation rates of rental property even from longitudinal data. The Apgar thesis suggests that the data in table 5.6 may understate the actual increase in real rents during the 1980s. There may also be biases due to "tenure discounts," the finding that tenants who live in a given property for a long period pay lower real rents than new tenants.

25. Vacancy data are drawn from the U.S. Bureau of the Census, *Report H-111: Housing Vacancies*.

26. Homeownership data are reported in the U.S. League of Savings Institutions (1989).

27. DiPasquale and Wheaton (1989) present empirical results showing that real rents respond to changes in tax incentives. They also present long-horizon forecasts of the effects of the 1986 Tax Reform Act on the rental market.

28. Mills (1987) discusses the efficiency costs of overinvestment in housing.

References

Apgar, William. 1988. Rental Housing in the United States. Harvard-MIT Joint Center for Housing Studies.

Berkovec, James, and Don Fullerton. 1989. The General Equilibrium Effects of Inflation on Housing Consumption and Investment. *American Economic Review* 79: 277−282.

Case, Karl, and Robert Shiller. 1989. The Efficiency of the Market for Single Family Homes. *American Economic Review* 79: 125−137.

DiPasquale, Denise, and William Wheaton. 1989. The Cost of Capital, Tax Reform, and the Future of the Rental Housing Market. Mimeo. MIT.

Gordon, Roger H., James R. Hines, and Lawrence H. Summers. 1987. Notes on the Tax Treatment of Structures. In M. Feldstein (ed.), *The Effects of Taxation on Capital Formation*. Chicago: University of Chicago Press.

Goulder, Lawrence H., and Lawrence H. Summers. 1989. Tax Policy, Asset Prices, and Growth: A General Equilibrium Analysis. *Journal of Public Economics* 38: 265−296.

Gravelle, Jane G. 1985. U.S. Tax Policy and Rental Housing: An Economic Analysis. Congressional Research Service Report 85−208E. Washington DC.

Hausman, Jerry A., and James M. Poterba. 1987. Household Behavior and the Tax Reform Act of 1986. *Journal of Economic Perspectives* 1: 101−119.

Hendershott, Patric H. 1987. Tax Changes and Capital Allocation in the 1980s. In M. Feldstein (ed.), *The Effects of Taxation on Capital Formation*. Chicago: University of Chicago Press.

Hendershott, Patric H., and David C. Ling. 1984. Trading and the Tax Shelter Value of Depreciable Real Estate. *National Tax Journal* 37: 213–223.

Mankiw, N. Gregory, and David Weil. 1989. The Baby Boom, the Baby Bust, and the Housing Market. *Regional Science and Urban Economics* 19: 235–258.

Mills, Edwin S. 1987. Dividing Up the Investment Pie: Have We Overinvested in Housing? *Federal Reserve Bank of Philadelphia Business Review* (March–April): 13–23.

Olsen, Edgar O. 1987. The Demand and Supply of Housing Service: A Critical Survey of the Empirical Literature. In Edwin S. Mills (ed.), *Handbook of Regional and Urban Economics*, vol. 2. Amsterdam: North Holland.

Poterba, James M. 1984. Tax Subsidies to Owner Occupied Housing: An Asset Price Approach. *Quarterly Journal of Economics* 99: 729–752.

Poterba, James M. 1987. Tax Reform and Residential Investment Incentives. *Proceedings of the National Tax Association-Tax Institute of America*, pp. 112–118.

Poterba, James M. 1989. Lifetime Incidence and the Distributional Burden of Excise Taxes. *American Economic Review* 79: 325–330.

Randolph, William C. 1988. Estimation of Housing Depreciation: Short-Term Quality Change and Long-Term Vintage Effects. *Journal of Urban Economics* 23: 162–178.

Rosen, Harvey S. 1984. Housing Subsidies: Effects on Housing Decisions, Efficiency, and Equity. In M. Feldstein and A. Auerbach (eds.), *Handbook of Public Economics*, vol. 1. Amsterdam: North Holland, pp. 375–420.

Rosen, Harvey S., and Kenneth T. Rosen. 1980. Federal Taxes and Homeownership: Evidence from Time Series. *Journal of Political Economy* 88: 59–75.

Scholes, Myron, Eric Terry, and Mark Wolfson. 1988. Tax Policy in a Complex and Dynamic Economic Environment: Challenges and Opportunities. Mimeo. Stanford University.

Slemrod, Joel. 1982. A General Equilibrium Model of Taxation with Endogenous Financial Behavior. In M. Feldstein (ed.), *Behavioral Simulation Methods in Tax Policy Analysis*. Chicago: University of Chicago Press.

Titman, Sheridan. 1982. The Effects of Anticipated Inflation on Housing Market Equilibrium. *Journal of Finance* 37: 827–842.

U.S. League of Savings Institutions. 1989. *Savings Institutions Sourcebook 1989*. Washington, DC.

COMMENTS

Michelle J. White
One of the major goals of the TRA86 was to "level the playing field," namely, to eliminate tax subsidies that favored particular types of investments. This was intended to increase the efficiency of investment incentives by forcing all types of investments to compete with each other based on economic return rather than on tax subsidies. The issue of tax subsidies is particularly relevant to housing since housing investments were heavily tax favored before 1986, as the figures given by Poterba demonstrate. These subsidies gave investors an excessively high incentive to invest in housing rather than in machinery or equipment. Using a general equilibrium model, Mills (1987) has calculated that the resulting distortion caused the housing stock to be 25% larger than the efficient level.

How well did the TRA86 succeed in equalizing incentives to invest in housing versus in machinery or equipment (i.e., in reducing the incentive to overinvest in housing)? Ideally, a general equilibrium model could both answer this question and predict how the housing stock will adjust in the future. Since I do not have a general equilibrium model at hand, I will instead follow the approach of comparing the social rate of return on a marginal investment in machinery versus in housing both before and after the TRA86. The social rate of return on an investment equals its private return (the user cost) minus the real costs of the investment. Poterba's chapter provides estimates of the user cost of rental and owner-occupied housing. Parallel estimates are therefore needed concerning the user cost of machinery. I calculate the user cost of machinery for the years 1982 and 1988, following Poterba's procedure as closely as possible.

The user cost of machinery is

$$c_r = \left[\left(\frac{1 - \tau z(1 - 0.5k) - k}{1 - \tau} \right) [(1 - \tau)i + \delta - \pi_e] + \tau_p + \alpha + m \right] * P_r. \tag{1}$$

This equation is similar to that given by Poterba for rental housing except for the addition of the term involving the investment tax credit, referred to as k. Machinery investors are eligible to receive the ITC but must subtract one-half of the credit from the depreciable basis of the asset.[1]

The machinery being analyzed is assumed to be a machine that incurs economic depreciation at the rate of 10% per year, so that $\delta = 0.1$. Since the lifetime of machinery is shorter than that of housing, the risk premium is also assumed to be smaller, and I use a value of $\alpha = 0.02$. Maintenance costs m, however, are higher for machines than for housing; I assume that $m = 0.05$. Property taxes τ_p are assumed to have the same value as Poterba uses for housing, or $\tau_p = 0.02$. Note that property taxes are treated here as a tax, whereas the Tiebout model suggests that property taxes are primarily a fee for services provided by the community. The nominal interest rates and inflation rates used are the actual figures, as given by Poterba in table 5.4.

For the marginal investor's income tax rate τ, I assume that the marginal investor is in the highest tax bracket, which was 0.50 in 1982 and 0.33 1988.

For the year 1982 the investment in machinery qualifies for a 10% tax credit so that $k = 0.1$. For depreciation purposes the investment qualifies as five-year property under ACRS. The allowable depreciation deductions are listed in my table 5C.1. For 1988 there is no investment tax credit for machinery, but the investment qualifies as 5-year property. The depreciation deductions are also listed in my table 5C.1. These deductions are discounted at the aftertax nominal interest rates, given by Poterba in table 5.4, which are $0.151(1 - 0.5)$ in 1982 and $0.091(1 - 0.33)$ in 1988. The resulting present value of depreciation deductions z is 0.81 in 1982 and 0.90 in 1988.

Substituting these figures into equation (1), we find that the user cost of machinery was 0.175 in 1982 and 0.22 in 1988. Thus the combination of tax changes and lower inflation rates caused the user cost of machinery to rise between 1982 and 1988, similar to what occurred for owned and rented housing.

The social return to an investment equals the private return (the user cost) minus economic depreciation δ, maintenance cost m, and the risk premium α. Economic depreciation and maintenance cost are subtracted

Table 5C.1
Allowable depreciation deductions for machinery, 1982 and 1988

	Year					
	1	2	3	4	5	6
1982	0.15	0.22	0.21	0.21	0.21	—
1988	0.20	0.32	0.192	0.1152	0.1152	0.0576

Note: Because of the half-year convention, the depreciation allowances on five-year property in 1988 extend into the sixth year.

since they are real costs. Since investors are typically risk averse, risk is also a real social cost, whose magnitude is measured by the risk premium if we assume efficient risk allocation through the securities market.[2] The social return to an investment in machines in 1982 and 1988 is shown in table 5C.2. The social return to investments in rental and owner-occupied housing is also shown, where the figures are calculated by subtracting $\delta + m + \alpha$ from the user costs of rental and owned housing in 1982 and 1988, using the figures given in Poterba's table 5.4.

Table 5C.2 shows that the social return to an investment in owner-occupied housing was negative in 1982. In contrast, the social return to both rental housing and machinery was positive in both years. The combination of lower inflation and tax changes reduced the tax subsidy to all three types of investments in 1988 relative to 1982 and therefore increased the social return.

For investment incentives to be efficient, the social return to all types of investment should be equal. A measure of whether the "playing field" is more level in 1988 than in 1982 is the difference between the social rates of return for machinery versus housing in the two years. If this difference equaled zero, then investors would have had an incentive to make efficient choices. Table 5C.2 shows that the social rate of return to machinery was higher by 4.2 percentage points than the social rate of return to owner-occupied housing in 1982 and was higher by 3.7 percentage points in 1988. This suggests that there was overinvestment in owner-occupied housing relative to machines in both 1982 and 1988, with little change in incentives over the period. Similarly the social rate of return on machines was lower by 1.2 percentage points than the social rate of return on rental housing in 1982 and was 1.7 percentage points lower in 1988. This implies that there was underinvestment in rental housing relative to machines during both years, but the distortion was less severe than the distortion in the incentive to invest in machines relative to owner-occupied housing. Overall, the gap between the social return to the three types of investments was little affected by the changes that occurred during the 1980s.

Table 5C.2
Social returns to investments in machinery, rental housing, and owner-occupied housing

	1982	1988
Machinery	0.005	0.053
Rental housing	0.017	0.07
Owner-occupied housing	−0.037	0.016

Thus the results suggest that the TRA86, combined with the lower inflation rates of the late 1980s, has not leveled the playing field. Owner-occupied housing remains heavily tax favored. The owned housing stock thus is likely to remain too large as a fraction of the total capital stock. Rental housing, however, is less heavily subsidized than either owned housing or machines. Investors' incentives to invest in rental housing have been too low throughout the 1980s and they remain so.[3] Congress will just have to try harder next time around.

The other topic that I would like to address concerns the provision of low-income housing and whether or how it has been affected by the TRA86. In the past, U.S. policy toward low-income housing has taken two forms: direct subsidies to local governments and other providers of low-income housing, and tax subsidies to private landlords providing rental housing. The cutbacks of the Reagan administration sharply reduced direct provision of new or rehabilitated low-income housing and, judging from the recent scandals at HUD, seems to have turned what remains into a subsidy program for developers who have friends in high places. This leaves tax subsidies to private landlords as the remaining U.S. policy toward low-income housing. Landlords providing rental housing of any type receive the subsidies detailed by Poterba. Landlords providing rental housing to low-income tenants are also allowed to depreciate their investments at the rate of 20% per year (straight-line depreciation based on a five-year lifetime) and can defer capital gains taxes if they sell low-income housing but reinvest the proceeds in other low-income housing. Also some low income housing is financed with tax exempt bonds. These relatively small tax subsidies remained intact through the passage of the TRA86, but their value was reduced by the reduction in income tax rates.

The major remaining tax subsidy to low-income housing is a deep tax credit with a present value of 70% of the qualified basis of the building. The credit is received over 10 years, and the building must comply with the various eligibility requirements for 15 years or else the credit is recaptured. Low-income tenants are defined as having no more than 50% or 60% of the area's median income, adjusted for family size. There are limits on the total amount of tax credit that investors in each state may receive of $1.25 per resident per year. Also the project must be approved by the relevant state or local government credit authority. The credit applies only to housing placed in service after 1987 (i.e., to new housing). There is a lower tax credit for existing low-income housing or for new low-income housing receiving other subsidies such as financing with tax-exempt bonds.

This large tax credit has the advantage that it is unaffected by the TRA86's cuts in marginal tax rates. However, it is so hedged with restrictions that it is difficult to evaluate its impact on investors' incentives to invest in low-income housing. Also the tax credit provides for low-income housing to be distributed around the country, but according to total population rather than according to low-income population. This is likely to mean that tax credits will be unavailable in some of the regions where they are most needed. The requirement that the project be approved by a state or local government credit authority is also difficult to evaluate and may make the program subject to abuse. Hanging U.S. policy toward low-income housing on a single heavily constrained tax credit seems generally unwise since a single provision that turns out to be overly restrictive could wipe out a large fraction of low-income housing investment activity. A rethinking of housing policy for low-income households in the post-TRA86 environment is needed.

Notes

1. Investors who purchased rental housing units were also eligible in some cases to receive a 10% ITC, although the rules changed during the 1980s. At the beginning of the period, investors received the ITC for investments in new rental housing units, and throughout the period they received the credit for investments in rehabilitation of used rental housing units if the units were in buildings at least 30 years old. There also was and is a 20% ITC for rehabilitating buildings that are certified historic structures. These provisions were not considered by Poterba in his user cost calculations. They make it difficult to calculate user costs since the credit goes to some investors but not others. Some of the value of the ITC is probably capitalized into the value of buildings eligible to receive it.

2. Tax distortions to the allocation of risk may in fact cause private costs to exceed social costs.

3. Actually investors in rental housing benefit to some extent from the more favorable tax treatment of machines since some elements of rental housing, such as furniture, appliances, or elevators, are subject to the same tax treatment as machines.

References

Mills, Edwin S. 1987. "Dividing up the Investment Pie: Have We Overinvested in Housing?" *Federal Reserve Bank of Philadelphia Business Review* (March–April): 13–23.

GENERAL DISCUSSION

Henry Aaron commented on the author's use of recent housing starts data and recommended that he carry the time series back farther. In response to Michelle White's discussion of the chapter, he noted that as much as 90%–95% of the housing subsidy for low-income families has shown up as an income transfer.

Daniel Feenberg observed that rents should be determined by demand and supply for the stock of existing rental units; prices therefore would be expected to move only gradually.

Alan Auerbach questioned White's measure of a 49% decline in the user cost of machinery, adding that he would expect the cost of capital to have gone up from 1982. James Poterba agreed and noted that the result depends critically on what one assumes about the effect of TRA86 on interest rates.

Charles McLure pointed out that in the post-TRA86 environment, owner-occupied housing may be the only remaining tax shelter. We should expect therefore to see increased investment in such housing post-TRA86. As a separate point McLure noted that rent control may be an important factor in some regions and suggested that researchers look for data on rents that are not controlled. Later in the discussion Poterba agreed that this would be a worthwhile study and that it may well be feasible.

In reference to the housing starts data in table 5.5, Patric Hendershott questioned whether the observed significant results should be attributed to TRA86. As an alternative explanation he proposed that favorable tax treatment of ERTA led to increases in vacancy rates, which has in turn led to a decline in housing starts now.

Burton Smoliar added that condominiums and cooperatives are classified as multifamily housing, and that overhang in this area resulting from generous depreciation available over the period 1981–84 has depressed recent investment.

Don Fullerton expressed his disenchantment with the marginal investor model used by Poterba. The model implies that contrary to observed behavior, only the wealthy will own housing and only low-income individuals will hold bonds. It would be better to employ a portfolio model in which each investor is at the margin. Later in the discussion Poterba responded that although individuals from a variety of income strata own housing, ownership is heavily skewed toward the top of the income distribution. Hendershott remarked that the weighted average tax rate for an investor in rental housing in the early 1980s was approximately 30%, which is lower than the marginal investor model would suggest.

Jeffrey MacKie-Mason observed that limited partnerships, and not general partnerships, had been included in the data on tax shelter behavior. This is arguably incomplete because investors may now be offered general partnerships with liability insurance, making them comparable to limited partnerships. MacKie-Mason asked if these kinds of investments had gone down over the test period too.

Roger Gordon was interested in seeing data on changes in ownership patterns, namely, conversions from individual property-owners to corporate property-owners.

Poterba agreed with McLure's suggestion that it may be important to consider tax changes that affect alternative investments such as tax shelter assets. To study this, a general equilibrium model would be appropriate. In such a model the impact on housing of these other tax changes would show up in their effect on the real interest rate.

Hendershott noted that upward pressure on rents would be a long-term response to the tax changes, whereas in the short run they would be reflected in lower asset values.

6

The Impact of the Tax Reform Act of 1986 on Foreign Direct Investment to and from the United States

Joel Slemrod

6.1 Introduction

At first glance, reconciling the post-1986 behavior of foreign direct investment (FDI) to the Tax Reform Act of 1986 (TRA86) presents an unusual puzzle. On the one hand, changing the tax treatment of foreign direct investment, either absolutely or relative to domestic investment, was not a major theme of TRA86 or the tax reform movement in general. On the other hand, since the act's passage in 1986, foreign direct investment both into and from the United States has apparently surged. As figure 6.1 shows, the standard measure of inward FDI reached an all-time high of $58.4 billion in 1988, continuing a secular increase that began in the late 1970s. Outward FDI also reached an all-time high of $44.2 billion in 1987 which, contrary to the case of inward FDI, represented a sharp turnaround from the situation of the early 1980s. Outward FDI in 1988, though, fell back to $17.5 billion, which is approximately its level in 1985 and, after adjusting for capital gains and tax haven transactions, is lower as a fraction of GNP than it was in the late 1970s.

Was tax reform responsible for the surge in FDI, or is the timing of the two events purely a coincidence? Furthermore, has the mix of investment, its financing, and its timing been affected by the tax law change? These are the principal questions addressed in this chapter. I conclude that it is impossible to establish a clear link between tax policy and the aggregate behavior of FDI, both because the a priori impact of the change is not clear and because it is impossible, with less than three years of post-TRA86 data, to sort out any tax effect from other influences on FDI. Several aspects of recent FDI performance are, however, consistent with the effect of TRA86 on incentives, including the strength of outward FDI to low-tax countries and the increase in net transfers of debt abroad. For inward FDI the predominance of investment from Japan and the United Kingdom, the

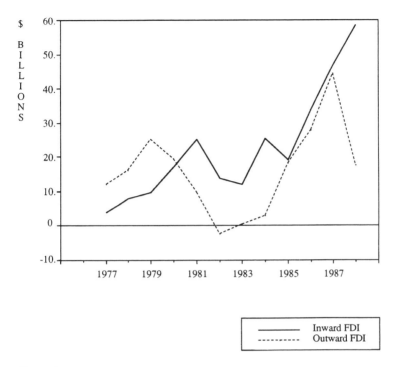

Figure 6.1
Inward and outward foreign direct investment, 1977–88. Source: *Survey of Current Business* (various issues).

relative decline of debt transfers, and the increased reported rate of return on investment are consistent with tax incentives.

To reach these conclusions, the chapter proceeds as follows: Section 6.2 briefly reviews the U.S. tax treatment of FDI. Section 6.3 discusses the changes wrought by TRA86 and how they affected the incentives for the real and financial decisions of multinational firms. The evidence about FDI since 1986 is presented in section 6.4, and compared to the predictions made in section 6.3. Some concluding comments are offered in section 6.5.

6.2   The Taxation of the Income from Foreign Direct Investment

An Overview

Each country in the world asserts the right to tax the income that is generated within its borders, including the income earned by foreign multinational corporations. Countries do, however, differ widely in the tax rate they apply, the definition of the tax base, and in the special incentives they offer for investment. Nevertheless, the first and quantitatively most important tax burden on FDI comes from the government of the country (known as the "host" country) where the investment is located.

Many countries, including the United States, Japan, and the United Kingdom also assert the right to tax the worldwide income of its residents, including its resident corporations. As a rule the income of foreign subsidiaries is recognized only upon repatriation of earnings through dividends, interest, or royalty payments. In order to avoid the potentially onerous burden of two layers of taxation, those countries that tax on a worldwide basis also offer a credit for income and withholding taxes paid to foreign governments. The total credit available in any given year is usually limited to the home country's tax liability on the foreign-source income, although credits earned in excess of the limitation may often be carried forward or backward to offset excess limitations for other years. Several other countries, including France and the Netherlands, operate a "territorial" system of taxing their resident corporations, under which foreign-source business income is completely exempt from home country taxation.[1]

This would be the end of the story if the geographical location of income was not a matter of dispute. In fact, even if all the information necessary to ascertain the location of income was costlessly available, the conceptual basis for locating income is controversial (Ault and Bradford 1990). In reality corporations do not have the incentive to fully reveal all the information on which to base a determination of the geographical source of income. For any pattern of real investment decisions, a multinational has the incentive to shift the apparent source of income out of high-tax countries into low-tax countries. This can be accomplished for example, through the pricing of intercompany transfers of goods and intangible assets, or by doing borrowing through subsidiaries in high-tax countries. Note that this incentive applies regardless of whether the home country operates a territorial or worldwide system of taxation.

Much of the complexity of the taxation of foreign-source income arises from the attempt of countries to defend their revenue base against the fungibility of income tax bases. Complex rules cover standards for acceptable transfer pricing, allocation rules for interest expense and intangibles, and taxing on an accrual basis certain types of income. It is impossible to concisely summarize the variety of rules that countries employ to determine the location of income. In some countries the statutes are not as important as the outcomes of case-by-case negotiations between representatives of the multinationals and the countries involved. In other cases the source rules are governed by bilateral tax treaties. What is clear, however, is that the de facto rules that govern the sourcing of income are at least as important for understanding the effective taxation of foreign direct investment as the tax rates, depreciation rules, and tax credits.[2]

The U.S. System of Taxing the Income from Foreign Direct Investment

Outward Investment
The U.S. operates a worldwide system of taxation. Thus both domestic-source and foreign-source income of U.S. multinationals are subject to U.S. taxation. The income of foreign subsidiaries[3] is not, however, taxed as accrued but instead enters the tax base of the U.S. parent only upon repatriation of dividends, at which time it is "grossed up" by the average tax rate paid to foreign governments. The grossed-up dividends, minus certain expenses of the multinational allocated to foreign-source income, enter into the taxable income of the parent. Foreign-source income of the parent also includes interest and royalty payments from subsidiaries and certain types of "passive" income on an accrual basis, plus the foreign-source income of foreign branch operations.

In general, income taxes paid by foreign affiliates to foreign governments can be credited against U.S. tax liability. This credit is, however, limited to the U.S. tax liability on the foreign-source income, which is approximately equal to the U.S. statutory corporation tax rate multiplied by the net foreign-source income of the subsidiary. Multinationals whose potentially creditable foreign taxes exceed the limitation on credits are said to be in an *excess credit* position. These excess credits may be carried forward for five years (or backward for two years) without interest to be used if and when the parent's potentially creditable taxes fall short of the limitation. If the potentially creditable taxes are less than the limit on credits to be taken in a given year, the corporation is said to be in an *excess limitation* (or *deficit of credit*) position. Distinguishing the excess credit and excess limitation situation is critically important because the tax-related incentives for real and financial behavior are often quite different for a corporation depending on which situation it is in.

6.3   The Tax Reform Act of 1986 and the Changed Incentives for Foreign Direct Investment

Outward Investment

Tax Law Changes
The three most significant aspects of TRA86 for outward investment, in order of importance, were as follows:

1. The reduction in the statutory corporate rate from 46% to 34%, and the resulting increase in the number of firms in an excess credit situation.

2. The change in the rules governing the sourcing of income and the allocation of expenses (most significantly interest) between domestic- and foreign-source income.

3. The tightening of the foreign tax credit limiting the averaging of different types of income.

The Reduced Statutory Corporate Tax Rate   The single most important aspect of TRA86 for outward FDI was the reduction in the statutory rate of corporation income tax from 46% to 34%. Many of the repercussions of the new law follow from this change.

To see this, a brief digression on the impact of TRA86 on domestic investment is required. It is well-known that the net effect of the tax system on the incentive to invest depends not only on the statutory rate but also on, among other things, the schedule of depreciation allowances, the rate and scope of investment tax credits, the source of financing, and the rate of inflation. TRA86 eliminated the investment tax credits that previously applied to equipment and machinery, and generally provided less generous depreciation allowances, both of which tended to offset the tax rate reduction. Most analysts concluded that the net effect of these provisions was to slightly increase the effective corporate-level tax on new domestic investment, an important alternative to FDI.

An analysis of how these same changes affected the effective tax rate on FDI must proceed quite differently because, with certain exceptions, foreign-source income of foreign subsidiaries enters the parent's tax base only to the extent that dividends are repatriated. There is thus no calculation of foreign-source taxable income from which depreciation allowances are deducted and against which investment tax credits can be offset. The tax base is simply dividends received minus allocable deductions, grossed up by the average rate of foreign taxation (calculated using an earnings and profits measure of taxable income, which is not sensitive to legislated changes in the tax depreciation schedules used for domestically located assets,[4] investment credits, etc.). To that base is applied the corporate statutory tax rate.

Thus, ignoring the source-of-income rules discussed below, the corporate tax changes of TRA86 reduced the statutory rate from 46% to 34% but did not broaden the tax base, resulting in an unambiguous reduction in the tax rate on income from FDI. Assuming that the taxes imposed by the foreign governments remained unchanged,[5] it follows that the amount of additional taxation imposed by the United States upon repatriation either stayed the same or declined. It stayed at zero for multinationals whose average[6] tax rate paid to foreign governments exceeds 46%. Any multinational subject to an average tax rate by foreign governments between 34% and 46% had formerly been paying taxes upon repatriation but, under the new rate, would no longer be liable for any additional taxes. For firms paying less than a 34% average tax rate to foreign governments, the tax due upon repatriation would fall substantially, although not to zero.[7]

The other important implication of the reduction of the U.S. statutory rate from 46% to 34% is that a much higher fraction of U.S. multinationals are likely to be in an excess credit situation, because the average tax paid to foreign governments exceeds 34%.[8] For a firm in excess credit status, every additional dollar paid in tax to a foreign government generates a foreign tax credit that cannot be used immediately. The foreign tax credit has some value to the multinational only if the firm either will be in an excess limitation position in the next five years (the carryforward limit) or had been in an excess limitation position in the previous two years (the carryback limit). Thus a U.S. multinational in an excess credit position is likely to be much more sensitive to differences in foreign effective tax rates than a firm in an excess limitation situation.[9] This increases the relative attractiveness of investment in a low-tax foreign country such as Ireland compared to a high-tax country such as West Germany.

New Source Rules A firm in excess credit status can reduce the present value of its tax burden to the extent it can increase the limit on foreign tax credits. This increases the importance of the rules determining the source, for U.S. tax purposes, of worldwide income. Holding worldwide income constant, if a dollar of income is shifted from domestic source to foreign source, it increases the foreign tax credit limitation by one dollar and allows 34 cents more of foreign taxes to be credited immediately against U.S. tax liability. Only to the extent that foreign governments enforce the same source rules will there be an offsetting increase in foreign tax liability.

One existing source rule that becomes more important applies to production for export. According to current regulations, between 40% and 50% of the income from domestic U.S. production of export goods can effectively be allocated to foreign-source income. For a multinational in an excess credit position, this has the effect of reducing the effective tax rate on domestic investment for export by as much as a half. Thus, if a contemplated FDI is to produce goods for sale outside the United States, the alternative of domestic U.S. production has become relatively tax favored for those firms that have shifted into excess credit status despite the base broadening aspects of TRA86. This reasoning would not, though, apply to FDI designed to reexport to the United States because the alternative of domestic production for internal consumption does not benefit from the export source rule.

Interest expenses of the U.S. parent corporation must be allocated to either U.S.- or foreign-source income. The general rule is to allocate on the basis of the book value of assets so that interest expenses deductible from foreign-source income are equal to total interest payments multiplied by the fraction of worldwide assets represented by assets expected to generate foreign-source income. Although TRA86 did not significantly alter this allocation formula, it did add a "one-taxpayer" rule under which corporations that are members of an affiliated group are consolidated for the purpose of allocating interest expenses between U.S. and foreign sources.[10] In the absence of this rule a multinational could load its debt into a U.S. subsidiary with no foreign-source income and have the interest expense be allocated entirely to U.S.-source income, thus maximizing foreign-source income and the limitation on foreign tax credits. With the one-taxpayer rule, a fraction of these interest payments has to be allocated to foreign-source income regardless of the legal structure of the multinational.

For multinationals in excess credit position that are forced to reallocate interest payments, this provision increases the average cost of capital of domestic or foreign investment to the extent debt finance is used. It also increases the marginal cost of foreign investment because foreign investment increases the amount of interest payments that must be allocated abroad, which decreases foreign-source income and therefore the amount of foreign taxes that are immediately creditable.[11] This provision is obviously most important for multinationals with a high debt-to-capital ratio.

Separate Baskets   TRA86 also changed the operation of the foreign tax credit by creating separate ("basket") limitations for certain categories of income. Foreign taxes imposed on taxable income in a particular basket can only offset U.S. taxes due on that category of income. There are eight separate baskets, including passive income, high withholding tax interest, and financial services income. In some cases (e.g., passive income) the objective was to prevent fungible income from being earned in low-tax rate foreign jurisdictions and thus increasing the amount of available foreign tax credits that could offset taxes paid on other income to foreign governments. In other cases (e.g., high withholding tax interest) the objective was to prevent multinationals (often banks) in an excess limit position from paying effectively high withholding taxes (which, due to the excess limit, could be immediately credited against U.S. tax liability) in return for favorable pretax terms of exchange (higher than otherwise pretax interest rates on loans). These objectives share the common thread of limiting the revenue loss to the United States than can arise from manipulation of the foreign tax credit mechanism.

In general, the creation of separate foreign tax credit baskets increases the effective taxation of foreign-source income because it makes it more difficult in certain cases to credit foreign income taxes against U.S. tax liability. In addition the baskets can add significant complexity to the typical multinational's compliance procedure, and to this extent the provisions add a hidden tax burden to multinational operation.

The Effect on Outward FDI

The preceding discussion touched only on the most important provisions of TRA86 that affect the incentives of U.S. firms to undertake and finance FDI. Because some of the provisions have offsetting incentive effects, its impact on aggregate outward FDI is unclear on a priori grounds. Moreover the net effect of the tax changes depends critically on firm characteristics such as its excess credit status (which in turn depends on such factors as the countries of operation and repatriation policy), its debt–capital ratio, and whether foreign production is for reexport to the United States or for sale abroad.

Before the actual impact of TRA86 could be discerned, Grubert and Mutti (1987) attempted a quantitative assessment of its impact on FDI using a two-country, multisectoral general equilibrium model. To quantify the changes in U.S. corporate taxation of foreign-source income, they relied on the revenue estimates that accompanied TRA86. Netting the tax increases on foreign income (due primarily to the new interest allocation rules and separate foreign tax credit limitations), estimated to be $2.9 billion, against the reduction in U.S. tax on foreign corporate income due to the statutory rate reduction, estimated at $3.2 billion, yielded a tax reduction on foreign-source income of 0.3 percentage points. Thus on net they judged that TRA86 provided a slight reduction in the tax on foreign-source income and a moderate increase in the corporate tax on domestic investment, and concluded that TRA86 would have a relatively small impact on capital flows and the trade balance. For the short run they forecast a capital outflow in response to lower aftertax returns in the United States, and an accompanying decrease in the trade deficit. In the long run, output in the import-competing sector was predicted to decline by between 1% and 2% due to the relatively large increase in that sector's capital costs, the tax incentives to exports, and the outflow of capital.

In a similar vein Sinn (1988) argued that TRA86 would result in a net outflow of direct investment. As in the Grubert and Mutti analysis, this conclusion is based on the judgment that the base broadening aspects of corporate taxation slightly outweighed the reductions in the statutory rate cut and thus increased the effective rate of taxation on domestic U.S. investment. Sinn also argued that TRA86's changes in the individual-level taxation of capital income would reinforce this conclusion. The cuts in marginal tax rates, by raising the aftertax return on financial assets, and the increased effective tax rate on capital gains would combine to raise the required rate of return to U.S. investors, who hold claims on predominantly U.S.-located real capital.

Although the impact on aggregate FDI is unclear on a priori grounds, as mentioned above investment in high-tax countries such as Germany should decrease compared to investment in low-tax countries such as Ireland. This is because the increased prevalence of firms in an excess credit position implies that incremental foreign-source income from Germany will often no longer generate offsetting foreign credits.

TRA86 also has implications for the financial and accounting decisions of multinationals, holding constant their real investment decisions. The relatively low U.S. statutory rate makes it attractive to have interest deductions taken against subsidiaries' income subject to tax by foreign governments. A movement toward this financial structure, depending on how it is structured, could show up in the data as transfers of debt capital from U.S. parent to its foreign affiliates and an offsetting transfer of equity from the affiliate to the U.S. parent.[12]

More generally, the relatively low U.S. statutory rate provides multinationals with the incentive to reduce taxable income subject to foreign taxes, even if there is a corresponding increase in U.S. source income for U.S. tax purposes. There are a host of techniques multinationals can use to achieve this purpose, including receiving income from foreign subsidiaries via payments deductible from host country taxable income (e.g., interest, royalties, and service fees) and the pricing of intrafirm transfers of goods and services. To the extent that this happens we would expect foreign-source income to decrease, which could show up in the data as a decreased rate of return on foreign investment.[13]

Because of the gradual reduction of the corporate tax rate (from 46% in 1986 to 40% in 1987 to 34% in 1988 and subsequent years), many multi-nationals had an incentive to postpone dividend repatriations from 1986 and 1987 into 1988 and beyond. Thus the dividend payment rate should be abnormally low in late 1986 and 1987, and abnormally high in 1988. This would increase measured undistributed earnings of foreign affiliates in 1986 and 1987 and reduce them in 1988.

Whether the rate of profit repatriation will be permanently affected is a distinct and interesting question. Lowering the U.S. corporation tax rate will generally reduce the amount of tax paid to the U.S. government upon repatriation. However, Hartman (1984) has persuasively argued that the amount of tax due upon repatriation should not affect a firm's choice of whether to repatriate or invest a dollar of its earnings because the repatriation tax reduces equally both the return and the opportunity cost of investment. In other words, the repatriation tax reduces equally the parent's aftertax return from a dividend today and a dividend in the future, and thus does not affect the optimal timing of dividends. If, though, the current tax rate on repatriations is expected to increase over time, Hartman's reasoning would imply an incentive for current repatriations because the tax system reduces the aftertax return to investing earnings (and future repatriation) more than it reduces the opportunity cost (current repatriation).

Inward Investment

Tax Law Changes
Foreign corporations that are engaged in a trade or business in the United States, and U.S. corporations controlled by a foreign corporation, are subject to taxation according to rules that are roughly comparable to those that apply to U.S. corporations. Thus the reduction of the statutory rate, elimination of the investment tax credit, and changes in depreciation schedules apply directly to foreign subsidiaries. The United States also imposes a "withholding" tax of 30%, modified by treaty to a much lower figure for many countries, on payments from corporations within the United States to foreign corporations. These withholding tax rates were not affected by TRA86.

TRA86 did introduce a new branch profits tax, which imposes a 30% tax (often reduced by treaty) on the repatriated profits and certain interest payments of a U.S. branch of a foreign corporation. This tax, which affects primarily financial institutions, was designed to equalize the tax treatment of foreign corporations operating through a U.S. branch and those operating through a wholly owned domestic subsidiary.

The Effect on Inward FDI

The conclusion of many observers that TRA86 increased the effective rate of taxation on new corporate investment dominated the forecasts about inward FDI made by those few brave souls who offered a prediction before the actual impact could be discerned. Both Grubert and Mutti (1987) and Sinn (1988) based their conclusions that inward FDI would fall on this aspect of TRA86.

After observing the surge of inward FDI to the United States immediately after the passage of TRA86, Scholes and Wolfson (1989) offered an ingenious argument that the increase in the effective tax rate on domestically located capital was a key element in the sharp increase of inward FDI. Their argument begins (as does the argument of Grubert-Mutti and Sinn) with the presumption that TRA86 increased the effective rate of taxation on domestically located capital. Now consider a foreign firm resident in a country that taxes on the basis of worldwide income and offers a tax credit for income taxes paid to foreign governments. If the U.S. average tax rate is below the foreign statutory rate, and ignoring the benefits of deferral, the total effective tax rate on a U.S. investment will be unchanged by the increase in the U.S. effective tax rate. To put it another way, the increased U.S. taxation is offset by increased credits offered by the foreign government. If the total effective tax rate faced by foreigners stays unchanged, when the tax rate faced by U.S. investors increases, the relative tax rate of foreigners declines, causing a shift in ownership of U.S.-located assets to foreign corporations. Thus the counterintuitive prediction of this analysis is that increases in U.S. corporate taxation will increase foreign ownership of U.S.-located capital. The Scholes-Wolfson hypothesis bears further discussion because of its startling predictions, its ability to apparently explain some of the post-TRA86 data (discussed below), and because it offers a convenient organizing focus for thinking about the effect of U.S. tax law on inward FDI.

The analysis rests on two assumptions which are subject to some qualification. First, of the six principal countries exporting capital to the United States, only two (Japan and the United Kingdom) operate a worldwide system with foreign tax credit. France and the Netherlands operate a territorial system so that foreign-source income of their resident multinationals is untaxed by the home country. Although Canada and West Germany in theory have a worldwide system, by treaty with the United States repatriated dividends bear no further taxation. For multinationals in these latter four countries, the effective tax rate on FDI in the United States is no different than for U.S. companies, so the analysis does not apply. Japan and United Kingdom have, however, accounted for slightly more than half of the six countries' FDI in the United States in the past several years. Nevertheless, the assumption that the investing country operates a worldwide system of taxation does not apply universally. Furthermore, even for Japan and the United Kingdom, TRA86 did not increase the tax rate on U.S. FDI only to the extent the multinationals are in an excess limitation position and are repatriating income that is subject to additional taxation in the home country. If most income is retained by the U.S. subsidiaries, then the U.S. tax rate is the relevant one for all investors and an increase does not reduce the relative tax rate faced by Japanese or U.K. investors.

Second, the Scholes-Wolfson hypothesis says that an increase in U.S. corporate taxation reduces the relative tax burden on foreign-owned investment, but not the absolute level of taxation. Thus the hypothesis suggests a change in the ownership pattern of existing capital that is consistent with a decline in the rate of increase of foreign-owned capital due to the heavier absolute tax burden imposed by TRA86.

Some of the changed incentives for financial behavior that apply to U.S. multinationals also apply to foreign multinationals operating in the U.S. The relatively low U.S. statutory rate makes it attractive to shift taxable income to a U.S. jurisdiction, either by shifting debt out of U.S. corporations or through transfer pricing. There is no change, though, in the incentives for dividend repatriation.

6.4 FDI since TRA86

Outward Investment

The usual measure of outward FDI surged immediately following the passage of TRA86. As figure 6.2 shows, the flow of outward FDI reached an all-time high of $44.5 billion in 1987, continuing a secular increase that began in 1983 and representing a sharp turnaround from the situation of the early 1980s. As recently as 1984, outward FDI was only $2.8 billion,

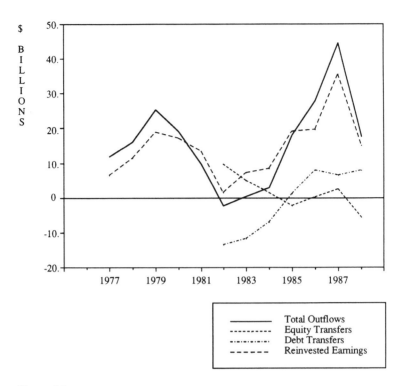

Figure 6.2
Outward foreign direct investment, by source of funds, 1977–88. Breakdown of transfers
of funds into debt and equity is available only from 1982 on. Source: *Survey of Current
Business* (various issues).

and it averaged less than $1 billion for the 1982–84 period. In 1988,
though, outward FDI fell from $44.2 billion back down to $17.5 billion,
below both the 1985 and 1986 levels but still significantly higher than in
the 1981–84 period.[14]

Figure 6.2 also shows that the 1987 increase in outward investment was
almost entirely comprised of an increase in retained earnings, with net
transfers of debt plus equity contributing very little to the total. Similarly
the 1988 drop was largely due to a decline in retained earnings. Furthermore a substantial fraction of the 1987 increase and 1988 decrease in
retained earnings can be ascribed to capital gains on foreign operations due
to the depreciation of the dollar. As an illustration, between 1984 and 1987
the increase in the flow of reinvested earnings was $24.6 billion and during
the same period the capital appreciation component of foreign-source income went from a capital loss of $8.4 billion to a capital gain of $15.6

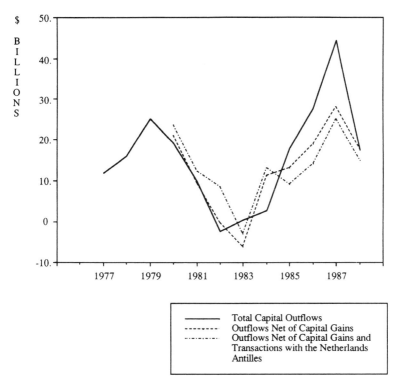

Figure 6.3
Outward foreign direct investment, adjusted for capital gains and transactions with the
Netherland Antilles. Capital gains are not available separately before 1980. Source: *Survey
of Current Business* (various issues).

billion, a net increase of $24.0 billion, or 97% of the total increase in
retained earnings and 58% of the increase in the overall outward flow of
FDI. The decline in retained earnings from $35.7 billion to $15.2 billion was
largely due to the change in capital gains from $15.6 billion to −$0.1
billion. Figure 6.3, which shows outward FDI measured net of capital gains
and losses, tells a somewhat different story about outward FDI in the
1980s, in particular a less dramatic rise from 1984 to 1987. However, still
evident is a large increase in 1986 and 1987 and a decline in 1988 to
slightly below the 1986 level.

   One further adjustment to the outward FDI data should be made. As it
stands now, it includes transactions between U.S. parent companies and
Netherlands Antilles affiliates. Most of these affiliates were established in
the late 1970s and early 1980s to borrow funds in European capital markets

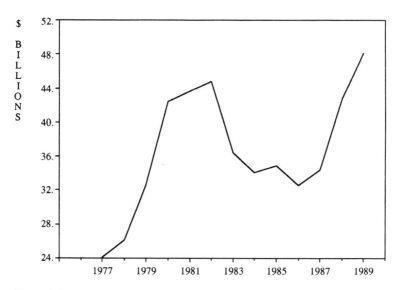

Figure 6.4
Capital expenditures by majority-owned foreign affiliates of U.S. companies, 1977–89.
Source: *Survey of Current Business* (various issues).

and reloan them to their U.S. parents. Due to the U.S.–Netherlands Antilles tax treaty then in force, this arrangement allowed the avoidance of U.S. withholding taxes. Upon the elimination of the withholding tax in 1984, this tax advantage was ended. Thus the data show large debt inflows from the Netherlands Antilles until 1984 and large outflows thereafter as the loans are repaid. Figure 6.3 shows the pattern of outward FDI after purging the data of transactions with the Netherlands Antilles (and capital gains). The upward trend of the 1980s looks smaller still, although 1987 still stands out as an all-time record, with 1988 falling back to the 1986 level.

All in all, the post-TRA86 performance of outward FDI has been strong relative to the early 1980s but not high relative to the late 1970s. This general conclusion is corroborated by other data on the strength of foreign direct investment. Figure 6.4 shows the recent history of capital expenditures by majority-owned foreign affiliates of U.S. companies.[15] The figures for 1987 and earlier represent actual expenditures, whereas those for 1988 and 1989 represent planned expenditures from a Bureau of Economic Analysis survey taken in December 1988. Consistent with the FDI numbers discussed above, these data indicate a surge in capital expenditures after TRA86. In this case the surge is expected to begin in 1988 rather than in 1987. Whereas 1987 investment was only 5.5% higher than 1986, planned

Table 6.1
Capital expenditures by majority-owned foreign affiliates of U.S. companies, by low-tax and high-tax countries in Europe, 1984–89 ($ millions)

	1984	1985	1986	1987	1988	1989	% increase 1985–89
Low-tax[a]	767	778	1,054	1,160	1,417	1,672	114.9
Low-tax plus Spain	1,234	1,193	1,505	1,793	2,253	2,653	122.4
High-tax[b]	6,836	7,187	8,385	7,928	9,306	10,424	45.0

Source: *Survey of Current Business*, various issues.
a. Low-tax European countries: Belgium, Ireland, Luxembourg
b. High-tax countries: Denmark, France, Germany, Greece, Italy, the Netherlands, Portugal

1989 expenditures are 47.5% higher than actual expenditures in 1986. The expected increase is widespread across industry group as well.[16]

In sum, two distinct sources of data indicate that outward FDI has been strong since the passage of TRA86. However, the 1988 FDI figure is substantially below the 1987 figure, and as a percentage of GNP it is below the FDI of the late 1970s. It is particularly difficult to detect the hand of TRA86 in this performance since its net impact on the incentive to undertake FDI is ambiguous on theoretical grounds due to the offsetting incentive effects of several of its aspects. To detect TRA86's influence, it may be necessary to look at specific aspects of the post-TRA86 FDI performance.

Geographical Distribution of FDI

Judging by the capital expenditures numbers, the planned increase in investment is broadly distributed across geographical areas. The overall increase between 1985 and 1989 is, however, higher for Europe and Japan (49.4% and 47.6%, respectively) compared to Canada and developing countries (19.1% and 15.7%, respectively). The strong European performance is no doubt partly stimulated by the planned dismantling of internal trade barriers in 1992 and fear of increased protectionism thereafter.

Is there any evidence of a post-TRA86 shift toward investment in low-tax countries? Table 6.1 assembles some evidence to assess that question. European countries are divided into groups based on their effective tax rates on investment as calculated by Crooks et al. (1988). The rate of growth of capital expenditures in low-tax countries (Belgium, Ireland, and Luxembourg) is notably higher than in high-tax countries (Denmark, France, Germany, Greece, Italy, the Netherlands, and Portugal).[17] This conclusion is robust to including as a low-tax country Spain, whose effective tax rate on new investment was assessed to be relatively high by Crooks and his coworkers but is generally understood to be a low-tax location for investment. Of course the prospect of reduced internal trade barriers is an alternative explanation for the growing importance of the relative tax burdens imposed by host countries. With a reduction in barriers to trade, there is less need to locate production facilities in the same country as the final market.

Financial and Accounting Responses

In situations where all governments agree on the source of income, the relative decline in the U.S. statutory rate gave multinationals (especially those in an excess credit situation) more incentive to have taxable income appear as U.S.-source income rather than foreign-source income. On the other hand, more U.S. multinationals are in an excess credit position, and in this situation an increase in foreign-source income *for U.S. tax purposes only* is advantageous because it increases the amount of foreign tax credit that can be taken immediately. Thus the incentive to shift income between U.S. and foreign sources depends on the relative strength of these factors and critically on the relationship between the income source rules of the U.S. and those of the host countries. Shifting of income can be accomplished through a great variety of financial and accounting transactions, the net effect of which would be to decrease net taxable income abroad and the reported rate of return on foreign assets.

Table 6.2 shows that there is evidence for one dimension of financial response, an increase in debt transfers from parent to foreign affiliate.[18] In the seven years since 1982 for which these data have been collected, until 1986 debt outflows had been substantially negative (except for a positive $187 million in 1982). Since 1986 debt transfers have averaged nearly $3 billion annually.[19] The evidence for complementary declines in equity transfers is more ambiguous because, although in 1988 equity transfers

Table 6.2
Debt and Equity outflows, net of transactions with the Netherlands Antilles, 1982–88 ($ millions)

	1982	1983	1984	1985	1986	1987	1988
Debt	187	−6,127	−3,118	−2,881	3,628	2,428	2,818
Equity	5,535	3,492	365	−1,350	−195	5,020	−2,944

Source: *Survey of Current Business*, various issues.

were at a seven-year low, in 1987 they were at their highest level since 1982. Note that subsidiary borrowing was made relatively more attractive not only by the reduced U.S. statutory rate but also by the one-taxpayer rule for interest allocations of the parent corporation. Under that rule the tax saving to a firm in an excess credit situation per dollar of U.S. interest expense is less than the U.S. statutory rate because some of the interest must be allocated to foreign-source income, reducing the available amount of foreign tax credits. Before TRA86 the interest deduction was fully effective if it was taken by a subsidiary with no foreign-source income.

As table 6.3 indicates, the rate of return on outward investment, calculated net of capital gains and transactions with Netherlands Antilles affiliates, shows no evidence of a post-TRA86 decline due to the incentive to shift income away from foreign taxable income now subject to relatively higher statutory tax rates. If anything, the trend is upward.

Timing Issues

The Tax Reform Act of 1986 was passed by both houses of the legislature on September 25 and 27, 1986 and signed into law by President Reagan on October 22. That many of the basic features of TRA86 would become law was widely perceived by May of 1986, when the Senate Finance Committee passed its tax bill, although some important details had yet to be decided by the conference committee.

Most details of the law were scheduled to take effect on January 1, 1987, although the cut in the corporate tax rate was phased in so that it was 40% in 1987 and 34% for 1988 and thereafter, and the investment tax credit was eliminated retroactively to January 1, 1986. The imminent change in the tax law provided corporations with the incentive to accelerate or decelerate decisions to attract more favorable tax treatment. Reflecting these incentives outward, FDI behaved strikingly in the fourth quarter of 1986 and, to some extent, in the first quarter of 1987.

Table 6.3
Rate of return on outward foreign investment, 1981–88

1981	1982	1983	1984	1985	1986	1987	1988
10.2	11.5	7.8	14.4	12.8	12.6	13.0	15.2

Source: Author's calculation using data from *Survey of Current Business*, various issues. Rate of return calculated excluding capital gains and transactions with the Netherlands Antilles affiliates.

The flow of net outward FDI was extraordinarily low in the fourth quarter of 1986, falling sharply to −$1.1 billion from an average of a $9.1 billion in the first three quarters and $11.2 billion in the first quarter of 1987. Equity transfers were extraordinarily large in both directions, four times as large as in previous quarters, with decreases exceeding increases. Gross decreases in equity amounted to $7.1 billion in 1986:4 alone, more than four times the rate of the first three quarters of 1986. Debt transfers moved from a substantial net outflow to a $0.3 billion inflow. Dividend repatriations were also unusually high in 1986:4—$10.0 billion, compared to an average of $4.4 billion in the first three quarters of 1986 and an average of $5.7 billion per quarter in 1987. There is some indication that the drop in net capital outflows in part reflected a timing change because outflows in the first quarter of 1987 were higher than any other period in the six quarters from 1986:2 to 1987:3.

What could have accounted for the extraordinary drop in net outward capital flows? The extraordinarily high volume of equity transfers was undoubtedly largely due to the imminent repeal (as of January 1, 1987) of the General Utilities doctrine (under which a corporation could liquidate and avoid paying a corporate-level capital gains tax on the sale of its assets) and other changes that would increase the tax cost of mergers and acquisitions after TRA86. Thus there was a tax incentive to accelerate a planned sale or reorganization into 1986:4.

The large volume of dividend repatriations in 1986:4 is an apparent puzzle in view of the argument made below that there is an incentive to postpone dividends from the high tax rate pre-TRA86 years to subsequent years when the tax rate would be lower. Dividend repatriations in 1986:4 could have been designed to beat the TRA86 clock concerning separate baskets for the foreign tax credit. As of 1987, excess credits earned for foreign-source income in certain categories could no longer be averaged against other kinds of income. By repatriating this income in 1986, the excess credits could have been of more value to the firm.

There is strong evidence that U.S. multinationals reacted to the declining statutory corporate rate between 1986 and 1988 by postponing dividend repatriations. Total distributed earnings jumped from $24.3 billion in 1987 to $37.2 billion in 1988. As a fraction of earnings before capital gains or losses dividend payments rose from 57.4% to 70.8%.[20] The fact that at 69.9% the 1986 payout rate was even higher largely reflects the extraordinarily high distributions in the fourth quarter of that year.

Inward Investment

As figure 6.5 shows, foreign direct investment into the United States has surged since the passage of TRA86. Inward FDI totaled $46.9 billion in 1987 and $58.4 billion in 1988, compared to an average of only $20.9 billion in the 1980–86 period. This statement needs less qualification than the earlier one about outward investment because capital gains have not been as important and because intrafirm transactions with financial affiliates in the Netherlands Antilles are not an important issue. Also in contrast to outward investment, retained earnings have, with the exception of 1988, been negligible. Equity transfers dominate the new investment, comprising over two-thirds of the capital inflows in 1987–88.

This post-TRA86 surge is corroborated by the data on investment outlays for U.S. business enterprises acquired or established by foreign

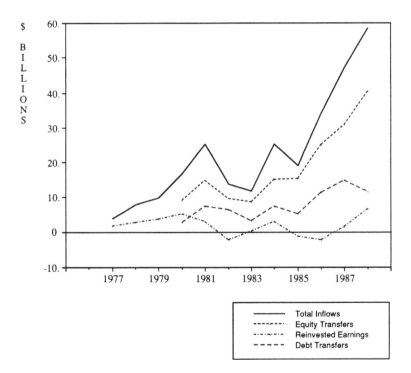

Figure 6.5
Inward foreign direct investment, by source of funds, 1980–88. Breakdown of transfers of funds into debt and equity is available from 1980 on. Source: *Survey of Current Business* (various issues).

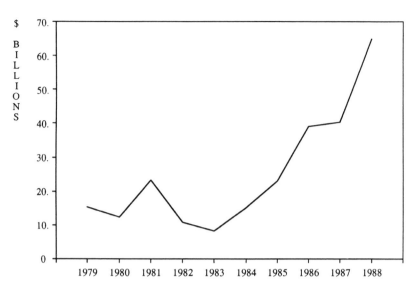

Figure 6.6
Outlays for acquisition of establishment of a U.S. business enterprise, 1979–88. Source: *Survey of Current Business* (various issues).

direct investors. This series differs from the equity transfer component of the FDI series because it excludes infusions (or reductions) of equity into existing affiliates and because it does not net out sales or liquidations of U.S. enterprises by foreign investors. As figure 6.6 shows, this series was marked by large growth from 1985 to 1986 and again from 1987 to 1988, putting the 1988 total at $65.0 billion, or six times the 1982–84 annual average. The total assets of U.S. businesses acquired or established also surged in 1986 and 1987, leveling off in 1988 to a level three times the 1984–85 average.

Geographic Distribution
Table 6.4 breaks down inward FDI by country of origin. Shown are the flow of FDI as well as outlays for acquisition or establishment of U.S. business enterprises by nonbank U.S. affiliates of foreign corporations. For the former, investments are classified by the country of the foreign parent. For the latter, investments are classified by the country of "ultimate beneficial owner," which is that person—proceeding up a U.S. affiliate's ownership chain, beginning with and including the foreign parent—who is not owned more than 50% by another person.

Table 6.4
FDI Inflows and Outlays for Acquisition or Establishment of a U.S. Business Enterprise by
Country of Origin, 1983–1988 ($ millions)

	1983	1984	1985	1986	1987	1988
Foreign direct investment inflows						
France	−201	774	30	1,017	2,471	962
Germany	1,007	1,291	2,292	1,982	3,150	2,306
Japan	1,653	4,374	3,794	7,268	7,504	17,838
Netherlands	2,778	3,520	2,776	4,374	8,293	4,766
United Kingdom	3,727	6,882	4,665	10,827	22,444	18,774
Total	11,946	25,359	19,022	34,091	46,894	58,435
Outlays for acquisition or establishment of a U.S. business enterprise						
France	295	330	754	2,491	2,044	3,753
Germany	584	685	2,270	1,351	4,664	1,375
Japan	392	1,806	1,152	5,416	7,006	14,166
Netherlands	492	562	771	4,700	391	1,937
United Kingdom	2,366	3,714	6,732	8,572	15,142	21,520
Total	8,091	15,197	23,106	39,177	40,310	65,019

Source: *Survey of Current Business*, various issues.

Although most investing countries participated in the post-TRA86 surge
in investment, the increase was dominated by investment from Japan and
the United Kingdom. These two countries account for about three-quarters
of the 1985–88 increase in FDI and outlays by foreigners for acquisition or
establishment of U.S. business enterprises.[21]

The recent predominance of FDI from Japan and the United Kingdom is
consistent with the Scholes-Wolfson hypothesis because they are two
countries that effectively operate a worldwide tax system with a foreign
tax credit, and their resident multinationals may be relatively less affected
by increases in the U.S. tax burden on investment. To some extent the
large rate of increase of FDI from Japan and the United Kingdom may
simply reflect the worldwide increase in FDI from these countries.[22]
Worldwide FDI from the United Kingdom (measured in pounds) did increase by 149% between 1984 and 1988, but this large growth rate is still
below the rate of increase in FDI located in the United States. Worldwide
FDI from Japan (measured in dollars) doubled between 1986 and 1988,
though the share going to the United States did increase over this period.
Although this pattern is consistent with the Scholes-Wolfson hypothesis,

the qualifications that must accompany its applicability are so important that I believe it is too early to accept their tax story as the principal explanation for the recent importance of FDI from Japan and the United Kingdom.

Financial Responses
The decreased U.S. corporate tax rate should reduce the incentive of foreign multinationals to locate debt in the United States, and more generally to induce them to have taxable income show up as U.S. source. Figure 6.5 shows that the former effect is indeed evident in 1988, when the ratio of equity transfers to debt transfers reached 3.5, the highest ratio since these data were tabulated in 1980.

Table 6.5 indicates that the rate of return on inward FDI did in fact increase substantially between 1986 and 1988. Since 1982 only 1984 shows a higher overall return, and for the manufacturing sector the 1988 rate of return is the highest since 1980. Although this evidence is consistent with the increased incentive of foreign multinationals to have income reported as U.S. source, the bottom row of table 6.5 indicates that between 1986 and 1988 there was also an increase in the rate of return for domestic manufacturing as a whole. It is too early to know to what extent the increased rate of return on inward FDI merely reflects the increased profitability of all U.S. located firms.

Timing
As was the case for outward investment, inward FDI in the fourth quarter of 1986 behaved differently than it had in the quarters before or after. Capital inflows, which averaged an annual rate of $28.7 billion in the adjacent four quarters, totaled $16.3 billion in 1986:4 alone. Compared to an average of the adjacent four quarters, both net debt and equity inflows were two and a half times higher. Not only were the net equity inflows unusually large but so also were gross equity flows (both increases and decreases). Much of the extraordinary activity in the fourth quarter of 1986 was probably pulled forward from the first half of 1987 because capital inflows, and particularly equity inflows, were significantly lower in the first half compared to the second half of 1987. As discussed above in the case of outward investment, the extraordinary behavior of 1986:4 was no doubt largely due to the prospective post-TRA86 increase in the tax costs of mergers and acquisitions, which accelerated sales and reorganizations planned for 1987, and perhaps beyond, into 1986.

Table 6.5
Rate of return on inward FDI and domestic manufacturing, 1977–88

	1977	1978	1979	1980	1981	1982	1983	1984	1985	1986	1987	1988
All FDI	8.7	10.9	12.7	15.6	9.4	2.6	4.3	6.1	3.5	2.7	3.9	5.6
Manufacturing	6.8	7.4	8.1	11.0	3.4	0.0	1.8	4.9	0.4	0.1	4.6	6.6
Petroleum	13.4	17.3	22.7	29.6	22.3	13.8	9.2	12.8	8.0	1.1	7.3	8.3
Wholesale trade	a	a	a	a	a	0.1	5.8	11.6	9.0	4.7	5.6	5.8
Other	a	a	a	a	a	1.9	4.2	2.4	2.0	4.6	1.3	3.6
All domestic manufacturing	14.2	15.0	16.4	13.9	13.6	9.2	10.6	12.5	10.1	9.5	12.8	16.4

Source: For FDI, *Survey of Current Business*, various issues. For domestic manufacturing, *Economic Report of the President*, 1989, table B-91 (1988 number is an average over the first three quarters).
a. Industry classification is not comparable to later years.

Conclusions

There is no question that multinationals' decision makers took notice of the Tax Reform Act of 1986. The extraordinary increase in the fourth quarter of 1986 of debt and equity flows as well as acquisitions was certainly due to the attempt to beat the January 1, 1987, expiration date of certain favorable tax provisions. A significant but unknown fraction of this extraordinary activity probably would otherwise have taken place in 1987 or 1988.

That TRA86 affected the timing of activity seems indisputable. But what of its permanent effect on FDI and its financing? This is, after all, a more interesting issue than the precise timing of investment. This is a more difficult question to answer because with less than three years of post-TRA86 data it is impossible to distinguish the tax explanation from other competing hypotheses. For example, the strength of inward FDI may be due to the decline in foreigners' rate of taxation relative to U.S. corporations, but it may also be the lagged response to the cheap dollar that, according to Froot and Stein (1989), enriches foreigners and thereby lowers their cost of raising capital. Moreover the theory does not offer a clear guide to expectations since the various provisions often have offsetting incentive effects.

The impact of TRA86 may be more transparent when the patterns of FDI are examined more closely. Since TRA86, the growth rate of outward FDI (actual and planned) into low-tax countries has greatly exceeded the growth rate of FDI into high-tax countries; this behavior is consistent with expectations. Furthermore the location of multinationals' debt finance has moved away from the United States to other countries, also as theory would predict. Observed trends in the rate of return to inward FDI are also consistent with tax incentives, although this is not clear in the case of outward FDI.

All of the analysis of this chapter has been conditioned on an assumption that foreign tax systems do not change in response to TRA86. As chapter 9 by Whalley makes clear, this may not be entirely true. The cross-border fungibility of taxable income was undoubtedly a prime motivation for Canada's reduction in the statutory corporate tax rate. Other countries have also moved toward a lower-rate, lower-allowance system. Such parallel changes, and the prospect of further parallel changes, would dampen the magnitude of the economic responses discussed here. In this case the lasting effect of TRA86 will be the induced change in the international system of taxation as much as changed patterns of cross-border flows of capital.

Although the evidence is often consistent with the changes in incentives due to TRA86, it does not establish that TRA86 has caused behavior to change. Less than three years of evidence cannot support such a claim. The preliminary evidence is, though, in line with other research documenting multinationals' responses to taxation, both with respect to financial behavior (Hines and Hubbard 1990) and real investment behavior (Slemrod, 1990).

Notes

I am grateful to Daniel Frisch, Timothy Goodspeed, Roger Gordon, David Hartman, Michael McIntyre, John Mutti, Robert J. Patrick, Jr., and Burton Smoliar for helpful comments on an earlier draft, to Jennifer Sumbler for able research assistance, and to Gregory Fouch and Richard McDermott for providing and interpreting critical data.

1. By statute, Canada and West Germany have a worldwide system of taxation. However, their tax treaties with the United States provide that repatriated dividends are generally subject to no further tax liability.

2. See Slemrod (1989) for a framework for measuring the effective tax rate on a foreign direct investment by a multinational firm.

3. The income of foreign branches of U.S. corporations is taxed as accrued. Partly for tax reasons, most foreign activity of U.S. corporations is carried out by subsidiaries rather than branches.

4. The depreciation rules used in the calculation of earnings and profits do, however, change. For example, since 1980 the depreciation rules that apply to property used overseas have been made less generous. These schedules have tax implications because, for any given amount of dividends remitted, they affect the calculation of tax deemed paid by subsidiaries to foreign governments and the amount of foreign tax credit available.

5. Since the passage of TRA86, many other countries have enacted tax reforms that share some of the corporate-rate-reducing, base-broadening aspects of TRA86. To the extent that TRA86 *caused* these reforms (or increased their likelihood), the host country's effective tax rate was influenced by the U.S. tax reform. The analysis that follows holds constant the foreign tax system.

6. The average tax rate paid to foreign governments is subject to a degree of control by the multinational through its repatriation policy. By repatriating income primarily from high-tax countries, the average tax rate on its foreign-source income is high and less likely to attract additional U.S. tax liability.

7. Hartman (1984) has argued that regardless of the excess credit status of the U.S. parent, the level of repatriation tax is irrelevant for the incentive to undertake FDI financed by earnings of the foreign subsidiary. This is because the repatriation tax reduces equally both the return to investment and the opportunity cost of investment (reduced dividends). This argument would not apply to the infusion of new equity capital from the parent. See Jun (1989) for a critique of this view.

8. Grubert and Mutti (1987) quote U.S. Treasury estimates that the fraction of manufacturing multinationals (weighted by worldwide income) in excess credit would increase from 20% to 69%. Goodspeed and Frisch (1989), using updated corporate tax return information, estimate that the fraction of foreign-source income subject to excess credits would rise from 50% to 78%, and from 32% to 82% in manufacturing. These calculations, however, consider only the change in statutory rate and do not consider changes in the allocation rules or the separate baskets, discussed later in this Chapter. In addition neither analysis considers changes, perhaps induced by the U.S. reform, in other countries' tax rates. Perhaps most important, the analyses do not take into account any behavioral response of the multinationals.

9. Of course Hartman's argument implies that for investment financed by retained earnings, only the host country's tax rate matters even for firms in an excess limitation position, so no post-TRA86 increased sensitivity to host country tax rates should be observed.

10. The one-taxpayer rule already effectively applied to the allocation of expenses on research and development.

11. This analysis presumes that the interest allocation rules of foreign governments have not changed.

12. This would happen if the parent loaned money to its affiliate, which in turn declared an equivalent dividend to its parent or returned equity capital to the parent. It would not appear this way if the change were effected by parallel transactions with a bank, such as a simultaneous bank loan to the affiliate and a repayment of principal by the parent company. Then no change in foreign direct investment would be indicated by the data.

13. Grubert and Mutti (1989a) discovered this phenomenon in a cross-sectional analysis, observing a highly significant negative relationship between the reported aftertax rate of profit for U.S. multinationals' subsidiaries and the host country's statutory corporate tax rate. This observation is consistent with the successful shifting of taxable income from high-tax countries to low-tax countries. By analogy, a reduction in the U.S. statutory rate relative to foreign rates would be associated with a decline in the rate of return on foreign-source income.

14. Note that the measure of FDI used in figure 6.2 is equal to net transfers of funds (debt and equity) from the parent to foreign affiliates plus earnings retained by the affiliates. Thus it is a financial flow rather than a real investment concept. For example, an investment of a foreign subsidiary that is financed by funds raised by the subsidiary from third parties would not be counted as FDI.

15. For affiliates other than those engaged in natural resource exploration and development, capital expenditures include all expenditures made to acquire, add to, or improve properties, plant, and equipment. For affiliates engaged in natural resource exploration and development, capital expenditures also include the full amount of exploration and development expenditures (whether capitalized or expensed). Capital expenditures are on a gross basis; sales and other dispositions of assets are not netted against them.

16. The difference in timing could be due to the accumulation of funds in 1987 in anticipation of capital expenditures to take beginning in 1988.

17. The United Kingdom is included in neither the low-tax nor high-tax group because, according to Crooks et al., its effective tax rate lies between the two groups and because the U.K. corporate tax system was undergoing rapid and fundamental changes over this period.

18. The relatively low U.S. statutory rate gives an incentive to have debt held by the foreign subsidiary (in a high-tax country) compared to the U.S. parent, as long as the foreign government allows the subsidiary's interest deductions. Such a shift need not be accomplished by increased parent-to-subsidiary lending but also by increased subsidiary borrowing from third parties. However, the interest allocation rules of TRA86 favored parent-to-subsidiary lending for firms in an excess credit position. This is because the interest receipts of the parent are considered foreign-source income. However, only a fraction of the parent's interest expenses would be deducted against foreign-source income, thus increasing net foreign-source income and the limit on the amount of foreign taxes that can be credited. This tax benefit in many cases more than offsets the withholding tax on interest paid by the subsidiary. The IRS has proposed a regulation that would eliminate the advantage of parent-to-subsidiary lending by requiring interest payments of the parent to be netted against interest received from subsidiaries before being subject to the allocation rules.

19. Note that these figures are all net of transactions with Netherlands Antilles affiliates.

20. The change looks even more striking if dividends are expressed as a fraction of earnings, including capital gains or losses, increasing from 41.5% in 1987 to 71.0% in 1988.
    To some extent tax-induced changes in the timing of dividend repatriations may not be reflected in the data. For example, subpart F rules treat certain kinds of income of subsidiaries as if they were remitted dividends, even if no dividends are actually paid (and therefore no withholding taxes are due to the foreign government).

21. The increase in United Kingdom activity would appear even larger if the measure of FDI was the change in a country's FDI position, which differs from capital inflows by including valuation adjustments that arise, for example, due to the transfer in ownership of a FDI from one owner to another. In 1988 a large holding in Shell Oil was transferred from a Dutch holding company to the British parent.

22. The impact of the U.S. tax system on investment from the United Kingdom is especially difficult to sort out because during this period there were major changes in the structure of U.K. corporate taxes. In the 1984 budget the corporate rate was reduced from 52% to 35% by 1987, and generous depreciation allowances were also phased out.

References

Ault, Hugh J., and David Bradford, 1990. Taxing International Income: An Analysis of the U.S. System and its Economic Premises. In Assaf Razin and Joel Slemrod (eds.), *Taxation in the Global Economy*. Chicago: University of Chicago Press.

Crooks, Ed, Michael Devereux, Mark Pearson, and Charles Wooley. 1989. Transnational Tax Rates and Incentives to Invest. Manuscript. Institute for Fiscal Studies. London. March.

Froot, Kenneth A., and Jeremy C. Stein. 1989. Exchange Rates and Foreign Direct Investment: An Imperfect Capital Markets Approach. Manuscript. March.

Goodspeed, Timothy J., and Daniel J. Frisch. 1989. U.S. Tax Policy and the Overseas Activities of U.S. Multinational Corporations: A Quantitative Assessment. Manuscript. July.

Graham, Edward M., and Paul R. Krugman. 1989. Foreign Direct Investment in the United States. Monograph. Institute for International Economics. Washington, DC. April.

Grubert, Harry, and John Mutti. 1987. The Impact of the Tax Reform Act of 1986 on Trade and Capital Flows. In *Compendium of Tax Research 1987*. Washington, DC: Office of Tax Analysis, Department of the Treasury.

Grubert, Harry, and John Mutti. 1989a. Taxes, Tariffs and Transfer Pricing in Multinational Corporation Decision Making. Manuscript. March.

Grubert, Harry, and John Mutti. 1989b. Financial Flows Versus Capital Spending: Alternative Measures of U.S.-Canadian Investment and Trade in the Analysis of Taxes. Manuscript. Presented at NBER Summer Institute. Cambridge, MA. August.

Hartman, David E. 1985. Tax Policy and Foreign Direct Investment. *Journal of Public Economics* 26: 107–121.

Hines, James R., Jr., and R. Glenn Hubbard. 1990. Coming Home to America: Dividend Repatriations by U.S. Multinationals. In Assaf Razin and Joel Slemrod, (eds.), *Taxation in the Global Economy*. Chicago: University of Chicago Press.

Jun, Joosung. 1989. What is the Marginal Source of Funds for Foreign Investment? NBER Working Paper No. 3064. August.

McIntyre, Michael J. 1989. The International Income Tax Rules of the United States. Stoneham, MA: Butterworth Legal Publishers. 1989.

Mutti, John, and Harry Grubert. 1988. U.S. Taxes and Trade Performance. *National Tax Journal* 41: 317–325.

Scholes, Myron, and Mark A. Wolfson. 1989. The Effect of Changes in Tax Laws on Corporate Reorganization Activity. Manuscript. Stanford Business School. April.

Sinn, Hans-Werner. 1988. U.S. Tax Reform 1981 and 1986: Impact on International Capital Markets and Capital Flows. *National Tax Journal* 41: 327–340.

Slemrod, Joel. 1989. A Framework for Measuring the Effective Tax Rate on Foreign Direct Investment. Manuscript. University of Michigan. August.

Slemrod, Joel. 1990. Tax Effects on Foreign Direct Investment in the United States: Evidence from a Cross-Country Comparison. In Assaf Razin and Joel Slemrod (eds.), *Taxation in the Global Economy*. Chicago: University of Chicago Press.

COMMENTS

Kenneth A. Froot

Slemrod's chapter provides a very useful overview of the link between FDI and the Tax Reform Act of 1986 (TRA86). One purpose of the chapter is to explain in simple terms the implications of the TRA86 for direct investment by foreigners in the United States and for direct investment abroad by U.S. entities. The chapter is excellent on this score. It also shows that U.S. FDI inflows and outflows do show signs of being affected by these tax changes. I have little quibble with Joel's conclusion that the TRA86 seems to have affected certain measures of FDI flows in the expected direction.

I want to spend a moment here on a kind of pretext to the chapter in order to clarify the nature of FDI and the kind of questions we might expect to answer by looking at the data. The first issue concerns what FDI actually is. Its name suggests that it involves international flows of capital as well as proper investment expenditures. But it actually involves neither: FDI is fundamentally about the extension of corporate control across national boundaries. When Ford takes control over the British firm Jaguar, plc, capital need not flow from Ford to or into the United Kingdom at all. That is, the purchase can be entirely financed within the United Kingdom by lenders other than Ford. In such a case there is merely a change across boundaries in the title of assets, but no investment expenditures (as would be measured in the national income accounts) takes place. Thus FDI is the right place to look if we are interested in such questions as, 'How did the TRA86 effect the equilibrium share of the U.S. capital stock controlled by foreigners, or the share of the foreign capital stock controlled by U.S. entities?'

Unfortunately, it is not possible to measure "control" directly. Instead, the most commonly used number for FDI comes from the balance of payments accounts, and it measures the funds committed by a parent (in the form of debt or equity) to finance an acquisition or expansion of productive facilities located abroad. In practice we might expect this to be a good measure of control. However, that will not always be the case. Recall that in a Modigliani-Miller world the composition of financing does not matter. In such a world FDI flows as measured by the balance of payments are simply undefined and may be completely unrelated to actual changes in control. Thus the data we have are more appropriate for answering the question, How did the TRA86 effect net commitments by parents to their foreign affiliates?

The ambiguity in the reasons behind international flows of direct investment means that the balance of payments numbers are likely to confound
the effects of changes in corporate taxation: Changes in the equilibrium
share of foreign control and changes in the incentives for parents as
opposed to other lenders to provide financing for the expansion or creation
of affiliates are likely to be mixed together. If taxes are one reason that
Modigliani-Miller fails in practice, then surely the balance-of-payments
numbers will be very imperfect measures of changes in control. It is important to keep this issue in mind as we look for measured effects in the data
of specific tax changes.

The second background issue concerns how substitutable ownership of
capital is. Does a given domestic corporation view acquisitions of physical
capital within the U.S. as a close substitute for acquisitions of capital
abroad? Increasingly, the representative FDI transaction suggests the answer is no. There is clearly no close substitute in Japan for recent acquisitions in New York such as Columbia Pictures or Rockefeller Center, or for
stakes in those U.S. firms that advise on mergers and acquisitions (e.g.,
Wasserstein-Perella, The Blackstone Group, and Lodestar). If spacial sub-
stitutability is low, then changes in the U.S. tax code that affect domestic
corporations' returns on domestic investment may have only a small impact on the incentive for FDI.

Yet who takes control of a given corporation being sold may be highly
substitutable. If tax changes have a differential effect on foreign rather than
domestic reservation prices for acquiring firms, then we might expect a
significant effect on FDI. In the case of FDI inflows into the United States,
Slemrod argues compellingly that this is going on: The less favorable treatment of corporate acquisitions imposed by the TRA86 falls more on U.S.
bidders than on foreign bidders (whose overall tax bills are less sensitive
to changes in U.S. taxation). Thus we would expect to see an increase in
FDI inflows into the United States following such a tax change.

Lastly, I want to reinforce Slemrod's conclusion that the data do not
necessarily support the view that tax changes had a *large* effect on U.S. FDI
inflows and outflows. Notice that figures 6.1 through 6.6 are within measurement error of being the same curve: increasing in the late 1970s, falling
in the early 1980s, and then rising to new heights thereafter. This naturally
suggests that a single force is at work. Several alternatives do come to
mind. First, there was a severe and synchronized worldwide recession that
roughly coincides with the turndown in FDI flows. Second, world real
interest rates fell, rose, and fell with the same turning points as the FDI
flows. Other arguments commonly given for the recent surge in U.S. FDI

inflows include the fear by foreign corporations of imminent trade protection in the United States and the low value of the U.S. dollar. All of these macroeconomic features are consistent with the data and could easily generate the kind of large changes that characterize them.

GENERAL DISCUSSION

James Poterba discussed work currently being undertaken at MIT by Deborah Swensen, which concludes that inward foreign direct investment has gone up most dramatically in those industries that have seen the greatest increase in tax burdens. This relationship is clearer when simple average tax rates, as compared to effective tax rates, are used to measure tax burdens.

Roger Gordon presented a clientele effect story that is consistent with the observed increases in inward foreign direct investment. In 1986 investors in the United States saw the disappearance of favorable treatment for capital gains together with a reduction of tax rates. In previous years equity had been held by high-tax U.S. investors, but in the post-1986 environment equity became relatively more attractive to foreigners. We would expect to have seen therefore a shift away from U.S. equity held by U.S. investors and increased ownership of U.S. firms by foreign investors.

Jack Mutti questioned how well greater inward investment can be explained by tax factors, since this rationale is most persuasive when parent firms report high U.S. profits and have an excess of foreign tax credits. Yet U.S. subsidiaries of Japanese firms report very low rates of profitability. Mutti also cautioned that in his own work with Harry Grubert on investment in Canada by U.S. firms, the regression results concerning the effect of exchange rates and cyclical variables varied significantly with the choice of dependent variable representing investment (i.e., financial flow or capital spending).

Disappointed with what she saw as an inadequate discussion of fundamentals, particularly with regard to risk and return, Ann Dryden Witte observed that investors spread their investments across countries in order to diversify their portfolios and thus reduce risk. Foreign investors, for instance, may see low political risks in the United States, making the United States an attractive target for investment.

Although compliance with the tax law covering foreign activity has improved dramatically, Fritz Scheuren recognized the need for the United States to join into partnerships with foreign governments to further improve compliance. The feeling is widespread that some large multinational corporations have simply "outgunned" the IRS. He then went on to indicate that considerable efforts are now underway to reverse this.

Gilbert Harter suggested that increased investment abroad by Japan may be the result of high savings there—the Japanese are generating more savings than they can use domestically.

Finally, Richard Musgrave encouraged researchers to consider the implications of climbing corporate tax rates on the withholding rates that will appear in future tax treaties.

7

The Impact of Tax Reform on Charitable Giving: A 1989 Perspective

Charles T. Clotfelter

In 1988 individuals in the United States contributed an estimated $87 billion to tax-exempt nonprofit organizations, including churches, community chests, museums, and colleges. This amount was more than seven times the total given by corporations and through bequests. Although not a large number in relation to total tax revenues, charitable contributions loom large for the nonprofit sector, which has come to depend on such giving as a major source of revenue. As debate over tax reform intensified during the 1980s, influential spokespersons for nonprofit organizations came to view such reform as a serious threat to that source of revenue, a view that was bolstered by economic models of charitable giving. Finding it uncomfortable to oppose tax reform itself, the nonprofits nevertheless fought to maintain tax incentives for giving, with the result that the treatment of charitable contributions provided some of the gloomiest predictions and most heated debate among the provisions involved in tax reform during the 1980s. There were many doubters who thought the sector's jeremiads amounted to little more than crying wolf.

The purpose of this chapter is to examine the predicted effects of tax reform in the 1980s on charitable contributions by individuals and to compare them to the actual and apparent effects, viewed from the perspective of 1989. Section 7.1 presents a description of the issues and tax provisions relevant to charitable contributions. Section 7.2 focuses on specific characteristics of the models used to predict the effects of tax reform on contributions and asks whether the predictions were in fact warranted by the models and indeed how one would test the models. Section 7.3 describes several approaches that can be used to assess the models and data that can be employed for that purpose, and the section 7.4 compares predicted with actual changes in contributions during the 1980s. Section 7.5 draws conclusions from the analysis.

7.1   The Tax Treatment of Charitable Contributions

The federal tax code accords special treatment to most nonprofit organizations, including exemption from corporate income taxation. For a large
subset of nonprofit organizations, it also allows individuals (as well as
corporations and estates) a tax deduction for the donations they make to
these organizations. The charitable deduction in the income tax, by virtue
of the preponderant importance of donations by individuals, is the most
important of these deductions. Applying only to taxpayers who itemize
their deductions, it is certainly one of the oldest personal deductions in
the tax code, having existed almost as long as the income tax itself. An
important effect of this provision is to lower an individual's net cost of
making gifts. For example, a taxpayer subject to a marginal tax rate of 30%
who is able to deduct a contribution of $100 will enjoy a tax reduction of
$30, thus reducing the aftertax net cost of the contribution to $70. The
taxpayer can be thought of as receiving a discount on the price of making
gifts; the deduction reduces the net cost of donating a dollar to 70 cents.
State income tax deductions reduce this net cost further, though data on
state tax rates are typically not available and thus are usually ignored in
statistical analyses.

There is an additional benefit of making contributions in the form of
appreciated property such as stock, real estate, and objects of art. Donors
of such gifts not only receive the tax deduction for the asset's current
market value, typically they also avoid paying tax on the capital gains that
would otherwise have been associated with the sale of the asset. For
example, if the gift described above had not been cash, but rather $100 of
stock that had originally been purchased for $50, the tax code's forgiveness
of the tax on the capital gain of $50 would further reduce the net cost of
giving if the stock would otherwise have been sold. If the capital gains tax
were 20%, for example, the taxpayer would save an additional $10 that
would otherwise have been due had the stock been sold, reducing the net
cost of the gift to $60, or 60 cents per dollar. As above, these calculations
generally apply only to taxpayers who itemize their deductions.

As a result of this tax treatment, the net cost of contributions comes to
depend crucially on two factors: first, tax rates and, second, how widespread the deductibility of gifts is. In general the latter equates to the
proportion of taxpayers who itemize their deductions, which depends in
turn on the size of the standard deduction and the number and size of other
itemized deductions.

Tax Reform in the 1980s

Each of the two major tax bills of the 1980s contained provisions that affected taxpayers' net cost of making contributions, and the most important of these are summarized in table 7.1. The 1981 act (the Economic Recovery Tax Act of 1981) modified the tax rate schedule by cutting the top marginal tax rate, from 70% to 50% and reducing other tax rates proportionally. At the same time the act failed to adjust the tax tables for inflation, thus allowing taxpayers to slide into higher tax brackets and largely nullifying the cut in rates for most people. The cut in the top rate of course meant an increase in the net cost of giving for those with high incomes. Working in the other direction was the likely increase in the number of itemizers that would result from a fixed standard deduction during a period of inflation. Surely the most obvious provision likely to affect contributions was a new charitable deduction for nonitemizers that was to be gradually phased in between 1982 and 1986. However, only in 1985 and 1986, when the very low dollar limits on this deduction were removed, was it likely to have an important effect on contributions.

The 1986 act (the Tax Reform Act of 1986) likewise contained several important changes having implications for charitable contributions. First, it continued the work of the 1981 act in cutting the top tax rate. The highest marginal tax rate was reduced to 33% for 1988, and taxpayers in the highest income brackets faced a rate of only 28%. Tax rates were not cut for all taxpayers, however. Hausman and Poterba (1987) estimate that only

Table 7.1
Major tax changes in the 1980s affecting individual contributions

Economic Recovery Tax Act of 1981	Tax Reform Act of 1986
Rate reductions scheduled	**Change in tax rate schedule**
1982: top rate reduced from 70% to 50%; other rates cut 10%	1987: top rate reduced from 50% to 38.5%; most rates cut
1983: lower rates cut 10%	1988: top rate reduced to 33%, 28% in highest class
1984: lower rates cut 5%	
Charitable deduction for nonitemizers phase-in scheduled	**Standard deduction increased**
	Charitable deduction for nonitemizers dropped
1982: 25% of first $100	
1984: 25% of first $300	**Capital gains in gifts of appreciated property included in alternative minimum tax**
1985: 50% with no dollar limit	
1986: full deduction	

59% of taxpayers saw their marginal tax rates decrease as a result of the new law. Second, the nonitemizer deduction was eliminated from the code after being fully in place for one year. Third, the number of taxpayers who would itemize their deductions would be reduced markedly due to increases in the standard deduction amounts, the elimination of the sales tax deduction, and the curtailment of the personal interest and miscellaneous deductions. The net effect of these three changes was to increase the net price of giving for virtually all taxpayers either by removing deductibility of gifts or reducing the value of the deduction for those who continued to itemize. A fourth important change related to charitable giving was made in the alternative minimum tax (AMT), a provision applying only to a comparatively small number of very wealthy taxpayers. To the existing list of "tax preference" items in the tax base of the AMT was included the heretofore untaxed appreciation of donated capital assets.[1] As discussed below, the effect of this provision was to diminish the attractiveness of giving away assets whose basis was small in relation to market value. A fifth and less important provision affecting contributions was the taxation of capital gains at regular rates. For taxpayers not subject to the AMT, this provision would in fact increase the relative desirability of giving away appreciated property since the forgone capital gains tax had increased. The 1986 act contained a number of other provisions affecting certain kinds of donations or nonprofit organizations more generally, but these provisions are of lesser importance for individual contributions in the aggregate.[2]

Two ready measures of the impact of the two tax acts on the net cost of making contributions are shown in table 7.2. The table shows that the proportion of taxpayers who itemized their returns increased steadily over the period in which the standard deduction was not adjusted for inflation. From 31%, the share of itemizers rose to 40% before being cut back to 30% by the large jump in the standard deduction contained in the 1986 act. The last column in the table chronicles the decline in the tax code's highest rate bracket. For a taxpayer subject to that rate, the cost of making cash donations more than doubled, from 30 to 67 cents per dollar. For those subject to the 28% rate in 1986, it increased even more.

7.2   Assessing the Impact on Charitable Giving

Models of Charitable Giving

In the decade between 1975 and 1985 there appeared at least a score of empirical studies of charitable giving based on a common basic economic

Table 7.2
Itemization status and maximum income tax rates, 1980–88

	Percentage of taxpayers with itemized deductions	Highest marginal tax rate
1980	31	70
1981	33	70
1982	35	50
1983	37	50
1984	38	50
1985	39	50
1986	40	50
1987	33	38
1988	30	33

Source: Internal Revenue Service, *Statistics of Income; SOI Bulletin* 8 (Spring 1989); *Taxpayer Usage Study*, Monthly Report, May 1989.

model of giving. As developed by Feldstein (1975) and modified in subsequent studies, this basic model takes charitable contributions to be a function of aftertax net income Y, the tax-defined price of contributions P, and other factors thought to affect charitable behavior X. Typically this relationship has been estimated using a log-linear specification:

$$\ln G = d + a \ln Y + b \ln P + cX + e, \tag{1}$$

where G is defined as contributions plus \$1 or \$10,[3] d, a, and b are parameters, c is a vector of parameters, and e is an error term. Price is defined as the dollar amount of consumption forgone per dollar of contributions. For donors who receive no tax deduction for their gifts—nonitemizers in most cases and all those owing no tax—this price is simply \$1. For an itemizer with a marginal tax rate of m, the price of making ordinary cash contributions is $1 - m$, since each dollar's worth of giving causes the person's tax liability to be reduced by \$m.

The model implies that taxes affect contributions in two ways: through net income and through the price of giving. Thus almost any change in the tax rate schedule or in the number of taxpapers who itemize their deductions will tend to have an impact on giving. It is straightforward to use such models to simulate the effects of tax changes on charitable giving. For example, if nontax factors remain the same, the simple model in equation (1) implies that contributions will change only as a function of changes in the tax-defined variables. Where $\hat{a}$ and $\hat{b}$ are, respectively, the estimated income and price elasticities, the predicted level of contributions in the second period is

$$G_1^+ = G_0 \left(\frac{Y_1}{Y_0} \right)^{\hat{a}} \left(\frac{P_1}{P_0} \right)^{\hat{b}}. \tag{2}$$

A similar approach can be taken with more complicated specifications. But whatever the exact specification, it is useful to emphasize what an approach of this sort implies about charitable behavior. It is not predicated on the assumption that taxes are the only or the major determinant of charitable giving but only that they are one influence. If the basic equation is correctly specified and estimated and if nontax factors are indeed unchanging, an equation such as (2) can be used to predict the effects of tax changes. It is important, however, to consider several issues that complicate the use and interpretation of this simple model.

Estimated Elasticities
The simple model given in (1) implies constant elasticities of contributions with respect to both the tax-defined price of giving and net income. Typical estimates for the price elasticity are greater than one in absolute value, which implies that contributions would fall by more than 10% in response to an increase in the net price of giving of 10%. The income elasticity has most often been estimated to be positive but less than one. Here I use estimates presented in Clotfelter and Steuerle (1981) to be representative of the empirical studies on this subject: -1.27 for the price elasticity and 0.78 for the income elasticity. The literature on this subject is not unanimous regarding the size or the constancy of these important parameters, however. There is some evidence, for example, that the elasticities differ by income level, with low-income households being less responsive to changes in price than others. And there are a few studies that suggest that both price and income elasticities are quite a bit smaller in absolute value than the majority of studies indicate.[4] In order to reflect these alternative views of charitable giving behavior, I compare the predictive success of the simple constant elasticity model using the above parameters with a variable elasticity model estimated in Clotfelter and Steuerle (1981), a model that incorporates price and income elasticities of zero, and one that assumes an income elasticity of one.

Gifts of Appreciated Property
In the past it has usually been advantageous for donors to make gifts in the form of appreciated property, such as stock, real estate, and works of art,

as opposed to giving the same amount in cash because no tax would be assessed on the capital gain that would have arisen had the asset been sold. This additional benefit is added to the value of the charitable deduction itself to make the net cost of giving such assets even less than that for giving cash. Because gifts of appreciated property are an important part of contributions for some types of donee organizations and among wealthy taxpayers, it is important to consider what this tax treatment implies for the price of giving. Where g^* is an asset's gain-to-value ratio in the year it is given away, n is the tax rate on capital gains income, and R is a dichotomous variable that takes on the value of 1 if the asset would have been sold immediately if it were not contributed and 0 if the asset would not otherwise have been sold, the net cost of contributing the asset is

$$P = 1 - m - Rg^*n. \tag{3}$$

Note that in the case of an unappreciated asset such as cash, this expression reduces to the $1 - m$ used above.[5] As noted above, the 1986 tax act modified this traditional treatment for taxpayers subject to the alternative minimum tax (AMT). For these taxpayers inclusion of the appreciation portion of the gift as a tax preference placed a penalty on the gift exactly equal to the capital gains tax that would have been due had the asset been sold. For a taxpayer who would have otherwise sold the asset, this penalty was equivalent to reducing the gift's benefit to that of giving cash.[6]

It is important to give attention to gifts of appreciated property for two reasons. First, this tax treatment ought to be integrated into simulations of the impact of tax reform just as it has been integrated into empirical studies of the impact of tax policy on contributions. Accordingly, the calculations given below calculate the price variable as a weighted average of the prices of giving cash and appreciated property. Following earlier work, the calculations use weights based on the proportion of contributions made in the form of cash in the initial year of observation. The price of giving appreciated property is calculated assuming an asset with a gain-to-value ratio of 50% that would have been sold immediately ($Rg^* = 0.5$). A second reason for being attentive to gifts of appreciated property is their potential to reveal another facet of the economic model of giving. If the relative price of making cash and noncash gifts varies over time, the economic model of giving would suggest that the pattern of giving would also vary accordingly.

To see what kinds of implications the model would have for tax changes in the 1980s, it is useful to examine the calculated net price for two specific cases. Since the tax circumstances of the wealthy were affected most dramatically, I present cases applying to high-income taxpayers. Table 7.3

Table 7.3
Impact of tax changes on high-income couple's net cost of making gifts

| Year | Current value of $1,000,000 AGI in 1985 dollars | Marginal tax rate[a] | Net cost of giving a dollar of[b] | |
			Cash	Appreciated property
1980	770,683	70	0.30	0.20
1985	1,000,000	50	0.50	0.40
1988	1,070,144	28	0.72	0.58

a. For each gross income, taxable income was estimated by multiplying the ratio of taxable income to adjusted gross income (AGI) for the corresponding AGI class in that year by the gross income figure. Using that taxable income, marginal tax rates were taken from the tax table for joint returns.
b. Assuming the taxpayer is an itemizer, the price of giving cash is $1 - m$, where m is the marginal tax rate. In general, the price of giving assets is $P = 1 - m - Rg^*n$. For this table, this price is calculated on the assumption that the asset would have been sold immediately had it not been donated ($R = 1$) and that the gain-to-value ratio ($g = g^*$) is 0.5.

shows the price of giving in three years for a hypothetical couple whose real AGI remained at $1 million in 1985 dollars over the period. This couple's marginal tax rate would have been cut sharply as a result of tax reform during the 1980s: from 70% to 50% by the 1981 tax act and down to 28% by the 1986 act. The result would have been more than a doubling in the price of giving cash, from 30 to 72 cents per dollar. For the net cost of giving an asset that consisted of 50% capital gains, the price would almost have tripled. The second example is based on an actual case that has been cited more than once as an example of the 1986 act's supposed discouragement of gifts of art. Having inherited Vincent van Gogh's *Irises*, valued then at $1.8 million, John Whitney Payson decided to sell the painting in 1987 rather than giving it, as he had planned, to Westbrook College in Portland, Maine. The painting sold in November 1987 for a record $53.9 million. Table 7.4 summarizes the tax consequences of donating the painting under the previous tax law, the regular tax under the 1986 law, and under the AMT provisions of the 1986 law. As a result of the drop in tax rates, the net cost per dollar of donating the painting under the regular tax increased by almost half as a result of the 1986 act. But because Mr. Payson would probably have been subject to the AMT, the price rose even more than that, from 31 to 79 cents per dollar as compared to selling the painting immediately. Although extreme, this example suggests one implication of the economic model of giving—that large gifts in the form of appreciated property would be particularly discouraged relative to cash and relative to gifts made before the tax act.

Table 7.4
The economics of donating art: An extreme example (asset value = $53.9 million; basis = $1.8 million)

	Regular tax, 1986 law ($m = 0.50; n = 0.2$)	Regular tax, 1988 law ($m = n = 0.28$)	Alternative minimum tax ($m = n = 0.21$)
(a) Value of deduction ($1,000s)[a]	26,950	15,092	11,319
(b) Tax preference penalty ($1,000s)[b]	0	0	10,941
(c) Forgone capital gains tax ($1,000s)	10,420	14,588	10,941
(d) Tax savings compared to immediate sale: $a - b + c$ ($1,000s)	37,370	29,680	11,319
Net cost per dollar (a) if alternative disposition were:			
(e) Immediate sale: $R = 1$	0.31	0.45	0.79[b]
(f) Bequest: $R = 0$	0.50[b]	0.72[b]	0.99

a. One minus the tax savings ($a - b + c$) for (e) and ($a - b$) for (f) as a percentage of $53.9 million.
b. Same as giving cash.

Dynamic Elements

The simple model in equation (1) takes no explicit account of time. Yet it seems reasonable that individual charitable behavior is unlikely to change overnight in response to changes in tax law. One model of charitable giving views equations such as (1) as a representation of the long-run or desired level of contributions. Individuals may not adjust right away to changes in this desired level, however, due to such factors as habit or established levels of solicitation that may be based on previous levels of giving. Applying an incomplete adjustment model to charitable giving behavior yields a model such as

$$\frac{G_1}{G_0} = \left(\frac{G^*}{G_0}\right)^h, \tag{4}$$

where G^* is the desired level of contributions and h is a coefficient of adjustment. A value of h close to 1 would imply that individuals adjust completely during a time period to changes in the desired level of contributions; values closer to 0 would imply a slower response. For the calculations made in this chapter, a value for h for a one-year period of 0.37 is used, based on an estimate given in Clotfelter (1980, 333). This value implies coefficients of adjustment of 0.60 for two years and 0.84 for four.[7]

The Nonprofits' Fear of Tax Reform

Although many of the details of the economic model of charitable giving were not widely understood, the essence of the price responsiveness argument did find its way into the debate over tax reform. Lobbyists for nonprofit organizations cited econometric models in warning of possibly harmful consequences of tax changes, while proponents of tax reform raised questions about the models being used. That such a seemingly esoteric piece of economic reasoning would become part of policy debate may seem surprising, but there were several factors that worked in its favor. Among these were the amount of attention that had been paid to tax effects on giving by the prestigious Filer Commission in the 1970s, the prominence of the economist (Martin Feldstein) who undertook econometric work under the commission's sponsorship, the relatively large number of confirmatory studies that followed the first work, and the easily overlooked fact that the conclusions of the economic studies generally resonated with the everyday experience of many people. The models served to lend specificity to the vague worries of nonprofit organizations about how tax reform might affect them.

Among the features of tax reform plans that were discussed during the 1980s, there were two that most worried leaders of nonprofit organizations. First, any drop in the number of taxpayers who received a charitable deduction was, understandably, seen as a threat to contributions. Not only was the nonitemizer deduction subject to a sunset provision after 1986, but many of the tax reform plans discussed, including the eventual 1986 act, would have reduced the number of taxpayers who itemized their deductions. The second source of concern was a feature common to all of the tax reform plans—rate reduction. Although few were prepared to speak out against rate reduction,[8] it was not hard to believe that the tax incentive for giving a gift under a 28% marginal tax rate, for example, would be a lot less than what existed under the previous 50% rate. In terms of the economic model of giving, both tax rate reduction and restrictions on the deductibility of gifts would raise the net cost of making gifts, but one did not have to be an economist to guess that the outcome would be unfavorable for nonprofit institutions. In addition to these two aspects of tax reform, a third challenge to the nonprofits arose at the eleventh hour of the debate over the 1986 act in the form of an attack on the tax-free status of capital gains in gifts of appreciated property.

Representatives of the nonprofit sector were quick to respond to major tax reform proposals, using economic models of giving to provide specific estimates of likely impacts. In response to the Treasury's first tax reform plan in 1985, Independent Sector, an umbrella group representing non-profit organizations, criticized that plan's elimination of the nonitemizer deduction and its introduction of a floor for itemized charitable donations, saying that contributions would drop by 20% if the plan were enacted.[9] Likewise spokespersons for the nonprofit sector criticized President Reagan's May 1985 tax proposal, which also eliminated the nonitemizer deduction. They publicized estimates that the proposal would cause contributions from individuals to drop by $10 billion.[10] When the details of the tax act itself were finalized in the summer of 1986, the story was much the same. Nonprofit representatives quoted research suggesting that the number of itemizers would decline as a percentage of all taxpayers from 38% to 20% under the new law.[11] Given certain caveats, models implied that contributions under the new law would be on the order of 14% to 16% lower than under the previous law.[12] Because of its special provisions affecting colleges and universities and gifts of appreciated property, those who spoke for arts and educational institutions were especially concerned about the bill's negative impact.[13]

7.3   A Closer Look at the Models

Before considering in detail the predicted and apparent effects of tax reform on charitable giving, it is useful to take a closer look at the economic model and some of its implications.

Using the Economic Model: Simulations, Limitations and Caveats

When a simplified model is applied to real-world policy analysis, caveats are usually in order, and this is certainly the case with models of charitable giving. Since behavioral equations such as (1) do not even purport to capture all of the factors that influence donative behavior, the analyst is well-advised to be careful in applying estimated parameters in simulating the likely effects of policy changes and modest in describing the validity of projections. Such care and modesty seldom come naturally, however, and they are furthermore counteracted by the frequent urge on the part of journalists, policymakers, and lobbyists to simplify and dramatize. In considering the policy applications of the economic model of contributions, it is useful to review the justification for using estimated models to assess likely policy outcomes.

As has been common practice in a number of applied topics in tax analysis, estimated models such as (1) have been used to simulate the likely effect of various planned or contemplated modifications in tax policy, in this case by translating such modifications into changes in the price and net income terms and using an estimated equation such as (2). What can such an exercise tell us? At most it can yield predicted levels of contributions for a hypothetical and most likely counterfactual situation, one in which none of the other factors contained in the vector X changes. Needless to say, simulations such as these are rarely described this way in newspaper stories. Because of their counterfactual nature, such projections tend to be inherently immune from factual verification: It is always impossible to eliminate the possibility that "other factors" have changed at the same time that tax policy has changed, thus confounding any pure tax policy effect. Although this may come as a relief to those who produce such projections, it is cold comfort to analysts and policymakers who are concerned about the actual impact of actual policies. Fortunately it is possible to devise indirect tests of the validity of such simulation models by examining various implications of the model under some reasonable assumptions. Several tests of this sort are discussed in the next subsection.

Besides their basic counterfactual nature, simulations based on a model such as (1) are subject to a variety of errors, and a policy of full-disclosure requires that these be aired as well. These may include statistical error emanating from the imprecise nature of all econometric estimates, errors associated with predicting such underlying variables as real income or the proportion of taxpayers who will itemize under different tax rules, and errors arising from ignorance of the characteristics of appreciated property that are contributed.[14]

There are two points on which the simulations are especially vulnerable: changes in other factors not reflected in estimated equations and dynamic aspects of giving behavior. "Other" factors motivating giving include personal beliefs and affiliations, aspects on which economists are by no means expert. Survey data on charitable behavior show, for example, that the best predictor of contributions are attendance at religious services and involvement in civic and other organizations.[15] To complicate matters further, it appears that issues within religious and other organizations may have a shifting effect on giving patterns over time. Contributions among Catholics, for example, have been found to be influenced by controversy between liberals and conservatives within the church over issues of faith.[16] More generally, donations to both religious and secular organizations appear to be highly sensitive to perceived social needs and capable of responding quickly to crises, such as the African famine and the problem of homelessness in the late 1980s.[17] Another entire category of outside influence on contributions is solicitation by charitable organizations themselves, and these efforts give every evidence of being responsive to changes in the giving environment, including changes in tax law. For example, Dartmouth and other universities have sent replicas of stock certificates to alumni as part of a reminder of the tax advantages of making gifts of appreciated stock. Charitable and educational institutions of all kinds have increasingly turned to "direct marketing" advisors to design solicitation campaigns.[18] Factors such as these are clearly outside of the realm of tax policy and are moreover difficult to measure, not to mention that their effects on giving have not been estimated. That they change over time seems quite probable; that some actually respond to changes in tax policy is likely. Thus the ceteris paribus assumption presents a significant complication in the use of simulations.

The second complication relates to dynamic elements in contributions behavior. Virtually all simulations of the effect of tax policy on charitable giving have used as their basic behavioral equation one that refers to long-run or desired levels of giving. Although such behavior is arguably the most important form of the response to tax policy, focusing on the long run has the drawback of ignoring two potentially important kinds of behavior. First, as noted in section 7.2, individual giving behavior probably does not respond immediately to changes in the desired level of giving. Second, since individuals usually have considerable latitude regarding when they make gifts, they may time their donations so as to minimize their total tax liability. This kind of timing might show itself, for example, in making donations early so as to have them counted for a tax year when the taxpayer faces a comparative high tax rate rather than the low tax rate anticipated for the following year. One might also imagine that a floor on the deductibility of contributions might inspire taxpayers to bunch their gifts, say, in alternating years so that a higher portion of their donations would be deductible.[19]

Some Implications Regarding Tax Reform

As noted above, it is impossible to perform a definitive test of the economic model's predictions, owing to the exclusion of other factors that affect contributions. Not only is it difficult to predict changes in these factors, they are for the most part not even measured. However, under a plausible assumption regarding these influences, the model does suggest several hypotheses concerning the effect of tax reform during the 1980s. One simple hypothesis suggested by the notion of price responsiveness in the model is that taxpayers would tend to accelerate their giving when a decline in the tax incentive is announced for the following year. For taxpayers facing declines in marginal tax rates between 1986 and 1987, for example, one would expect to observe a surge of contributions in 1986 as people try to take advantage of the high tax rates. Since there are few estimates relevant to such timing behavior, however, it is impossible to judge the size of this effect.

A second set of hypotheses is more useful in assessing the estimated parameters of the model. If one assumes that other factors have a uniform effect on all donations, unrelated to changes in tax variables, one can compare patterns of variation in contributions to patterns of variation in tax parameters and ask whether these patterns are consistent with the model's predictions. As an illustration, there is little to be learned from observing that an individual's contributions rose by 5% over a period in which income rose by 4% and price fell by 10%, for the simple reason that other factors may have changed as well over this period. If it is assumed, however, that all individuals were affected similarly by other influences and would have experienced the same percentage increase in giving in the absence of tax changes, one can sensibly compare *differences* in the changes in tax variables and in giving. One can then determine, for example, whether individuals with the biggest price increases also had the smallest increases in giving, as the model would predict. Specifically, one might expect to see evidence useful for judging the model by looking for three kinds of effects.

1. In comparing changes in contributions over time, the model would predict bigger declines (or smaller increases) in income classes in which the price of giving had increased the most. In order to examine this implication, the next section presents an examination of data on average income, price and contributions by income class over time. Since the 1986 tax act (and the 1981 act as well) cut tax rates the most at upper income levels, the model would predict that contributions by the wealthy would decline relative to contributions at middle and lower income levels, holding constant changes in income. But changes in aftertax income would also be predicted to affect giving. Both effects can be incorporated into the model to yield predicted changes in giving, and the pattern of predicted changes can be compared to the pattern of actual changes.

2. In the aggregate, changes by income class such as these would add up to a redistribution of contributions between the wealthy and the rest of the taxpaying public. If the income distribution did not change, the implication of these changes is that the share of total giving by the rich would decline. If the income distribution did change, one would still expect that contributions by the rich, relative to their income, would decline as a result of tax reform. A corollary effect would be that organizations traditionally supported by the wealthy, such as cultural and educational institutions, would suffer in comparison to those institutions traditionally favored by the middle and lower income groups, particularly religious organizations. These implications assume, again, that other factors affecting contributions had a similar influence at all income levels and that shifts in the distribution of income did not offset the pattern of changes in tax incentives.

3. A third implication of the model applies to one specific provision, the charitable deduction for nonitemizers. Between 1985 and 1986 that provision changed dramatically, increasing from a 50% deduction to a full deduction. For a nonitemizer facing marginal tax rate m, this change would have caused the net price of giving to fall from $(1 - 0.5m)$ to $(1 - m)$, implying an increase in contributions.

7.4   Evidence on the Impact of Tax Reform on Contributions

There is no reliable measure of total charitable contributions by individuals. Tax returns normally contain information for itemizers only, and estimates based on the receipts of nonprofit organizations is approximate at best, largely because there is no good information on giving to religious organizations. This data limitation plus the conceptual difficulties regarding non-tax effects discussed above make it impossible to devise definitive tests of the efficacy of economic models of contributions. However, one can gain insight from looking at the aftermath of the tax reform acts of 1981 and 1986. The current section examines, first, information from recipient organizations and, second, data from tax returns.

Evidence from Donees on Contributions

Probably the most consistent message contained in articles reporting trends in charitable giving in recent years is that, despite charities' fears regarding the effects of tax reform, contributions have continued to increase year after year. The widely quoted *Giving USA* has reported increases in aggregate donations each year for the past 37 years, with the total rising from $80 billion in 1985 to $98 billion in 1987 to $104 billion in 1988, increases well above the rate of inflation. (Unfortunately, the largest component of these figures, an estimate of the giving of individuals, is based largely on personal income and incorporates no direct evidence on charitable giving until several years after the fact.)[20] Corroborating the figures for the most recent years, articles on individual charities suggest that most had increases in contributions between 1986 and 1987 and between 1987 and 1988. For example, a group of 27 Protestant denominations, representing some 30% of U.S. church membership, reported a 3% increase in gifts between 1986 and 1987, the first year following the 1986 tax reform. Similarly an informal survey of charities the next year showed that most had modest increases.[21] One bellwether, the United Way, reported a 6.6% increase in giving from 1986 to 1987 and a 6.9% increase from 1987 to 1988.[22]

Such increases were not universal, however. Two groups of institutions that have traditionally relied on gifts from the wealthy, especially in the form of appreciated property, are museums and institutions of higher education. In both cases the 1986 act did appear to have its predicted impact on appreciated property gifts, although the overall effect of tax reform on them is still uncertain. For these donees the economic model would imply two things: a surge in contributions in 1986 relative to 1987,

Table 7.5
Contributions to universities and colleges, 1985–88 ($ millions)

	Average dollar amount of donations from individuals	
	Total	Appreciated property
16 private universities		
1985	16.9	4.8
1986	22.4	7.9
1987	22.9	5.3
1988	19.0	3.7
23 private four-year colleges		
1985	1.49	0.30
1986	1.72	0.62
1987	2.36	0.50
1988	1.92	0.40

Source: National Association of Independent Colleges and Universities, unpublished data, April 30, 1989, cited with permission.

with a further decline in 1988, owing to the decline in rates; and a larger drop-off in gifts of appreciated property after 1986, owing to the more stringent treatment of such gifts in the AMT. Tables 7.5 and 7.6 present some information for both types of institutions for years immediately before and after the 1986 act. In the case of colleges and universities, the findings on total contributions from individuals are mixed, as shown in table 7.5. Between 1986 and 1987 contributions to 16 private universities changed very little in real terms, while gifts to 23 colleges increased. In both cases total contributions at least kept up with inflation over the four-year period despite the decline in marginal tax rates. Gifts of appreciated assets to these educational institutions are a different story, however, with both groups showing large jumps in 1986 followed by declines in the following years. These declines are consistent with the economic model, of course, but they could equally well be explained by the October 1987 stock market crash. Perhaps a purer test of the effect of the 1986 provisions on gifts of appreciated property is provided by the experience of art museums, shown in table 7.6. For a group of 119 such museums, donations of artwork surged dramatically in 1986 and then fell to a level in 1988 below that achieved in 1985, a result that is consistent with the act's having a permanent effect on such contributions.

Data from Tax Returns

A tried and true source of data for examining charitable giving is tax returns: All itemized returns contain the dollar amount of reported contributions. The tax return data show, for example, that total contributions by itemizers rose from $48.0 billion in 1985 to $54.5 billion in 1986 and then fell to $49.3 billion in 1987 (U.S. Internal Revenue Service, various

Table 7.6
Contributions to 19 art museums, 1985–88

Fiscal year	Value of art donated ($ millions)	Number of artworks donated
1985	$76.1	28,305
1986	143.0	43,670
1987	94.6	20,900
1988	67.2	17,035

Source: Association of Art Museum Directors, *1989 Statistical Survey* (New York: AAMD, 1989, p. 190).

years). However, this slight 3% increase in contributions between 1985 and 1987 (a decline of 3% in real terms) was accompanied by an 11% decrease in the number of itemizers. Shifts in the itemizing population thus make it difficult to assess changes in total reported contributions.[23] Yet tax return information is very useful for the analysis of giving behavior by itemizers. Its ready availability is no doubt one of the reasons that there have been relatively many studies on the impact of taxes on contributions. A possible drawback is the possibility that taxpayers systematically overstate their contributions, and furthermore that the amount of overstatement is positively correlated with marginal tax rates, but these problems do not in fact appear to be very severe.[24] Subject therefore to the problem of observing the behavior of nonitemizers and to the usual lag in the availability of data, tax return data provide a useful source of information for assessing the impact of tax reform. In line with the discussion in section 7.3, the remainder of this discussion examines three hypotheses derived from the economic model of contributions.

Contributions by Income Class
A major effect of the tax reform acts of 1981 and 1986 was to modify rate structures, thus changing the price of giving especially in the upper income classes. By looking at years before and after these large changes, it is possible to compare income classes experiencing different amounts of change in price in order to see whether the economic model is a useful guide for predicting donative behavior. For the purpose of assessing the impact of tax reform in the 1980s, "predicted" and actual changes in contributions for itemizers, based on changes in income taxes and tax rates, were calculated for two pairs of years: 1980–84 and 1985–87.[25] No allowance was made in these calculations for the relatively small number of taxpayers subject to the alternative minimum tax. Each income class in the ending year was paired with the income class in the beginning year with the closest mean AGI in constant dollars. Equations (1) and (4) were used to calculate the predicted giving in real terms in the ending year, and the percentage change in actual and predicted giving were then compared. Figures 7.1 and 7.2 show this comparison for each pair of years using the constant elasticity model (price elasticity of -1.27 and income elasticity of 0.78; coefficients of adjustment equal to 0.84 for the four-year period and 0.60 for the two-year period).

Figure 7.1 compares actual percentage changes in contributions to "predicted" changes based only on the price and income effects in the constant elasticity model. Although far from perfect, the model does mimic the

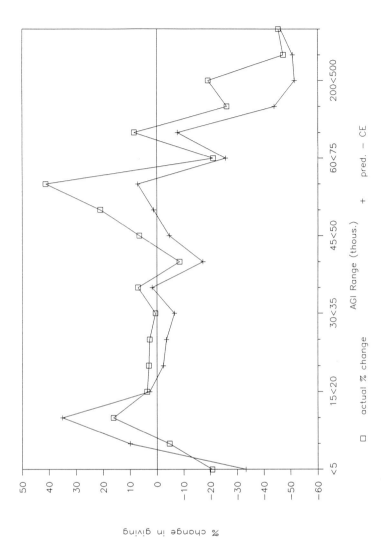

Figure 7.1
Predicted versus actual changes in giving, 1980–84

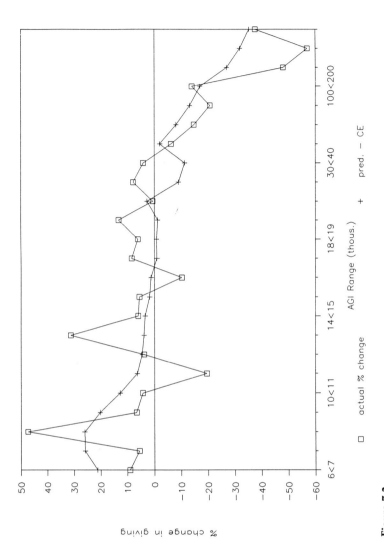

Figure 7.2
Predicted versus actual changes in giving, 1985–87

overall pattern of actual changes. Especially noteworthy are the actual and predicted declines in average giving for high-income taxpayers. For most income classes contributions increased by more than the model—with its implicit assumption that "other things" had not changed—predicted. For every class above $15,000 the predicted change is less than the actual change, sometimes by wide margins. Yet there is also a certain consistency in these errors, with both the predicted and the actual declines being the largest in the top income classes. It is obvious from looking at the graph that in this case this version of the economic model of giving would outperform a naive model based on the assumption that contributions do not change in real terms, or that both income and price elasticities are zero. But it is not obvious that it would be superior to another, somewhat less naive hypothesis that giving varies proportionately with net income, that is, the income elasticity is 1 while the price elasticity is 0.

In order to compare the performance of these various assumptions about giving behavior, I calculated the changes in contributions that each model would imply for the 1980–84 period. These calculations are summarized in the top panel of table 7.7.[26] Over this period the weighted average of itemizers' contributions declined by about 11%. Because the number and distribution of itemizers changes over time, this figure does not measure the actual change in contributions for all taxpayers or a specified group of taxpayers; it is rather one summary measure of the change in contributions over the period. The fourth and fifth columns in each row show the percentage change due to price and income changes predicted by each model.[27] The sixth column shows the average percentage by which each model misses the mark, which may be thought of as the result of changes in "other" variables unrelated to changes in income and tax policy. The last column gives the aggregate of all errors, measured in absolute value, as a percentage of 1984 total giving. For example, the basic constant elasticity model predicts that changes in the price of giving between 1980 and 1984 would have decreased total giving by itemizers by about 24% and that change in net income would have been responsible for a 2% increase. The net of these two effects—a "predicted" decline of 22.2%—and the actual decline in giving of 10.5% can be seen as a general shift in giving at all income levels of 11.7%. The remaining errors, added together without regard to sign, amount to 10.4% of total giving, the lowest ratio among the four models shown. This comparison supports the impression given by figure 7.1 that the pattern of changes in giving in response to the 1981 tax act were consistent with the economic model: Income groups facing the biggest price increases tended to show relative declines in giving.

Table 7.7
Tax reform and changes in contributions: A comparison of the performance of four alternative models

Period and Sample	Weighted change in contributions (logarithm)	Model	Predicted price effect	Predicted income effect	Shift	Weighted absolute errors as percentage of total giving
1980–84 Itemizers	−0.105	Constant elasticity	−0.237	0.015	0.117	10.4
		Variable elasticity	−0.335	0.013	0.217	22.2
		Zero elasticity	0	0	−0.105	19.7
		Income elasticity = 1	0	0.018	−0.128	18.5
1985–87 Itemizers	−0.227	Constant elasticity	−0.092	−0.067	−0.068	11.7
		Variable elasticity	−0.119	−0.063	−0.045	12.1
		Zero elasticity	0	0	−0.227	21.2
		Income elasticity = 1	0	−0.142	−0.084	12.9
1985–86 Nonitemizers	0.253	Constant elasticity	0.045	−0.007	0.214	14.2
		Variable elasticity	0.022	−0.004	0.235	14.5
		Zero elasticity	0	0	0.253	15.8
		Income elasticity = 1	0	−0.021	0.273	15.6

The same kind of comparison was performed by comparing contributions in 1985 and 1987. In order to make income definitions comparable between the two years, the portion of capital gains income excluded from AGI in 1985 was added in calculating 1985 net incomes. Actual and "predicted" changes in contributions are shown in figure 7.2. In this case the other-things-equal economic model predicts very little change in giving for the bulk of the income classes. At the lower end of the scale, where itemizers are scarcer, contributions were predicted to rise. At the very top they were predicted to drop, due to the cut in the top tax rates. As the figure shows, actual changes in giving at the lower end bounced around a good deal, reflecting the very small number of itemizers in those income classes, though the changes did remain positive as predicted. There was little change in giving in the middle ranges of income. At the top actual contributions fell by more than the amounts "predicted" by the basic model. This latter effect might be explained by one factor that certainly did not remain constant over this period: the stock market, which experienced its crash in October of the ending year of this comparison. It might also reflect the less favorable treatment of appreciated gifts by those taxpayers subject to the alternative minimum tax. Again, the simple constant elasticity model performs better than both naive models, with a gross error of 11.7% of total giving.[28]

The Distribution of Contributions
Because the tax rate cuts in the 1980s were concentrated at upper incomes, the price effects in the economic model imply that the share of contributions accounted for by the wealthy would decline unless increases in income among the wealthy overcame this price effect.[29] Because data on nonitemizers are not available for most years, it is impossible to examine how the whole distribution of giving has changed over time. In order to confine a comparison to a portion of the taxpaying population that is primarily composed of itemizers and also to keep a fairly constant population, I examined contributions among itemizers who fell into the top quintile of taxpayers in terms of income in each of three years.[30] The years chosen were 1980, 1984, and 1987, years before and after the two major tax reform acts of the 1980s. In order to describe the concentration of giving, the cumulative percentage of charitable contributions was compared to the cumulative percentage of two variables: the number of itemizing taxpayers and their income. The degree to which contributions are concentrated or evenly distributed can be summarized using a conventional index of inequality. This index ranges in value from 0, representing complete equality, to 1, representing complete concentration.[31]

The first approach—comparing the distribution of contributions to the distribution of households—showed little change in the distribution of giving among the top quintile of taxpayers. There was a slight increase in the inequality of giving among households, with the index of inequality increasing from 0.34 in 1980 to 0.38 in 1984 and 1987.[32] This contrasts with the *decrease* in the inequality of giving predicted by the economic models. However, when one compares contributions against income rather than the number of taxpayers, the distribution is shown to have become much more equal. On this basis the calculated index of inequality decreased from 0.15 in 1980 to 0.13 in 1984 and to 0.08 in 1987. In other words, within the top quintile of taxpayers, the portion of contributions given by the very wealthiest taxpayers has been declining. Relative to their incomes, these taxpayers gave less in 1987 than they did in 1980. How can these two results be reconciled? The answer is that the distribution of adjusted gross income in this top quintile became more unequal over the period, probably reflecting an underlying redistribution of economic income as well as the inclusion in AGI of all capital gains. This change in measured income distribution allowed the very richest to give a smaller percentage of their incomes but still account for approximately the same share of total giving in the top quintile.[33]

The 1981 Act and Contributions by Nonitemizers
A third implication of the economic model of giving relates to one specific provision of the 1981 act, the special deduction for nonitemizers. In 1985 and 1986 this deduction applied to all contributions made by nonitemizers, the only difference being that only 50 cents per dollar of contributions were eligible in 1985 compared to 100% in 1986. This change generally implies a decrease in the price of giving and thus an increased incentive to give. One might expect to see, then, an increase in nonitemizer giving between 1985 and 1986, other things equal, as well as increases in non-itemizer giving versus itemizer giving over that period.

Figure 7.3 presents a comparison of "predicted" and actual percentage changes in giving by nonitemizers between the two years, where predictions are derived using the constant elasticity model. Comparisons are made in this case between the same income group denoted in nominal dollars, although income and contributions continue to be expressed in constant dollars. Because of the small number of high-income nonitemizers, income classes above $75,000 are not shown. One notable feature of the figure is that the model predicts quite small changes in giving for all income classes, with most of the predicted changes being positive owing to the

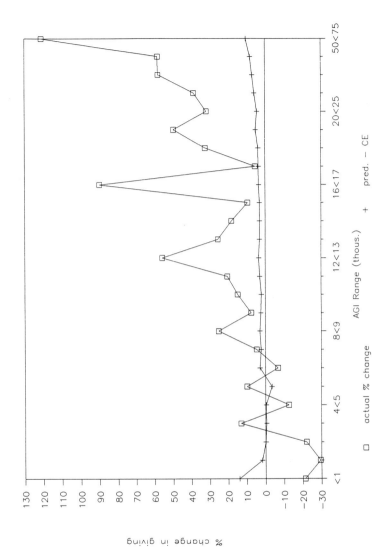

Figure 7.3
Predicted versus actual changes in giving, 1985–87: nonitemizers

increased rate of deductibility. The actual changes show substantial variability, but in general the average giving for nonitemizers rises over the period. This result is again consistent with the economic model. One alternative explanation for the increase is that especially generous donors switched from itemization to nonitemization status in 1986 because of the special deduction. This raised average giving by nonitemizers and lowered it for itemizers. The validity of this possibility can be assessed only by examining panel data when they become available. As shown in table 7.7, the constant elasticity model again performs better than the naive models in anticipating the pattern of changes in giving.

7.5 Implications

Both everyday experience and econometric analysis suggest that taxpayers' charitable giving would be sensitive to certain kinds of changes in tax law. The 1980s featured two significant changes in tax law that, according to the dominant economic model of contributions, should have had a sizable impact on incentives to contribute. The purpose of this chapter is to evaluate that model by determining whether these anticipated changes actually came to pass. The analysis yields implications that can be summarized in the form of three major points.

The first point is a reiteration of one that is made above: The economic model of charitable giving [summarized by equation (1)] is by no means a complete model of giving. Important nontax and noneconomic factors are excluded from the model. This fact implies, of course, that there is more to charitable giving than economic factors. More to the point of the current application, this fact implies that *changes* in contributions through time cannot be predicted. Only if the other excluded factors did not change could the model be used to predict changes in contributions. The best that the model can offer is a counterfactual statement, or a conditional prediction, for the hypothetical case in which nothing else has changed. If the coefficients of the model are correctly estimated—however incomplete the model itself—this kind of counterfactual statement can be a useful guide in evaluating the likely impact of tax changes. Accurate prediction of the future, however, is not a reasonable expectation.

A second implication arises from the comparison of simulated and actual effects of tax reforms. It is that the economic model performs reasonably well, in the sense that the changes in giving are broadly consistent with the model's implications. This consistency is apparent in three observations. First of all, the surge in contributions in 1986, particularly at the highest income levels, is consistent with the tax-sensitive timing of gifts. Second, after both tax acts, contributions tended to fall in income classes that experienced the largest price increases. More specifically, the basic model out-performed two naive models incorporating no price response. A third bit of empirical support for the economic model is the apparent redistribution in contributions among taxpayers in the highest quintile of income distribution. As predicted by the economic model, the most affluent gave a smaller share of total contributions—relative to their income—following the two tax acts.

A third implication arises in turn from these results. Because the results are generally consistent with the economic model, it follows that the predicted effects of tax reform based on the economic model are worth paying attention to. In the current policy environment, several possible changes in tax law are discussed from time to time, ranging from the reinstatement of the nonitemizer reduction to a floor for the itemized deduction. Since these and other changes could have large effects on the net cost of giving, they could also have a large impact on charitable contributions.

Notes

I am grateful to Marshall Adesman and Jane Farley Terrell for research assistance, to Henry Aaron, Gerard Brannon, Don Fullerton, Joel Slemrod, Steven Smith, and participants at the tax reform conference for helpful comments, and to the Duke Center for the Study of Philanthropy and Voluntarism for financial support.

1. For a description of this provision and its effect on donations of artwork, see Fullerton (1989).

2. For example, the law limited donations to private nonoperating foundations to the asset's basis except for certain kinds of stock, it limited the deductibility of travel costs associated with charitable deductions, it liberalized the deductibility of gifts out of inventory, it granted certain exceptions to the unrelated business income tax, it made the income of certain previously tax exempt nonprofits taxable, it made fellowships and scholarships taxable, it imposed limits on the ability of colleges and universities to issue tax-exempt bonds, and it lowered the excise tax on some foundations. For a fuller description of the act's provisions related to nonprofit organizaitons, see Chiechi et al. (1987).

3. Because the logarithm of zero is not defined, adding a small amount to reported contributions allows contributions to be expressed as a logarithm. This amount can be thought of as unreported contributions.

4. For example, Glenday et al. (1986), using cross-sectional data for Canada, obtain a price elasticity of -0.15 for high-income donors and 0 for other taxpayers.

Other studies, using first differences calculated from panel data, also yield esti-mated coefficients smaller than the benchmark estimates obtained from cross-sectional studies. See, for example, Clotfelter (1980) or Broman (1990). There are at least three reasons why equations estimated in first differences might produce elasticities smaller in absolute value. First, the cross-sectional equations could be subject to omitted variable bias. If price or income variables are systematically correlated to personal characteristics important in determining charitable giving, the estimated price and income coefficients could be overestimated in absolute value. Taking first differences would mitigate that problem. A second reason why elasticities estimated in first-difference equations might be smaller is that giving might not respond right away to changes in price and income. This explanation provides the motivation for developing a dynamic model of giving such as that described in the text. A third reason why the first difference model would produce smaller coefficients is errors in variables. Because individuals seldom know exactly what their tax rate is, particularly in the year in which the income is earned and contributions made, it is quite likely that donors have at best only an imprecise idea of the year-to-year change in income or price, making the actual change in those variables an error-prone estimate of the individual's own expected values, which are the variables more likely to be influencing behavior.

5. See Clotfelter (1986) for a discussion of the tax treatment of gifts of appreciated property.

6. Where the tax rate for the alternative minimum tax was 0.21, the price of giving under the AMT was $(1 - 0.21 - 0.21Rg^* + 0.21g)$, where g is the gain-to-value ratio in the year of the gift and g^* is the ratio in the year the asset would have been sold. If the donor has not sold the asset, but rather allowed it to pass into his or her estate, the price would approach 1 as g approaches 100%, as shown by the example given in the text. See Clotfelter (1986, 203).

7. Equation (2) implies in general that $\ln G_t = (1 - h)^t \ln G_0 + [1 - (1 - h)^t] \ln G^*$.

8. One frank statement came from arts lobbyist Anne G. Murphy, who was head of the American Arts Alliance, in the midst of final debate over the 1986 tax reform act: "I hope it breaks up. I hope it (tax reform) goes down the sewer. They're trading two lollipops for a piece of mayonnaise." Judith Michaelson, "Washington Lobbyist Figures Arts Organizations Come Away Losers," Los Angeles Times, August 19, 1986, p. VI-1.

9. "Treasury I" was a plan that would have cut rates, ended the nonitemizer deduction, and made the itemized deduction subject to a floor of 2% of adjusted gross income. For a description of the model used to project the 20% decline, see Clotfelter (1986, 199). For a description of the opposition by nonprofits, see David Johnston, "Charities Plan Deluge of Letters on Deduction Cuts," Los Angeles Times, January 5, 1985, p. I-1.

10. See Kathleen Teltsch, "Loss of Charity Deductions Would Hurt, Groups Assert," New York Times, May 30, 1985, p. I-19.

11. A study by Lawrence Lindsey is cited in Irvin Molotsky, "Charities Fear Effect of Changes," *New York Times*, August 20, 1986, p. IV-11.

12. Lindsey (1987, 67) cited a difference of 14% in the long run while Clotfelter (1987, 14) cited differences of 15% and 16%, depending on the model used, comparing contributions under the old and new tax regimes. An estimate made several years later by Lankford and Wyckoff (1989) implied a much larger percentage difference in giving for itemizers only, 26%, a prediction not necessarily inconsistent with the smaller figures applying to all taxpayers.

13. See, for example, Clotfelter (1987), Michaelson, "Washington Lobbyist," or Anne C. Roark, "College Students Could Be Tax Losers," *Los Angeles Times*, August 21, 1986, p. I-16.

14. For an illustration of a fuller listing of the limitations of simulations using such models, see Charles T. Clotfelter, "Tax Reform and Charitable Giving in 1985," *Tax Notes*, February 4, 1985, p. 481.

15. *Giving and Volunteering in the United States*, 1988 edition (Washington, D.C.: Independent Sector, 1988). For a description of the survey questions regarding attitudes and charitable behavior, see Kristin A. Goss, "In Charitable Giving, Volunteers Lead and the Wealthy Lag," *Chronicle of Philanthropy*, October 25, 1988, p. 9.

16. See Peter Steinfels, "Church Message This Season: Erasing Debt by Giving More," *New York Times*, November 14, 1988, p. 12.

17. Africare, an organization specializing in relief operations in Africa, experienced a surge in donations in 1987. The Salvation Army had much higher increases in donations between 1987 and 1988 than other religious organizations, which was attributed to concern over the homeless. See Anne Lowrey Bailey, "1988's Gifts Barely Keep Pace with Inflation, but Year-End Rise Heartens Charities," *Chronicle of Philanthropy*, January 24, 1989.

18. See, for example, Kathleen Teltsch, "Creative Fund-Raising Grows as Year Nears End," *New York Times*, December 23, 1985, p. I-12.

19. The standard deduction could result in similar multiyear timing behavior if contributions represented the difference in deductions that would make itemization worthwhile. For a detailed treatment of such behavior in general, see Martin Feldstein and Lawrence Lindsey, "Simulating Nonlinear Tax Rules and Nonstandard Behavior: An Application to the Tax Treatment of Charitable Contributions," National Bureau of Economic Research Working Paper No. 682, 1981.

20. The variables used to estimate individual contributions include personal income, a time trend, population, a stock market index, and an indicator of the party of the incumbent president. For an explanation of the estimation used, see the appendix A of *Giving USA*.

21. "Protestant Churches Saw 3-Pct. Increase in Giving between 1986 and 1987, Survey Finds," *Chronicle of Philanthropy*, July 11, 1989, p. 4, and Bailey, "1988's Gifts."

22. "United Way Contributions up 6.9 Pct.," *Chronicle of Philanthropy*, May 2, 1989, and personal communication from Russy Sumariwalla, United Way of America.

23. An additional limitation of tax return data on contributions is the existence of upper limits on the deductibility of contribution. For most types of contributions, the deduction is limited to 50% of AGI; any excess can be carried foward into the following five years. The limit for gifts of appreciated property is 30% of AGI, and for gifts to foundations, 20%. Relatively few taxpayers are subject to these limits, however.

24. See Slemrod (1989).

25. Comparisons were also made for the 1980–82 period, with very similar results to those shown for 1980–84.

26. One way of seeing the components of changes in contributions is to rewrite the basic equation for an individual as

$$\frac{G_{1i}}{G_{0i}} = \left(\frac{d_1}{d_0}\right)\left(\frac{Y_{1i}}{Y_{0i}}\right)^{ah}\left(\frac{P_{1i}}{P_{0i}}\right)^{bh}\left(\frac{X_{1i}}{X_{0i}}\right)^{ch} E_i,$$

where all "other" factors are assumed to enter as one variable logarithmically and E_i is a multiplicative error term. The term $(Y_{1i}/Y_{0i})^{ah} = A_i$ is the predicted effect due to the change in income, $(P_{1i}/P_{0i})^{bh} = B_i$ is the comparable price effect, and the effect of shifts in the intercept and changes in the "other" variable can be combined as $C_i = (d_1/d_0)(X_1/X_0)^{ch}$. The percentage change in giving can then be decomposed as

$$\ln G_{1i} - \ln G_{0i} = \ln A_i + \ln B_i + \ln C_i + \ln E_i.$$

If all individuals are assumed to be subject to the same proportional changes in "other" variables, including the intercept, then $C_i = C$ becomes a shift parameter common to all individuals. The extent to which a model fails to explain differences in behavior between individuals, or income classes in the case of observations based on income classes, will be reflected in the error term E_i.

Table 7.7 shows weighted averages for $\ln A_i$ and $\ln B_i$ along with the average value of $\ln C$ for each of several models, effectively decomposing the actual percentage change in total giving. For example, the portion due to price is calculated as $(\sum_i N_i G_{0i} \ln A_i)/(\sum_i N_i G_{0i})$, where i refers to income class.

A useful measure of the degree to which a model fails to explain all changes in giving is the sum of absolute errors expressed as a percentage of actual giving in the second period: $(\sum_i N_i G_{0i} |\ln E_i|)/(\sum_i N_i G_{0i})$. The measure is calculated for each model and sample and is presented in the last column of table 7.7.

27. More precisely, the second column in the table is the weighted average of the log difference in average real contributions between 1980 and 1984, which is

approximately the percentage change. Analogously, the fourth and fifth columns are weighted averages of the logarithm of the implied price and income effects which are also interpreted as percentage changes.

28. The limitations inherent in the calculations of the weighted total giving figures are worth emphasizing. Actual total contributions by itemizers in 1987 were $49.3 billion ($46.4 billion in 1985 dollars). Using the 1987 distribution of itemizers as weights, the changes in actual contributions between 1985 and 1987 imply a total giving figure of $56.3 billion in 1985, markedly higher than the actual figure of $48.0 billion for itemizers in that year. The reason for this discrepancy is the significant increase between 1985 and 1987 in the number of taxpayers in the upper income classes, the classes experiencing the largest percentage decline in giving. As noted in the text, this increase in the number of high-income taxpayers is probably the result of changes in the distribution of economic income and the inclusion of all capital gains in AGI. As long as data from income classes (as opposed to individual returns) are used for such comparisons, there will be no entirely satisfactory set of weights to use for this purpose.

29. See, for example, Clotfelter and Salamon (1982, 177–180).

30. For each year, I calculated 20% of the total taxpaying population and based my calculation on that group. The top income classes corresponding to this population were identified and used for the analysis. In the income class where the top quartile began, I weighted the class's mean values by the percentage of class members who fell into the top quartile. The transitional income classes, with the percentage of the class falling into the top quintile by year were $25,000–$30,000 in 1980 (68.5%), $30,000–35,000 in 1984 (31.8%), and $30,000–40,000 in 1987 (17.3%). Because the ratio of total taxpayers to total households did not change appreciably over this period, basing the quintile calculations on the number of households seemed appropriate. Calculations were then based on itemized contributions, number of itemizers, and AGI for itemizers (the latter was estimated for 1987 as the total AGI for the class multiplied by the percentage of taxpayers who itemized in each class). For these income classes, the percentage of itemizers was very high. For example, the percentage of itemizers in 1987, the year with the lowest rate, was 84%.

31. The index can be defined by reference to a graph with the cumulative percentage of households (or income) on the x-axis and the cumulative percentage of contributions on the y-axis. Where A is the area between the diagonal line connecting the 100% points and the curve and B is the area under the curve, the index of inequality is $A/(A + B)$.

32. All of the indices presented in this section are calculated in the manner of gini coefficients for Lorenz curves. If A is the area under the curve and T is the area of the triangle under the diagonal, the index is $(T - A)/T$. For the distribution of AGI versus contributions, this index could take on a negative value, signifying a curve above the diagonal and a generally decreasing percentage of income devoted to contributions.

33. The gini coefficient calculated by comparing AGI and number of itemizers for the top quintile was 0.22 for 1980, 0.27 for 1984, and 0.31 for 1987.

References

Broman, Amy J. 1989. Statutory Tax Rate Reform and Charitable Contributions: Evidence from a Recent Period of Reform. *Journal of the American Taxation Association* 11: 7–21.

Chiechi, Carolyn P., Robert E. Atkinson Jr., and Miriam Galston. 1987. Impact of the 1986 Tax Reform Act on Exempt Organizations. *Journal of Taxation* 66: 344–348.

Clotfelter, Charles T. 1986. The Effect of Tax Simplification on Educational and Charitable Organizations. In *Economic Consequences of Tax Simplification*. Boston: Federal Reserve Bank of Boston.

Clotfelter, Charles T. 1985. *Federal Tax Policy and Charitable Giving*. Chicago: University of Chicago Press.

Clotfelter, Charles T. 1987. Life after Tax Reform. *Change* (July–August): 12–18.

Clotfelter, Charles T. 1980. Tax Incentives and Charitable Giving: Evidence from a Panel of Taxpayers. *Journal of Public Economics* 13: 319–340.

Clotfelter, Charles T., and Lester Salamon. 1982. The Impact of the 1981 Tax Act on Individual Charitable Giving. *National Tax Journal* 35: 171–187.

Clotfelter, Charles T., and C. Eugene Steuerle. 1981. Charitable Contributions. In Henry J. Aaron and Joseph A. Pechman (eds.), *How Taxes Affect Economic Behavior*. Washington, DC: Brookings Institution.

Feenberg, Daniel. 1987. Are Tax Price Models Really Identified: The Case of Charitable Giving. *National Tax Journal* 40: 629–633.

Feldstein, Martin. 1975. The Income Tax and Charitable Contributions. Part I— Aggregate and Distributional Effects. *National Tax Journal* 28: 209–226.

Feldstein, Martin, and Lawrence Lindsey. 1981. Simulating Nonlinear Tax Rules and Nonstandard Behavior: An Application to the Tax Treatment of Charitable Contributions. NBER Working Paper No. 682.

Fullerton, Don. 1989. Tax Policy toward Art Museums. In Martin Feldstein (ed.), *The Economics of Art Museums*. Cambridge, MA: NBER.

Glenday, Graham, Anil K. Gupta, and Henry Pawlak. 1986. Tax Incentives for Personal Charitable Contributions. *Review of Economics and Statistics* 68: 688–693.

Hausman, Jerry, and James Poterba. 1987. Household Behavior and the Tax Reform Act of 1986. *Journal of Economic Perspectives* 1: 101–119.

Lankford, R. Hamilton, and James H. Wyckoff. 1989. Modeling Charitable Giving. State University of New York at Albany. Unpublished paper.

Lindsey, Lawrence B. 1987. Gifts of Appreciated Property: More to Consider. *Tax Notes*, January 5, pp. 67–70.

Slemrod, Joel. 1989. Are Estimated Tax Elasticities Really Just Tax Evasion Elasticities? The Case of Charitable Contributions. *Review of Economics and Statistics* 71: 517–522.

U.S. Internal Revenue Service. 1987–88. *SOI Bulletin* 7(Winter): 39–52.

U.S. Internal Revenue Service. 1982–88. *Statistics of Income—Individual Income Tax Returns*. Washington, DC: Government Printing Office.

U.S. Internal Revenue Service. 1989. *SOI Bulletin* 8(Spring): 5–26.

COMMENTS

Don Fullerton

In the economics of tax policy toward charitable giving, Charles Clotfelter "wrote the book" (Clotfelter 1985). In his chapter we get an important evaluation of that seminal work. The chapter includes excellent discussions of the basic econometric model used to estimate the effects of tax policy on giving, the major vulnerabilities of this model, the major tax policy changes in the 1980s that might be expected to affect charitable giving, and some juicy quotes about tax reform from representatives of the charitable sector. These details could only be provided by someone who keeps his finger on the pulse in this area by doing regular searches of newspapers and of trade journals like the *Chronicle of Philanthropy*.

From Clotfelter, however, we also get important new empirical tests of the model. These econometric models are designed for the conceptual purpose of isolating the effect of one variable while abstracting from changes in other variables. They are often used, however, for the practical purpose of "predicting" the effect of a change in the one variable. Since other variables never in fact remain unchanged, actual outcomes that differ from the prediction are not taken as evidence against the model and do not discourage economists from its continued use! Clotfelter avoids this complacency by undertaking not one, not two, but three different kinds of tests. In doing the tests, Clotfelter does not get stuck trying to pinpoint the level of gifts because other variables can change. Instead, he makes use of the insight that if these other variables affect all taxpayers similarly, then the pattern of giving among taxpayers in the outcome should match the pattern in the prediction. His results suggest a satisfactory match.

My discussion will follow the outline of Clotfelter's chapter by noting pitfalls in the model and then suggesting a fourth possible test.

First, the model usually employs too much aggregation. Early work often aggregated taxpayers by income group, but even later work with individual tax returns necessarily lumps together different kinds of commodities in estimating a single price elasticity of demand for charitable giving. The price elasticity of demand for gifts to the church is probably quite different from the price elasticity of demand for gifts to the arts, even for the same individual. The IRS has not provided data on the type of gift in each income class since 1962; ideally it should undertake to show the types of gifts for a sample of individual returns. Rather than wait indefinitely for such data, I would encourage the use of alternative information on gifts of particular types. For example, Kingma (1989) estimates a similar model for 3,541 gifts to 63 public radio stations. He is also able to estimate the crowding-out effect of others' gifts and of direct government spending on this good (excluded variables not emphasized by Charles Clotfelter). However, I think Kingma overstates his conclusions about "the correct model" and the "true" measure of crowding out.

Second, and especially if the model can employ specific gifts, further work is required to calculate the individual's price. The model currently employs proportions for cash gifts and appreciated property given by the average for the AGI group, but the individual's gift may be all cash or all property. Another example is given by the pernicious alternative minimum tax (AMT). Clotfelter notes that a taxpayer on the AMT is not forgiven capital gains tax on the appreciated portion of a gift of property. Since the value of the gift is deducted at the AMT's 21% rate, the price of a dollar gift is 79 cents. But consider a gift that is lumpy (like a piece of art), that is basically all appreciation, and that is enough to *put* the individual onto the AMT. Then the alternative of selling the art for consumption would result in a capital gains tax at the regular 28% tax rate. Since the donation results in a deduction at the 21% AMT rate *and* capital gains tax at the same 21% rate, these AMT effects wash, and the net tax saving of the donation relative to consumption is the 28% rate. In other words, the price is 72 cents, not 79 cents. Because of credits and carryforwards, it also matters how long the individual expects to remain under the AMT. See Lyon (1989) for other pernicious incentive effects of the AMT. Even for art donations the credit against future regular tax depends on the taxpayer's mix of "exclusion" preferences and "deferral" preferences.

Third, we know almost nothing about intertemporal substitution. Clotfelter notes the vulnerability of the model to dynamic aspects of giving behavior, and he uses an incomplete adjustment model that implies 60% adjustment in two years. In some cases we might expect immediate overadjustment rather than slow underadjustment. For example, I personally have given considerably less to charity in years when I went on leave and had lots of business expenses that put me in a lower tax bracket, and have given proportionately more in other years. For those with volatile incomes, marginal tax rate effects can compound apparent income effects. Another example of intertemporal substitution is that a nonitemizer in the 1980s with correct expectations would anticipate that the deduction would be increased between 1984 and 1985, increased again for 1986, and then expire. He or she might well shift gifts both from earlier years and from later years into 1985 and especially 1986. One of Clotfelter's tests involves the changes in gifts of itemizers and nonitemizers from 1985 to 1986, but it should involve changes in all years from 1984 to 1987. A final example involves Clotfelter's table 7.5, where the value of art donated to museums rose from $76 million in 1985 to $143 million in 1986, the last year before appreciated property was to be placed under the alternative minimum tax, and then fell to $94 million and $67 million in the next two years. Museums conclude that the AMT provision caused the 53% reduction in gifts of art between 1986 and 1988, but clearly the 1986 figure was inflated by the anticipated subsequent loss of this tax benefit. In addition the 1988 figure is depressed because (1) some gifts were moved up to 1986, (2) the AMT now discourages such gifts, and (3) many in 1988 anticipated that the provision would soon be repealed (as was just voted by the Senate Finance Committee in October of 1989). We cannot yet know the long-run effect of factor 2 alone (i.e., a permanent AMT provision).

Fourth, Clotfelter's tests give the econometric model a leg up, essentially by doing an ex post prediction rather than using an ex ante prediction. He feeds into the model the actual change in the level of income and marginal tax rate for each group and multiplies by the regression coefficients to see what the model would predict for gifts. For the model to be useful in predicting the effect of some tax change proposal, however, it must use predictions of the change in tax variables and income between the two years. He has in fact done just such predictions (for the 1981 act in Clotfelter and Salamon 1982, and for the 1986 act in Clotfelter 1987). Why not compare the outcome to those predictions?

I also did some such predictions (Fullerton and Goodman 1982). In a point not strongly emphasized in Clotfelter and Salamon, or in Clotfelter's chapter in this book, the 1981 act has a certain "twist" in it that gives the model a fairly strong qualitative prediction. That act immediately lowered marginal tax rates, especially for high-bracket taxpayers who give more than proportionately to education and the arts. Thus we might expect fewer such gifts. It also provided a nonitemizer's deduction for 1986, especially for low-bracket taxpayers who give more than proportionately to religious organizations. Thus we might expect more such gifts (or less of a reduction in the total for high- as well as low-bracket donors). The specific numbers in my study, under one set of assumptions including a full nonitemizer's deduction, were 22% less for education and only 1% less for religion. What has happened to relative donations by type of donee? *Giving USA* reports:

Year	Religion		Education		Arts	
	$ billions	%Δ	$ billions	%Δ	$ billions	%Δ
1980	22.2	10.2	5.0	9.3	3.2	15.4
1981	25.1	12.7	5.8	16.3	3.7	16.2
1982	28.1	12.0	6.0	4.0	5.0	35.5
1983	31.8	13.5	6.7	10.8	4.2	−15.1
1984	35.4	11.3	7.3	9.6	4.5	6.9
1985	37.5	5.7	8.2	12.1	5.1	12.9
1986	41.7	11.3	9.4	14.9	5.8	14.8
1987	44.5	6.9	9.8	4.8	6.3	8.2
1988	48.2	8.2	9.8	−0.6	6.8	8.1

This numbers seem to go in the wrong direction. Growth in 1981 for education and the arts is bigger than that for religious organizations. Furthermore the jump in 1986 for giving to religious organizations is smaller than the jump for education and the arts. Unfortunately, these numbers are fairly meaningless since *Giving USA* relies very little on real data after 1985, using a time-series econometric model without tax variables to project individual gifts for more recent years!

This discussion brings me, finally, to another suggested test. All three of Clotfelter's tests, though useful, rely on tax return data that contain no information about nonitemizers (except in 1985 and 1986 when they received partial and full deductions) or about donee organization. One might, in addition, look at the Consumer Expenditure Survey. The data for each household in that survey contain enough information to construct a decent guess at their marginal tax rate and itemization status. The data also show the recipient of their charitable gifts. Thus, even though these are not panel data, one could look at nonitemizers' gifts in each year from 1984 through 1987, rather than rely on tax return data that only have such gifts for 1985 and 1986. Also, without necessarily assuming who is an itemizer, one could check the strong qualitative prediction of the model about total relative gifts to religious and educational or other organizations.

In summary, I think that this chapter by Charles Clotfelter is a fine piece of art, with great value. If he were to donate it to a charitable institution such as the University of Michigan's Office of Tax Policy Research, he definitely would subject himself to the alternative minimum tax.

References

Clotfelter, Charles T. 1985. *Federal Tax Policy and Charitable Giving.* A National Bureau of Economic Research Monograph. Chicago: The University of Chicago Press.

Clotfelter, Charles T. 1987. Life after tax reform. *Change* (July/August): 12–18.

Clotfelter, Charles T., and Lester M. Salamon. 1982. The impact of the 1981 tax act on individual charitable giving. *National Tax Journal* 35: 171–187.

Fullerton, Don, and Shira D. Goodman. 1982. The Economic Recovery Tax Act of 1981: Implications for charitable giving. *Tax Notes* (September 20): 1027–1036.

Giving USA, The Annual Report on Philanthropy for the Year 1988. 1989. Nathan Weber (ed.). A Publication of the AAFRC Trust for Philanthropy.

Kingma, Bruce Robert. 1989. An accurate measurement of the crowd-out effect, income effect, and price effect for charitable contributions. *Journal of Political Economy* 97: 1197–1207.

Lyon, Andrew B. 1989. Understanding investment incentives under parallel tax systems: An application to the alternative minimum tax. NBER Working Paper No. 2912. March.

GENERAL DISCUSSION

Larry Langdon posed two questions pertaining to changes in charitable giving patterns. First, is it clear that giving by the wealthy has declined over time? Second, does giving increase as people get older? Later in the discussion Charles Clotfelter replied that contributions do, indeed, increase with age.

Noting that most giving occurs at the end of the year, Ann Dryden Witte suggested that the stock market crash in late 1987 may have depressed giving in that year.

Recalling that the size distribution of charitable giving is surprisingly even across income classes, John Whalley wondered if it could be the case that the income distribution itself is more concentrated than the distribution of giving.

Fritz Scheuren warned that researchers who use these data should be aware that the definition of adjusted gross income changed over the study period. It is necessary to adjust for these changes to arrive at a consistent income concept.

Michael McIntyre proposed classifying givers into two groups: those who give only for altruistic reasons, and those who make their contribution decisions based on the "rate of return" from the gift. The distinction is important because tax effects are relevant to the rate-of-return group but not to the altruistic givers.

Charles McLure thought it would be interesting to see a tabulation of the size distribution of the nonitemizer contribution deduction. He posited that many nonitemizers probably claimed contributions up to the limit, regardless of their actual contributions.

Richard Musgrave recommended that researchers look at the reduction of contributions by income bracket and compare these changes to the reduction in tax rates by the same income brackets.

Burton Smoliar asked if any studies had been done comparing bequests to lifetime gifts.

Now that this study was done, Joel Slemrod wondered if the author could report a new estimate for the price elasticity of charitable giving.

Daniel Feenberg argued that as a result of changes that broadened the definition of adjusted gross income, some taxpayers have moved into new tax brackets.

Gerard Brannon requested a clarification of the lag structure the author used to estimate the model.

Referring to the windfalls enjoyed by some investors who are involved in corporation takeovers, James Poterba asked if the current wave of take-overs, and the resulting return from the forced realization of capital gains, has made an impact on the contributions data. He also wondered about the tax treatment of a one-time donation of assets to a charitable trust that will continue to give money into the future: Is the deduction taken when the original contribution is made, or each time the trust makes a contribution thereafter?

Paul Menchik pointed out that donations of time and donations of money have been found to be complements; that is, a reduction in an individual's ability to donate time to a charity may lead to a reduction in monetary gifts. He asked if the author had seen any evidence of this.

Robert Haveman asked about ways to relate charitable giving to wealth instead of to income.

Randall Weiss suggested that the author consider the effects of estate and gift taxes on charitable contributions. Because these taxes allow a deduction for charitable contributions, recent changes in the rates of these taxes should affect the taxpayer's effective price of giving.

8

The Impact of the Tax Reform Act of 1986 on State and Local Fiscal Behavior

Paul N. Courant and Edward M. Gramlich

Just three years have elapsed since TRA86 was signed and most of its provisions regarding states and localities became widely known. Most of these provisions have been in effect for less than three years. One or two years of post-TRA86 aggregate data on states and localities are available, one or no years of data for some of the key micro variables. This is not very much information, given various lags in behavioral responses and the degree to which subtle effects emanating from TRA86 can be concealed by more dramatic behavioral shocks. Our purpose here then is to take a first look at whether TRA86 is having the various impacts it was thought likely to have. There is no question that these early indications may become revised or outmoded as time passes, behavior changes, and new data become available.

We investigate three main topics:

1. The impact of TRA86 on the aggregate fiscal policy of states and localities—spending, the level and composition of taxes, and asset stocks.

2. The impact of TRA86 on the economic activity, property values, and tax bases of local jurisdictions.

3. The impact of TRA86 on the market for state and local bonds.

The first topic is investigated by comparing aggregate national income accounts data for 1987 and 1988 with those of earlier years through time series regression analysis. The second is investigated by a form of event study. Rather than conducting what seemed to be a hopeless examination of mobility and property values for all jurisdictions, we focus on adjacent border jurisdictions in states that should be quite differentially affected by TRA86. We then look for shocks in a variety of indicators of population shifts, including building permits, assessed values, and county employment levels. The third topic is investigated by comparing the return on state and local bonds relative to taxable bonds, both before and after TRA86.

8.1   State and Local Fiscal Behavior

We first discuss a simple theory of state and local fiscal behavior in the presence of differential federal tax treatment of different taxes and the pre-TRA86 empirical predictions of its impact. We then give our own early empirical estimates of what seemed to have happened and compare these estimates with more informal reports of what is going on.

A Simple Theory

Consider a jurisdiction that levies a variety of taxes and user fees, receives grants from other governments, and spends the money on goods, services, and transfers. Without going into the underlying social choice mechanism, we can posit that the jurisdiction has a demand for public spending that varies positively with the community's resources and negatively with the total cost to the jurisdiction's residents of a dollar's worth of public expenditure (E). Thus jurisdictions will have demands for public spending that are downward sloping in the cost per dollar of such spending, drawn as the MB schedule in figure 8.1.

The supply schedule for this jurisdiction's public expenditure is more complicated. If the jurisdiction behaves rationally, this supply schedule will be the usual horizontal sum of the marginal cost functions of the various sources of revenue. First will come lump-sum grants (G). These are fixed in total amount and, once this amount is reached, are supplied inelastically. Then come the various taxes the jurisdiction can assess. To anticipate later analysis of TRA86, these taxes will be disaggregated into those that were deductible (D) before and after TRA86, those taxes and fees that were nondeductible (N) before and after TRA86, and sales taxes (S) which were deductible before but not after TRA86. The marginal cost for each of these taxes is weakly increasing in revenue raised because of direct burden, excess burden, or political costs. These marginal cost schedules are shown as D, N, and S respectively in figure 8.1.

The jurisdiction will choose its revenue sources so that the three marginal costs are equalized. At this point the marginal benefits of public spending will also equal these common marginal costs, as shown in figure 8.1. The line indicated by MC is the horizontal sum of all revenue sources before TRA86 and E is the equilbrium level of public spending, which is financed by the fixed level of G and the designated level of each of the taxes.

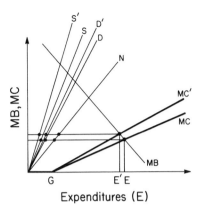

Figure 8.1
Impact of TRA86 on state and local budgets:

Budget constraint

$\Delta E = \Delta D + \Delta S + \Delta N$

TRA86 impact

$$D' = D\left(\frac{1 - a't'}{1 - at}\right)$$

$$S' = S\left(\frac{1}{1 - at}\right)$$

Predictions

$\Delta E < 0$

$\Delta S < 0$

$\Delta D < 0$

$\Delta N > 0$

Now assume a federal tax change such as was made by TRA86. This bill would change the fiscal position of the jurisdiction by

1. lowering the marginal federal tax rate faced by most itemizers in the jurisdiction,

2. lowering the fraction of taxpayers who itemize,

3. removing the sales tax deduction altogether.[1]

TRA86 did not affect the marginal cost schedule for nondeductible taxes and fees, so there would be no shift in the N schedule.

The standard way of representing the impact of changes such as this has become to focus on the mean voter in the jurisdiction. With this focus, even if the median voter in the jurisdiction does not itemize deductions, the loss of, say, the sales tax deduction is costly for the jurisdiction because some voters in the jurisdiction are worse off and now find public services to be more costly.[2] Letting t stand for the average marginal federal tax rate of itemizers in the jurisdiction before TRA86, t' for this rate after TRA86, a for the share of taxpayers who itemize before TRA86, and a' for the share of taxpayers who itemize after TRA86, the other two tax schedules would shift as follows:

$$D' = \frac{D(1 - a't')}{1 - at}, \tag{1}$$

$$S' = \frac{S}{1 - at}. \tag{2}$$

These shifts are shown in figure 8.1, as is the shift in the horizontal sum schedule to MC'. The jurisdiction would reoptimize at the new expenditure level E' and the higher aftertax marginal tax cost of all three taxes.

One could then make the following predictions of the impact of TRA86 on state and local budgets:

State and local spending E would fall.

Nondeductible taxes and fees N would rise.

Sales taxes S would fall.

Deductible taxes D would fall.

The first two predictions would be true with any normally sloped spending demand function and marginal cost function for nondeductible taxes. These two predictions in turn imply that the sum of S and D will fall. If the pretax cost functions of these two taxes are similar, S is likely to fall by more in percentage terms because its aftertax cost increases by more. But there are some instances where either tax may not drop, although the sum still will.

One such complication is mentioned by Inman (1989), who gives a reason why sales taxes could rise in response to TRA86. Inman points out that in eliminating a tax deduction primarily used by the rich, TRA86 might have thrown the distributional balance of states and localities out of whack, forcing these governments to raise regressive sales taxes to restore their distributional balance. Another complication that works in the same direction is raised by Metcalf (1989), who shows that when sales taxes are exported to other jurisdictions, the relative cost of sales taxes could rise less than that of income taxes with TRA86: The price of the component borne at home rises more than for income taxes, but the price of the exported component does not rise. This latter effect would be shown on figure 8.1 with a very elastic S schedule, so even a higher percentage change than for the D curve might raise the marginal cost at the initial revenue mix by less.

These predictions are also only relevant for changes in the aftertax cost of certain taxes, which in effect pivot the MC curve counterclockwise. Further complications ensue when some of the schedules in figure 8.1 also shift for independent reasons. If, for example, there were an outward shift in the MB function, the new intersection would be on the MC' schedule at a higher expenditure level. The higher aftertax marginal cost and benefit would lead to greater use of all taxes, with the consequence that S and D might both rise in order to finance this higher spending. If, on the other hand, grants were cut, the MC' schedule would be shifted in, the new equilibrium would be at a lower spending level but again a higher aftertax cost of all taxes, and again all taxes could be increased to finance the cut in grants.

One final factor is what is known as the "windfall effect" of TRA86. TRA86 raised the federal tax base, and many states use this federal tax base as the base for their own tax. In such a case TRA86 could shift the D curve outward because of this windfall effect, again making it more likely that D would increase.

Pre-TRA86 Empirical Predictions

Before the fact almost everyone predicted that TRA86 would lower state and local spending. Using various estimates of marginal rates and numbers of itemizers before and after, Courant and Rubinfeld (1987), Kenyon (1988), and Gramlich (1987) predicted very slight declines in state and local spending, on the order of 1%. Using empirical estimates from a sample of local governments, Holtz-Eakin and Rosen (1988) predicted very sharp declines in local spending, on the order of 8%. Applying their elasticity estimates to state spending gives even larger percentage declines for states.[3] This is one battle to be joined.

The second prediction is that TRA86 should have raised the share of nondeductible taxes and fees. Although this prediction is clear from the theory, nobody was able to get very sensible parameter estimates before the fact. Feldstein and Metcalf (1987) obtained mixed results on the question, whereas Holtz-Eakin and Rosen (1988) and Inman (1989) estimated coefficients, albeit insignificant ones, that implied that fees would fall, not rise, in response to TRA86.

The third and fourth predictions are that the mix would shift away from those taxes where marginal costs are increased . Hettich and Winer (1984), Inman (1989), and Noto and Zimmerman (1985) found relatively small effects of TRA86 on the revenue mix. In contrast, Feldstein and Metcalf (1987) and Holtz-Eakin and Rosen (1988) found much larger effects. Feldstein and Metcalf estimated very high elasticities (with large standard errors) of revenue from deductible taxes with respect to marginal cost. At face value their estimates implied that TRA86 should reduce income taxes by at least 12% and sales taxes by 30% or more. The similar numbers for Holtz-Eakin and Rosen (with smaller standard errors) were that local deductible taxes should fall by 6% and state sales taxes by 14%. Another battle to be joined.

As mentioned above, all of this gets much more complicated when other large changes are occurring simultaneously. And there were no shortage of these. One of the most dramatic is the change in the fiscal relationship between the federal government and states and localities. Grants from the federal government have been cut significantly. A decade ago grants were 3.4% of GNP and rising as a share; by 1988 grants were 2.3% of GNP and falling as a share. Provisions on the big income distribution grants'—AFDC and Medicaid—have been tightened, general revenue sharing has been cut out altogether, categorical grants have first been converted to block form and then killed or reduced. But while these cuts were occurring, the federal government has actually mandated increased state in local spending in areas such as health care, environmental protection, and human services.

Regarding windfalls, Gold (1988) estimated the state personal income tax windfall to be $6.3 billion, of which only $1.1 billion was likely to be retained after all discretionary rate cuts took effect. Aten (1987) initially estimated the state corporate tax windfall to be \$3.4 billion, though subsequent data suggest it was less (Aten and Gold 1989).

A Time-Series Model

To see whether the various theoretical and empirical predictions of the impact of TRA86 stand up, we fit a model to aggregate time-series data. Obviously it would have been possible to take a case study type look at the behavior of particular state or local governments, as Chernick and Reschovsky (1989) recently did, but there is always the problem of generalizing to the whole on the basis of particular governments. And there are so many individual local governments (about 80,000 right now) that one could never say anything sensible about local governments with this approach.

Our first approach then was to do what researchers would naturally do in investigating any other aspect of TRA86—its effect on investment, saving, housing, or whatever. That is to use aggregate national income accounts data. These can now be broken down by state general governments and local general governments separately, which also makes sense in view of the fact that different taxes and types of spending are used by the different levels of government. Separated state and local fiscal data are now available on an annual basis from 1959 to 1988 (Levin and Peters 1986, 1987; Peters 1988). We applied a time-series model modified from Gramlich (1978) to annual time-series observations from 1959 to 1986, the period of the old tax law, and then made out-of-sample extrapolations for the post-TRA86 years 1987 and 1988. From these extrapolations we can see whether the residuals moved in line with the theoretical and empirical predictions.

The model postulates a state or local objective function made up of three arguments:

Spending

Aftertax private income

Fund balances

The latter is included because available fund balances can be turned into future spending or private income. Utility is maximized subject to the budget constraint:

$$\Delta B = D + S + N + G - E, \tag{3}$$

where ΔB refers to the change in the stock of fund balances, or the surplus, of governments and all other variables are as defined above. The level or stock of fund balances B is defined as:

$$B = B_{-1} + \Delta B. \tag{4}$$

Combining equations (3) and (4), it can be seen that

$$B_{-1} + G = E - D - S - N + B, \tag{5}$$

which is the basic budget identity of the model. The left side variable of equation (5) is grants and previously unallocated balances. These can be distributed to spending E, tax cuts $-D$, $-S$, and $-N$, and currently unallocated balances B according to the actions of state or local politicians.

To focus on shifts in tax shares resulting from TRA86, we estimate separate regressions for seven or six dependent variables:

1. Direct spending (E for localities, one component of E for states).

2. Grants to localities (the other component of E for states).

3. Deductible personal taxes (one component of D, mainly income taxes, for states, mainly property taxes for localities).

4. Deductible business or corporate taxes (the other component of D).

5. Sales taxes (S).

6. Nondeductible taxes, fines, and user fees (N).

7. Currently unallocated balances (B).

Following the standard utility maximization calculation (detailed in Gramlich 1978), each of these variables can be shown to be a function of income (GNP less federal taxes plus federal transfers to persons), a price term, and grants and previously unallocated balances ($B_{-1} + G$).

A model such as this could be fit either in money or real terms. The budget identity actually works in money terms and since most state tax systems are not indexed for inflation, most tax equations should also be formulated in money terms. On the other side, spending equations are usually fit in real terms, as if voters make decisions about real spending levels. Since our main interest is on the tax side and in the budget identity—to see how impacts are allocated across all budgetary categories—we fit the model in money terms. Each dependent variable and dollar flow independent variable is measured in money terms, and each equation includes the state and local purchases deflator as a separate independent variable. Previous versions of this model disaggregated grants according to whether they reduce the prices of favored activities at the margin. But since most actual grants these days do not reduce prices at the margin (are closed-ended), and since there is little time-series variation in matching rates for open-ended grants, we simplified the model to treat all grants from higher-level governments as exogenous closed-ended grants with no price effect at the margin.

There was serial correlation in the level version of the model, so we fit the equations under the assumption that the time-series residuals for all equations u followed the first-order process

$$u = 0.75u_{-1} + e, \tag{6}$$

where e represents the new shock in any period. The coefficient 0.75 must be the same in the equations for all budgetary components to preserve the budget identity, and it was selected by examining the uncorrected residuals from all seven or six budgetary equations.

The set of identities given above requires that the sum of all dependent variable equals $(B_{-1} + G)$, so the coefficients of this variable sum to one and the constants and coefficients of all other variables sum to zero. This constraint was automatically built into the coefficient estimates by the simple expedient of including every independent variable in the equation for every dependent variable. There are more elaborate ways to incorporate constraints if some of the coefficients have to be zeroed out, but most of our coefficients made reasonable sense. Since our main interest was in the residuals anyway, we followed golfers' summer rules and played the coefficients as they lay.[4]

The estimates for state governments are shown in table 8.1. The row sum of coefficients for the constant and each independent variable other than grants and previously unallocated balances is zero and that for grants and previously unallocated balances is one, as discussed above. Hence in this first year a dollar of federal grants raises direct spending by 0.2935, grants to localities by 0.3155, causes 0.0371 worth of tax cuts and raises the surplus by 0.3538. Next year this 0.3538 goes into unallocated balances and is further distributed to spending increases and tax cuts. On the other hand, in the first year a dollar rise in GNP raises all taxes by 0.1013 (0.0312 + 0.0121 + 0.0442 + 0.0138), spending by 0.0682 (0.0473 + 0.0209), and the surplus by 0.0332. Next year this amount too causes further rises in spending and this time slight cuts in taxes. Since the spending coefficient on untied grants is well above that for private income, there is an important "flypaper" effect—funds' inflows stick where they hit. Such an effect is quite characteristic of empirical models of state and local

Table 8.1
Budget constraint model, state governments annual observations, 1960–86

Independent variable	Dependent variables						
	Direct spending	Grants to localities	Minus deductible personal taxes	Minus deductible business taxes	Minus sales taxes	Minus nondeductible taxes	Unallocated balances
Constant ($ billion)	−14.38	−2.56	4.67	−2.32	−6.78	4.44	16.96
Grants and previously unallocated balances	0.2935	0.3155	0.0617	−0.0113	0.0382	−0.0515	0.3538
	(2.3)	(4.4)	(1.2)	(0.3)	(0.6)	(1.1)	(2.5)
Income less federal withdrawals	0.0473	0.0209	−0.0312	−0.0121	−0.0442	−0.0138	0.0332
	(5.3)	(4.1)	(8.7)	(5.4)	(9.2)	(4.3)	(3.3)
Gross price	34.54	23.26	30.30	23.66	47.63	−4.67	−154.72
	(1.1)	(1.3)	(2.4)	(2.8)	(2.8)	(0.4)	(4.4)
Residual statistics (after correction for serial correlation)							
R^2	0.9912	0.9902	0.9881	0.9318	0.9893	0.9828	0.5617
Standard error ($ billion)	2.05	1.16	0.82	0.55	1.09	0.74	2.52

Note: semi-first differences ($\rho = 0.75$); t ratios below coefficients.

behavior, and there have been many, many theoretical rationales developed to explain it.

A 1% increase in the gross price deflator raises money spending by $.58 billion, implying a price elasticity of spending demand of about -0.8 at present levels of the variables. The finding that state spending demand is inelastic is standard, though it is puzzling that a rise in the gross price and money spending is coupled with tax cuts, leading to a large decline in fund balances. But the gross price variable (the state and local purchases deflator) in a time-series analysis is certainly measured very poorly, it behaves pretty much as a trend, and it should not interfere with our attempt to discern TRA86 induced changes in residuals.

Table 8.2 gives the residuals for these equations. Since the equations were fit assuming a first-order serial correlation process, it is not straightforward to know which residuals to give. The upper part of the table contains the residuals before any correction for serial correlation, u in equation (6), for 1987 and 1988 in comparison with those for the rest of the 1980s. Up to 1986 the residuals were within the regression sample, the 1987 residuals are out-of-sample extrapolations based on 1987 values of the exogenous variables, and for two of the series—deductible personal taxes and sales taxes—this calculation could also be done for 1988. As before, the residuals sum to zero across all budgetary components for each date.

The next panel shows the component of these residuals that would have been predicted at the end of 1986, the last year before TRA86 went into effect. To measure these predicted residuals, we have used whatever information was available at the end of 1986. The uncorrected 1986 residuals were known and forecast through equation (6). Given these, the model solved for the 1987 value of B, which in turn was used to generate predicted 1988 residuals across all seven budgetary equations. As the footnote to the table explains, since the 1986 prediction of 1987 stocks was higher than actual by $2.5 billion, this $2.5 billion was allocated across all seven budgetary equations by the estimated coefficients to give predicted 1988 residuals that sum to the same amount. Then these predicted residuals were subtracted from the uncorrected residuals to give the new shocks for 1987 and 1988, shown in the bottom panel.

These new shock residuals suggest the following story about the first year impact of TRA86 on state budgets:

1. There was a positive shock in the direct spending residual of $6.6 billion for 1987. The authors who predicted a small decline in state spend-

Table 8.2
1980s residuals, state budget model (billions of current $)

| | Uncorrected residuals (u) | | | | | | |
Date	Direct spending	Grants to localities	Minus deductible personal taxes	Minus deductible business taxes	Minus sales taxes	Minus nondeductible taxes	Unallocated balances
1980	−5.3	0	0.1	−1.9	1.0	2.0	3.8
1981	−8.1	−2.4	1.8	−1.1	2.9	0.1	6.5
1982	−4.7	−2.9	1.1	0.6	2.7	−0.6	3.6
1983	−3.0	−3.0	0.9	0.5	2.5	−0.3	1.9
1984	−3.2	−2.4	−0.7	0.5	1.5	−0.5	4.6
1985	0.0	−0.7	−1.0	0.6	−0.5	−0.8	2.1
1986	4.3	0.3	−0.1	0.2	−0.7	−1.0	−3.3
1987	9.8	2.9	−4.8	−3.4	−1.5	2.6	−6.1
1988	na	na	0.1	na	−0.7	na	na
1987 value	248.6	135.2	−83.4	−25.7	−123.8	−57.7	−23.1
Predicted as of 1986[a]							
1987	3.2	0.2	−0.1	0.2	−0.6	−0.8	−2.5
1988	3.1	1.0	0.1	0.1	−0.4	−0.7	−1.0
New shock (uncorrected less predicted)							
1987	6.6	2.7	−4.7	−3.6	−0.9	3.4	−3.6
1988	na	na	0	na	−0.3	na	na

a. Since 1986 prediction of 1987 unallocated balances was higher than actual by $2.5 billion, this amount is allocated across all seven components according to the regression coefficients.

ing, such as Courant and Gramlich, were wrong, but not nearly as far wrong as those who predicted a large decline in spending, such as Holtz-Eakin and Rosen. The shock could be partly caused by the nongrant mandating of expenditures discussed earlier, but even the extreme estimates of the governors would not peg it as this large.

2. There was a positive shock in the residual for state grants to localities of $2.7 billion. This shock could well be due to federal grant policy, because federal grants to localities were cut by the large total of $4.5 billion between 1986 and 1987. This rise in state grants to localities could then be compensating for some of the decline in federal grants to localities.[5]

3. There was a positive shock in deductible personal taxes of $4.7 billion (the residual of the negative of taxes was negative). Gold's windfall amount mentioned earlier would seem to account for only a small share of this total, but there are many reasons why our residual could be above the net calculated by Gold. States could still be benefiting from a capital gains windfall in their 1987 refunds, or their discretionary measures to return the windfall could simply not have been made yet or taken effect yet. In view of these possibilities, our shock of $4.7 billion is likely to be quite close to the mark.

4. There was a positive shock in deductible business taxes of $3.6 billion, again very close to Aten's windfall amount.

5. Sales taxes showed a positive shock of $0.9 billion. Apparently the financing effect described above outweighed the price effect, belying the predictions of those who argued the reverse.

6. Nondeductible taxes and user fees showed a negative shock of $3.4 billion, a change that does not makes sense under any of the hypotheses discussed earlier. Even Inman's ingenious account of why sales taxes might have increased cannot simultaneously explain why regressive user fees might have decreased. The simultaneous decline in oil prices could explain some drop in severance taxes, part of the reason for the decline in this catchall, but there is no obvious story for the sharp drop in "fines," which accounts for most of the drop. The only consolation is that all other pre-TRA86 estimates of user fee sensitivity also had the wrong sign.

7. The surplus showed a negative shock of $3.6 billion, the net implied by all of these spending and tax changes.

Then we move on to 1988. At present data are available for only two of the taxes; personal deductible taxes and sales taxes. But they both show that taxes are moving in the expected direction. The personal tax windfall now seems like it is down to zero, much as Gold might have forecast, and the positive shock in sales taxes is also very small. So price effects are not of the wrong sign, but they are obviously not of the right sign either. In fact the 1959–86 equation works remarkably well for these two taxes through 1988.

Given the large state spending residuals and the windfalls, it is not terribly surprising that state deductible taxes rose in the short run. And it may not even be surprising that state sales taxes rose. But what is very definitely surprising from almost any standpoint is that state nondeductible taxes and fines went down.

Regressions for localities are shown in table 8.3. The equations are presented in the same form, the only change being that there is no analogue for state grants to localities—all local spending is direct. The equations again show a powerful flypaper effect and again imply a price elasticity of spending demand in the neighborhood of −0.5, a standard result. This time rises in the gross price do not lead to any noticeable changes in taxes but are entirely financed by drawing down balances.

The residuals in table 8.4 tell a very similar story about the impact of TRA86:

1. The first year new shock for direct spending is $10.3 billion, only about $1 billion of which could be attributed to the cuts in higher government grants to localities (federal grants down by $4.5, state grants up by $2.7, and the coefficient of grants on spending is 0.6600).

2. Both types of deductible taxes show a positive new shock of $2.1 billion. Since these deductible taxes are mainly residential property taxes, there is no windfall, and the entire rise must be attributed to the need to finance the rise in direct spending.

3. There is no new shock for sales taxes. Indeed, the 1987 value of $24.9 billion shown in the table indicates that local sales taxes are pretty minor to begin with.

4. User fees have a slight positive shock of $1.4 billion.

5. Fund balances show a negative shock of $6.8 billion.

Again we have the large positive residual in spending, also observed at the state level. There is some rise in deductible taxes to finance this spending demand, and this time some rise in nondeductible taxes and fees as well. But for the most part in 1987 local governments had not gotten around to financing the spending increase but just let balances fall.

Table 8.3
Budget constraint model, local governments annual observations, 1960–86

Independent variable	Dependent variables					
	Direct spending	Minus deductible personal taxes	Minus deductible business taxes	Minus sales taxes	Minus nondeductible taxes	Unallocated balances
Constant ($ billion)	8.20	−8.48	−0.10	1.59	5.20	−6.42
Grants and previously unallocated balances	0.6600 (4.4)	0.0395 (0.4)	−0.0026 (0.7)	−0.0312 (2.7)	−0.0216 (0.5)	0.3561 (2.4)
Income less federal withdrawals	0.0097 (0.5)	−0.0289 (2.3)	−0.0009 (1.8)	−0.0049 (3.3)	−0.0176 (3.3)	0.0426 (2.3)
Gross price	151.71 (2.9)	−3.03 (0.1)	2.06 (1.5)	−0.65 (0.2)	7.53 (0.5)	−157.62 (0.5)
Residual statistics (after correction for serial correlation)						
R^2	0.9888	0.9534	0.8137	0.9890	0.9763	0.8275
Standard error ($ billion)	3.23	2.12	0.09	0.25	0.90	3.13

Note: semi-first differences ($\rho = 0.75$); t ratios below coefficients.

Table 8.4
1980s residuals, local budget model (billions of current $)

Date	Uncorrected residuals (u)					
	Direct spending	Minus deductible personal taxes	Minus deductible business taxes	Minus sales taxes	Minus nondeductible taxes	Unallocated balances
1980	−3.0	7.8	−0.2	1.0	3.7	−9.5
1981	−2.8	6.6	−0.3	0.9	3.0	−7.6
1982	−3.9	2.5	−0.3	0.2	−0.1	1.3
1983	−3.6	2.4	−0.2	0.1	−0.9	2.1
1984	−7.1	2.7	−0.2	−0.1	−0.3	4.8
1985	−6.7	0.4	−0.4	−0.5	−1.3	8.3
1986	1.9	−2.6	−0.5	−0.3	−1.6	2.9
1987	11.7	−3.6	−0.8	−0.3	−2.6	−4.6
1988	na	−3.8	na	−0.9	na	na
1987 value	368.2	−124.6	−2.2	−24.9	−62.6	29.6
Predicted as of 1986[a]						
1987	1.4	−2.0	−0.3	−0.2	−1.2	2.2
1988	−0.4	−1.6	−0.2	−0.2	−0.9	0.9
New shock (uncorrected less predicted)						
1987	10.3	−1.6	−0.5	−0.1	−1.4	−6.8
1988	na	−2.2	na	−0.7	na	na

a. Since 1986 prediction of 1987 unallocated balances was less than actual by $2.2 billion, this amount is deducted from all six components according to the coefficients in table 8.4.

By 1988 some of these tax responses begin to occur but not in directions pleasing to those who predicted large price effects. Unlike for state governments where the embarrassing positive shocks in deductible and sales taxes are at least getting smaller, at the local level these shocks seem to be getting larger. That could reflect the financing effect of continued spending pressures for higher revenue: It certainly does not confirm a change in the revenue mix due to tax price changes.

In the theory outlined above state and local spending are endogenous and are reduced by TRA86. These econometric estimates make it hard to see price impacts on the revenue mix because instead of falling, both state and local spending are rising so rapidly. To see if our results were being driven by the spending residuals, we reestimated the model, this time making state and local spending exogenous so that their residuals are constrained to equal zero. Then the equations are refit with only the tax and unallocated balances residuals adding to zero. Instead of equation (5), the constraining identity becomes

$$B_{-1} + G - E = -D - S - N + B. \tag{7}$$

This variant of the model is given in tables 8.5 through 8.8. The equations are, if anything, more sensible than before because prices can be assumed to affect spending, spending to affect taxes, and the puzzling direct link between prices and taxes can be suppressed. But the residuals tell

Table 8.5
Recursive budget constraint model, local governments annual observations, 1960–86

Independent variable	Minus deductible personal taxes	Minus deductible business taxes	Minus sales taxes	Minus non-deductible taxes	Unallocated balances
Constant ($ billion)	8.52	1.20	−1.22	4.02	−12.52
Grants—spending and previously unallocated balances	0.0621 (1.1)	0.0037 (0.1)	0.2103 (3.1)	−0.0054 (0.1)	0.7292 (5.3)
Income less federal withdrawals	−0.0168 (3.7)	−0.0055 (1.8)	−0.0140 (2.6)	−0.0165 (4.6)	0.0528 (5.0)
Residual statistics (after correction for serial correlation)					
R^2	0.9847	0.9087	0.9894	0.9817	0.5885
Standard error ($ billion)	0.91	0.62	1.06	0.75	2.14

Note: semi-first differences ($\rho = 0.75$); t ratios below coefficients.

Table 8.6
1980s residuals, state model (billions of current $)

| Date | Uncorrected residuals (u) | | | | |
	Minus deductible personal taxes	Minus deductible business taxes	Minus sales taxes	Minus non-deductible taxes	Unallocated balances
1980	1.3	−0.9	1.6	1.5	−3.5
1981	2.5	−0.2	2.4	−0.3	−4.4
1982	2.6	2.1	4.7	−1.0	−8.1
1983	1.5	1.7	3.8	0	−7.0
1984	−1.4	1.0	0.9	0	−0.6
1985	−1.2	0.9	−0.8	−0.7	1.9
1986	−0.7	−0.1	−1.5	−1.1	3.4
1987	−5.0	−3.7	−0.4	−2.8	6.3
1988	−1.8	na	−3.6	na	na
1987 value	−83.4	−25.7	−123.8	−57.7	−23.1
Predicted as of 1986[a]					
1987	−0.5	−0.1	−1.2	−0.8	2.6
1988	−0.5	−0.1	−1.4	−0.6	0
New shock (uncorrected less predicted)					
1987	−4.5	−3.6	0.8	3.6	3.7
1988	−1.3	na	−2.2	na	na

a. Since 1986 prediction of 1987 unallocated balances was less than actual by $2.6 billion, this amount is deducted from all five components according to the regression coefficients.

Table 8.7
Recursive budget constraint model, local governments annual observations, 1960−86

Independent variable	Minus deductible personal taxes	Minus deductible business taxes	Minus sales taxes	Minus non-deductible taxes	Unallocated balances
Constant ($ billion)	0.55	0.36	1.84	5.48	−8.22
Grants—spending and previously unallocated balances	0.2519 (3.0)	0.0013 (0.3)	−0.0187 (1.5)	−0.0380 (0.9)	0.8036 (6.5)
Income less federal withdrawals	−0.0191 (6.3)	−0.0005 (3.0)	−0.0074 (16.4)	−0.0179 (11.9)	0.448 (10.0)
Residual statistics (after correction for serial correlation)					
R^2	0.9659	0.7848	0.9865	0.9764	0.8743
Standard error ($ billion)	1.78	0.09	0.27	0.88	2.62

Note: semi-first differences ($\rho = 0.75$); t ratios below coefficients.

Table 8.8
1980s residuals, recursive local model (billions of current $)

| Date | Uncorrected residuals (u) | | | | |
	Minus deductible personal taxes	Minus deductible business taxes	Minus sales taxes	Minus non-deductible taxes	Unallocated balances
1980	8.3	0.3	0.9	3.8	−13.0
1981	7.6	0.2	1.2	3.1	−11.8
1982	4.2	0.3	0.5	0.2	−4.9
1983	3.5	0.4	0.5	−0.7	−3.4
1984	1.8	0.3	0.5	−0.1	−2.2
1985	1.3	0.1	−0.2	−1.2	3.0
1986	3.5	0	−0.4	−1.9	6.3
1987	2.0	−0.3	−0.5	−3.3	6.5
1988	−5.2	na	−0.4	na	na
1987 value	−124.6	−2.2	−24.9	−62.6	−29.6
Predicted as of 1986[a]					
1987	−2.6	0	−0.3	−1.5	4.7
1988	−3.1	0	−0.1	−1.0	0.3
New shock (uncorrected less predicted)					
1987	0.6	−0.3	−0.2	−1.8	1.8
1988	−2.1	na	−0.3	na	na

a. Since 1986 prediction of 1987 unallocated balances was less than actual by $4.7 billion, this amount is deducted from all five components according to the regression coefficients.

about the same story as before. The new state shocks in table 8.6 still show the windfall gradually dying out for deductible taxes. This time the sales tax shock begins negative and then becomes positive in 1988, exactly the reverse pattern of the earlier estimates. Nondeductible fees and fines are still down. Hence by and large the recursive model for states still gives no comfort to those who believe in large price effects.

The new local shocks in table 8.8 are generally pretty small. As in table 8.4, local user fees move the right way, and sales taxes' residuals are very small. Deductible taxes rise for some reason (the windfall effect is still inoperative for local property taxes), as do balances.

Hence as regards fiscal flows, it is frankly hard to see a big impact of TRA86 on either state or local governments. For some reason direct spending went up at both levels of government. This put pressure on governmental finances and led to some nonwindfall-induced rises in deductible taxes at both levels. Sales tax residuals were generally positive, if fairly small, indicating that the financing effect seemed to dominate the price effect. Nondeductible taxes and fees, which should have risen sharply at both levels of government, in fact did not, rising only slightly at the local level and falling at the state level. The main financing of the spending surge was then left over for fund balances. To the extent that taxes changed to finance this surge, knowing about TRA86 would not have helped one to make very good predictions of changes in the revenue mix. And the predictions of large budgetary effects by Holtz-Eakin and Rosen and Feldstein and Metcalf are simply not supported by the experience so far.

Other Evidence

These regression residuals seem quite consistent with other evidence of post-TRA86 fiscal changes for state and local governments. It is hard to document the puzzling fall in nondeductible taxes and fees made up of countless items not even recorded separately in the aggregate accounts. But sales tax changes are generally made at the state level, and there it is easier to see what is going on. According to Gold (1988), Gold and collaborators (1987, 1988), and Fabricus and collaborators (1989), the behavior of many states was consistent with the pattern of our residuals. In 1987 and 1988 seven states substantially increased their sales taxes, in 1989 five more states significantly increased sales taxes, and a number had less significant increases. Both the regression results and this more informal evidence then confirm the puzzling move toward greater use of state sales taxes.

The situation with income taxes is more interesting, and it goes beyond a simple explanation of the residuals. Even though no clear story emerges from these residuals, there does seem to be evidence of deeper structural change in state income tax systems that mirrors changes at the federal level. Gold (1988) and Fabricus and collaborators (1989) detail a number of these:

1. By 1989, 8 states had restructured their entire income tax, generally increasing conformity with the federal income tax.

2. By way of redistributing their windfall gains, 19 states reduced income tax rates and only 6 increased them as of 1989.

3. By 1988, 18 states had increased their personal exemption or credit, 20 states had increased their standard deduction, and 12 states eliminated all taxes on poor families. More states moved in these directions in 1989.

The net result of these changes is to reduce administrative costs by increasing the conformity between state and federal tax systems, and to enhance economic efficiency by generally lowering state marginal tax rates. Equity is also improved, to the extent that many poor families are removed from state as well as federal tax rolls. In the long run these structural effects of TRA86 should be much more important than the price effects economists spend much more time discussing. And we might say that even if we could find some price effects.

8.2 Mobility and Capitalization

As was seen already, TRA86 affected the tax price of state and local public expenditure differentially in different states. Tax prices rose in all states because of the drop in marginal federal tax rates and the elimination of the sales tax deduction. But because the incidence of deductible and sales taxes varies a good deal across states, the effect of TRA86 on effective tax burdens also varied a good deal. In this section we try to exploit that variation by looking at economic and fiscal behavior in adjacent cities (sometimes counties) on opposite sides of state lines before and after TRA86.

By looking at adjacent cities, we can make the convenient assumption that everything other than tax prices changed in the same way on both sides of the state boundary between 1986 and 1987. Take two cities—say, Fargo, ND, and Moorehead, MN. These cities are in the same labor market, the same grain market, and the same tractor market. Even fairly localized changes in economic environment should affect them in about the same way. But TRA86 will not: It will cause a much higher rise in effective tax burdens in high-tax Minnesota than in low-tax North Dakota.

What would then happen? A first possibility is that governments would adjust, with Minnesota, say, eliminating its sales tax. In the first part of the chapter we found minimal evidence of such adjustments to take advantage of TRA86 for states and localities as a whole, though it is always possible that there would be more adjustment in our key border towns. If there is no governmental adjustment, then the private sector may adjust its location of business or residential activity. Our basic strategy then is to pick pairs of cities where the differential effect of TRA86 on tax prices was large and to analyze a number of measures of economic behavior for each pair. The reason for looking exclusively at cases where the differential effect was large is simply that little time and less data have passed since TRA86; if TRA86 is going to have measurable effects, it is most likely to have them across these pairs of cities.

Even in this purposely biased sample, there are probably few cases where differences in the change in the local cost of public services are large enough to induce people to bear the cost of moving across a state border (the biggest differences are on the order of 0.5% of annual income for the average taxpayer). But the differences could be large enough to affect the behavior of both households and firms that are potentially moving within or into the economic area. Such effects are both a consequence of local and state fiscal policy and impose a constraint (or opportunity) on the fisc. The town on the favored side of the border will enjoy a fiscal windfall at the expense of the town on the unfavored side. Direct evidence on these fiscal effects with one year of data seems too much to hope for, but direct evidence for the economic effects has a better chance. The capitalized value of a half percent of annual income is perhaps $1,000 for the average household, much more for the average itemizing household or the average rich household.[6] If all of the change is capitalized immediately, there should be noticeable changes in property values. If some of the change remains available to new entrants, there should be noticeable increases in population and economic activity on the favored side of the border.

Ideally, we would look at changes in the market value of existing real property, which would measure the extent to which changes in local tax benefits were valued in local markets. In practice, none of the measures available is anywhere near that good. For some of our pairs we have data on changes in assessed value, but we have no idea how much the change is due to improvements and how much to revaluation of existing property, nor do we know the relationship between assessed value and market value. Moreover none of the data sets we use has complete information for every city, and this makes things especially difficult when the unit of analysis is the city pair. If, for example, data of tolerable-looking quality are available for 60% of the cities, we will only be able to use 36% of the pairs.

In order to choose pairs of cities (sometimes counties) that might be expected to show effects of TRA86, we constructed a measure of the change in the cost of state and local taxes collected from residents. As before, t stands for the mean marginal tax rate faced by itemizers in a state, a for the fraction of taxpayers who itemize, S for sales taxes, and D for deductible taxes. If governments do not change their tax structure as a result of TRA86, the increase in state and locally borne cost of tax collections as a share of state income ($\Delta C/Y$) can be expressed as

$$\frac{\Delta C}{Y} = \frac{atS}{Y} - \frac{\Delta(at)D}{Y}. \tag{8}$$

We calculated $\Delta C/Y$ for each of the contiguous 48 states (Alaska and Hawaii did not seem promising sources of city pairs), using Metcalf's NBER TAXSIM calculations of a and t for 1985 (the most recent year available) and actual state budget data for 1986. $\Delta(at)$ was estimated by assuming that $\Delta(at)/(1 - at) = -0.46$ in all states, the average estimate that Courant and Rubinfeld (1987) derived from data used by Hausman and Poterba (1987).

Having estimated $\Delta C/Y$ for 48 states, we plotted the values on a map and looked for those pairs of states that had cities near to each other and that had the largest differences in $\Delta C/Y$. We required that there be cities of noticeable size, both because that increased the probability of finding useful data and because it enhanced the plausibility of the maintained hypothesis that the relevant labor market conditions would be the same on both sides of the border.[7]

Fourteen pairs of adjacent states had values of $\Delta C/Y$ of 0.002 or greater. The largest difference (Pennsylvania–New York) was 0.004. For each of the 14 pairs of states, we looked for adjacent cities on both sides of the border. Some (Greenwich, CT–Port Chester, Rye, NY; Portsmouth, NH–Kittery, ME) are very close indeed. Others (Billings, MT–Sheridan, WY) are much farther apart. And some simply do not exist, such as on the border between Oregon–California or, curiously, Massachusetts–New York. For some states there is more than one potentially usable pair. Pennsylvania and New York, for example, have a long border, and cities (or counties) can be matched across it in more than one place. Information about the city pairs and their data availability is given in table 8.9.

For each city (or county) pair for which data were available, we analyzed data on building permits, assessed property values, and county employment. In all cases we computed the share of the favored member of the pair in the total volume of activity in the pair and measured the change in the share between 1986 and 1987.

Usable building permit data for single-family houses are available for 11 pairs of cities; for multifamily houses, no cities. TRA86 should have caused the share of building permits to rise in the favored state. But it did so in only 4 of the 11 cases, with an average change in share of -7.5%. When these data were smoothed by subtracting the average of available 1984–86 shares from the 1987 share, the share rose in 5 of the 11 cases, with an average change in share of -4.8%. It is also possible that some building permits taken out in 1986 could have been in response to TRA86, so we compared the 1986 and 1987 average share with the share in the previous three years. In this test 6 of the 11 cases were positive, with an average

Table 8.9
Information on city and state pairs

States	$100\Delta C/Y$	City or county	Data
NY–PA	$0.73 - 0.33 = 0.4$	Jamestown–Warren	
		Olean–Bradford	
		Binghamton, Johnson City, Endicott	BP
		–Dunmore, Carbondale	
MA–NH	$0.47 - 0.12 = 0.35$	Lawrence, Lowell, Methuen–Nashua	BP
		Essex, Middlesex–Hillsborough,	CBP
		Rockingham counties	
		Dracut–Nashua	AV
		Lawrence, Methuen–Salem	AV
WA–OR	$0.61 - 0.27 = 0.34$	Vancouver–Portland	BP, AV
WY–MT	$0.47 - 0.13 = 0.34$	Sheridan–Billings	BP
NY–CT	$0.73 - 0.41 = 0.32$	Rye–Greenwich, Stamford	BP
MN–ND	$0.51 - 0.21 = 0.30$	Moorehead–Fargo	BP
		Clay–Cass counties	CBP
UT–ID	$0.58 - 0.29 = 0.29$	No places	
VT–NH	$0.39 - 0.12 = 0.27$	Brattleboro–Keene	BP
		Windham–Cheshire counties	CBP
MD–DE	$0.50 - 0.24 = 0.26$	No data	
NY–MA	$0.73 - 0.47 = 0.26$	No places	
CA–OR	$0.51 - 0.27 = 0.24$	No places	
ME–NH	$0.34 - 0.12 = 0.22$	Kittery–Portsmouth	BP, AV
		York–Rockingham counties	CBP
NM–TX	$0.42 - 0.22 = 0.20$	Las Cruces–El Paso	BP
		Clovis–Amarillo, Lubbock	BP
NJ–DE	$0.43 - 0.24 = 0.20$	Pennsville–Wilmington	BP

Note: AV = assessed value; BP = building permits; CBP = county business patterns.

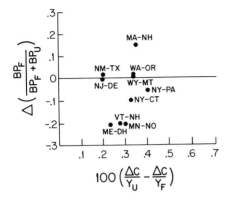

Figure 8.2
Change in building permit shares and tax costs: BP_F = building permits in state favored by TRA86; BP_U = building permits in state not favored by TRA86; $\Delta C/Y_F$, $\Delta C/Y_U$ = as defined in equation (8), 1985–86 data. Building permit shares are based on 1987 data over the 1984–86 average.

change in share of 0.1%. All of this leads to the conclusion that *1986* was an unusually good year for the favored cities, but 1987 an unusually bad year. TRA86 could explain the first change but not the second, and certainly not the fact that the two-year average was unchanged from the previous three-year average. One example of this relationship between $\Delta C/Y$ and changes in the share of building permits is plotted in figure 8.2. What should be a neat positive relationship entirely in quadrant I is in fact a jumble.

Regarding assessed values, the use of the Moody's (1988) series for calculations such as these can be seriously misleading if there are changes in assessment rules from year to year. But excluding those city pairs where neither element had a change in assessment practices between 1986 and 1987 left only four city pairs.[8] The share for the favored pair did rise in three of them, but this is hardly a statistically significant finding.[9]

Finally, *County Business Patterns* provides extensive information on economic activity in U.S. counties and is in principle suited to shedding some light on the problem at hand. Unfortunately, the Census Bureau has not yet released 1987 for most regions of the country. New England and the Mountain states are all that are available as of September 1989, giving us three New Hampshire pairs and Montana–Wyoming. Shares of total employment and total payroll did rise in three of our four pairs, but again these are awfully sparse data from which to generalize.

The upshot of our attempts to look at early evidence on mobility and capitalization is more randomness. In the previous section there was some suggestion from the early data that TRA86 was not having large effects on the budget position of states and localities: Here a more appropriate conclusion is that it is just too early to do analyses of this sort.

8.3   The Market for State and Local Bonds

TRA86 was also predicted to have powerful effects on the market for state and local bonds. The most important reason is that the value of the exemption of state and local bond interest is now reduced, both by the lower personal and corporate tax rates and by the fact that half of bond interest is now included in the base for the corporate alternative minimum tax. Other provisions that could have an effect are those that eliminate the interest deduction for banks that use the borrowing to buy tax-exempt securities, and those that limit the issuing of private-purpose tax-exempt bonds by state and local governments.

To see how all this works, a general expression for the impact of the interest rate on tax-exempt municipal bonds m can be written as

$$m = r(1 - bt), \tag{9}$$

where r is the interest rate on taxable securities, t is now the marginal federal tax rate applied to the taxable interest income of the highest income taxpayers, and b is an adjustment factor.[10] Were all marginal tax rates the same and state and local securities perfect substitutes for private securities, b would equal one. But if municipal bonds are held by investors with lower tax rates than this maximum, b can be less than one empirically. Poterba (1989, from whom much of the following analysis is taken) shows that over the 1980s b has been about 0.93 for short-term bonds (based on the corporate rate paid by banks, alleged to be the marginal investors in this market) and about 0.55 for long-term bonds (based on the rate paid by high income individuals, alleged to be the marginal investors in this market). The different top-bracket tax rates are used because historically there has been a good deal of segmentation between the short- and long-term markets—governments are either forced to use, or find it advantageous to use, long-term bonds to finance construction projects even though the implied interest rate is higher, and banks have been arbitrageurs in the short- but not the long-term market (Mussa and Kormendi 1979).

When m and r differ, Gordon and Slemrod (1986) point to the existence of a number of separate arbitrage opportunities involving state and local bonds:

1. Classic governmental arbitrage, where the government borrows at the tax-exempt rate m and lends at the taxable rate r. Citizens gain $r - m$ on every dollar borrowed. The Internal Revenue Service (IRS) has rules against this form of arbitrage. But Gordon and Slemrod show how difficult it is for the IRS to enforce these rules, and Metcalf (1989) shows that a lot of this form of arbitrage does seem to exist.

2. Brokerage arbitrage, where citizens use their government as a broker. Citizens borrow at $r(1 - t)$ and prepay taxes so their government can invest and earn r. Citizens must trust their friendly local government to credit them the prepaid taxes. If they are so willing, they can gain rt. Note that bonds are not involved in this transaction.

3. High-income arbitrage, where citizens borrow at $r(1 - t)$ and invest in municipal bonds at m, gaining $m - r(1 - t)$. The citizens' own local government plays no role in this transaction. The gap between m and $r(1 - t)$ also corresponds to the annual gain per dollar borrowed realized by high-income people from this sort of tax subsidy for state and local governments, in that these high-income people earn $m - r(1 - t)$ more than they would if they were the marginal investors and b were equal to one.

4. Low-income arbitrage, where low-income citizens have their government borrow at m, cut taxes, and then let the citizens invest the proceeds at $r(1 - t_1)$, where t_1 is the tax rate faced by low-income people, gaining $r(1 - t_1) - m$ in the process. Unlike the above form of arbitrage, where it is assumed that high-income citizens face a high marginal rate, these low-income citizens face much lower effective progressive marginal rates. They are able to make more in aftertax returns on taxable securities than they pay on tax-exempt municipals. Gordon and Slemrod do find that in 1977 communities with low marginal tax rates borrowed more than communities with high marginal tax rates, other things equal.

How is all this changed by TRA86? There are at least five provisions that could have an impact:

1. The reduction in individual and corporate marginal tax rates means that the gap between r and m should diminish. To state and local governments, this means that the tax-exempt rate should rise relative to other interest rates.

2. That marginal tax rates are compressed eliminates at least one of the arbitrage channels that previously benefited low marginal tax rate communities.

3. That banks can now no longer deduct interest when they buy tax-exempt securities means that they are now less likely to hold, and arbitrage, short-term state and local bonds.

4. That tax-exempt interest is now included in the base for the corporate alternative minimum tax means that municipal bonds are now not tax free for some banks, again reducing banks demand for short-term state and local securities.

5. Volume caps on private purpose tax-exempt securities should lower the supply of these.

The cut in marginal tax rates and the bank provisions should raise the tax-exempt rate relative to other rates, reducing the tax subsidy for state and local governments. This prediction has come true: According to Poterba's (1989) calculations, the short-term tax-exempt rate averaged $0.564r$ from 1982–85 and $0.685r$ in 1988; the long-term tax-exempt rate averaged $0.792r$ from 1982–85 and $0.845r$ in 1988.[11] If banks are no longer the marginal investors in the short-term market, this short-term rate could also become more volatile. Over time the reduced subsidy should show up in higher state and local interest costs and perhaps in reduced state and local construction spending. However, given all the opportunities for financial market arbitrage, it is not at all clear that m, rather than r, sets the hurdle rate for state and local physical capital formation.[12]

Second, the cut in the high-income individual rate from 0.5 to 0.28, and in the corporate rate from 0.46 to 0.34, means that all of the gaps leading to arbitrage possibilities should either diminish or disappear altogether:

1. The return to classic governmental arbitrage has fallen from $r(1 - 0.564) = 0.436r$ to $r(1 - 0.685) = 0.315r$ for short-term bonds and from $r(1 - 0.792) = 0.208r$ to $r(1 - 0.845) = 0.155r$ for long-term bonds (Poterba 1989). These declines, and the volume caps on private purpose bonds, should reduce both the reward from and the ability of governments to engage in this sort of arbitrage.

2. The return to brokerage arbitrage has fallen from $0.46r$ to $0.34r$ if done by corporations and from $0.5r$ to $0.28r$ if done by high-income individuals. Even when this return was much larger, Gordon and Slemrod found little of this sort of arbitrage, perhaps because high-income investors did not

trust their governments as brokers, but just in case the trust grows, the opportunities are now constricted.

3. The return to high-income arbitrage fell from $r(0.792 - 0.5) = 0.292r$ to $r(0.845 - 0.72) = 0.125r$ for high-income personal investors in long-term bonds, and by similar large amounts for other combinations of individual and corporate investors in long- and short-term securities. Since state and local governments play no role in this form of arbitrage, it will be hard to notice anything on state and local books, but there will, as stated, also be an implied reduction in the excess returns realized by high-income taxpayers from the tax subsidy for state and local bonds.

4. The return on low-income arbitrage is made negative. There are now no positive taxpayers for whom $r(1 - t_1)$ exceeds m. This change would seem to block out entirely this arbitrage channel and should make it difficult to replicate the Gordon-Slemrod finding that low marginal tax rate communities borrow more in the post-TRA86 world.

Third, there is at least indirect evidence that the volume caps on private purpose securities are having an impact. There was a flood of these offerings in late 1986, after TRA86 was passed but before its provisions took effect, confirming again the proposition that the best place to look for impacts of taxes on behavior is in the timing of actions that groups are planning to take anyway.

In all cases credit market efficiency is improved and both the revenue losses and the social losses associated with tax arbitrage are mitigated. One must go through financial data much more carefully than we have to make definitive quantitative estimates of the gains from this side of TRA86, but the gains could be sizeable.

8.4 Conclusions

The most widely discussed aspect of the impact of TRA86 on state and local behavior is in its alteration of the locally borne cost of different types of taxes. Sales taxes are made much more costly and income and property taxes somewhat more costly. Despite many predictions and some econometric work that suggested that these tax changes would have large effects, as of 1988 they had not seemed to have had much impact on state or local budgets as measured by out-of-sample fiscal data. Generally spending went up, contrary to both theoretical and empirical predictions, fines and user fees went down, contrary to theoretical predictions, and one has to squint very hard to make sense of the movements in deductible taxes and sales taxes. In any case the movements are quite small, even in those rare cases where they are in the expected direction.

Another way to search for effects of TRA86 is to compare activity measures for pairs of state border communities affected quite differently by TRA86 but quite similarly by everything else. Using border communities introduces a very large bias toward finding large effects, and even with this large bias, the effects on measures of activity such as building permits seem miniscule. Indeed, our point estimate is that they have the wrong sign. Here, however, we are mining early data so hard that our conclusions must be quite tentative.

So what are the effects of TRA86 on the state and local sector? In the end we are forced back to rather subtle factors. TRA86 stimulated an unusual amount of state legislative activity regarding taxes, and the result will be state income taxes that generally have lower rates, broader bases, and less taxation of the poor, mimicking the federal tax changes. TRA86 reduced the value of the tax exemption for state and local bonds, and the result will be higher interest costs for states and localities, reduced efficiency losses, reduced arbitrage revenue losses, and perhaps reduced capital spending. TRA86 may have done some other things as well, but three years after the fact its impacts are much smaller than predicted, and there is no evidence that its long-run effects will be large.

Notes

We are grateful to Steven D. Gold, Donald Peters, and Gilbert Metcalf for making available recent data, interpreting recent events, and commenting on earlier drafts of the chapter. We are also grateful to Charlotte Mack, who provided able research assistance.

1. Other changes affecting the state and local bond market will be discussed later.

2. The issue is dealt with in more depth by both Courant and Rubinfeld (1987) and Feldstein and Metcalf (1987).

3. Holtz-Eakin and Rosen's estimate of the elasticity of local spending with respect to the price of deductible taxes is -1.8. The tax price of local spending rose by 4% or 5% as a result of TRA86; that for state spending, because of the sales tax, by about 6%.

4. Using the constraint in this way does lead to one complication we have not been able to resolve. The constraining variable B is a lagged dependent variable, which means that there could be serial correlation in the residuals beyond that taken out by our correction. One might want to construct an instrument for B and use that in the estimation. Knowing what to do about the constraints is then

not straightforward, however, because in principle all dependent variables should then be recomputed.

5. A recent paper by Helen Ladd (1989) finds strong evidence of such behavior.

6. For high-income itemizers differences in the change in the local cost of public services across neighboring jurisdictions could exceed 1% of a much higher income. The annual change for high income itemizers could be on the order of $600; the capitalized value more than $10,000.

7. But we were unable to use data on the fiscal policies of the cities themselves. Each of these cities had to be assigned the average fiscal policy of all state and local governments in the state, a potential source of measurement error.

8. Although Moody's does not report a reassessment for either Billings, MT, or Portland, ME, it is clear from the numbers that there must have been one.

9. We can only interpret these data qualitatively, not quantitatively, because the denominator of the share, "total assessed value" for the pair, does not mean anything when different jurisdictions have different ratios of assessed to market value. The sign of changes in the share are still meaningful, but only when assessment rules have not changed.

10. In principle one could use either the highest marginal rate (0.33) or the rate for the highest-income taxpayers (0.28) in equation (9). That there is now a difference is one of the little nuggets of TRA86. Since most wealth available for investment in state and local bonds is in the highest income range, we will use 0.28 throughout this section.

11. In the spirit of giving all pre-TRA86 predictions however embarrassing, we should report that Courant and Rubinfeld (1987) speculated that by cutting back on other tax shelters, TRA86 "might" actually lower m relative to r. As the numbers show, it did not.

12. This could go either way, and it bears further study. If state and local governments are constrained by various antiarbitrage provisions, they would exhaust arbitrage opportunities as far as possible and then buy tangible capital to the point where the return was m. In this case TRA86 would reduce real capital formation by raising m. If the constraint were instead on the amount of debt that they could issue, they would only buy tangible capital that earned at least r, and TRA86 would have no effect on real capital formation.

References

Advisory Commission on Intergovernmental Relations. 1988. *Significant Features of Fiscal Federalism*, vol. 2.

Aten, Robert H. 1987. The Magnitude of Additional Corporate Income Taxes Resulting from Federal Tax Reform. *Tax Notes* 37 (3 August): 529–534.

Aten, Robert H., and Steven D. Gold. 1989. Where's the Corporate Tax Windfall? *Tax Notes* (2 October): 107–114.

Bureau of the Census. 1985–87. *County Business Patterns.* Washington, DC.

Bureau of the Census. 1983–87. *Housing Units Authorized by Building Permits and Public Contracts.* Washington, DC.

Chernick, Howard, and Andrew Reschovsky. 1989. The Distributional Politics of Fiscal Adjustment: A Case Study of Four Northeastern States. Mimeo. October.

Courant, Paul N., and Daniel R. Rubinfeld. 1987. Tax Reform: Implications for the State-Local Public Sector. *The Journal of Economic Perspectives* 1: 87–100.

Fabricus, Martha A., Steven D. Gold, and Corina L. Ecki. 1989. *State Budget Actions in 1989.* National Conference of State Legislatures.

Feldstein, Martin S., and Gilbert E. Metcalf. 1987. The Effect of Federal Tax Deductibility on State and Local Taxes and Spending. *Journal of Political Economy* 95: 710–736.

Gold, Steven D. 1988. Tax Reform Activity in the States. *Publius* 18: 17–35.

Gold, Steven D., Corina L. Eckl, and Brenda M. Erickson. 1987. *State Budget Actions in 1987.* National Conference of State Legislatures.

Gold, Steven D., Corina L. Eckl, and Martha A. Fabricus. 1988. *State Budget Actions in 1988.* National Conference of State Legislatures.

Gordon, Roger H., and Joel Slemrod. 1986. An Empirical Examination of Municipal Financial Policy. In Harvey S. Rosen (ed.), *Studies in State and Local Public Finance.* Chicago: University of Chicago Press.

Gramlich, Edward M. 1978. State and Local Budgets the Day after It Rained: Why Is the Surplus So High? *Brookings Papers on Economic Activity* 1: 191–216.

Gramlich, Edward M. 1987. Federalism and Federal Deficit Reduction. *National Tax Journal* 40: 299–313.

Hausman, Jerry A., and James M. Poterba. 1987. Household Behavior and the Tax Reform Act of 1986. *Journal of Economic Perspectives* 1: 101–119.

Hettich, Walter, and Stanley Winer. 1984. A Positive Model of Tax Structure. *Journal of Public Economics* 24: 67–87.

Holtz-Eakin, Douglas, and Harvey S. Rosen. 1988. Tax Deductibility and Municipal Budget Structures. In Harvey S. Rosen (ed.), *Fiscal Federalism: Quantitative Studies.* Chicago: University of Chicago Press.

Inman, Robert P. 1989. The Local Decision to Tax: Evidence from Large U.S. Cities. NBER Working Paper No. 2921. April.

Kenyon, Daphne A. 1988. Implicit Aid to State and Local Governments through Federal Tax Deductibility. In Michael G. Bell (ed.), *State and Local Finance in an Era of New Federalism.* Greenwich, CT: JAI Press.

Ladd, Helen F. 1989. State Aid to Local Governments in the 1980s. Mimeo. October.

Levin, David J., and Donald L. Peters. 1986. Receipts and Expenditures of State and Local Governments: Revised and Updated Estimates, 1959–84. *Survey of Current Business* 66: 26–33.

Levin, David J., and Donald L. Peters. 1987. Receipts and Expenditures of State Governments and of Local Governments: Revised and Updated Estimates, 1983–86. *Survey of Current Business* 67: 29–35.

Metcalf, Gilbert E. 1989. Arbitrage and the Savings Behavior of State Governments. NBER Working Paper No. 3017. June.

Metcalf, Gilbert E. 1989. A Note on the Sales Tax after Reform: Why Hasn't It Disappeared? Mimeo. June.

Moody's Investor Service. 1985–87. *Moody's Municipal and Government Manual.* Chicago.

Mussa, Michael L., and Roger C. Kormendi. 1979. *The Taxation of Municipal Bonds.* Washington, DC: American Enterprise Institute.

Noto, Nanna, and Dennis Zimmerman. 1984. Limiting State-Local Tax Deductibility: Effects among the States. *National Tax Journal* 37: 539–550.

Peters, Donald L. 1988. Receipts and Expenditures of State Governments and of Local Governments: Revised and Updated Estimates, 1984–87. *Survey of Current Busines* 68: 23–25.

Poterba, James M. 1989. Tax Reform and the Market for Tax-Exempt Debt. *Regional Science and Urban Economics* 19: 537–562.

COMMENTS

Steven D. Gold

Courant and Gramlich's chapter is methodologically sophisticated, both in the econometric model employed in its first section and in the analysis of paired border communities in its second section. Its methodology provides a good starting point for future studies of the effects of federal, state, and local tax changes.[1] Moreover it reaches the correct conclusion—that the most important effect of federal tax reform on state and local fiscal behavior has been to inspire state governments to reform their own income taxes.

Unfortunately, however, the chapter's analysis of how federal reform affected state and local tax systems is flawed. There are two interrelated problems:

1. The national income and product accounts (NIPA) are a blunt instrument for tracking changes in state and local behavior. This is generally true, but some of NIPA's early indications about what happened to the states in 1987 were particularly far off the mark.

2. The authors do not give sufficient recognition to two factors that affected state revenue in 1987—the timetable that determines when state policy changes affect tax collections, and the transitory effects of federal reform on revenue from capital gains.

Most of my comments relate to the analysis, in the first part of the chapter, of how reform affected personal and corporate income taxes. But I also have some brief comments about how reform affected other revenue, spending, and the market for state and local bonds.

Even if Courant and Gramlich had avoided the flaws in their chapter, I doubt that their results would have been much more definitive because it is just too early to draw any conclusions about the long-run effects of federal reform on state and local tax systems. They are correct that the short-run effects on revenue have been minor, but they should have examined revenue in 1988 and 1989 to draw that conclusion, not 1987. Alternatively, they could have devoted more attention to the discrete policy changes enacted in 1987.

Personal Income Tax

Courant and Gramlich find that deductible personal taxes were $4.7 billion higher in 1987 than their model based on the period from 1960 to 1986 predicted, and that my estimate of the portion of the personal income tax windfall retained by states can account for only a small share of this extra revenue.[2]

The answers to this riddle are mentioned in the chapter but not adequately emphasized. Much of the extra revenue flowed in because investors rushed to realize capital gains in the last several months of 1986 before the maximum federal tax on gains rose from 20% to 28%. The value of capital gains realized in 1986 was approximately twice as great as in 1985. This led to a one-time bulge in both federal and state tax collections in the spring of 1987. Although the gains were realized in 1986, virtually all of the additional tax revenue was received by states in 1987. Capital gains probably accounts for about half of the extra 1987 revenue.

Courant and Gramlich also do not give sufficient attention to the timetable for state policymaking. When state legislatures met in the first half of 1986, the prospects for passage of federal reform were not very bright, so no more than one state passed legislation in anticipation of it.[3] By the time federal reform was passed in the late summer of 1986, the great majority of legislatures had adjourned for the year. After TRA86 was passed, only one state (Ohio) changed its income tax in response in late 1986.

Most of the states did respond to federal reform during their sessions in the first half of 1987. State actions were diverse, with many of them reducing tax rates and raising standard deductions and personal exemptions. Generally, states with above-average marginal and effective tax rates acted to avoid receiving the "windfall" they would have reaped if they had merely conformed to the broadening of the tax base implicit in federal reform, without making any adjustments in their tax rates, personal exemptions, or standard deductions. On the other hand, states with relatively low income taxes tended to retain the entire "windfall." Two important results were to reduce the dispersion of state income tax rates and to increase progressivity.

In terms of the question on which Courant and Gramlich have focused, what is important is that these state responses to federal reform did not have their full effect on state tax revenue in many cases until 1988. In part, this is because most of the state reforms did not take effect until July 1987 or later. Even when they were retroactive to January 1987, withholding often did not reflect the full-year effect of the state response, so part of the effect of the reforms was not reflected until taxpayers filed their returns in early 1988.

In other words, one cannot discern the state response to federal reform from revenue received in 1987. Part of the $4.7 billion residual found by Courant and Gramlich was due to state conformity with federal base-broadening before states had a chance to offset it, and another part was due to the one-time capital gains phenomenon.

Corporation Income Tax

In analyzing the corporation income tax, Courant and Gramlich were blindsided by a peculiar set of developments. The chapter says that an estimate by the U.S. Treasury Department's Robert Aten (1987) that state governments would receive a $3.4 billion windfall is very close to the $3.6 billion positive shock generated by their model. In fact, Aten and I recently completed a study (Aten and Gold) that attempted to figure out why the $3.4 billion windfall had not materialized.

Here's what happened:

1. Aten made his estimate in early 1987, relying on national estimates by the Treasury and the Bureau of Economic Analysis (BEA) of the component parts of federal reform that were likely to be picked up by the states.

2. Then, since actual data on tax collections were not yet available, BEA relied in part on Aten's analysis to estimate NIPA state corporate tax accruals for 1987. Note that NIPA estimates *accruals*, not *actual collections*, in dealing with the state corporation income tax. As of June 1989 BEA was reporting that state corporate income tax accruals had soared from $22.5 billion in 1986 to $27.9 billion in 1987, a $5.4 billion increase. It reported a further increase to $31.3 billion in 1988.

3. State governments' actual collections from the corporation income tax were disappointingly low in 1987 and 1988. Apparently, for reasons not fully understood, there has not yet been a windfall.

4. In the July 1989 NIPA revisions, corporate tax accruals were chopped from $27.9 billion to $23.7 billion for 1987, and from $31.3 billion to $26.5 billion in 1988. In other words, the increase from 1986 to 1987 was $1.2 billion, not $5.4 billion.

To summarize, Courant and Gramlich found that Aten's estimate was accurate because the BEA, in developing the NIPA estimates, initially relied partly on Aten's estimates; cause and effect were reversed. Now that NIPA estimates are rolled back, the windfall has disappeared.

Several factors help to explain why the corporate windfall has not materialized. One is that corporations have adjusted their behavior to minimize the increase in their tax liability. In part, this entails specific developments like the spread of LBOs, the conversion to subchapter S status, and the migration of passive losses from individual to corporate returns, but in part it also reflects corporations' taking a harder line in complying with state tax provisions. Another factor is that the stacking order in which the tax increases resulting from federal reform were estimated by the Treasury Department led Aten astray in his estimates, attributing too much of the increase to the portions of federal reform that states were likely to conform to.

There are probably also timing issues, such as (1) corporations accelerating their state payments while they were more valuable in reducing federal tax liability because federal tax rates were higher before 1988, and (2) a delay by corporations in complying with the complex new federal accounting provisions because of delays in the publication of IRS regulations on how they should be implemented. To the extent that timing factors are responsible, they imply that the windfall did not evaporate but was either accelerated (factor 1) or delayed (factor 2).

Other Revenue and Spending

Courant and Gramlich are perplexed by the finding that nondeductible taxes and user fees show a negative shock of $3.4 billion, saying that "there is no obvious story for the sharp drop in 'fines,' which accounts for most of the drop." In fact, a small amount of detective work uncovers the fact that fines paid by oil companies for overcharging customers—which were received in 1986—are the primary reason why fines fell sharply in 1987. Revenue from fines was $1.5 billion in 1984, $1.6 billion in 1985, $3.8 billion in 1986, and $1.9 billion in 1987.

Some unknown data problems may also account for Courant and Gramlich's finding that spending had a large positive shock in 1987. They imply that state and local governments went on a spending binge, when in fact the rate at which spending increased actually fell. For example, real spending on goods and services rose 5.5% in 1986 (before reform), 3.4% in 1987, and 3.2% in 1988. The rise of transfer payments also slowed in 1987 from its 1986 growth rate.

Reliance on National Income and Product Accounts Data

This study is handicapped by its use of NIPA data. A much better way to analyze state and local finances is with data that disaggregate national totals by state. There are at least four important advantages of state-specific data:

1. The biggest states have such a large effect on national aggregates that important developments in many small states can be swamped. New York and California alone, for example, account for 35% of state corporate income tax revenue.[4]

2. State data are available more quickly than NIPA data. We now have two full fiscal years of data (1988 and 1989) that reflect state policy responses to federal reform. (Remember that most state fiscal years end by June 30.)[5]

3. The high degree of aggregation of NIPA data sometimes tends to obscure the reality of what is occurring in state finances. At the time this is written (late 1989), for example, NIPA seem to be flashing false signals, indicating that state and local governments are running large operating deficits, although surveys of state general funds suggest that most states have relatively large surpluses (Fabricius, Gold, and Eckl 1989; Howard 1989).

4. Because NIPA data are usually discussed on a calendar year basis, they represent averages of data for state and local fiscal years. Since changes of spending policies tend to coincide with the dates of fiscal years, NIPA do not reveal them as clearly as do fiscal year data.

There are three alternatives to using NIPA data to study the state-local response to federal tax reform. (1) For states, surveys by the National Conference of State Legislatures (NCSL) and the National Association of State Budget Officers (NASBO) provide timely information on general fund spending and revenues. (2) The U.S. Census Bureau also publishes quarterly reports on state and local tax revenue and detailed reports on state and local finances; although the quarterly tax reports have a relatively short publication lag, the detailed reports are much less timely than NIPA data. (3) The explicit changes in state tax rates and other provisions can be analyzed as a supplement to the econometric analysis of revenues. Knowledge of the number of states raising income and sales tax rates (and reducing income tax rates), for example, enhances understanding of how states have responded to federal reform. It is not, however, sufficient to analyze only explicit rate changes without considering the increase of revenue resulting from economic growth. Because of the high elasticity of the income tax, for example, its effective tax rate may increase even when nominal tax rates are falling.

State and Local Bonds

Courant and Gramlich's discussion of bonds focuses too heavily on how TRA86 affected the opportunity for governments to earn interest arbitrage. They devote little attention to the new definition of nongovernmental bonds, the restrictions on private activity bonds, volume caps, and other features of the act that have resulted in a large decrease in the volume of tax exempt borrowing (Petersen 1987). Municipal financing fell from $204.3 billion in 1985 and $151.0 billion in 1986 to $105.5 billion in 1987 and $117.0 billion in 1988 (The Bond Buyer 1989).

Conclusion

Federal tax reform fundamentally changed the fiscal environment in which states operate. It was unrealistic to expect that states would immediately make major changes in the shape of their tax systems in response. The incentives and disincentives provided by the federal tax code are only one of the many factors that influence the choice of state tax instruments and spending levels. After three years there is still no clear response on the part of states to the new incentives produced by federal reform, but it is premature to write off the possibility of important long-run effects.

I agree with Courant and Gramlich that the demonstration effect of federal reform was important, in that it spurred on a movement toward reforming state taxes that was already underway. Now, with the likelihood that federal reform is going to unravel in some significant respects through the reintroduction of preferential treatment for capital gains and the enactment of numerous new tax credits, the question is how the crumbling of federal reform will affect the state tax reform movement. My prediction is that it will hurt the prospects for state reform but that a considerable amount of state level reform will nevertheless occur in the 1990s.

Notes

I appreciate helpful suggestions from Robert Aten and Daphne Kenyon, who are not responsible for any of the remaining shortcomings of these comments.

1. One possible refinement of the methodology might be to allow for a structural difference in state-local fiscal behavior after 1978, when the tax revolt signaled by Proposition 13 began. Studies by Bahl and Duncombe (1988) and Skaperdas (1983–84) both found evidence that states and localities were more fiscally conservative after that date.

2. The $6.3 billion figure for the total potential personal income tax windfall was derived by aggregating estimates prepared by individual states. Because numerous states made these estimates conservatively, it is probably an underestimate to some degree. A number of the states that badly underestimated the size of the windfall (e.g., Hawaii, Utah, and Virginia) made further reductions in their income taxes in 1989 to compensate for the earlier low estimates. For a disaggregated discussion of the accuracy of the original windfall estimates, see Gold (1990).

3. New Mexico decoupled its income tax from automatic conformity with the federal definition of taxable income as a precaution against unforeseeable impacts of federal changes on state tax revenue.

4. This calculation for fiscal 1988 excludes Michigan because its single business tax is not technically a tax on corporate income, as the U.S. Census Bureau treats it.

5. The only states with fiscal years that do not end June 30 are New York (March 31), Texas (August 31), Alabama (September 30), and Michigan (September 30).

References

Aten, Robert H. 1987. The Magnitude of Additional State Corporate Income Taxes Resulting from Federal Tax Reform. *Tax Notes* 37 (3 August): 529–534.

Aten, Robert H., and Steven D. Gold. 1989. Where's the Corporate Tax Windfall? *Tax Notes* 45 (2 October): 107–114.

Bahl, Roy, and William Duncombe. 1988. State and Local Government Finances: Was There a Structural Break in the Reagan Years? *Growth and Change* 19: 30–48.

The Bond Buyer. 1989. *1989 Yearbook.* New York: The Bond Buyer.

Fabricius, Martha A, Steven D. Gold, and Corina L. Eckl. 1989. *State Budget Actions in 1989.* Denver: National Conference of State Legislatures.

Gold, Steven D. 1990. Did the Windfall Stay or Blow Away? *Fiscal Letter* (January–February): 3–4.

Howard, Marcia. 1989. *Fiscal Survey of the States: September 1989.* Washington, DC: National Association of State Budget Officers.

Petersen, John E. 1987. *Tax Exempts and Tax Reform: Assessing the Consequences of the Tax Reform Act of 1986 for the Municipal Securities Market.* Washington, DC: Academy for State and Local Government.

Skaperdas, Peter D. 1983–84. Quantifying State and Local Discretionary Policy Changes. Unpublished appendix to "State and Local Governments: An Assessment of Their Financial Position and Fiscal Policies." Federal Reserve Bank of New York, *Quarterly Review* (Winter).

GENERAL DISCUSSION

Robert Mattson cited evidence that called into question the absence of a corporation income tax windfall at the state level. States have reported that revenues from corporate minimum taxes rose over the period, corporate taxes went up by 70% at the federal level, and state taxes have increased to 40% of all taxes paid. Each fact points to the existence of a corporate tax windfall for state and local governments. Mattson also discussed a study done by Emil Sunley that found an increase in state corporation income tax collections.

Larry Langdon made several points concerning Steven Gold's comments. First, the deduction against federal income taxes for state tax payments is allowed on an accrual basis, not a cash basis. Second, most states provide conformity with federal tax law, which for some tax law changes, such as repealing the completed contract method, would have resulted in a windfall to the states. Finally, there was an incentive for firms to shift income forward into periods of relatively low income rates.

Burton Smoliar warned against underestimating the importance of taxes that are in dispute. It often takes years for a firm to sort out such a dispute with the state, so a corporation may settle or simply pay tax early in order to take advantage of the federal deduction, especially if the federal rate is declining. In this sense corporations are accelerating their state income tax payments. Patrick Moran supported this hypothesis by remarking that Merck did, indeed, accelerate payments, resulting in a huge windfall.

Michael McIntyre commented on the "gestation period" for state tax reforms. He claimed that federal reform clearly facilitated state reform in New York, where reforms were already being planned. Action may simply be taking longer in other states, and there is a good chance that some may still respond to the federal changes.

Fritz Scheuren clarified some issues concerning the authors' data. The State GNP numbers, like the National Income and Product Account totals, are benchmarked to federal tax return data. Since the data available are estimates, the real effects of TRA86 are not built into them. More accurate numbers will not be available until the first tax figures are reported by the IRS.

Moving to a broader issue, Robert Haveman observed that embedded in Gold's comments is a methodological approach that differs from that of the authors in that it places greater emphasis on state-by-state analysis. According to this approach one should be able to model state legislative behavior based on known federal action. Haveman wondered if any data were available that would make such a study possible.

Paul Courant explained what he thought to be the biggest puzzles posed by the results. First, the data do not show much downward movement in sales tax revenues, even though the tax price rose significantly, and second, the unambiguous prediction of the importance of user fees is not reflected in the results.

Courant then presented Robert Inman's hypothesis about the political economy of tax changes. According to this hypothesis the federal base broadening made state taxes less regressive, and the states, in an effort to maintain the distribution of burden, reacted by raising a regressive tax—the nondeductible sales tax. Edward Gramlich observed, however, that Inman's argument does not work for nondeductible user fees. Such fees are regressive, and their use did not increase.

Another argument suggested by Courant pertains to the perceived fairness of different kinds of taxes. Taxpayers generally think that income taxes are unfair, property taxes are *very* unfair, and sales taxes are *not* unfair. Thus raising sales taxes appears to a be an attractive tool.

Gramlich argued that the puzzling results do not necessarily mean that TRA86 had an insignificant effect on state and local fiscal behavior. In response to federal tax reform, many state tax laws are now in conformity with federal law. The fact that so many states have revamped their tax systems is, indeed, important. What are difficult to find in the data are price and incentive effects.

Alan Auerbach argued that we should not have expected short-run shifts in state tax bases post-TRA86. After all, many state treasuries were surprised by the effect of federal reform on capital gains realizations, and this outcome really was predictable, at least at the federal level. Since state planners did not see this coming, we should not have expected them to react swiftly to federal action.

David Bradford broached the broader question of whether it was still too early to be doing these kinds of analyses. He argued that it was productive to explore what the early data had to tell us, at least insofar as it helped researchers identify which issues and questions were going to be important. Supporting Auerbach's assessment of state legislative action, Bradford argued that any observer who is familiar with the workings of state legislatures would be reluctant to predict swift, rational action on their parts. We should not therefore have expected to see a lot of adjustments even by now.

9　Foreign Responses to U.S. Tax Reform

John Whalley

9.1　Introduction

This chapter discusses the responses of foreign countries to recent U.S. tax reforms, and specifically to the 1986 Tax Reform Act. The 1980s have been a decade of worldwide tax reform, with major changes occurring in personal, corporate, and other taxes in a wide range of countries. The directions of reform for both personal and corporate taxes have been similar in nearly all countries: rate reductions and consolidation of brackets at personal level, elimination (or weakening) of investment incentives, and reductions in statutory rates at corporate level.

The chapter examines how central U.S. reforms have been in triggering these changes. Is the global economy integrated to such an extent that tax change in the largest economy inevitably triggers corresponding tax changes in other countries? Or does the similarity of outcome largely reflect common intellectual influences, and despite these seemingly comparable changes, substantial diversity in tax structure across countries remains.[1]

The chapter particularly considers the experiences of seven countries outside the United States: Japan, Canada, the United Kingdom, Sweden, New Zealand, Australia, and Mexico. The picture that emerges suggests that despite common elements, the tax reform experiences have been deceptively different. Any similarity in the pattern of tax reforms in fact cannot be attributed solely to integration pressures that force smaller countries to make a direct policy response to changes in larger economies.

Indeed, the lesson we learn from this experience is that defining and dating reform and then attributing direct foreign response to U.S. tax reform is difficult in many cases. There are clearly conditions under which a direct response in tax policy by smaller countries in response to reforms enacted by a larger country will occur. Changes in the large country will more likely directly trigger changes in small countries where trade and/or investment flows are large and the taxes at stake are marginal instruments that directly affect these flows. Conversely, changes in tax policy in small countries will be conditioned by the tax structure of the large country. This is particularly the case for Canada and Mexico, and to a lesser extent Japan, in the corporate tax area.

In other areas, however, direct foreign policy responses to the 1986 U.S. reforms have been somewhat limited. The common elements suggest similar intellectual influences on tax policy as much as incentive-driven interdependence among country tax structures. More interconnections between country tax policies may occur with continued future global integration and a further weakening or removal of barriers to factor and goods flows. At the same time, however, if the relative importance of the United States in these global flows continues to fall, as it has in recent decades, the direct bilateral links to U.S. tax policy could become even weaker. Whether more or less similarity will be present in future comparisons between foreign and U.S. tax structures thus remains to be seen.

9.2   The Content and Timing of Recent U.S. and Foreign Tax Reforms

While recent global tax reforms contain the common elements of rate reductions and bracket consolidation at personal level, and rate reductions and elimination of investment incentives at corporate level, they also contain a wide variety of other features. They have also taken place at different points in time.[2]

Tables 9.1 and 9.2 summarize the broad features of the more major tax changes in the United States over the period 1979–89, along with those in seven other countries. These countries have been somewhat arbitrarily chosen in light of availability of information and variety of experience, but between them they provide a reasonably broad coverage of different continental experiences. Table 9.1 summarizes the main features of the reforms, and table 9.2 gives a brief chronology of the more major changes involved.

In these tables the common elements of reforms—namely, personal and corporate rate reductions and base-broadening features in both taxes—can clearly be seen in the experiences of all eight countries. But the timing, path, and content of other elements of the reforms also emerge as clearly different.

Although helpful as an overview, to fully evaluate what lies behind these reforms in each country, more detail is needed than can be presented in summary tables such as tables 9.1 and 9.2.

Table 9.1
Broad features of tax reform outcomes in the United States and seven other countries in the 1980s

	United States	Australia	Canada	Japan	Mexico	New Zealand	Sweden	United Kingdom
Personal tax								
Bracket consolidation	14 → 2	5 → 4	10 → 3	15 → 5	28 → 12	5 → 2	11 → 4	13 → 6 → 2
Top marginal rate reduction	50 → 28(+5)	60 → 49	34 → 29	70 → 50	55 → 40	66 → 43	80 → 50 (by 1991)	80 → 40
Other changes	Deductions eliminated; full taxation of capital gains	Deductions eliminated; full taxation of capital gains	Deductions converted to credits; inclusion rate for capital gains	New tax on interest income; increased exemptions	Some limited base broadening	Deductions eliminated	Planned removal of 90% of taxpayers from national income tax by 1991	Personal deductions eliminated
Corporate tax								
Rate reduction/ increase	46 → 34	46 → 49 → 39	36 → 28 (Fed. only)	42 → 37.5	40 → 35	42 → 48 → 28 → 33	58 → 30 (by 1991)	52 → 35
Investment incentives	ITC eliminated; accelerated depreciation withdrawn	Accelerated depreciation withdrawn	ITC eliminated; accelerated depreciation withdrawn	Accelerated depreciation withdrawn	Lump-sum deductions for some fixed assets	Accelerated depreciation withdrawn	Limits on write-offs	Accelerated depreciation withdrawn
System change	None	Classical → imputation	None	Split rate → classical	Planned cash flow for 1991	Classical → imputation	None	None

Sales tax								
VAT introduced/ increased	None	RST proposed but not implemented	VAT introduced	VAT introduced	VAT introduced	VAT introduced	VAT rate increased	VAT rate increased
Tax abolished	None	None	Manufac- turers' sales tax	Commodity tax	Selective excises	Wholesale sales tax	None	None
Property/ wealth/ inheritance taxes	None	None	None	Inheritance tax rates reduced	2% net worth tax on corporate equity (creditable against income tax)	None	New real estate tax; reduced wealth tax	Inheritance tax rates and brackets reduced
Balance of taxation	CIT ↑ PIT ↓	None intended in proposals enacted; but RST proposal was to ↑ indirect taxes	None intended	Direct ↓ indirect ↑	Direct ↓ indirect ↑	Direct ↓ indirect ↑	Direct ↓ indirect ↑	Direct ↓ indirect ↑

Table 9.2
A chronology of major tax changes in the United States and seven other countries,
1979–89

	United States	United Kingdom	Sweden	Canada
1979		PIT rates and brackets ↓; VAT rate ↑		
1980				
1981	PIT rates and brackets ↓; ACRS depreciation system introduced			
1982				
1983			VAT rate ↑	
1984		CIT rate ↓; PIT and CIT allowances and deductions eliminated	CIT rate ↓; CIT base broadened	
1985				
1986	PIT and CIT rates and brackets ↓; investment incentives weakened; PIT and CIT bases broadened		PIT rates and brackets ↓	CIT rate ↓; ITC eliminated; mininum personal tax introduced
1987				
1988		PIT rates and brackets ↓; separate taxation of husband and wife introduced	PIT and CIT rates ↓; VAT base expanded; deductions eliminated[a]	PIT rates and brackets ↓; CIT rate ↓; PIT and CIT base broadened
1989		VAT base expanded; NISS rates and brackets ↓[a]	Net wealth tax rates and brackets ↓[a]	9% GST (VAT) announced

	Japan	Australia	New Zealand	Mexico
1979				
1980				10% VAT introduced
1981				
1982				

Table 9.2 (continued)

	Japan	Australia	New Zealand	Mexico
1983				VAT rate ↑
1984				1980–84 PIT and CIT base-broadening measures introduced
1985		PIT rate and brackets ↓; CIT rate ↑	PIT rates and brackets ↓; CIT rate ↑ 10% GST introduced	
1986		PIT and CIT bases broadened		CIT rate ↓; new tax assessment scheme introduced
1987	PIT rates and brackets ↓			
1988	PIT rates and brackets ↓; CIT rate ↓; 3% VAT introduced	CIT rate ↓; withdrawal of concessions[a]	PIT rates and brackets ↓; CIT rate ↓; elimination of deductions	PIT rates and brackets ↓
1989			CIT rate ↑; GST rate ↑[a]	2% net worth tax on companies introduced

a. Proposed.

The United States

The main features of the more major U.S. reforms as enacted in the 1986 Tax Reform Act are by now well known.[3] At the personal level the previous multibracket rate structure, with marginal rates ranging from 11% to 50%, has been replaced by a two-rate structure of 15% and 28% with a 5% surcharge for some higher income individuals. There are increased personal and dependents exemptions, along with an expanded tax base through the elimination of several deductions, including sales taxes, the dividend deduction, and with an increased inclusion rate for capital gains.

At the corporate level, the top 46% rate has been reduced to 34%. In addition there has been a substantial reduction in investment incentives, with an elimination of the investment tax credit and a weakening of acceleration in depreciation allowances. A number of industry-specific tax preferences have been restricted, including those for oil and gas producers, and for financial institutions. A previous 15% add-on minimum tax has been replaced with a 20% alternative minimum tax for corporations and a 21% alternative minimum tax for individuals.

These tax reforms followed a fairly clear chronology. Major changes were first introduced in June 1981 in the early years of the Reagan administration under the Economic Recovery Tax Act. This reduced individual tax rates, which previously ranged from 14% to 70%, to 11% to 50% by 1983, with a reduction in the capital gains tax rate from 28% to 20%. More important, the 1981 act introduced a new accelerated depreciation system, termed the Accelerated Cost Recovery System (ACRS).

Substantial debate followed these reforms, reflecting the ongoing debate in the United States on tax issues originating in the 1970s. This was to lead to the 1984 U.S. Treasury Tax Reform proposals and the Tax Reform Act of 1986 which finalized the changes outlined above.

Australia[4]

In the Australian case recent tax reforms have their origins in the 1975 Asprey Taxation Review Committee and a 1981 Government Committee of Inquiry into the Australian Financial System. A subsequent June 1985 government draft White Paper proposed three alternative approaches to tax reform. The first was to reduce direct taxes, with an increased dependence on indirect taxes, a proposed change in the tax mix not present in the U.S. debate. A second was to change the tax mix further by supplementing the reduction in direct taxes with a 5% broadly based consumption tax. The third was to go beyond both of these approaches with larger reductions in direct taxes and a 12.5% consumption tax. Major attention also focused on how to achieve better integration between the tax and social welfare systems.

These proposals generated substantial debate, which also occurred during a period that immediately preceded a national election. A nationally televised taxation summit was called to discuss these alternative approaches, which only served to undermine the political support for much of this tax reform.[5] The changes that were eventually announced in September 1985 effectively dropped both the consumption tax proposals, instead consolidating personal tax brackets from 5 to 4, with top marginal rates falling from 60% to 49%, an elimination of deductions and rebates, and an increase in corporate tax rates from 46% to 49%. The latter, opposite from the direction of change in the United States, reflected plans to introduce a European-style imputation system (dividend tax credit system) at a higher rate.

In June 1986 a capital gains tax at full-income rates was introduced, and the corporate tax base broadened to include tax shelters, capital gains, and other items, with the introduction of the imputation system scheduled for July 1987. Subsequently, however, the 1988–89 Economic Statement proposed a reduction in corporate tax rates from 49% to 39% with a withdrawal of accelerated depreciation and other deductions. Interestingly, the driving force behind this policy reversal and lowering of corporate tax rates seems to have been a tax competition effect, stemming in large part from the substantial reduction in New Zealand rates in February 1988 and not the 1986 reduction in U.S. rates.[6]

This reform episode therefore finished up with a result not dissimilar to that of the United States but reflected concerns and followed a path that were quite different. The initial thrust of reform was to change the balance between direct and indirect taxes, quite opposite to the U.S. approach to reform, and initially involved increases in corporate tax rates as the imputation system was introduced. Only subsequently, two years after the initial reform was enacted, did corporate tax rates fall, and this was largely sparked by New Zealand rather than U.S. rate reductions.

Canada[7]

Tax reforms in recent years in Canada have involved actual or planned changes at all three levels of federal taxation: corporate, personal, and sales. At the personal level there has been consolidation of brackets with a previous ten-bracket federal rate structure of 6% to 34% being replaced by a three-bracket structure of 17% to 29%. Most exemptions and deductions have been converted to tax credits, and an alternative minimum tax of 17% has been introduced. The inclusion rate for capital gains has increased from 50% to 75% (with no indexing). At the corporate level the federal rate has been reduced from 36% to 28%, the investment tax credit has been eliminated, accelerated depreciation has slowed, and there is increased taxation of financial institutions. At the sales tax level there has been a major change proposed, but not yet enacted, involving a multistage federal Goods and Services Tax (VAT) to be introduced at a 9% rate in 1991, with an elimination of the existing federal manufacturers' sales tax.

These changes in Canada, as in Australia, have different origins from those of the United States.[8] In May 1985 a discussion paper on corporate tax reform was released[8] along with the budget of that year. It suggested a reduction in statutory rates and an elimination of investment incentives. In January 1986 a minimum personal tax was introduced, and in the February 1986 budget the corporate tax rate was reduced from 36% to 33%, along with the elimination of the general investment tax credit. In late 1986 a planned release of a discussion paper on sales tax reform was shelved ostensibly because of the passage of U.S. tax reform legislation, and the argument that Canadian tax reform should consider a wider range of reform options, including income tax reform.[9] The result was a 1987 White Paper on tax reform, which proposed further changes in individual, corporate, and sales taxes.[10] The legislation that resulted in December 1987, as in the United States, consolidated personal rate brackets and enacted the changes in personal and corporate taxes, further lowering the corporate tax rate to 28%. This latter change clearly was seen as needed since, with lower U.S. corporate rates, increased debt financing in Canada by cross-border-integrated multinationals would erode the Canadian tax base. Changes in personal taxes were also seen as following the U.S. pattern, but the arguments made were individual incentive (effort) based rather than reflecting tax competitive effects. Distinctive Canadian elements, such as the conversion of deductions and exemptions into credits, were also consciously included in the reform package.

In January 1988 changes also occurred in the then-existing federal manufacturers' sales tax that were close to shifting the tax from a manufacturing level tax to a wholesale tax for a limited range of products. The recent April 1989 budget has subsequently reiterated plans to introduce a value-added tax[11] to replace this tax. The details of this proposed tax are expected to be completed by this summer.

The Canadian experience therefore is much closer to U.S. experience than the Australian case. Nonetheless, it has a number of features different from the U.S. case. Much of it has been focused on reform of the sales tax, motivated in part by the inherent problems and difficulties of the present tax. However, despite a number of the key elements in the corporate tax reform similar to those introduced in the United States, the debate in Canada, to some degree, predates the release of the details of U.S. plans and, like the U.S. and other countries, was influenced by the 1984 U.K. changes.

Japan[12]

Tax reform in Japan, like that in the United States and other countries, has involved consolidation of rate brackets at personal level and rate reductions at corporate level. The previous 15-bracket national rate structure from 10.5% to 70% has been replaced by a 5-bracket structure from 10% to 50%.

An inhabitants' tax, a local tax applied to the personal income tax base, has been reduced from a 4-bracket rate structure of 4.5% to 18% to a 3-bracket structure of 5% to 15%. A 20% flat-rate tax on interest income received by individuals has also been introduced. Along with these changes have come increased personal exemptions.

At the corporate level rates will be reduced from 42% to 37.5% by 1990. Lower rates on income distributed as dividends will be removed along with this, signaling a move from a split rate to a classical corporate tax system. There have also been major changes involving sales and excise taxes. A broadly based 3% consumption-type value-added tax has been introduced, and several national and local excise taxes have been limited in their application. In addition inheritance tax rates have been reduced from 75% to 70%.

As in the Australian and Canadian cases these reforms, though following the U.S. pattern in terms of the final result, reflect concerns and a process quite different from U.S. experience. In 1985 the Nakasone administration declared its commitment to undertake major tax reform in Japan, and in October 1986 the Tax Council, a government tax commission, reported. They proposed consolidating personal rate brackets from 15 to 6, with a top rate reduction from 78% to 60%. However, dealing with the perceived unfairness in Japan in the relative tax treatment of salaried earners, small businesses, and farmers (the so-called 9–6–4 problem; see Noguchi 1988 and discussion below) was a key issue. A reduction in corporate tax rates and an introduction of a broadly based indirect tax were also planned. Part of the rationale for lowering corporate taxes was clearly stated as a perceived need to lower corporate tax rates in light of pending rate reductions in the United States. The concern was stated in terms of a threat to international competitiveness.

The reform outcome was largely shaped by an influential Liberal Democratic Party Tax Commission report in December 1986 that proposed consolidating personal rate brackets from 15 to 13, and then to 6, with the top rate falling from 70% to 50% by 1988, a corporate tax rate of 37.5% by 1989, and the introduction of a 5% value-added tax along with a review of the current sales tax. Legislation in September 1987 consolidated national rate brackets from 15 to 12, and local brackets from 14 to 7, with top national and local rates falling from 70% to 60% and 18% to 16%, respectively. A 20% flat-rate income tax was enacted on many types of interest.

In 1988, after heated debate on the value-added tax proposal, the government announced its commitment to a continuation of tax reform, and in December reform legislation was introduced enacting on the features listed above, including the 3% value-added tax.

Japanese reform therefore also has strong similarities to U.S. reform while revealing important differences. There has been a major focus in the reform debate on changes in indirect taxes and the introduction of a value-added tax. And changes in the income tax have focused heavily on the vertical equity issues of equal taxation of interest and labor income, and within labor income, equal taxation of different types.

Mexico[13]

Mexico represents an example of a semi-industrialized country that has also undergone major tax change in recent years, but with once again different emphasis and outcomes from the U.S. case. At the personal level the previous 28-bracket rate structure running from 3% to 55% has been replaced by a 12-bracket rate structure, with top marginal rates by 1989 having fallen from 55% to 40%. Base-broadening measures have also been adopted in the personal tax, including limited taxation of capital gains. At the corporate level the investment tax credit has been substantially limited, and rates will have been reduced from 40% to 35% by 1991.

As far as sales and excise taxes are concerned, the main change has involved a 10% value-added tax, with preexisting taxes on soft drinks, gasoline, alcoholic beverages, and other selected excises replaced with a special new tax on production and services.

These reforms, however, cover a much longer period of time than is the case for Canada, Japan, or Australia. The 10% value-added tax was introduced in January 1980, and in January 1981 taxes on soft drinks, alcoholic beverages, beer, gasoline, processed tobacco, life insurance, and telephone services were replaced with the special new tax. In January 1983 the general value-added tax rate was increased from 10% to 15%, and over the period between 1980 and 1984 base-broadening measures were also adopted, including the elimination of preferences for capital gains and dividends. Accelerated depreciation in the corporate tax was reduced, and itemized deductions in the personal tax eliminated in favor of a single deduction. However, changes in tax structure that occurred over this time were driven, in part, by the need to raise revenue to both replace declining natural resource revenues and lower the deficit.

January 1986 saw a 10% surcharge for high-income earners introduced, and the June 1986 tax reform bill reduced corporate tax rates from 42 to 35 after 1991. Two accounting schemes will coexist during the transitional period: One will preserve the traditional corporate tax base with an unindexed graduated rate structure of 5% to 42%; the other will use an indexed base and a fixed rate of 35%.

January 1988 also saw further changes with personal brackets consolidated from 28 in 1985 to 12 in 1988, with the top marginal rate falling from 55% to 50% in 1988 and 40% in 1989. In January 1989 a 2% net-worth tax on companies' net equity was also introduced.

The picture that emerges therefore is that Mexico, like many other countries, has followed rate consolidation and rate reductions at both personal and corporate levels and reductions of incentives. Different concerns from other countries, however, have been paramount in the Mexican case. Portions of the tax reforms were enacted in part to aid compliance by simplifying taxes, broadening bases, and lowering rates and on that basis to eventually raise revenues. Serious compliance problems have been well-known in both the personal and sales tax areas in Mexico for some years, and lower rates and simplification were felt to help both. Also, with high inflation rates, large structural adjustment, and other difficulties, domestic macro policy has oscillated, and at times quite wildly. Stability and predictability have become central Mexican policy themes, and the mirror image in tax policy has been broadened bases and lower rates.

New Zealand[14]

In the New Zealand case the major elements of recent tax reforms have been the replacement of the previous five-bracket personal tax rate structure of 20% to 66% by a two-bracket rate structure of 24% and 33% and the elimination of several deductions, including gifts and employment-related expenses. At the corporate level rates have been reduced from 45% to 33%, with a European-style imputation system (dividend tax credit) introduced.

Sales and excise taxes have also changed, with the introduction of a broadly based consumption-type goods and services tax (VAT) at a 10% rate. The previous wholesale tax has been eliminated, with a continuation of existing selective taxes on alcoholic beverages, tobacco, and motor vehicles. In addition deductions and preferences in the tax treatment of pension schemes have been eliminated.

As in the Australian case these tax reforms had their origins in events in the mid-1980s. In August 1985, following both the election of a new government and a wider series of liberalization measures which the government of the day introduced, a budget statement on taxation and benefit reform announced the consolidation of personal tax rate brackets from five to three, with the top marginal rate falling from 66% to 48%. At the same time a 10% value-added tax was announced, along with the abolition of the existing sales tax and an increase in the corporate tax rate from 45% to 48%, and with a European-style imputation scheme planned for 1988–89.

In the fall of 1987, however, a subsequent Treasury paper proposed a sharp reduction of both personal and corporate tax rates and a simplification of the indirect tax base along with an increase in the rate for the goods and services tax. In February 1988 the corporate tax rate was reduced from 48% to 28%. A two-bracket personal rate structure of 24% and 35% was also announced, along with an abolition of all existing deductions and full taxation of pension income. In March 1989 a consultative committee proposed corporate tax rate increases from 28% to 33% and an increase in the goods and services tax rate from 10% to 12.5%. In March 1989 there was also increased taxation of and elimination of deductions in revisions to the tax treatment of pensions.

New Zealand tax reform therefore at the end of the day also has a similar outcome to U.S. reforms, with consolidation of personal rate brackets, and personal and corporate rate reductions. The appearances of similarity is, however, deceptive. Much larger change has occurred in New Zealand, and with wider oscillations with corporate rates first up and then down. This in part is consistent with the turbulent pace of New Zealand policy change in other areas during this period. Also the concerns central to New Zealand reforms were different to those in the U.S. case. A substantial shift in the balance of taxation between direct and indirect taxes has occurred, with the introduction of a value-added tax at the same time that personal tax rates were reduced. In addition a major initial thrust of the corporate reform was to move to an imputation-style corporate tax system, hence the initial perception of a need to raise rather than lower rates.

Sweden[15]

Swedish tax reforms in the 1980s have focused primarily on changes in a previous 11-bracket personal rate structure. By the late 1970s this tax had basic and supplementary national rates effectively running from 4% to 50%, plus a 30% local tax. It has, for now, been replaced by a four-bracket basic and supplementary rate structure of 5% to 42%, which, with a 30% local tax, has resulted in top combined marginal tax rates falling from 80% to 72%. However, more major change is planned for 1991, which may lower top marginal tax rates to 50% and, even more dramatically, remove

90% of taxpayers from the rolls for the national income tax. At the corporate level statutory rates have been reduced from 58% to 52% with base-broadening measures adopted such as limited write-downs on inventories. Once again, dramatic change is to follow in 1991, with the statutory tax rate falling to 30%.[16]

At indirect tax level, the basic value-added tax rate has increased from 17.7% to 19% over the 1980s, and real estate (property) taxes (on assessed values) have been introduced at rates of 1.4% and 2%. Other tax changes have included a 1% turnover tax on sales of equity and increases in employers' social security contributions to 37.47% of gross of tax wages and salaries, and a one-time 7% net-worth tax on insurance companies.

These reforms, unlike the New Zealand, Australian, and Canadian reforms, have taken place over a long period of time and clearly predate recent U.S. changes. Reform can be dated to 1981, to the so-called "wonderful night" agreement between the Centre Party, the Liberals and the Social Democrats. This was to lead in 1983 to an increase in the basic value-added tax rate from 17.7% to 19%, and in 1984 to a reduction in the national corporate tax rate from 40% to 32% (a combined national plus municipal rate of 58% to 52%), along with a broadened corporate tax base.

In 1986 basic and supplementary personal tax brackets were consolidated from 11 to 4, with the combined top marginal rate falling from 80% to 72%. In 1987 the combined municipal and national corporate tax was replaced by a single national tax at 52%, and a real estate tax was introduced at rates of 1.5% and 2%. Also in 1987 the one-time 7% net-worth tax on insurance companies was announced.

The fall of 1988 saw the release of a Ministry of Finance paper detailing plans for a wide-ranging tax reform for 1991. This is supposed to remove 90% of taxpayers from income tax rolls, with a further reduction in the top marginal rate from 72% to 50% for those remaining. Increased taxation of capital income at personal level is planned, but with a further sharp fall in the corporate tax rate from 52% to 30%. The corporate tax base will be broadened through the elimination of several deferral-based deductions, and a substantial widening of the value-added tax base is planned. In 1989 there was also a further proposal for a reduction in the current net-wealth tax, with the present four brackets from 1.5% to 3% replaced by a single rate of 1% to 1.5%.

The striking feature of these reforms is both the length of the period over which change has been underway, and the sweeping nature of the changes now planned for 1991. Much of the reform seems largely independent of U.S. changes. The more major changes are those proposed for 1991, with a radical restructuring of the whole personal income tax system and major change at the corporate level. Earlier changes involved consolidation in rate brackets well before change was underway in the U.S. case, and lowering of corporate tax rates also well before U.S. changes occurred.

United Kingdom[17]

The United Kingdom has also seen major tax change over the last decade. The multi-rate personal tax structure of a decade ago (13 brackets in 1978), which had rates running from 30% to 83%, has been replaced by a two-bracket structure of 25% to 40%. The 14-bracket capital transfer tax, now called the *inheritance tax*, has been consolidated into a four-bracket rate structure running from 30% to 60%. Separate taxation of husbands and wives has been introduced, and capital allowances and personal deductions have been eliminated at the personal level.

At the corporate level rates have been reduced from 52% to 35% and acceleration in depreciation allowances sharply reduced. All previous investment allowances and incentives were replaced in 1984 with 25% annual declining balance depreciation. Tax preferences for occupational and personal pensions have been introduced. At the indirect tax level the value-added tax base has been broadened and the basic VAT rate increased from 8% to 15%. The most recent 1989 budget also reduced national insurance (social security) employer contributions.

As in the Swedish case tax reforms in the United Kingdom have taken place over a much longer period of time than in other countries, and noticeably longer than in the United States. In 1979, shortly after the election of the Conservative government, a budget consolidated personal tax brackets to six, with the top marginal rate falling from 83% to 60%, and increased the basic value-added tax rate from 8% to 15%. This pace of change continued with the 1984 budget which announced a phased reduction in corporate tax rates from 52% to 35% and reduced both depreciation allowances at the corporate level and deductions in the personal income tax. The 1985 budget consolidated capital transfer tax brackets from 14 to 4, with marginal rates ranging from 4% to 60%, abolished a previous development land levy and introduced graduated social security contributions.

March 1986 saw further changes to the structure of the capital transfer tax, renamed the inheritance tax, and introduced new incentive schemes in personal and corporate taxes. March 1987 saw a further reduction in personal tax rates and made cash received and paid the basis of accounting for the value-added tax.

The March 1988 budget consolidated personal tax brackets from six to two, with the top marginal rate falling from 60% to 40%, the basic rate falling from 27% to 25%, and separate taxation of husbands and wives, which was a major change for the United Kingdom. March 1989 saw a further reduction in social security contributions and an expansion of the value-added tax base to include new construction, water, and fuel as power for business. New tax preferences for occupational pensions were also announced.

In the United Kingdom therefore the period over which tax reforms took place is considerably longer than in the U.S. case, and reform is hard to separate from ongoing yearly change in budget announcements. These changes also contain many different elements from the U.S. case, including changes in value-added taxes, consolidations of rate brackets in the inheritance and social security taxes, and other components. Also the 1984 corporate rate reductions and changes in investment incentives clearly predate the subsequent U.S. changes.

Thus, although the similarity in the broad directions of change at personal and corporate levels compared to the United States seems clear in all those countries, the diversity of tax reform experience across these countries is also striking. Besides the clear common features of rate reductions, bracket consolidation and weakening of investment incentives at personal and corporate levels, there are the noncommon features of corporate system changes, value-added tax introductions, and changes in the balance of direct and indirect taxes. Thus, although there are instances of direct foreign response to U.S. tax reforms, particularly in countries that are the most integrated with the United States, such as Canada, pinpointing how extensive these are and in which countries and tax areas they have occurred is more difficult.

9.3 Disentangling the Direct Effects of U.S. Reforms on Foreign Tax Systems[18]

In the preceding discussion we have seen that recent U.S. and foreign tax reforms suggest both a similarity of outcome in the corporate and personal tax areas and substantial differences of detail and timing. In addition in a number of these countries indirect taxes and other issues, such as system change at the corporate level, have played a prominent role. To what extent therefore have U.S. reforms helped shape these changes abroad?

On the one hand, one might argue that tax changes in the largest country will automatically tend to trigger comparable changes in other countries because of pressures that arise toward erosion of tax bases, migration, and relocation.[19] On the other hand, the diversity of experience summarized earlier seems to suggest that this view might place too much weight on direct bilateral incentive effects in determining foreign tax changes. Because many countries were already moving in the directions in which the United States eventually moved, the similarity of reform outcome could, instead, be taken to reflect common intellectual influences, as much as direct incentive effects to follow U.S. reforms. Also other bilateral links between pairs of countries (Australia–New Zealand, West Germany–United Kingdom) might have been more important in shaping reform outcomes.

Common and Distinctive Intellectual Issues

Tracing out the intellectual issues behind any tax reform is difficult, and this is no more apparent than in the U.S. case. It would, for instance, be simplistic to say that TRA86 had its origins in the 1984 U.S. Treasury document, Tax Reform for Fairness, Simplicity and Economic Growth, because this document in fact reflected pressures that had been building for tax reform in the United States for many years.[20]

There was a feeling that the tax system had become overcomplex, with a proliferation of exclusions, adjustments to income, deductions, and other complexities. This in turn had led to substantial erosion of the tax base through loopholes that violated principles of vertical equity, giving unequal treatment to equals and distorting resource allocation. This lack of a broad comprehensive tax base was felt to further distort savings and investment through nonneutralities with respect to asset and financing decisions, adversely affect work effort, retard invention and innovation, and encourage unproductive investment in tax shelters.

There was also a view that the tax system had created unfair treatment within families since tax burdens had increased relatively more for large families with many dependents than for other taxpayers. And in the 1980s high inflation rates and the interaction of inflation and taxes were felt to create further inequities and distortions. The tax system of the day thus did not accurately measure real income from capital in most cases.

The stated objectives of reform in the 1984 U.S. Treasury tax reform document mirrored all these concerns—economic neutrality, lowering tax rates, equal treatment of equals, fairness for families, fairness across income classes, and simplicity and perceived fairness—and aimed at achieving an inflation-proof tax law. Despite the machinations of the U.S. political process, in TRA86 these principles were never either fundamentally challenged or restated.

Intellectual issues behind tax reform in many of the other countries discussed in this chapter were broadly similar, but at the same time each had its own different interpretation and slant. Thus in the New Zealand case[21] there was a strong view that increases in average and marginal tax rates as a result of bracket creep from inflation had redistributed taxes heavily onto middle-income individuals and compounded problems of tax evasion and avoidance. On the other hand, there was also major emphasis in the New Zealand debate on selective export and tax incentives that had been previously designed to increase investment and exports. These were felt to have resulted in a lack of uniformity and neutrality in the tax system as well as to have generated economic inefficiency.

In the Japanese case there were again intellectual issues similar to those shaping the U.S. reforms, but as Noguchi (1988) notes, additional issues also entered the debate. A central issue that arose early in Japanese debate was that of horizontal equity, the so-called 9–6–4 problem in Japan. It was argued at the time that the tax burden of salaried workers was heavier than those of small business owners, self-employed, and farmers at similar income levels. This inequality in assessments was referred to as the 9–6–4 or 10–5–3 problem because the portion of the income subject to taxes was alleged to be 90% to 100% of the actual earned income for salaried income earners, 50% to 60% for business income, and only 30% to 40% for agricultural income. This was seen as one of the central problems that needed to be addressed through tax reform and, though closely related, a different notion of horizontal equity from the U.S. case.

Another major reform issue in Japan was the preferential treatment of interest income for small savings (mainly postal savings). The claim was that the system was abused by wealthy individuals because they held numerous accounts in banks and post offices, substantially beyond the legal limit that was allowed. It was even argued that this favorable tax treatment was the main cause of high savings in Japan.

Canada, as has already been mentioned above, also represents shared but different intellectual issues on its tax reform compared to those of the United States. In the mid-1980s, as Mintz and Whalley (1989) document, the Canadian tax reform debate began with a discussion of corporate reform a little before the debate fully got underway in the United States. The influence of the 1984 U.K. reforms was clearly noticeable. In early 1985 a discussion paper released with the budget detailed corporate tax changes that were to be enacted. These reflected concerns similar to those of the United States—nonneutralities in the tax system and the need to have uniformity of treatment—but dealt with the specifically Canadian problem of an overhang of large corporate losses. The 1985 Government Corporate Tax Discussion Paper (p. 17) reports that in 1981 over 60% of Canadian corporations were nontaxpaying and over 46% of nontaxpaying corporations were making profits as indicated by their financial statements.

The reform debate accelerated in 1987, with a change in focus first toward sales tax reform and then toward personal tax reform. Debate on personal taxes reflected the U.S. reform debate. Concerns over high rates were prominent, but because of the limited scope for further broadening the tax base in the Canadian case, concerns over vertical equity were less prominent.[22]

In contrast to the United States, however, major attention began to gravitate toward the sales tax component of Canadian tax reform. The existing federal manufacturers' sales tax was seen as something of an anachronism. It had a narrow base and high rates and a complex administrative structure with many biases that had to be removed. Thus the thrust of the reform became the replacement of the federal sales tax by a value-added tax, with the continuing enactment of the corporate tax changes. A further corporate rate reduction announced in 1987 reflected the view that Canadian rates had to fall to match the reduction in the statutory rates introduced in the United States in 1986. Once again, the outcome of Canadian and U.S. reforms is similar at the personal and corporate levels but has different origins and concerns.

Swedish tax reform represents a substantially different case from that of the United States. As Andersson (1988a,b) stresses, the dominant concern in tax reform throughout the 1980s has been high marginal tax rates at personal level, which has been viewed as encouraging tax evasion, tax planning, and "grey" activity, along with low savings rates within the household sector. Problems with the unevenness of existing capital income taxation have been emphasized but with less profile than in other countries.

These problems therefore led the Swedes in the directions documented in the previous section: dealing with deductions (including interest deductions at the personal level), moving the tax system toward neutrality so that income from different sources is not treated differently, and removing the complexity of tax regulations to facilitate administration and compliance. Although the results seemed similar to those of the United States in that reductions were made at the corporate and personal levels, unlike the U.S. reform, Swedish tax reforms were mainly concerned with both changing and lowering income taxes, particularly in the latest proposed changes.

Australian reforms also fit a picture different from the U.S. case but reflect similar underlying concerns. The objectives of the reforms were vertical equity, improved economic efficiency, and increased simplicity in the tax system. The coordination of tax policies with social welfare programs, however, was a distinctive Australian concern. Australia, once again, finishes with a similar outcome to that for the U.S. as far as personal and corporate tax reductions go, but the intellectual drive behind reform contains several different elements. There was an initial proposal to introduce a sales tax, with the objective of moving the tax system more heavily toward indirect taxation. Likewise initially there was a move toward a new system of corporate taxes that raised statutory rates.

Direct Triggers in the Foreign Response

A different approach to identifying the direct effects of U.S. reforms is to look for evidence of direct triggers operating between components of U.S. reforms and tax changes abroad. As far as I am able to determine, such direct trigger effects are most striking at corporate level and largely involve changes in statutory corporate tax rates.

In the Canadian case in 1985 the government announced its commitment to corporate tax reform through a reduction in statutory tax rates, to be accompanied by a phased elimination of investment tax credits and acceleration in depreciation allowances. However, by the time these changes were to be enacted in 1986, the U.S. Tax Reform Act had passed, resulting in a larger reduction in statutory rates in the United States. Thus in 1987 further Canadian rate cuts were announced, rationalized by the argument that because of the large size of U.S. investment in Canada (approximately 25% of manufacturing industry in Canada is foreign owned, and 95% of foreign-owned capital originates from the United States), it would pay integrated multinational corporations to do their debt financing in the high-tax jurisdiction (in Canada rather than in the United States). This in turn would result in a substantial erosion of the tax base, unless Canada followed the U.S. rate reduction down. The commitment in the 1987 tax reform documents was thus to produce a combined federal-provincial corporate tax rate in Canada approximately equal to the U.S. rate.

Canada provides the most dramatic of these examples, but similar arguments can be found in the debates on corporate tax reform in Japan. In the Japanese case the argument was that high corporate tax rates undermine international competitiveness.[23] The argument was not stated in quite the same direct form as in the Canadian case, which stressed the threatened erosion of the tax base. Rather it maintained that unless corporate tax rates were lowered in Japan to match U.S. rate reductions, there would be an outflow of business activity from Japan and eventually loss of jobs and incomes. Therefore the U.S. rate reduction had to be followed.

As far as this author is able to determine, however, these are the only two cases where in government documents, and related debate within the country, such arguments were made at the corporate level. There were undoubtedly arguments in similar vein made at the personal level about the impact of tax reform on migration patterns with the threatened loss of more mobile, highly skilled workers. Such arguments were made in Japan, Canada, and New Zealand, but in the latter case in reference to threatened migration to Australia more so than to the United States. In the income tax case, however, these concerns over migration effects were also clearly stated as supplementary to the basic arguments for reducing tax rates, namely, improving work incentives, aiding compliance and reducing tax evasion, dealing with problems of vertical equity, and other concerns.[24] Among the countries discussed in this chapter, Japan and Canada seem to exhibit the most significant direct tax responses to U.S. reforms.

These cases then would seem to support the notion of direct trigger effects from U.S. tax policy changes to tax policies in other countries. They are strongest in the corporate area because of the high degree of mobility involved, particularly of financial capital. They are also strongest for countries where there are large trade and investment linkages with the United States, for example, Canada, Japan, and Mexico.

Timing—Who Moved First?

A further issue in disentangling the direct effects of U.S. reforms on foreign tax systems is the question of timing. Who moved first, and with what effect? Dating tax reforms and determining their underlying intent is a hazardous exercise under the best of circumstances, but comparing reforms across countries is even more hazardous.

One of the complexities of trying to determine which country changed its tax system first is that what constitutes a tax reform is somewhat vague in a number of the countries considered here. In the U.S. congressional system, because of the need for eventual consensus, a date of agreement can be taken to date the reform. For the other countries discussed in this chapter which have parliamentary systems, a number of tax measures through a series of budgets cumulatively constitute reform over a much longer period of time. Thus in the United Kingdom one can date reform from the 1979 budget with major cuts in personal income tax rates, but changes have continued all the way through to the recent 1989 budget, with further major tax cuts. Swedish reforms, similarly, begin in the late 1970s but have major changes still scheduled for 1991. It is therefore often difficult to determine the timing of reform and assess who moved first.

What seems clear, however, is that the tax area where direct linkages most forcefully come into play, namely, at the corporate level, did undoubtedly involve changes by other countries prior to the recent tax reforms in the United States. The 1984 budget in the United Kingdom involved a clear commitment to a reduction in the statutory corporate tax rate through phased reductions from 52% to 35% and a weakening of investment incentives. In the Canadian case the government discussion paper of February 1985 reflected thinking and discussion that had been underway within the tax policy circles in the Canadian government in previous years. Once again, this discussion partially predated the release of the 1984 U.S. Treasury documents and, if anything, was more heavily influenced by the 1984 U.K. changes. The 1984 U.K. changes also had their effect on the 1984 Treasury proposals announced in the United States. Thus it seems clear that the tax reforms of the 1980s do not reflect a clear and unambiguous first move by the United States on the corporate tax front.

On the other hand, once the United States moved, other countries equally clearly began to modify their positions. Some went further in direction they were already moving, while others reversed direction. The Canadians, for example, modified their corporate tax reform in 1987 through deeper cuts in rates in light of the U.S. actions of 1986, even though they had been moving in the same general direction from 1985 onward. Reversals of corporate rates followed in both Australia and New Zealand.

It also seems unreasonable to claim that there was a first U.S. move at the personal level. Reductions in marginal tax rates and consolidation of brackets were clearly present in the 1979 budget in the United Kingdom, and Sweden and other countries moved in this direction starting in the early 1980s. But the U.S. actions of 1986 clearly do not seem to have triggered the same direct response that their corporate tax measures did in other countries.

Thus despite the ambiguity of defining tax reform and detailing the content of tax reform packages in both the corporate and personal tax areas, other countries were indeed moving in the tax reform directions prior to U.S. actions in the mid-1980s. This seems to weaken the claim that the global tax reforms reflect the direct effects of U.S. reforms on foreign tax systems.

Lack of Complete Replication

A final factor relevant to disentangling the direct effects of U.S. tax reforms on foreign tax systems is the lack of complete replication of either U.S. tax changes abroad or foreign tax changes in the United States. Thus the major elements of U.S. tax reforms—reduction in marginal tax rates and consolidation of rate brackets at personal level, and reductions in statutory rates and elimination of investment incentives—are common to the United States and the other countries whose experiences are discussed here, but there are many elements that are not replicated.

In the U.S. case corporate revenues were raised with a clear intent to change the tax mix between corporate and personal taxes. As far as I am able to determine, this direction of tax change is unique to the United States. In the Canadian case tax reforms at personal level converted existing exemptions and deductions into credits, something that was not replicated in the U.S nor elsewhere.

In addition at the sales tax level, countries with sales taxes seemed to become embroiled in major debates on the appropriate balance of direct and indirect taxes. This issue was hotly debated in New Zealand, Australia, Sweden, the United Kingdom, and, to some extent, Canada. Because the United States had no broadly based indirect tax, this element of the debate was lacking in the United States.

Thus, although there are broad similarities, the lack of complete replication of the U.S. tax changes once again weakens the claim that foreign tax policy responses were a direct reflection of the 1986 U.S. tax act.

9.4   Conclusion

This chapter has discussed recent tax reforms in New Zealand, Australia, Japan, the United Kingdom, Canada, Sweden, and Mexico and has compared them to recent U.S. tax reforms. These reforms, of course, have complex details, but they are striking in their broad similarities at both the personal and corporate levels. All of the countries discussed in the chapter have moved to consolidate rate brackets and reduce marginal rates at the personal level. At the corporate level statutory rates have been reduced, while investment incentives have either been weakened or removed. The broad nature of these simlarities suggests common forces at work.

Two alternative hypotheses were discussed. One is that the United States, the largest country, initiated tax reforms, and other countries simply accommodated their tax systems to the U.S. changes. In that case U.S. changes elicited the response abroad. The other hypothesis is that common intellectual issues were at work in all of the countries analyzed here, and direct interactions were relatively small.

The chapter argues that neither hypothesis alone is able to account for the similarities in the tax changes. In fact a number of countries had started tax reforms prior to the U.S. tax acts, and they subsequently influenced U.S. tax reforms. It is also clear that many differences in the details of the various reforms were not replicated among countries. Evidence that the United States may have directly triggered foreign tax changes seems to be largely limited to the corporate tax and to those countries with major investment links with the United States.

Common intellectual issues may well have led to some similarity of result. This would negate the importance of direct trigger effects at the personal level because many impediments exist between countries, such as immigration restrictions and trade barriers. But where the bilateral linkage to the U.S. economy is large, policy concerns to follow U.S. actions forcefully come into play.

Notes

I am grateful to Charles McLure, Joel Slemrod, and other conference participants for helpful comments, and to Dale Hancocks and Leigh MacDonald for research support.

1. This same issue of foreign response to the 1986 U.S. tax reforms is also discussed in Tanzi (1987), Bossons (1987, 1988), and Whalley (1990). Tanzi, writing soon after the reforms and without having the full range of foreign response available to him, suggested that the similarity of outcome reflects common intellectual forces more so than direct cross-country pressures. Bossons (1987), in contrast, emphasizes the importance of cross-border U.S. pressures on Canada as far as corporate taxes are concerned, and emphasizes the role played by U.S. income taxes in redirecting Canadian reforms. Whalley (1990) also highlights the role played by U.S. pressures at the corporate level on Canadian reforms. Bossons (1988) seems to assign a larger weight to common intellectual features and influences from tax reform elsewhere (especially the United Kingdom) in non-Canadian cases.

2. One of the more recent compendia of country tax reforms is the volume from OECD (1987); see also OECD (1988).

3. See, for instance, Deloitte, Haskins, and Sells (1986), Pechman (1987, 1988), and Herber (1988).

4. This section draws on various issues of the *Tax News Service* of the International Bureau of Fiscal Documentation, Amsterdam, Keating (1984), Morgan (1986), and Porter (1988).

5. See Porter (1988), p. 12.

6. See the discussion of this in Porter (1988), p. 18.

7. The material in this section draws on Government of Canada (1985, 1987b, 1989), Mintz and Whalley (1989), Dodge and Sargent (1988), and Whalley (1990).

8. See Government of Canada (1985).

9. See the discussion in Bossons (1987).

10. See Government of Canada (1987a,b,c,d) for more details.

11. See Government of Canada (1989).

12. Material in this section draws on Shoven (1988), Keitaro (1988), Noguchi (1988), Government of Japan (1989a,b), and Ishi (1988).

13. Material in this section draws on Price Waterhouse (1988a,b), Gil Diaz (1988), and International Bureau of Fiscal Documentation, *Tax News Service*.

14. Material in this section draws on Stephens (1987) and the *Tax News Service* of the International Bureau of Fiscal Documentation (various issues).

15. The material in this section is based on Andersson (1988a,b) and the *Tax News Service* of the International Bureau of Fiscal Documentation (various issues).

16. These dramatic reductions in tax rates at personal and corporate levels are expected to cost approximately S.Kr.60 billion. They will be financed by increased taxes on capital income (S.Kr.25 billion) (the largest revenue sources are increased taxation of private dwellings, taxation of sheltered pension income, and increased capital gains taxes), increased taxes on fringe benefits (S.Kr.15 billion), a widened VAT base (S.Kr.10 billion), new taxes on energy (S.Kr.10 billion), and reduced public housing subsidies. See Andersson (1988a) for more details.

17. The material in this section draws on the discussion in Renwick (1987), Stuart Buttle and Whitehouse (1988), and the *Tax News Service* of the International Bureau of Fiscal Documentation (various issues).

18. A related but different issue is the extent to which countries already consciously design their tax policies in light of tax policies in the United States. Recent reforms in Colombia covering the tax treatment of capital income reflect this. I am grateful to Charles McLure for bringing this to my attention.

19. See Musgrave's (1988) arguments regarding this case.

20. See, for instance, the discussion in Herber (1988) and Musgrave (1987).

21. See the more detailed discussion in Stephens (1987), p. 332.

22. Bossons (1987) also points this out as a key difference from U.S. experience.

23. See Shoven (1988), pp. 19–20.

24. Also see the discussion of the Canadian case in Bossons (1987).

References

Andersson, Krister. 1988a. Tax Reform in Scandinavia during the 1980s. Mimeo. Prepared for the American Economic Association's annual meetings, New York, December 28–30.

Andersson, Krister. 1988b. Tax Reforms in Scandinavia during the 1980s—A Summary. Mimeo. Prepared for the American Economic Association's Annual Meetings, New York, December 28–30.

Boidman, Nathan, and Gary J. Gartner. 1987. *U.S. Tax Reform: The Canadian Perspective*. Don Mills: CCH Canadian Limited, pp. 1–11.

Boskin, Michael J. 1988. Tax Policy and Economic Growth: Lessons from the 1980s. *Journal of Economic Perspectives* 2, 4: 71–97.

Bossons, John. 1987. The Impact of the 1986 Tax Reform Act on Tax Reform in Canada. *National Tax Journal* 40, 3: 331–338.

"Budget Speech." 1989. *Times* (London), March 15, pp. 16–17.

Byatt, Ian C. R. 1988. United Kingdom. In Joseph A. Pechman (ed.), *World Tax Reform: A Progress Report*. Washington, DC: Brookings Institution, pp. 219–236.

Canada, Department of Finance. 1985. *The Corporate Income Tax System: A Direction for Change*. Department of Finance, Ottawa. May.

Canada, Department of Finance. 1987a. *Tax Reform 1987: The White Paper*. Department of Finance, Ottawa. June 18.

Canada, Department of Finance. 1987b. *Sales Tax Reform*. Department of Finance, Ottawa, Canada. June 18.

Canada, Department of Finance. 1987c. *Tax Reform 1987*. Department of Finance, Ottawa, Canada. December 16.

Canada, Department of Finance. 1987d. *Supplementary Information Relating to Tax Reform Measures*. Department of Finance, Ottawa. December 16.

Canada, Department of Finance. 1989a. *Budget '89: Budget Papers*. Department of Finance, Ottawa, Canada. April 27, pp. 31–58.

Coopers & Lybrand International Tax Network. 1986. *International Tax Summaries 1986: A Guide Planning and Decisions*. New York: Wiley. 1986.

Deloitte, Haskins and Sells. 1986. *The Tax Revolution: A New Era Begins*. Washington, DC: Deloitte, Haskins and Sells.

Dodge, David A., and John H. Sargent. 1988. Canada. In Joseph A. Pechman (ed.), *World Tax Reform: A Progress Report*. Washington, DC: Brookings Institution, pp. 43–69.

Evans, Edward A. 1988. Australia. In Joseph A. Pechman (ed.), *World Tax Reform: A Progress Report*. Washington, DC: Brookings Institution, pp. 15–40.

Galper, Harvey. 1988. Editor's Overview. In *Portfolio—International Economic Perspectives*, vol. 13, no.3. St. Louis, MO: George Washington University.

Gil Diaz, Francisco. 1988. Tax Reform issues in Mexico. Mimeo. Presented at a conference on World Tax Reform, ICEG, San Francisco, October 7.

Goode, Richard. 1988. Overview. In Joseph A. Pechman (ed.), *World Tax Reform: A Progress Report*. Washington, DC: Brookings Institution, pp. 269–275.

Government of Japan. 1989a. Explanatory Document on Japan's Tax Reform. Mimeo. Tokyo.

Government of Japan. 1989b. *An Outline of Japanese Tax Reform*. Tax Bureau, Ministry of Finance, Tokyo.

Grubert, Harry, and John Mutti. 1987. Taxes, International Capital Flows and Trade: The International Implications of the Tax Reform Act of 1986. *National Tax Journal* 40, 3: 315–329.

Herber, Bernard P. 1988. Federal Income Tax Reform in the United States: How Did It Happen? What Did It Do? Where Do We Go from Here? *American Journal of Economics and Sociology* 47, 4: 391–408.

Ishi, Hiromitsu. 1988. Why Tax Reform Now? *Japan Echo*, 15, 2: 36–39.

Keating, Paul J. 1984. The Government's Taxation Objectives. *Australian Tax Form* 1: 2–7.

Keitaro, Hasegawa. 1988. Tax Reform from a Global Perspective. *Japan Echo* 40, 2: 46–49.

Ljungh, Claes. 1988. Sweden. In Joseph A. Pechman (ed.), *World Tax Reform: A Progress Report*. Washington, DC: Brookings Institution, pp. 187–211.

Messeve, Kenneth C. 1988. Overview. In Joseph A. Pechman (ed.), *World Tax Reform: A Progress Report*. Washington, DC: Brookings Institution, pp. 277–289.

Mintz, J., and J. Whalley (eds.). 1989. *The Economic Impacts of Tax Reform*. Canadian Tax Paper No. 84. Canadian Tax Foundation, Toronto.

Morgan, David R. 1986. The Government's Tax Reform Package: An Overview. *Australian Tax Forum* 3: 3–30.

Musgrave, P. 1988. Comments on paper by J. Bossons (1988), "The Competitive Issue: The Foreign Government Response in Canada and Other Countries." *National Tax Journal* 41, 3: 365–366.

Musgrave, R. A. 1987. Short of Euphoria. *Journal of Economic Perspectives* 1, 1: 59–72.

Nagono, Atsushi. 1988. Japan. In Joseph A. Pechman (ed.), *World Tax Reform: A Progress Report*. Washington, DC: Brookings Institution, pp. 155–162.

Noguchi, Yukio. 1988. Tax Reform Debates in Japan. Mimeo. Presented at a conference on World Tax Reform, ICEG, San Francisco, October 7.

Organization for Economic Cooperation and Development. 1987. *Taxation in Developed Countries: An International Symposium Organised by the French Ministry*. OECD, Paris.

Organization for Economic Cooperation and Development. 1988. Tax Reform: The Present State of Play. Mimeo. Committee on Fiscal Affairs, IMF Fiscal Library, Washington, DC.

Pechman, Joseph A. 1987. Tax Reform: Theory and Practice. *Journal of Economic Perspectives* 1, 1: 11–28.

Pechman, Joseph A. 1987. Introduction: Recent Developments. In J. A. Pechman (ed.), *Comparative Tax Systems: Europe, Canada and Japan*. Arlington, VA: Tax Analysts.

Pechman, Joseph A. (ed.). 1988. *World Tax Reform: A Progress Report*. Washington, DC: Brookings Institution.

Porter, Michael G. 1988. Tax Reform in Australia. Mimeo. Presented at a conference on World Tax Reform, ICEG, San Francisco, October 7.

Price Waterhouse. 1988a. *Individual Taxes: A Worldwide Summary*. New York: Price Waterhouse. USA. July.

Price Waterhouse. 1988b. *Corporate Taxes: A Worldwide Summary*. New York: Price Waterhouse. USA. July.

Renwick, G. F. 1987. United Kingdom. *National Business Lawyer*, pp. 21–25. London.

Shoven, John B. 1988. The Japanese Tax Reform and the Effective Rate of Tax on Japanese Corporate Investments. NBER Working Paper No. 2791. December.

Sinn, Hans-Werner. 1988. U.S. Tax Reform 1981 and 1986: Impact On International Capital Markets and Capital Flows. *National Tax Journal* 41, 3: 327–340.

Stephens, Robert J. 1987. Tax Reform in New Zealand. *Australian Tax Forum* 4: 327–346.

Stuart Buttle, Elizabeth, and Chris Whitehouse. 1988. Lawson's Great Tax Reform. *New Law Journal*, March 18, pp. 177–180.

Tanzi, Vito. 1987. The Response of Other Industrial Countries to the U.S. Tax Reform Act. *National Tax Journal* 40, 3: 339–355.

Tax News Service. Vol. 14–19. (Countries: Sweden, Japan, Canada, United States, United Kingdom, Australia, New Zealand and Mexico.) International Bureau of Fiscal Documentation, Amsterdam. Various years.

U.S. Treasury Department. 1984. *Tax Reform for Fairness, Simplicity and Economic Growth.* Washington, DC: Government Printing Office. November.

U.S. President. *The President's Tax Proposals to the Congress for Fairness, Growth and Simplicity.* Washington, DC: Government Printing Office. May.

Whalley, John. 1990. "Recent Tax Reform in Canada: Policy Responses to Global and Domestic Pressures. In M. J. Boskin (ed.), *World Tax Reform.* San Francisco: Institute for Contemporary Studies, pp. 73–92.

COMMENTS

Richard A. Musgrave

John's interesting review of international responses to the U.S. tax reform of 1986 shows that the type of adjustment made in the United States was widely shared, but that there is no clear pattern as to sequence: In some instances the United States led, while in others it was preceded by similar changes elsewhere. This is not surprising. It is not easy to pinpoint the precise timing of tax changes, and there may be responses to anticipated as well as actual legislation. To the extent that the U.S. change was the triggering factor, the causal evidence is stronger with regard to adjustments in the corporation tax. This is as may be expected since capital is the most mobile factor and the United States is a major force on both the giving and receiving end of capital flows. However this may be, the most interesting and striking fact that emerges from the chapter, as it did from earlier surveys, is the high degree of similarity in most of these reforms. Although overall levels of taxation did not change greatly during the 1980s, there were important changes in how the revenue is raised, and these changes were widely shared.

Regarding the income tax, there has been a general trend toward base broadening, reduction in the number of rate brackets, and reduction in top marginal rates—all changes in the direction of a more comprehensive and flatter tax. Regarding the corporation tax, we find a similar trend toward rate reduction and base broadening, including reduced reliance on investment incentives and accelerated depreciation. In addition we note a transition from turnover to value-added taxes, and with it some increase in the revenue share drawn from indirect as against direct taxation. These have been the major changes, and John raises the intriguing question to what extent they reflect forces of tax competition and to what extent they may be taken to implement common intellectual findings, which, I take it, is a modest way of referring to our (i.e., the tax economist's) constructive influence. I would like to explore this assignment of influences a bit further, and in the process add a third factor, that is, the common experience of a changing political climate in the capitals of the Western world.

As John notes, tax competition has been a factor, especially so regarding the corporation tax. Capital originating in high-rate countries will seek the safe haven of low-rate countries, and capital originating in low-rate countries will suffer excess credits when investing in higher-rate countries. The system thus offers a built-in mechanism for a mutual downward adjustment in rates, a mechanism for tax avoidance of capital income. The problem is less marked at the level of personal income tax, naturally so since residency is less mobile than capital. Competition is thus a less dominant factor at the personal level, but not absent, as the uniform pattern of reduction in top bracket rates suggests.

But tax competition has not been the entire story; "intellectual" influences and political climate have been at work as well. Beginning with the income tax, one of the two main features of the reform pattern may be imputed to the former source—the move toward implementation of the Schanz-Haig-Simons concept of accretion, a concept that has dominated academic thinking on income taxation of my generation. Beginning with Simons in the early 1940s, it has been extended by a long chain of authors, Groves, Goode, Surrey, Vickrey, Shoup, Pechman, and myself, to mention but a few. In the United States, Blueprints and Treasury I, and in Canada, the Carter Commission Report, are in the same vein. What has transpired may be credited to our "intellectual" efforts, and even though much remains to be done such as the treatment of housing and full inclusion of capital gains without writeup of base at death—there have been some results. Even intellectual efforts may pay off if there is sufficient patience. However, as one victory is won, new challenges arise, such as the difficulties posed by inflation adjustments.

Intellectual victory may be claimed also for the recent tendency to move from a separate set of corporation taxes to integration with the individual income tax. Once more, in line with the Schanz-Haig-Simons tradition, it is only the individual who has ability to pay and to whom corporate source income should be imputed. Such integration, I hasten to add, is not to be confused with transition to a cash-flow tax. Far from integration with the income tax so as to tax corporate source income but once, the cash-flow version aims at transition to a consumption base and exclusion of most capital income from taxation.

The pedigree of reform is less clear, however, when it comes to the second component of income tax change—the flattening of the rate structure, including (1) reduction in the number of rate brackets and (2) frequently sharp cuts in upper-bracket rates. Of the two, the former is of only minor importance. The claim that reducing the number of brackets results in great simplification is phony since people use tax tables anyhow. The sharp reduction in upper-bracket rates is, however, of major importance. Such is the case even though this reduction, especially so in the United States, did not really change the actual pattern of effective rates. The high marginal rates had previously been rendered ineffective by loopholes, so the repeal of loopholes, combined with rate reduction, left effective rates by brackets more or less unchanged. Now it is evident that the two changes in combination were an improvement, on equity as well as efficiency grounds. But instead of matching the closing of upper-bracket loopholes with reduction of high-bracket rates, it would also have been possible to close loopholes while maintaining the underlying structure of rates. The package could then have been rendered revenue-neutral by combining loophole closing with a moderate across-the-board cut in all rates. This would have validated rather than voided the earlier if ineffective goal of progressive taxation over the middle and upper range.

The retreat from progressive taxation, so it might be argued, also had an "intellectual" input. Concern with deadweight loss and optimal taxation theory during the 1970s and 1980s has shown the burden of high marginal rates to be more severe than had been thought, and growth considerations also pointed in that direction. But as I see it, these influences have been relatively minor. The major factor has been a change in political climate toward a less egalitarian view of distributive justice—an upper-end flattening of the accepted social welfare function—which has occurred since the 1960s. Although a progressive burden distribution continues to be held desirable over the lower to middle range of the scale, such is no longer the case over the middle to upper range.

As individuals we may applaud or regret this change, and there is no scientific basis on which to prove it correct or mistaken. The question here is this: If this flattened view of the social welfare function is to be the wave of the future, what will it mean for the income tax? Putting it bluntly, does not the shift from a progressive to a flat rate remove much of the raison d'être of income taxation? Or, putting it more correctly, does it not remove much of the raison d'être of personal taxation, be it on an income or a consumption base? Note that this question cuts across the issue of income versus consumption base, and indeed applies especially to the latter. If lower-end progression can be achieved via exclusion of low-income products and/or via transfers from the expenditure side of the budget, the value-added tax will do and in a much simpler fashion than the expenditure tax. Viewed in this way, we can understand that the major intellectual innovation of the period—the academic enthusiasm for a personal expenditure tax—has had so little impact. In a period moving toward in rem taxation, the restructuring of personal taxation from an income toward a consumption basis had little appeal and may be a stillborn idea.

This change in political climate, with its turn away from middle–upper-income progression, also helps explain John's other finding—the rise in the share of indirect taxation. Here the major intellectual contribution has been to work out the mechanics of value-added taxation, and this has contributed to its sweeping advance over the past decade. I have some doubts about this. Although the VAT is more effective in reaching parts of the base such as services, the retail sales tax has the great advantage of visibility. It also avoids the need for border adjustment in the common market, allowing rate differences to be retained without border adjustments. But this may be a minor point. The main point is that the success of the VAT has been the main factor in the rise of indirect and, more important, impersonal taxation.

As someone dedicated to personal taxation with a reasonable degree of middle- to upper-bracket income progression—whether on an income or a consumption base is of lesser importance—these trends do not make me especially happy. Such is the case especially in the United States where the trend toward the value-added tax is supported by a rather unholy alliance, including those who wish to render the tax system less progressive as well as others who favor an invisible tax, no matter how bad it may be, because it will permit larger budgets. There is no denying that this has been an exciting decade for tax reform or, using a more careful term, of tax change. Not all "reforms" need be an improvement.

GENERAL DISCUSSION

Alan Auerbach began the discussion by making three points. First, he questioned whether competition in capital income taxes would increase investment incentives. Reductions in corporate tax rates have often been accompanied by broadening the corporate tax base. Second, he observed that the United States appears to be unique in how it coupled federal tax reform with deficit spending in the 1980s. Finally, Auerbach responded to John Whalley's argument that Mexico has been reluctant to adopt a corporate cash-flow tax because such a tax, not being based on income, might not be creditable against U.S. tax liability. Auerbach suggested that Mexico might adopt a cash-flow-type tax and *call* it an income tax for foreign tax purposes.

Charles McLure observed that the fact that tax reform in the United Kingdom preceded reform in the United States was instrumental in bringing about reform in the United States because it increased its political acceptability, particularly to the then secretary of the treasury, Donald Regan.

McLure brought up the case of Colombia as a clear example of the intellectual impact of U.S. tax reform. As evidence, he claimed that the Colombian government's exposition of motives for reform echoed that of the United States. Further the proposal for inflation adjustment gained credibility by having been included in Treasury I—more credibility, that is, than if it had been considered only by other South American governments. Finally, McLure noted that Colombia's recent tax reform act contains specific wording allowing the president to change Colombia's taxation of foreigners in direct response to changes in the international tax environment.

McLure offered the cases of Indonesia and Jamaica as counterexamples to the hypothesis of U.S. influence. In both countries tax reform reduced rates and broadened the tax base, but in neither case did the changes come in direct response to TRA86 or Treasury I.

Robert Mattson pointed out that the intellectual influence of U.S. reform could be dated from 1981 with the debate surrounding the Bradley-Gephardt and Kemp-Roth bills. He also suggested that whether U.S. reform had been a direct trigger or not, it probably accelerated the adoption of changes that European governments had already been considering.

Mattson also explained that the Japanese have *not* reduced their corporate tax. Previously, Japan had a two-rate corporate tax system, with a lower rate due on earnings paid out as dividends. Since Japanese firms traditionally do *not* pay dividends, they faced a high tax rate relative to U.S. firms, which have generally paid a lower rate. Recently the Japanese have moved away from this two-rate system, equalizing the rates effectively paid by Japanese and foreign firms.

While Whalley had emphasized the importance of common intellectual influences on policymakers, Roger Gordon argued that we should consider common economic pressures. Increasing reliance on international trade, for example, stimulates reform because differing tax rates across countries tend to distort trade. Further distortions occur because countries compete for the location of mobile accounting profits and savings. Finally, mobility of the labor force in Europe has created pressure to adopt a value-added tax.

10   Lessons for Tax Reform

Henry J. Aaron

Public finance economists have long preached that tax systems should be judged on the basis of their effects on economic efficiency, ease of administration, and fairness. Few public economists thought that the Tax Reform Act of 1986 would do much to ease administration of the income tax. Some gains in simplicity were anticipated from the hoped-for reduction in the number of tax shelters. Some former itemizers would become standard deducters. But these gains in simplicity were substantially offset—some would say, swamped—by additional headaches for taxpayers with large interest deductions, passive losses, and other complicated capital transactions. Any added complexity, it was hoped, would be amply repaid in the coin of reduced horizontal inequities.

Nor did TRA86 hold out much promise for those who dislike the current distribution of tax burdens, since distributional neutrality became virtually a binding constraint on the tax debate. In the end TRA86 slightly increased progressivity, as conventionally measured (Pechman 1990). But wealthy taxpayers may have been the major welfare gainers because TRA86 reduces the risk they bear in equilibrium (Galper, et al. 1988).

The major disputes among economists before enactment of TRA86 dealt rather with its effects, hoped for or feared, on economic efficiency. Advocates claimed that reduced marginal rates would increase labor supply, a prediction supported by empirical research (Hausman and Poterba 1987). They also claimed that reduction in the dispersion of effective rates of tax on tangible investment would improve efficiency by excluding projects with low before-tax but high aftertax rates of return. Critics of TRA86 held that increased effective rates of tax on capital income would reduce saving, which most economists regard as too low. They also held that the increased dispersion of effective rates between tangible and intangible investments would cause the efficiency of investment to fall, not rise.

Nothing has happened during the three years since passage of TRA86 to confirm either the worst fears of its opponents or the best hopes of its supporters. Investment rates have not moved outside the range of past fluctuations. Saving rates rose modestly, but no one I have seen has suggested the tax reform deserves the credit. Some slight increase in labor supply may have occurred, but it is hard to detect (Burtless 1989). No point of inflection is visible in trends in investment rates or growth of total factor productivity, but none probably should have been expected at all and certainly not this fast.

Most of the papers presented at this conference reinforce casual observation that TRA86 has had little effect on the broad measures of real economic activity in which most economists are interested. In fact several of the chapters indicate that predicted effects were, if anything, much larger than anything actually observed. Clotfelter (chapter 7) finds that charitable giving has not fallen off, as it was predicted to do. Courant and Gramlich (chapter 8) find that the types of taxes state and local governments impose and the amounts they spend bear almost no relationship to what a standard equation would have forecast. Auerbach and Hassett (chapter 2) fail to find any of the shift from equipment to structures that past investment equations indicate TRA86 should have caused. Poterba remains convinced that TRA86 will reduce construction and drive up rents, because of theoretical reasoning but not because of anything that has yet happened. Skinner and Feenberg (chapter 3) join a long list of researchers who cannot find much evidence that aftertax real rates of return are consistently related to household saving. We have no paper on labor supply, probably because no good microdata are yet available with which to measure possible effects, but perhaps also because nothing dramatic was expected.

In contrast, tax changes may have affected asset values, corporate organization (according to Gordon and Mackie-Mason, chapter 4), and the international flow of capital (according to Slemrod, chapter 1), but even these judgments must be hedged because so much else was going on.

As of now, in short, both casual observation and the research unveiled here make one wonder what all the fuss concerning gains or losses of economic efficiency was about. If Congress forbears from legislative infanticide on tax reform, it is of course possible that previously obscure effects will become apparent and that today's namby-pamby judgments may have to be modified. Although major effects may one day became apparent, I am going to assume in the remainder of this chapter that the verdict does not change, that no major effects of tax reform, currently obscured from our view, emerge.

This preliminary appraisal of the most important tax legislation in a generation provokes a number of observations about the future course of tax reform and of analyses of taxes. First, is it possible that our original models were correct and that the findings of little or no tax-induced response are false? Second, if we reject this possibility, what are the implications of this finding for tax research? Third, what are the implications of the findings of this chapter for debate about tax policy?

10.1 How Could We Turn Out to Be Wrong?

Any reasonably imaginative theorist or econometrician can come up with several reasons why the models of economic behavior that predict large behavioral effects of tax policy are right and the findings of the papers at this conference are misleading.

The first is that TRA86 was not a clear signal in most dimensions. Marginal personal rates rose for a significant minority of taxpayers, even if they fell for a plurality. Although marginal corporation income tax rates fell, the investment tax credit was repealed, and depreciable lives were lengthened. Hence effective tax rates for most types of investment actually increased. Furthermore the tax reform modified a host of other provisions that affect various capital transactions in different ways but that do not enter the usual calculations of effective tax rates or most investment equations.

Second, taxpayers may have regressive expectations regarding tax legislation. They may believe that changes enacted in 1986 will prove evanescent. The current debate over capital gains and individual retirement accounts lends substance to such views. The existence of such expectations could serve to rehabilitate the models of behavior of state and local governments, for example, whose attachment to sales taxes would then be recognized as percipient, not perverse. Investors could be seen as making long-term plans dependent, not on short-lived aberrations in tax law, but on the average tax environment they anticipate over the life of current projects. Although regressive expectations may explain the imperturbability of investors, they deepen the puzzle about charitable donors. Why, if taxpayers see higher rates in their futures, has giving been so well maintained?

Third, we may simply have gotten lags wrong. People may expect current law to remain in effect but adjust their behavior slowly, which is just another way of saying that data next year or the year after may return to predicted patterns.

Fourth, the experience of 1986 may be rationalized by appeal to excluded variables. In the case of saving, there is nothing really to rationalize since past empirical efforts to establish the effects of taxes—really, of real, aftertax rates of return—on saving have been so inconclusive. But the fact that marginal personal tax rates on saving went down for taxpayers who do most of the saving, while capital taxes at the entity level went up, provides an almost infinite menu of specifications that can explain any conceivable sequence of events. One can almost pity journal editors perspiring under the heavy load of studies reaffirming the insubstantiality of the corporate veil. Future efforts to explain the rise of state and local spending after 1986 may cite the drop in exhaustive federal spending for nondefense programs; in such models state and local voters not only would be influenced by tax prices and income but also would use services of lower level governments as alternatives for declining national outlays.

The problem with each of these explanations, and with many others like them that we are likely to see, of course, is that they are all ex post and ad hoc. Any set of facts can be rationalized ex post by sufficient data mining. Even if new equations showing large responses to taxes can be found, they should do little to revive our confidence that such responses will in fact occur. If the goal of fitted relationships is to help us predict, the failure, chronicled in papers presented at this conference, of previously estimated relationships to predict the consequences of tax reform should instill a new and unaccustomed modesty in us all. Although the past two years may end up as outliers in equations that reaffirm what we thought we knew, let us proceed, following the papers presented at this conference, as if TRA86 should cause us to reduce our estimate of the power of taxes to influence economic behavior.

10.2   Implications for Research

Like ambulance-chasers who profit from injury and death, econometricians prosper from the demise of old economic relationships. TRA86 is for economists what the San Francisco earthquake is for construction companies—a splendid opportunity to build replacements for structures that collapsed under stress. One of the safer predictions about the effect of TRA86 is that it will lead to a bull market in dissertations and journal articles trying to match specification to fact.

Although this prosperity will trickle down to many branches of public economics, I want to focus especially on the importance of the results presented here for analysis of tax incidence. The history of tax incidence studies reflects the gradual abandonment of naive notions of burden. For decades economists warned lawyers and others not to identify legal liability with economic burden. Early tax incidence studies assigned burdens without much empirical basis or even economic justification. In general, the burden of taxes on labor income has been assumed to fall on workers, although most studies have always found that elasticities of labor supply are positive. Taxes on capital income were assigned in ways that now seem arbitrary in the extreme—half of the property tax to renters and half to consumers, for example. The next generation of studies chose rules of thumb consistent with theoretical developments—assign corporation income taxes to all owners of capital, following Harberger's classic analysis, for example. Recently full-blown general equilibrium models based on the assumptions of utility and profit maximization have been used to incorporate the effects of taxes on pretax incomes. The strength, and it now appears perhaps the weakness for incidence analysis, of these models is that their calculations rest on independent estimates of the relevant elasticities.

But if such elasticities lead to exaggerated predictions of the effects of tax changes, they may well spawn misleading estimates of tax incidence. To put matters more simply, if behavioral effects on saving as well as on labor supply are small, the relatively naive methods of estimating tax incidence according to rules of thumb look far more attractive than they did before. Furthermore the validity of revenue estimates made with relatively naive methods widely scorned by economists for failing to take adequate account of induced behavioral effects looks better in direct proportion to the shrinkage of estimates of behavioral response.

The kinds of results reported here would, if replicated and sustained in future work, cast a shadow over the celebrated conclusion of optimal tax literature that welfare-maximizing tax rates leave little room for progressivity and that actual tax schedules almost certainly exceed those levels. As marginal excess burden of taxes drops, so does the marginal social cost of public spending, which suggests that cost-benefit analyses done without regard to excess burdens may not be far off the mark. As behavioral effects shrink, the utilitarian case against public spending weakens and the case for progressivity strengthens. If the behavioral elasticities are small, the relative importance of administrative effects such as those analyzed by Slemrod (1990) also increase.

10.3   Implications for Policy

If behavioral effects are smaller than we thought, the importance of efficiency gains and losses falls. But the relative importance of equity, both horizontal and vertical, increases, at least for end-state theorists who work in the utilitarian mainstream of economics.[1] In particular, it is useful to consider how debates concerning some of the major issues of tax policy now under debate would be changed, if at all, by a judgment that previous estimates of behavioral effects, and hence efficiency losses, were too high. Such an exercise is inescapably speculative because each person's answer will depend on the shape of his or her trade-offs between efficiency and equity.

Capital Gains

Some proposals for cutting tax rates on realized capital gains, such as those before Congress in 1989, are so outlandish from the standpoint of tax policy that it is hard to take them seriously. Accordingly I shall consider instead the simple proposal to return to a permanently lower tax rate on gains from sale of assets held more than a minimum period. The case for a reduced rate on income from long-term capital gains rests on three claims.

The first is that nominal gains overstate real gains because of inflation. The problem is indisputably real, but the solution of reducing gains is clearly dominated by indexing. As Brinner (1976) showed, a concessionary rate designed to offset inflation should rise steadily with the length of holding period, a very counterintuitive and legislatively implausible idea.

The second is that incentives to undertake risky investments will be increased if rates are reduced, partly because reduced lock-in will augment the supply of capital and partly because increased rewards to entrepreneurs will spur demand. The third is that revenues will rise permanently because realizations grow.

Evidence to support the second argument, other than bald assertion put forward as if it were self-evident, is virtually nonexistent. Evidence to support or to refute the third argument is abundant but contradictory. Everyone acknowledges that cuts in capital gains rates have been associated with increases in realizations, but Auerbach (1988) has shown that past studies do not clearly establish whether the effect is temporary or permanent and that data available now or likely to become available are unlikely to settle the issue.

The papers presented here can be read in either of two ways. On the one hand, the papers by Gordon and MacKie-Mason (chapter 4) and by Slemrod (chapter 6) lend some support to the proposition that asset transactions, as divorced from real investment or saving, are sensitive to tax rules. They support the view that decisions about when and, more important, whether to realize capital gains are sensitive to tax rates. But no one ever doubted the qualitative argument. The debate is quantitative, and none of the papers bears on that question.

On the other hand, the insensitivity of investment to rather blunt tax incentives should, I think, marginally increase one's skepticism that reduced capital gains rates will affect supposedly high-expected-payoff, high-risk investments enough to matter. Those who hold that reduced capital gains rates will spur such investment have not even tried to pick up the burden of proof to show that such an effect will be quantitatively significant. The papers presented here reinforce my prior view that until someone shoulders this burden of proof, their claims should not be taken seriously.

This line of reasoning suggests that the distributional effects of the proposed reductions in capital gains rates are the principal substantive consideration in appraising concessionary rates. Calculation of such distributional effects is straightforward with respect to gains that would have been realized in any event; the old and simple methods of allocation are about right.

The benefits from induced realizations are more difficult to calculate. One knows that households sell some assets at reduced rates that they would have sold later or not at all if rates were not cut. On income from such sales households certainly enjoy a welfare gain, but the gain is smaller than the difference between tax at the old and tax at the new rates. Indeed, it is not possible to calculate either incidence or overall welfare effects without knowing whether realizations are increased permanently or temporarily and how the increased realizations are distributed over income classes.

It seems clear, however, that the tables compiled by the Joint Committee on Taxation, which show that more than half of the gains from the proposals before Congress this year accrue to taxable units with incomes in excess of $200,000 per year, describe the distribution of benefits with rough accuracy. To focus on these distributional tables should not be seen as inflaming class warfare, but as attending to the only evidence of any solidity advanced so far in the debate.

Individual Retirement Accounts

Skinner and Feenberg (chapter 3) point out that some provisions of TRA86 discouraged and others encouraged personal saving. The net effect is hard to sort out. They claim to have found in data for the 1980s a positive relationship between real aftertax rates of return and household saving. However, strikingly absent from their story is any mention of household net worth or the stock market or the anomalies associated with the agricultural drought of 1988. Their paper certainly does not strengthen the case that individual retirement accounts perceptibly add to household saving. This case rests largely on microdata as analyzed in a succession of papers by Venti and Wise (1987, 1988) that were criticized in turn by Gale and Scholz (1989) and even more fundamentally by Gravelle (1989). On balance, the Skinner and Feenberg paper does nothing to strengthen and may marginally weaken the credibility of claims that IRAs boost saving.

The general tone of the papers surely undercuts faith that the new version of the IRA, in which deposits are taxable but withdrawals are not, will have any meaningful effect on household saving. For households to react to this version, they have to be motivated by tax savings that they will enjoy some years or decades in the future, rather than by tax savings realized currently. For fully rational households such discounting poses no difficulty. But some of the better arguments that old-style IRAs boosted household saving pointed to the irrationality of households to support their claims. In particular, rational households would make their IRA deposits as early in the tax year as possible. In fact deposits were found to be bunched just before deadlines for filing tax returns, a pattern of behavior that suggests deposits were motivated to an irrational degree by current tax savings. While such evidence provides some support for a belief that old-style IRAs boosted household saving by some fraction of deposits, it also suggests that new-style IRAs, which do not reduce current taxes at all, are likely to be far less effective.

Integration

Economists and tax lawyers have long supported some form of integration of personal and corporation income taxes. The only opponents were business leaders, who have preferred to take out their tax cuts as liberalized depreciation and investment tax credits or reduced rates, and labor leaders, who opposed any cuts in corporation taxes at all.

Resurgent concern about corporate borrowing, in general, and leveraged buy-outs, in particular, have revived interest in integration. Recent
theoretical work by Gravelle and Kotlikoff (1989) suggests that a non-
integrated corporation income tax may produce larger welfare losses than
prior work had suggested. Their argument rests on alleged efficiency advantages of corporations that are not realized because corporations are
handicapped in competition with unincorporated competitors. The paper
by Auerbach and Hassett (chapter 2) finds that real investment has not
responded as predicted to past changes in the relative and absolute treatment of structures and equipment. It elevates the question of whether the
claimed efficiency gains would actually be realized from elimination of
the corporate tax wedge, gains that would allegedly result from a shift in
real investments to efficient companies, now operating as corporations, from
inefficient companies, now operating as partnerships and proprietorships.

In contrast, however, the papers alleging the sensitivity of asset transactions to relative tax rates leave undamaged the hope that elimination or
reduction of the corporate tax wedge would reduce tax-motivated corporate restructuring and leveraging.

Cash-Flow Taxation

Many of the economists here have argued that cash-flow taxes are superior
to income taxes. Some take this position only if gifts and bequests are
subject to tax, others don't much care, and still others actively oppose
their inclusion. All share the view that the annual focus of the income tax
leads to horizontal inequities and inefficiencies based on the timing of
consumption.

Work by Hall (1988) that finds little evidence to support an intertemporal elasticity of consumption different from zero weakens the efficiency arguments. So does the drift of the papers presented here that report
less sensitivity of most real economic decisions to tax rates than prior
analysis led the authors to expect. These calculations call into question the
estimates of welfare gains from consumption taxation that have emerged
from numerous simulations, including those by Summers (1981), Auerbach
and Kotlikoff (1987), and various combinations of Stanford authors. In
general, it seems that we ought to estimate the welfare effects based on
utility functions in which the timing of consumption is less sensitive to tax
rules than we supposed. Since the welfare gains estimated in these models
from the switchover were very large, even reduced estimates may still
seem to justify an eventual conversion to cash-flow or other consumption-

type rules. But I am skeptical whether efficiency considerations will justify the rather considerable upheaval necessary to reverse the movement toward comprehensive income taxation initiated in 1986. If we wish to justify cash-flow taxation, we may have to have recourse to the weak reed of horizontal inequity. (Pechman 1990)

10.4   Conclusion

I recognize that I may be exaggerating the ramifications of the kinds of findings reported in the papers presented here for tax incidence and for how we think of the use of the tax system for income redistribution. But the economics profession has been part of a large and powerful intellectual movement that has undermined the respectability of egalitarian impulses. If the case for progressive taxation was never better than uneasy, economic analysis in recent years has made it seem to be a product of hormonal excess rather than clear thinking. The desire to curb "distinctly evil or unlovely" inequality (in Henry Simon's characterization) has been put to shame by careful analyses showing that efforts to cut inequality would detract from welfare by producing rampant inefficiency. Results such as those presented here cast doubt on the models, even those that sported high coefficients of inequality aversion, that found welfare maximized at low marginal tax rates, and that contributed to the respectability of inequality.

I confess also to being influenced in the drafting of these comments by the memory of Joseph Pechman, who always retained more interest than was sometimes fashionable in the distribution of income and in the power of taxes to change it. He would have chuckled as he read the papers written for this conference.

Note

1. For those who adhere to process theories of distribution, which hold that any distribution of income is just if the processes that generated it were just, a drop in estimates of behavioral effects has little to do with the desirability of policies to change the distribution of income.

References

Auerbach, Alan J. 1988. Capital Gains Taxation in the United States: Realizations, Revenue, and Rhetoric. *Brookings Papers on Economic Activity* 2: 595–631.

Auerbach, Alan J., and Laurence J. Kotlikoff. 1987. *Dynamic Fiscal Policy*. Cambridge: Cambridge University Press.

Brinner, Roger E. 1976. Inflation and the Definition of Taxable Personal Income. Henry J. Aaron (ed.), *Inflation and the Income Tax*. Washington, DC: Brookings Institution, pp. 121–145.

Burtless, Gary. 1989. The Supply-Side Legacy of the Reagan Years: Response of Labor Supply. Paper prepared for a conference on "The Economic Legacy of the Reagan Years: Euphoria or Chaos?" Oakland University, June 30–July 1.

Gale, William G., and John Karl Scholz. 1989. IRAs and Household Saving. Unpublished manuscript.

Galper, Harvey, Robert Lucke, and Eric Toder. 1988. A General Equilibrium Model of Tax Reform. In Henry J. Aaron, Harvey Galper, and Joseph A. Pechman (eds.), *Uneasy Compromise: Problems of a Hybrid Income-Consumption Tax*, Washington, DC: Brookings Institution, pp. 59–107.

Gravelle, Jane G. 1989. Capital Gains Taxes, IRA's, and Savings. Congressional Research Service. CRS Report for Congress #89–543 RCO. September 26.

Gravelle, Jane G., and Laurence J. Kotlikoff. 1989. The Incidence and Efficiency Costs of Corporate Taxation When Corporate and Noncorporate Firms Produce the Same Good. *Journal of Political Economy* 97: 749–780.

Hall, Robert E. 1988. Intertemporal Substitution in Consumption. *Journal of Political Economy* 96: 339–357.

Hausman, Jerry A., and James M. Poterba. 1987. Household Behavior and the Tax Reform Act of 1986. *Journal of Economic Perspectives* 1: 101–119.

Pechman, Joseph A. 1990. The Future of the Income Tax. *American Economic Review* 80: 1–20.

Slemrod, Joel. 1990. Optimal Taxes and Optimal Tax Systems. *Journal of Economic Perspectives* 4: 157–178.

Summers, Lawrence H. 1981. Capital Taxation and Accumulation in a Life-Cycle Growth Model. *American Economic Review* 71: 533–544.

Venti, Steven, and David Wise. 1987. IRAs and Saving. In Martin Feldstein (ed.), *The Effects of Taxation on Capital Accumulation*. Chicago: University of Chicago Press, pp. 7–48.

Venti, Steven, and David Wise. 1988. The Evidence on IRAs. *Tax Notes*, January 25, pp. 411–416.

COMMENTS

Charles E. McLure, Jr.
Much of Henry Aaron's paper is concerned with one asserted common characteristic of the findings reported in the papers presented at this conference and the implications of those findings for both future research and future policy. As Henry sees it, "Most of the papers presented at this conference reinforce casual observation that TRA86 has had little effect on the broad aggregates in which most economists are interested." Henry implicitly contrasts the following policy-relevant effects of changes in the tax law: If behavior is highly sensitive to changes in tax prices, there is a change in economic efficiency; if behavior is not sensitive, there is a change in fairness. (As Bailey 1974, p. 1174, put it, "Apparent horizontal inequities as a rule shake out in competitive resource allocation and translate into misuse of resources.") Henry also notes that if behavioral elasticities are small, administrative effects are more important.

Rather than focus on Henry's characterization of findings, I would like to begin by supplementing this implicit discussion in several ways, especially to emphasize (1) that tax preferences are generally undesirable, no matter *what* one thinks about the sensitivity of behavioral responses to taxation, and (2) that administrative considerations are more important than most economists seem to think. (Perhaps I should acknowledge at this point that it is not primarily to Henry that I am addressing these remarks. For evidence that he is probably sympathetic with much that I say, see Aaron 1989.) Then I will discuss some lessons for future tax reform.

Expanding Concerns

Horizontal Equity

Perhaps through oversight, Henry seems to equate lack of fairness primarily with vertical inequity or progressivity, to the relative neglect of horizontal equity. My own view—validated if economic behavior really is as is insensitive to changes in tax prices as suggested—is that one of the true triumphs of the 1986 act is the reduction of horizontal inequities. For what it is worth, I believe that its attack on horizontal inequity is also one of the political reasons tax reform succeeded in 1986 when it had failed so often before when based primarily on appeals to vertical equity.

Equity, Efficiency, and Other Matters

I would take issue with the following statement by Henry, presumably made tongue in cheek, "As of now, in short, both casual observation and the research unveiled here make one wonder what all the shouting was about." The finding that tax reform did not eradicate serious distortions because there are no serious distortions if economic behavior is insensitive to tax prices, if it were true, would not invalidate the case for tax reform. There is more to life than Harberger triangles.

Now I am not suggesting that we should not attempt to measure the welfare loss resulting from distortionary tax policy. Welfare loss is certainly a potentially important element of the case for (or against) tax reform. But we economists should not allow ourselves to be deluded into thinking that excess burdens are all that matters. (I refer to deluding ourselves advisedly. No one else is going to delude us in this way because no one else believes it!) Both inefficient resource allocation and inequity are undesirable.

Perception of Inequity

The existence of tax preferences—and the tax shelters they spawn—gives the impression that the tax system is unfair—at least horizontally and usually vertically. This is true no matter whether we produce theory—or even evidence—that burdens and benefits of differential tax treatment are spread beyond their initial impact incidence, for example, via the Harberger mechanism, and thus affect efficiency but not equity. I believe that such perceptions of inequity are undesirable in a democratic society in which the tax system is based on voluntary compliance. Indeed, perhaps the perception of fairness should be elevated to equal status with the traditional goals of taxation, equity, efficiency, and simplicity. (I am not suggesting acceptance of the cynical view that gives a policy high marks if it is perceived to be fair, even if it is not. I am saying a policy should generally be given low marks if it is perceived to be so inequitable that taxpayer morale is seriously harmed.)

I believe that the curtailment of preferences and the strict antishelter provisions of the 1986 act were crucial for improving the perception of fairness despite the complexity of the latter. Again, this is something Harberger triangles—or economic analyses of any type—are not going to tell us about.

Tax Rates

Tax preferences mean that higher tax rates are required to raise a given amount of money. Whether one is worried about distortions, about inequities, or about the perception of inequity, problems are aggravated by high tax rates.

Simplification

Henry seems to pay too little attention to simplification. This may be understandable if one is discussing the 1986 act, which greatly increased complexity for many taxpayers. But I would make two points here, and will return to this issue below. First, the 1986 act did simplify matters for those with simple financial affairs (who admittedly already filed simple returns), and it removed some 6 million low-income taxpayers from the tax rolls. It also increased complexity primarily for corporations and for individuals in business and those with complicated financial affairs, especially if they were involved in tax shelters. (In this regard it might be noted that though antishelter provisions are quite complex, they can reduce complexity on balance by reducing shelter activity; see McLure 1990.) Second, the complexity for the latter group has become so great that we may finally want to consider whether to replace the income tax with a system of direct taxation based on consumption. The remainder of my comments relate to this possibility.

Schedular Income Taxes

One standard piece of advice given developing countries, where applicable, is to replace schedular taxes with a "global" income tax; any country that retains an explicitly schedular income tax is usually thought to be hopelessly benighted. Yet in 1986 the United States took a giant step toward schedular taxation. It is true that for the most part (with the exception of income from municipal bonds and, before the 1986 act, long-term capital gains), we do not explicitly levy different tax rates on income from different sources. But we do now distinguish, inter alia, income from the active pursuit of a trade or business, passive income, investment income, and income from municipal bonds; similar distinctions determine whether expenses will be deductible, and against which type of income. (One can easily name at least seven types of interest expense.) We have also tightened the alternative minimum tax. The natural question is whether we have merely retrogressed, or is there some logic to what we have done.

The answer, it seems, is that there is, indeed, some logic to this. To some extent we have merely come to realize—and acted on that realization—that if we are going to continue to provide tax preferences, we must use "backdoor" techniques—including schedular elements such as the limitations on investment interest and the deductibility of passive losses—to limit the availability of preferences and thereby avoid abuse and the perception of inequity. This is partly a matter of preventing expenses incurred to earn tax-preferred income from being deducted against fully taxed income. But more than this is involved.

Much advocacy of global income taxes has been rather naive, focusing almost entirely on patently preferential treatment of some types of income and neglecting the very real difficulties that inevitably result from the uneasy marriage of realization concepts and accrual concepts in the same tax code. Let me explain, using the example of long-term capital gains.

Partial exclusion of capital gains (or a preferential rate) clearly creates opportunities for tax arbitrage, inequities, and distortions; these alone might lead to demands for backstop measures such as recapture rules intended to prevent the benefits of accelerated depreciation from being taxed as capital gains on disposition of assets. But such explicitly preferential treatment is not the only source of these problems; the deferral of tax until gains are realized (and step-up of basis in the case of assets transferred at death) is every bit as great a problem. These opportunities for tax arbitrage would be even worse in the absence of limitations on the deduction of passive losses and investment interest that prevent current deduction of the expense of earning income that is deferred for tax purposes or not taxed because assets are transferred at death. (That such gains might be taxed at a preferential rate, the previous point, is not relevant for this purpose; benefits of deferral would exist even if real capital gains were taxed as ordinary income.) In short, the schedular approach adopted in the 1986 act reflects the inevitable difficulty of avoiding opportunities for tax arbitrage in a system that contains both accrual and realization features, as well as an unwillingness to eliminate preferential treatment—treatment that could, in principle, be eliminated without administrative difficulties. Of course the 1986 act did eliminate the preference at issue at the beginning of this paragraph, the partial exclusion of long-term capital gains. I have argued in McLure 1990 that perhaps in reaction to previous experience with tax shelters, the 1986 act may contain a bit of overkill—what I call the vampire approach (wooden stakes, crosses, mirrors, and wolfsbane)—to dealing with tax shelters.

The theoretical solution to the second problem is to tax everything on an accrual basis, as Haig and Simons suggested. There are, however, insuperable technical problems with this advice, as well as severe political difficulties. It is difficult to know accurately the "change in net wealth" part of the Haig-Simons equation and even more difficult to write a tax code that will always capture the changes with sufficient accuracy in an administratively feasible manner. One of the important manifestations of this difficulty is what we might call "timing issues." For example, what is the true pattern of depreciation (the loss of present value of future income) of various assets? What is the appropriate pattern for taking account of the interest income and expense generated by an original discount obligation, especially when interest rates are changing? At best these issues are often complex; at worst they yield no generally accurate solution that can be administered simply.

Capital Gains, Indexing, and the SAT

The one feature of TRA86 that has come under the most intense pressure for change is the taxation of long-term capital gains as ordinary income, without benefit of adjustment of basis for inflation. The reform adopted is clearly wrong conceptually; it is sometimes too generous and sometimes too harsh, depending on whether the benefits of deferral exceed the costs implied by the absence of inflation adjustment. One can only speculate as to whether President Bush would be advocating a preferential rate for capital gains if inflation adjustment had been adopted in 1986. (I actually have some sympathy to the view that because of external benefits it would be desirable to have preferential treatment of gains resulting from entrepreneurial activity. On the other hand, I see little justification for preferential treatment of gains from what I call "vanilla" investment (investment not likely to be characterized by external benefits), or even those from investment of venture capital. Moreover it would be extremely difficult for technical reasons to construct an administratively feasible means of distinguishing between gains from different sources.)

Suppose for the moment that sanity prevails and that indexation of basis, rather than (or even in addition to) a preferential rate, is ultimately adopted. This raises the crucial question of whether that would put us on a slippery slope that would ultimately but almost inevitably lead to indexation of the remainder of the calculation of income from business and capital, notably depreciation allowances, inventories, and interest income and expense. (This could be achieved either through ad hoc adjustments or through an integrated approach, such as that used in Chile and recently adopted by Colombia for introduction in 1992. Treasury I proposed an ad hoc approach in which various items in the income statement would be indexed. Under the integrated approach selected "real" balance sheet items are adjusted for inflation, and these adjustments are reflected in the income statement, producing a measure of net income that is accurately adjusted for inflation. See Harberger 1988 for a brief exposition of the integrated approach and McLure et al. 1989, ch. 7, for a more extended discussion and comparison with the ad hoc approach.)

Regardless of whether inflation adjustment is extended beyond capital gains—and I think that it ultimately must be to avoid both arbitrage opportunities and even more maddening complexity—the income tax will have been made more complex. This, together with other complexities in the 1986 act based on timing issues, leads me to suggest that we might better consider seriously the possibility of shifting to a system of direct taxation based on consumption, rather than on income. (For a more detailed discussion of this issue, see McLure 1988. Some may be tempted to ask why Treasury I, which I helped prepare, did not propose a consumption-based direct tax. The answer is contained in three short words: dead on arrival. Had Ronald Reagan made such a proposal, no one would have given it serious consideration.)

I was surprised that in his discussion of cash-flow taxation Henry mentioned only efficiency considerations and the horizontal inequity of the income tax. In my view it is the simplification benefits of consumption-based taxes, and not the equity and efficiency advantages, that we should be concentrating on in our attempts to determine whether to go down this route. After all, horizontal equity is, as Henry notes, a "weak reed" on which to lean in this debate, and if we want to do something about the lack of saving in the economy (admittedly only a close relative of the distortion of the saving-consumption choice), we have, in principle, the possibility of reducing the federal budget deficit. By comparison, if we want to simplify the income tax, we have no alternative but to simplify it!

The most important simplification benefits of such a tax, which we thought deserved to be called the simplified alternative tax in our recent report to the government of Colombia, are (1) that it does not require inflation adjustment and (2) that most timing issues vanish since tax liability is based on cash flow rather than on accrual. (This is not to say that consumption-based taxes raise no difficult practical problems. For some of these, see the papers presented at the 1988 World Bank workshop on cash-flow taxes. In addition to the well-known general problems of distributional effects, inconsistency with the tax systems of our trading partners and our treaty obligations, and transitional problems, Howitt and Sinn 1989 have noted the difficulty of phasing in a system of expensing with tax rates that increase over time.)

The work I have done with George Zodrow suggests that the so-called prepaid approach (the R-base tax of the Meade commission) is substantially simpler than the individual cash-flow approach (the R plus F base of the Meade commission) (see Zodrow and McLure 1988 or McLure et al. 1989, ch. 8 and 9. Bradford 1986 and Hall and Rabushka 1983, 1985, also favor the prepaid approach; Aaron and Galper 1985 advocate the individual cash-flow approach.) Rather than using qualified accounts, the prepaid approach allows no deduction for interest and does not include interest income or dividends in the tax base of individuals. As in all consumption-based taxes, immediate expensing is allowed for all investment, including additions to inventories, as well as depreciable assets.

Some may object that it is unfair and unrealistic to compare an ideal consumption-based tax with the present income tax, which reflects the political cross-hauling of three-quarters of a century. My point is that even a conceptually pure income tax would be complex because of inflation adjustment and timing issues. To see this, it is instructive to read the following partial list of timing issues, which sounds like a "rogues gallery" of complexity, especially for small business: original issue discount, installment sales, multiperiod contracts, and capitalization of such expenses as construction-period interest and costs of acquiring and holding inventories. None of these issues would exist under a consumption tax based on cash flow.

References

Aaron, Henry J. 1989. Politics and the Professors Revisited. *American Economic Review* 79, 2: 1–15.

Aaron, Henry J., and Harvey Galper. 1985. *Assessing Tax Reform*. Washington, DC: Brookings Institution.

Bailey, Martin J. 1974. Progressivity and Investment Yields under U.S. Income Taxation. *Journal of Political Economy* 82: 1157–1175.

Bradford, David F. 1986. *Untangling the Income Tax*. Cambridge: Harvard University Press.

Hall, Robert E., and Alvin Rabushka. 1983. *Low Tax, Simple Tax, Flat Tax*. New York: McGraw-Hill.

Hall, Robert E., and Alvin Rabushka. 1985. *The Flat Tax*. Stanford, CA: Hoover Institution Press.

Harberger, Arnold C. 1982. Notes on the Indexation of Income Taxes. Memo. Prepared for the Ministry of Finance of Indonesia, August. Summarized in Henry J. Aaron, Harvey Galper, and Joseph A. Pechman (eds), *Uneasy Compromise: Problems of a Hybrid Income-Consumption Tax*. Washington, DC: Brookings Institution, pp. 380–383.

Howitt, Peter, and Hans-Werner Sinn. 1989. Gradual Reforms of Capital Income Taxation. *American Economic Review* 79, 1: 106–124.

McLure, Charles E., Jr. 1988. The 1986 Act: Tax Reform's Finest Hour or Death Throes of the Income Tax? *National Tax Journal* 41, 3: 303–315.

McLure, Charles E., Jr. 1990. The Budget Process and Tax Simplification/Complication. Presented at a joint AICPA/ABA conference on Reduction of Income Tax Complexity, Washington, January 11–12. Forthcoming in the *Tax Law Review*.

McLure, Charles E., Jr., Jack Mutti, Victor Thuronyi, and George R. Zodrow. 1988. *The Taxation of Income from Business and Capital in Colombia*. Bogota: Ministerio de Hacienda y Credito Publico. Also Durham, NC: Duke University Press, 1990.

Zodrow, George R., and Charles E. McLure, Jr. 1988. Implementing Direct Consumption Taxes in Developing Countries. World Bank Discussion Paper Series.

GENERAL DISCUSSION

Fritz Scheuren asked what data are needed for further analysis of the effects of the TRA86 and offered the assistance of IRS' Statistics of Income Division with locating useful data. In particular, he was interested in the data needs of researchers planning to study potential future tax reforms, such as consumption taxes.

With reference to his paper with Daniel Feenberg (chapter 3), Jonathan Skinner cautioned that it is difficult to make inferences about savings incentives from a single series of savings rates. He also contrasted the conservative position he and Feenberg took regarding the effect of IRAs on savings incentives with results they have reported in earlier work.

Michael McIntyre noted that the 1986 act contained some schedular elements, but a pure Haig-Simons tax would not be schedular. Any tax on realizations, he claimed, is inherently schedular.

Remarking that tax policy is complicated by political compromise, Randall Weiss suggested that it is misleading to compare, for example, the ideal cash-flow tax to the ideal income tax. The more interesting comparison is between the versions of these two taxes that might emerge from the political process.

John Whalley responded to Henry Aaron's conclusion that we have not observed a significant impact from the TRA86. First, he noted that strong effects were reported in an area where they were not expected: foreign direct investment. Next, he claimed that Aaron's conclusions regarding simplicity and distributional effects were premature, as these issues had not been addressed by this conference.

Joel Slemrod suggested that there is a hierarchy of responses to tax reform. At the top of the hierarchy, most susceptible to taxation, are the timing of transactions, such as capital gains realizations, mergers, and acquisitions made to avoid General Utilities costs, and the timing of appreciated asset gifts. Next in importance are the financial and accounting responses, including changes in corporate leverage and personal portfolio shuffling. At the bottom of the hierarchy are the responses that we have had the most difficulty identifying: the real effects of tax reform. Slemrod added that if real effects are found to be insignificant, tax simplicity ought to be a major focus of tax design.

Aaron agreed that simplicity issues should be considered of first-order importance. He added that he felt too little attention was being paid to horizontal equity.

Alan Auerbach remarked that the real impact of simplicity would be seen by examining the narrowly focused provisions of the TRA86 but added that the precision of such analysis would be limited by the complexity of the law. He encouraged researchers to think about why some of these narrow rules were adopted. Why did policymakers want to discourage the specific transactions that these provisions discouraged? Many of these changes, he claimed, were never adequately justified.

Martin Zimmerman remarked that in areas where tax incentives are dominant and changes are easily implemented, the impact of reform should be immediately observable. Where decisions are complicated by a variety of influences, as is the case for investment decisions, we should not expect to see effects until much later.

Patrick Moran argued that tax reform appears to have succeeded in the goal of removing taxes from business decisions. He also noted that the United States has become more attractive as a tax haven, bringing additional income into the country.

Commenting on the political limits of moving toward a cash-flow tax, Charles Ballard claimed that it would be infeasible to remove all taxation of capital income. He also observed that tension among the standard goals of equity, efficiency, and simplicity often leads to complicated hybrid tax policies.

Robert Haveman requested an elaboration of Moran's claim that tax issues have been removed from business decisions. Moran replied that although the law is more complex than before, the complexities are narrowly focused. Some decisions, such as plant location, are now made with less consideration to tax effects. Taking issue with Moran, Gilbert Harter argued that the foreign tax credit has become a primary determinant of plant location. Larry Langdon added that although the law that become increasingly complex with respect to international issues, he agrees with Moran that taxes play less of a role in domestic operations.

Burton Smoliar argued that due to tax return complexity, the TRA86 has increased the compliance burden.

James Wheeler recommended that the Social Security payroll tax be considered in any discussion of equity issues.

Don Fullerton claimed that most of the economists' input to TRA86 took place within Treasury before it went to Capitol Hill. After May 1989, discussions in the House and Senate were weighted heavily toward revenue considerations.

Observing that few aspects of tax law are simple, McLure argued that even the ideal income tax would be very complicated, much more complicated than the ideal tax based on consumption.

Index

Accelerated depreciation. *See* Depreciation
Accounting responses
  and FDI, 176, 184–185, 190
  after TRA86, 9
Accrual basis taxation, 336
Acquisitions
  and integration, 329
  after TRA86, 107, 111–114
Administration, simplification of, 7–9, 321,
  334
  from cash-flow taxation, 337
  as intellectual issue, 302
Affiliated corporations. *See* Foreign direct
  investment; Multinational corporations
Alternative minimum tax
  in Canada, 293
  and complexity, 8
  and donations, 206, 209, 237
  and fairness, 10
  for S corporations, 116–117
  in United States, 292
Appreciated property, donations of, 204,
  208–211, 218–219, 238–239
Arbitrage, 269–270
Artwork, donations of, 210, 218–219,
  238–239
Assets
  vs. personal savings, 80–81
  shifting of, 66–69, 83, 100–101
Australia
  intellectual issues in, 305
  and New Zealand, 306
  tax reform by, 292–293, 307
Automobile sales and personal saving, 60

Baby boomers, and housing, 153
Bankruptcy cost, and corporate financing,
  92, 106–107, 132–134

Banks, interest deductions by, 268, 270
Baskets for FDI, 174–175, 186
Bonds
  and corporate financing, 95, 97
  state and local, markets for, 268–271, 281
Border towns, in fiscal behavior study,
  263–268
Borrowing. *See* Credit; Financing
Broadening of tax base, 2–3
Brokerage arbitrage, 269–270
Built-in gains, and organizational form, 117
Business saving
  effect of, on personal saving, 85–86
  vs. personal, 59

Canada
  foreign investments in, 183
  housing in, 152–155
  intellectual issues in, 303–304
  tax reform in, 6, 293–294, 307
  TRA86 effects on, 287, 305, 308
Capital gains, tax treatment of
  in Australia, 293
  in Canada, 293
  and corporate financing, 92–93, 96, 99,
    105, 110–111
  and dividends, 71–72, 96
  and donations, 204, 209–210, 225, 237–
    238
  fairness of, 9, 335
  for housing, 146–147, 164
  and inflation, 326, 336–338
  and investment, 32, 327
  in Mexico, 296
  and organizational form, 115–116
  and personal saving, 52–55, 69–73,
    321–322
  policy implications of, 326–327

Captial gains, tax treatment of (cont.)
  and simplification, 7
  and state and local fiscal behavior, 277
  in United States, 292
Cash flow
  and investments, 25
  taxation based on, 329–330, 337–338
Charitable contributions, 203
  incentives for, 214–215, 228–229
  by income classes, 220–225, 236
  tax impact on, 206–217
  tax treatment of, 204–206
  after TRA86, 5, 8, 217–229, 322–323
  TRA86 provisions affecting, 212–217
Churches, donations to, 214–215, 236,
    238–239
Cities, adjacent, in fiscal behavior study,
    263–268
Colleges, donations to, 218–219, 238
Complexity, 7–9, 321, 334
  from cash-flow taxation, 337
  as intellectual issue, 302
Computing, investment in, 14, 33, 35, 41,
    46
Consumer credit. See Credit; Home
  mortgages; Interest deductions
Consumption taxes
  in Australia, 292
  in New Zealand, 297
  in United States, 337
Contributions. See Charitable contributions
Corporate taxes
  in Australia, 293
  in Canada, 293
  integration of, with personal, 328–329
  and investments, 31
  in Japan, 295
  in Mexico, 296–297
  in New Zealand, 297–298
  and state and local fiscal behavior, 278–
    279
  in Sweden, 299
  in United Kingdom, 300
  in United States, 291
  worldwide, 315
Corporations. See also Financing;
  Investments; Organizational form
  multinational, 102–103, 133–134 (see
    also Foreign direct investment)
  and rental housing, 150–151
  savings by, 85–86

Credit. See also Financing; Home
  mortgages; Interest deductions
  and personal saving, 51–52, 55, 66–69,
    83
  shifting of, 66–69, 83, 100–101

Debt vs. equity financing, 91, 133–136
  and corporate distributions, 108–113,
    136
  theories of, 92–100, 103–104
  after TRA86, 9, 104–108
  TRA86 provisions affecting, 100–108
Deductions
  for donations (see Charitable contributions)
  for housing, 145–146
  for interest (see Interest deductions)
  and personal saving, 73
  and simplification, 7
  for state and local taxes, 244–246, 248,
    255–256, 261, 279
Deindustrialization of America, 1
Depreciation
  and accrual taxation, 336
  in Canada, 293
  and corporate financing, 94
  and fairness, 335
  on housing, 145–146
  and investment, 31
  in Mexico, 296
  in United Kingdom, 300
  in United States, 291–292
  worldwide, 315
Dividends
  and capital gains, 71–72, 96
  and corporate financing, 108–113, 136
  and equity financing, 91
  and FDI, 177, 186
  vs. interest deductions, 92
  and personal saving, 53, 55–57, 84
  predictions for, 95–96
  after TRA86, 4, 111–114
Donations. See Charitable contributions

Economic efficiency, 321–322
Education, donations to, 218–219, 238
Endowment effect in saving and
  investment, 58
Equipment investment, 13–15
  incentives for, 15–25
  vs. structure investment, 20, 26, 31
  after TRA86, 32–33, 41, 43–46, 322

Equity cost of capital, 18, 20
Equity financing, 91
  vs. debt financing (see Debt vs. equity
    financing)
  with FDI, 184–187
Equity in taxation. See Fairness
Equity lines of credit, 52
Euler equation approach for personal
  saving, 62–63
Excess credit and limitation positions, 171,
  173
Excise taxes
  in Japan, 295
  in Mexico, 296
  in New Zealand, 297

Fairness, 8
  of capital gains, 9, 335
  and depreciation, 335
  horizontal equity, 332
  and inflation, 302–303
  as intellectual issue, 302
  of interest deductions, 335
  and passive losses, 10, 335
  perception of, 333–334
Farm support payments, 60
Financing
  and capital gains, 92–93, 96, 99, 105,
    110–111
  debt vs. equity (see Debt vs. equity
    financing)
  and FDI, 176, 184–185, 190
  sources of, 91
Flow method of personal saving
  determination, 51
Foreign direct investment, 3, 8, 168
  and corporate financing, 106
  definition of, 198–199
  taxation of, 169–171
  after TRA86, 179–191, 199–200
  TRA86 provisions affecting, 172–
    179
Foreign response to TRA86, 286
  content and timing of, 287–301
  direct, 301–308
Foreign tax credits, and corporate
  financing, 103
France, taxation of foreign investments by,
  170, 179
Fringe benefits, and organizational form,
  117

General Utilities doctrine
  and corporate financing, 111, 114
  and organizational form, 116–117
Geographical location of income, and FDI,
  170
  inward, 188–190
  outward, 183–184
Global income taxes vs. schedular, 334–
  336
Governmental arbitrage, 269–270
Government retirement plans, and personal
  saving, 81
Grants for state and local governments,
  244
  predictions for, 248
  after TRA86, 255–256

High-income arbitrage, 269, 271
Home mortgages
  and housing, 155–156
  and personal saving, 52, 66–69, 83
  TRA86 provisions affecting, 100–102
Horizontal equity, 332
Housing, 141–142, 161–165
  analysis of, 143–145
  in Canada, 152–155
  and capital gains, 146–147, 164
  cost of owning, 143–145, 148–149
  and interest rates, 155–156
  multifamily, 5, 9, 34, 151
  and passive losses, 147–151
  and personal saving, 81
  prices of, 142–143, 149–150, 153
  after TRA86, 151–156
  TRA86 provisions affecting, 145–151

Incentives
  for donations, 214–215, 228–229
  for equipment investment, 15–25
  for FDI, 172–179, 190
  for housing investments, 141–142, 161
  for personal saving, 50–52, 56–58
Income classes, donations by, 220–225,
  236
Income shifts, and personal saving, 61
Income taxes, state and local, 248, 262
Indexation for capital gains, 336–338
Industrial buildings, investment in, 35
Inequality. See Fairness
Inflation
  and capital gains, 326, 336–338

Inflation (cont.)
 and fairness, 302–303
 and housing costs, 150
 and real cost of funds, 18
Information processing, investment in, 14,
 33, 35, 41, 46
Inhabitants' tax in Japan, 295
Inheritance tax in United Kingdom, 300
Integration of taxes, 328–329
Intellectual issues, 302–305, 316
Interest deductions, 100–101
 by banks, 268, 270
 and corporate financing, 93
 vs. dividends, 92
 fairness of, 335
 and FDI, 174
 and investment, 20, 32
 and personal saving, 51–52, 55, 57,
 60–61, 66–69, 83–84
Interest income and rates
 and housing, 155–156
 in Japan, 303
 and personal saving, 51–52, 55–57,
 60–61, 66–69, 83–84
Investments, 13–14
 behavior of, 15, 25–31
 and capital gains, 32, 327
 foreign (see Foreign direct investment)
 incentive for, 15–25
 and investment tax credit, 13
 and personal saving, 73, 80–81
 predictions for, 3
 present value considerations for, 19
 and productivity of capital, 19
 and real cost of funds, 18
 technological, 14, 33, 35, 41, 46
 timing of, 19–25
 after TRA86, 32–36, 41, 43–46,
 322–323
 TRA86 provisions affecting, 31–32
 in United Kingdom, 300
 in United States, 291
 worldwide, 315
Investment tax credit, 13, 31
 in Canada, 293–294
 and corporate financing, 93–94, 98, 105
 in Mexico, 296
 predictions for, 3
 in United States, 291
Inward foreign investment
 after TRA86, 187–188
 TRA86 provisions affecting, 177–178

IRAs, 10
 and personal saving, 51, 63–66, 73, 83
 policy implications of, 328
Itemized deductions. See Deductions;
 Interest deductions

Japan
 foreign investments in, 183
 intellectual issues in, 303
 investments from, 189–190
 taxation of foreign investments by, 170,
 178–179
 tax reform in, 6, 294–296
 TRA86 effects on, 287, 305–306

Labor supply, increases in, 321–322
Leverage, and corporate financing,
 134–135
Leveraged buy-outs
 and integration, 329
 after TRA86, 107, 111–114
Local governments. See State and local
 fiscal behavior
Location of income, and FDI, 170
 inward, 188–190
 outward, 183–184
Loopholes. See also Fairness; Passive losses
 elimination of, 316–317
 and perception of fairness, 333–334
Losses. See also Passive losses
 and corporate financing, 94, 98
 and organizational form, 119
Low-income arbitrage, 269, 271
Low-income households
 housing for, 142–143, 164–165
 state and local taxes for, after TRA86,
 263

Mergers
 and integration, 329
 after TRA86, 107, 111–114
Mexico
 tax reform by, 296–297
 TRA86 effects on, 287
Mining exploration, 34–35, 41
Models, problems in, 323–324
Mortgages. See Home mortgages
Multifamily housing after TRA86, 5,9, 34,
 151
Multinational corporations, 102–103,
 133–134. See also Foreign direct
 investment; Foreign response to TRA86

Municipal bonds, 268
Museums, donations to, 218–219, 238

Netherlands, taxation of foreign
   investments by, 170, 179
Netherlands Antilles affiliates, 181–182,
   185, 187
Net wealth change method of personal
   saving determination, 51
Net-worth tax
   in Mexico, 297
   in Sweden, 299
New Zealand
   and Australia, 293, 306
   intellectual issues in, 303
   tax reform by, 297–298, 307
NIPA (national income and product
   accounts)
   saving measure by, 64–65
   for state and local fiscal behavior, 276,
   280–281
Nonitemizers
   deductions for, 205–206, 213, 217
   donations by, 226–228, 239
Nonprofit sector. *See* Charitable
   contributions
Nuclear war fears, and personal saving,
   60–61

Oil exploration, 35, 41
Organizational form
   and capital gains, 115–116
   theoretical considerations for, 115–117
   after TRA86, 118–120
   TRA86 provisions affecting, 136–137
Outward foreign investment
   taxation of, 171
   after TRA86, 179–183
   TRA86 provisions affecting, 172–177
Overhang of existing structures, 45
Ownership. *See* Organizational form

Partnerships, 115
   and personal saving, 57
   after TRA86, 120
Passive losses, 7, 102
   and complexity, 10
   and housing, 147–151
   and investments, 45
   and personal saving, 57
   and S corporations, 117
   and tax arbitrage, 335

Personal exemptions, 262
Personal expenditure tax, 317
Personal saving, 50–51
   vs. assets, 80–81
   vs. business, 59
   business tax influence on, 73, 85–86
   and capital gains, 52–55, 69–73,
   321–322
   and dividends, 53, 55–57, 84
   incentives for, 50–52, 56–58
   and interest deductions, 51–52, 55, 57,
   60–61, 66–69, 83–84
   and investments, 73, 80–81
   and IRAs, 51, 63–66, 73, 83, 328
   after TRA86, 4, 10, 58–63, 322, 324
   TRA86 provisions affecting, 52–58,
   83–86
Personal taxes
   in Canada, 293
   and corporate financing, 92–93, 95
   integration of, with corporate, 328–329
   in Japan, 295
   in Mexico, 296–297
   in New Zealand, 297–298
   and state and local fiscal behavior,
   277–278
   in Sweden, 298–299
   in United Kingdom, 300–301
Policy implications of TRA86 effects
   for capital gains, 326–327
   for cash-flow taxation, 329–330
   for integration, 328–329
   for IRAs, 328
Present value, and investment incentives,
   19
Productivity, and investment incentives,
   19, 42–43
Progressive taxation, 317–318, 321, 323,
   325, 330
Property for donations, 204, 208–211,
   218–219, 238–239
Property taxes in Sweden, 299
Proprietorships, 115

Real estate taxes in Sweden, 299
Religious groups, donations to, 214–215,
   236, 238–239
Rental investments, 141
   in Canada, 152–153
   depreciation for, 145
   losses from (*see* Passive losses)
   and personal saving, 57

Rental investments (cont.)
  after TRA86, 5, 141–143
  user costs of, 150
Repurchase of shares, 4, 91, 110, 113
Research, economic, 324–325
Retained earnings, 121
  and corporate financing, 105
  and FDI, 180–181, 187
Retirement plans, and personal saving, 81
Risk
  and capital gains, 326
  as social cost, 162–163

Sales taxes
  in Australia, 308
  in Canada, 293–294, 304, 308
  in Japan, 295
  in Mexico, 296
  in New Zealand, 297, 308
  predictions for, 247
  state and local, 244–246
  in Sweden, 308
  after TRA86, 6, 255–256, 262
  in United Kingdom, 308
Saving. See Business saving; Personal
    saving
Schedular income taxes, 334–336
S corporations, 91, 115–117
  and personal saving, 57
  after TRA86, 4, 118–120
  TRA86 provisions affecting, 137
Share repurchases, 4, 91, 110, 113
Shelters. See also Fairness; Passive losses
  elimination of, 316–317
  and perception of fairness, 333–334
Simplification, 7–9, 321, 334
  from cash-flow taxation, 337
  as intellectual issue, 302
Single family housing
  in Canada, 153
  after TRA86, 34, 151
Social rate of return, and housing, 161–
    163
Social security contributions
  in Sweden, 299
  in United Kingdom, 301
Source rules, for FDI, 173–174
Standard deductions
  and donations, 206
  and simplification, 7
  and state and local fiscal behavior, 277

State and local fiscal behavior, 243
  and bond markets, 268–271, 281
  and corporate income tax, 278–279
  grants for, 244, 248, 255–256
  mobility and capitalization in, 263–268
  NIPA data for, 280–281
  and personal income tax, 277–278
  predictions of, 247–249
  theory of, 244–247
  time-series model for, 249–262
  timing of, 276, 279
  after TRA86, 6, 322, 324
Stock
  foreign-owned, 198
  repurchasing of, 4, 91, 110, 113
Stock market
  and corporate financing, 106–108
  and donations, 225
  and personal saving, 72, 86
Structure investments
  vs. equipment investment, 20, 26, 31
  after TRA86, 33–34, 45, 322
Subsidiaries, foreign. See Foreign direct
    investment; Multinational corporations
Substitution effect for saving and
    investment, 58
Sweden
  intellectual issues in, 304
  tax reform in, 298–300, 307

Tax credits for low-income housing,
    164–165
Taxes, state and local, 244, 248
Tax rates
  in Australia, 292
  in Canada, 293
  and corporate financing, 94–96, 98, 105
  and donations, 205–206, 212
  and FDI, 172–173, 178–179
  and housing, 145, 150
  and interest costs, 67–68
  and investments, 31
  in Japan, 295
  in Mexico, 296–297
  in New Zealand, 297–298
  and personal saving, 52–58, 60, 83
  reduction of, 2
  and shelters, 334
  and state and local fiscal behavior, 277
  in Sweden, 298–299
  in United Kingdom, 300–301

in United States, 291–292
worldwide, 287, 315–316
Tax reform, viability of, 9–10
Tax shelters. *See also* Fairness; Passive
   losses
 elimination of, 316–317
 and perception of fairness, 333–334
Tax studies, history of, 325
Tax systems
 accrual basis, 336
 cash-flow, 329–330, 337–338
 consumption, 337
 integrated, 328–329
 personal expenditure, 317
Timing, 323
 and accrual taxation, 336
 and donations, 211, 215–216, 229,
   237–238
 and FDI, 185–186, 190
 and indexation of capital gains, 337–338
 of investments, 19–25, 43
 and state and local fiscal behavior, 276,
   279
 TRA86 effect on, 8
 worldwide, 287, 287–301, 315
Transitory income shifts, 61

United Kingdom
 Canada influenced by, 303–304
 investments from, 189–190
 taxation of foreign investments by, 170,
   178–179
 tax reform in, 6, 300–301, 306–307
United States
 intellectual issues in, 302–303
 taxing of FDI by, 170–171
 tax reform in, 291–292
Universities, donations to, 218–219, 238
User fees
 state and local, 244
 after TRA86, 6, 255–256, 262, 279

Value-added tax
 in Canada, 293
 in Japan, 295–296
 in Mexico, 296
 in New Zealand, 297–298
 in Sweden, 299
 in United Kingdom, 300–301
 worldwide, 315, 317–318

Welfare distribution, 9
Welfare loss, 333
West Germany, taxation of foreign
   investments by, 179
Windfall effect, 247–249, 255–256,
   261–262, 277–279
Withholding taxes for FDI, 177, 182